SOCIO-STYLES

This book is an English adaptation of *Socio-Styles-Système* (1990) published in French by Les Editions d'Organisation, Paris.

OTHER BOOKS BY THE SAME AUTHOR

Styles de Vie, Volume 1: Maps and Portraits; Volume 2: Currents and Scenarios (1985, revised 1989), Les Editions d'Organisation, Paris
With Robert Ebguy: *Styles de Pub: 60 Manières de Communiquer* (1987, revised 1989), Les Editions d'Organisation, Paris
With Monique Cathelat: *Collection mémento* (1991), Les Editions d'Organisation, Paris
Les Styles de Vie des Français 1978–98 (1977), Editions Stanké, Paris
Publicité et Société (1976, revised 1982 and 1987), Editions Payot, Paris
With Gérard Mermet: *Vous et les Français* (1975), Editions Flammarion, Paris

OTHER BOOKS BY CCA

Mike Burke (1983) *Les Styles de Vie des Cadres et des Entreprises, portraits de famille*, Interéditions, Paris
Mike Burke (1987) *A chacun son Style d'Entreprise*, Interéditions, Paris
Mike Burke (1991) *Les Styles de Pouvoir*, Dunod, Paris

SOCIO-STYLES

*The New Lifestyles
Classification System
for Identifying
and Targeting
Consumers and
Markets*

Bernard Cathelat

KOGAN
PAGE

LES ÉDITIONS
D'ORGANISATION

NETWORK

*Kogan Page is the UK member of the Euro Business Publishing Network.
The European members are: Les Editions d'Organisation, France; Verlag Moderne
Industrie, Germany; Liber, Sweden; Franco Angeli, Italy; and Deusto, Spain.
The Network has been established in response to the growing demand for interna-
tional business information and to make the work of Network authors available in
other European languages.*

First published in 1990 in France
by Les Editions D'Organisation
26 Avenue Emile-Zola, 75015 Paris

This edition published in Great Britain by Kogan Page Limited

Kogan Page Limited
120 Pentonville Road
London N1 9JN

© Bernard Cathelat 1990, 1993
Translated by Roger Jones
Illustrations by *Vincent Moreau* and *Christian Pommerol*

British Library Cataloguing in Publication Data
A CIP record for this book is available from the British Library.
ISBN 0 7494 0696 8

Typeset by Saxon Graphics Ltd, Derby
Printed in England by Clays Ltd., St Ives plc.

CONTENTS

INTRODUCTION

THE SOCIO-STYLES SYSTEM IN BRIEF

This book describes the socio-styles system, which is an innovative method for studying the lifestyles of individuals and society. It is equally applicable to social, cultural and political problems as well as economics and business. The book describes our extensive experience over two decades experimenting with and applying this method. It develops the key concepts and outlines the theory behind the socio-styles system and its scientific contribution within the general context of other socio-cultural study methods and schools of thought in the social sciences.

The book explains the principles of the research and data processing methods which represent a radical innovation with respect to opinion polls and market studies. It also describes the principal operational applications of this tool and explains how it can be used. Examples are given from the various international applications of the socio-styles system in Europe and the USA.

For more details on the sociological theory, statistical methods and the sociological applications, please refer to the French version of this book: *Socio-Styles-Système* (1990) published by Les Editions d'Organisation, Paris.

THE METHOD

The socio-styles system method was created in 1970 and has since been developed by a group of researchers, initially in France at the Centre de Communication Avancé (CCA) and later in the USA (with US Mapping), in 15 countries of Western Europe (in conjunction with CCA and Europanel) and in the Caribbean region (with M Consultants). It takes quite a different approach to other 'socio-cultural' studies, as explained in chapter 3.

The socio-styles system can be used for research, analysis and databank management of both socio-cultural and socio-commercial data. The data are assembled using unique sampling and statistical techniques to describe and measure:

❑ a practical typology of society profiles of attitudes, behaviour and feelings organized in a series of maps;
❑ the principal socio-cultural trends (major and minor) in public opinion.

The study also describes in each sector or market how customers or audiences divide into specific groups and locates the competing positions of ideas, products, brands, images, messages, etc. This information enables us to analyze the variety of target groups in all sectors: politics and social life, culture and information, advertising and merchandising, and all consumer sectors.

An initial foundation study creates a general analytical tool that can be applied to all forms of opinion polls, studies of brand images, advertising and communication trials, audience and media measurement, and research into consumer practices and attitudes. It creates in a given geo-cultural zone (such as a region, a country, a continent) a databank covering several sectors and including commercial, cultural and political information. It can be updated and enhanced regularly with additional sector-based or theme-based research focused on a specific market or subject.

The socio-styles system is a new tool for analysis and strategic choice for social and economic decision makers in all sectors. It offers:

❑ an understanding of the structure and development of their socio-cultural environment;
❑ an analysis of their positioning on the competitive chessboard;
❑ a definition of their current and future target groups;
❑ a description of dynamic social currents that bring about change.

The system aims to produce authentic social science research which measures new social structures and evolving systems of values, models and stereotypes. It also aims to be a complete tool for the commercial marketing of goods and services, for merchandising and distribution networks, for advertising and public relations strategies, for press and media marketing, for social and political marketing, and so on.

A PRACTICAL TOOL

The socio-styles system databank makes it possible to observe the interaction and mutual influence of different markets, different social sectors, and different lifestyles. Because the study is not rigidly specialised but analyzes at the same time politics and consumption, private family life and commerce, the media and advertising, it enables a better analysis to be made of the different variables that influence behaviour and attitudes. It draws a more complete portrait of a customer group than normal motivation research or marketing studies, describing both its psychology and its actual way of life.

The socio-styles system enables us to define customers and groups in different sectors according to the same typology. Because of this multi-sector approach, it is a practical tool for comparing the customers for different products, for moving on from market analysis to media planning, for analyzing developments in consumer behaviour in different markets, for establishing correlations between two groups on social problems and economic questions, and so on.

SOME CONCEPTS

Any effort to create and structure a method requires a very clear definition of specific concepts and tools. This gives rise to a specialized vocabulary that may sometimes lapse into the obscurity of jargon.

We define below the principal terms that have been created specifically to define the concepts and tools of the socio-styles system in its different applications. The method aims to provide a general check-up of a society and its population both in terms of the different segments within it and in terms of its structural and socio-dynamic organization. Six terms are in current use to describe this tool:

❑ *Socio-styles* refer to the different models of behaviour, thought, motivation and living conditions making up a typology that describes the lifestyles of a given population. The term has been coined in order to emphasize the specific nature of our method. The socio-style combines variables relating to behaviour, attitudes and opinions, inner motivations, emotional feelings, demographics and economics. It is a general portrait gallery of the public applicable to all sectors and markets. In the study and databank reports socio-styles are described in the form of detailed portraits which are sometimes summarized and represented by a code name and an illustration to make them easier to remember.

❑ *Socio-mentalities* are a simpler typology with a restricted number of profiles. If the socio-styles system is imagined to be a tree, socio-styles are the boughs and mentalities the branches. In practical terms mentalities are sociological families of socio-styles.

❑ *Cultural flows* or *socio-cultural currents* refer to value systems, drives and general attitudes whose social importance and penetration into different social groups can be measured at a given moment, and whose evolution can be followed over time. These currents form part of the socio-style, but only represent one of its facets, that of fashionable and social stereotypes. The 'hit-parade' of cultural flows measures the mood of the time.

❑ *Socio-waves* represent oppositions between two different values of cultural flows representing ethical, ideological and practical choices which can then be applied to all sectors, forms of behaviour and thought. While socio-cultural flows or currents measure theoretical ideals, wishes, dreams and passions, socio-waves measure an actual choice which takes account of the attraction of these ideas and the realities of how people live.

❑ The *socio-compass* shows the range of concepts which attract each socio-style and measures the dominant trends. We can use it by placing it over any map from the report as a 'compass chart' of society.

❑ The *socio-map* organizes socio-styles into a socio-structure. This mathematical diagram, resulting from correspondence analysis, can be compared to a geographical map on which different lifestyles are grouped together in families or placed in opposition to one another according to their similarities and differences. The map is defined by two or three principal mathematical axes and serves as the base diagram for presenting all the data in the socio-styles-system reports.

These general tools are adapted specifically for each sector or market studied:

❑ *Socio-targets* represent population, audience or customer segments specific to a given market. A socio-target is made up of several socio-styles which have the same motivation, behaviour and sensitivity profile in this sector, presented in the form of a map. The sector-based typology of the socio-targets can be superimposed on the macro-social socio-styles typology on the same socio-map.

❑ *Socio-niches* are the principal competitive niches identified in a market or sector. On the same map we can see how product brands concepts or images are grouped into territories in which they compete or share the same customers. The socio-niche map represents how products and services are distributed and can be superimposed on the socio-target map which pictures the demand for them.

❑ *Socio-contrasts* define the significant contrasts in concepts or behaviour separating two opposing families of socio-styles, often in two remote regions on the map. They are a structured interpretation of contrasts between customer segments or market niches. Socio-contrasts are presented in the form of maps, each devoted to a significant pair of opposites, and are derived from synthesis and interpretation, not from raw study data.

❑ The *sector-based compass* or *socio-compass* is a tool for identifying and measuring trends in behaviour and psychology peculiar to an activity in a particular market. Several sector-based compasses are presented in each market analysis of the socio-styles system, covering motivation, behaviour and habits, and in particular communication concepts and images.

AN INNOVATION AND A STEP FORWARD

Socio-cultural studies in general, and socio-styles studies in particular, have marked a turning point in professional practice and social science research since the beginning of the 1970s.

The socio-styles system has introduced real innovations:

❑ social innovation, by combining sociological, political, cultural and commercial analyses in the same survey and in a single databank, in contrast with the partial specialization of market studies and polls;

❑ methodological innovation, by synthesizing data relating to behaviour, opinions and even feelings on each subject, in contrast with the partial view of the classical methods;

❑ technical innovation with a radically new style of questionnaire;

❑ statistical innovation with a process for reducing and structuring information;

❑ conceptual innovation, particularly with the idea of the socio-style, a multi-thematic and multi-dimensional, synthetic portrait of an individual balancing past conditioning and the desire for change, negotiating between the different facets of personality and the habit of social conformity. This contrasts with caricatures based on social class and demographic criteria;

❑ information innovation with the presentation of data in the form of a map which transforms tables of figures into an ordnance survey map, a diagram for reflection, simulation and decision making;

❑ professional innovation by multiple applications of this tool to commercial, cultural, social and political marketing: innovation concepts, diversification plans, positioning for a range of products or services, communication strategy.

The method relies less on theory than on years of application, firstly through empirical experimentation and then professional application in all sectors — for businesses, the media and the public sector. While never claiming to be a panacea, the socio-styles system has become accepted in numerous professions as a trustworthy, useful and stimulating method.

PART ONE

WHAT IS THE SOCIO-STYLES SYSTEM?

The socio-styles system provides social and economic decision makers with three main types of operational and practical information, which can be used:

- ❏ to analyze markets and social problems;
- ❏ to identify target groups of people;
- ❏ to explore different possible strategic scenarios;
- ❏ to choose the main tactical tools for action, sales or communication in order to reach the desired audience.

THE SYSTEM IS TYPOLOGICAL

The foundation study for the socio-styles system defines, measures and analyzes a socio-styles typology which represents the whole variety of behaviours, attitudes and motivations among the public, media audiences and consumers of products and services. This typology is formed from all the responses relating to behaviour, attitude and motivation at all stages of life, in all areas of social life and in all business markets. This general typology offers a new standard of analysis that is valid for all opinion polls, audience studies and market analyses. It is the most complete, extensive and intelligent basis in existence for classifying individuals in order to find basic explanations of consumer behaviour.

THE SYSTEM IS MULTI-SECTORIAL

In each sector of activity and of the market the foundation study describes how the population can be divided into several socio-targets which represent different segments of consumers, audiences, voters or employees. The basic segmentation takes account of both individual motivation and behaviour.

THE SYSTEM PROVIDES A MAP OR A STRUCTURE

The foundation study analyzes the principal mathematical axes which explain the market segmentation into socio-targets and the general typology of the various lifestyles. It defines the social landscape in the form of a mathematical map of three main dimensions on which the socio-styles are placed and on which all the individual responses are positioned. This socio-map is a cultural and commercial chessboard for analyzing a product according to the position of its consumers, its brand image or its manufacturer's image, or the public impact of a commercial – set against the positions of other competitive brands and products. It is a strategic ordnance survey map for identifying the current position, competitors' positions and consumers to be won over.

THE SYSTEM IS DYNAMIC

The socio-styles survey measures socio-waves, the choice of dominant values, the most attractive themes and the most stimulating socio-cultural trends throughout society. In addition the survey measures the most attractive prospective scenarios for private and social life, the economy and consumption, media and culture, business and products for the future.

THE SOCIO-BANK IS MULTI-FUNCTIONAL

It is a multi-dimensional databank. The typological socio-style portraits synthesize all the dimensions of a person's life: an economic and demographic identity card, describing living conditions and behaviour, attitudes and opinions, feelings and subconscious motivations.

It is a multi-thematic databank. The socio-styles portraits synthesize people's ways of life and thinking in all areas: politics and religion, work and leisure, family and private life, knowledge and culture, finances and consumption. It is the most complete portrait in existence of people considered as citizens, consumers and media audiences.

It is a multi-sectorial databank. The socio-styles typology and the socio-map of positionings are applied to the study of all markets: home and household equipment, house decoration and maintenance, food and drink, hygiene, health and nutrition, clothing and fashion, cars, holidays, sport and leisure, financial products, banking and insurance.

CHAPTER I
PRINCIPLES OF THE SOCIO-STYLES SYSTEM

A SOCIO-CULTURAL VISION

The socio-styles concept is intended to be complete and complex in order to reflect a complex reality:

❑ a multi-dimensional person imbued with reason and emotions, dreams and habits;
❑ who as an individual is torn between his or her basic personality and social role;
❑ who chooses a life of compromise within a range of accepted but changeable models of behaviour;
❑ who adapts these models at all stages in life in the search for both inner coherence and freedom of action;
❑ who remains in unstable equilibrium between the weight of the past and the possibilities of the future.

This is a reality that the socio-styles system tries to grasp in all its complexity and rebuild in the form of a simple tool for understanding and decision making.

A multi-thematic principle

The socio-styles system attempts to offer a more complete classification system than the partial and incomplete segmentations carried out in market research. It defines socio-styles through all stages of an individual's life (or at least the most that can be tackled in one investigation). Each stage helps to explain others within a complete personality. This method is currently the only one to offer a general portrait of the whole of a social subject aimed at greater understanding. This is achieved, not with the partial blinkers of a precise study focused on a particular objective, but by attempting to grasp the place of each action or attitude in the way a person is adapting his or her model of life.

A multiple variable

The typologies of socio-styles and mentalities can be viewed and understood in three complementary ways:

❑ as styles of life, behaviour and thought that are indicative of the ways that individual personalities adapt, particularly to the social environment. In this socio-styles bring out the dominant integrating mechanisms of the time;

❑ as a social segmentation revealing the divisions or homogeneity of society, its tolerance of diversity or its repressive uniformity. In this way the socio-styles typology analyzes the cohesion of society (or the group being studied) when faced with a particular problem;

❑ as a social dialectic establishing the divergence and convergence of values, accommodation and opposition of micro-cultures, domination and subordination of lifestyles. Here the socio-map shows struggles for influence within the social arena.

This three-way reading is useful in all social sectors: from political analysis to culture and consumption. It applies equally to a continental population, to a national one, and to sub-samples by region or category.

A multi-dimensional principle

The socio-styles system offers a comprehensive classification system where the socio-style is defined simultaneously by psychological variables (motivations), socio-objective variables (living conditions), symbolic psycho-social variables (opinions, attitudes, language) and praxis variables (behaviour). In this multi-dimensional, identikit portrait of static variables (habits), dynamic variables (ambitions), rational variables (opinions) and imaginary sensitivities (revealed by projective questions), there exist at the same time the motivation, the way it is translated into thought and how it takes physical shape, taking into account living conditions and effective behaviour.

A complex variable

This lifestyles typology offers multi-faceted portraits of socio-cultural groups, each one able to be used either to analyze a social situation in relation to others or to work on known segments of the population. However, a socio-style is by definition a synthetic variable; its object is to describe the complexity of lifestyles at all levels (behaviour, attitudes, feelings, aspirations) and at all stages of the lifecycle.

In this way it is not a simple variable like sex or age intended for research into the strongest mathematical correlations with other simple variables such as vote or the purchase of a product. In classical marketing usage the typological lifestyle variables sometimes appear less discriminating and less predictive than demographic or economic criteria (see examples in chapter 5); they have to be considered principally as a more intelligent and interpretative, complementary approach.

The goal and interest of the socio-styles system lie not in the statistical correlation between two simple variables but in the search for an intelligent structural link between two complex wholes: a description of logic and equilibrium in life (the lifestyle) and a comprehensive description of psychology and behaviour (political, commercial, etc).

Since this method was first used more data have continued to be collected on the socio-styles and their interpretation has become more complex. This has happened of its own accord since life itself is complex and we have to try to analyze the mechanisms of this complexity without over-simplifying them. They are therefore increasingly removed from simple variables such as professional and demographic categories. We must therefore neither evaluate nor use the socio-styles typology as an alternative to or a competitor with these simple variables, but as another, complementary approach, whose aim is not so much to discriminate as to understand the interaction between two complex phenomena.

A structural principle

The socio-styles system is a structured and organized classification, and it is in this way that the socio-map should be read. It is an ordnance survey map on which we can see how the socio-styles are grouped in families, which ones are related, which ones are in opposition. We can therefore see which ones respond to the same language and which ones respond to different types of media. This structural analysis gives each type its place without considerations of hierarchy or value judgements about progress. Contrast with this Yankelovich and RISC which judge profile types according to an alleged sense of progress, or VALS which considers social success.

A synthetic variable

A socio-style and a mentality are mathematically synthetic data which integrate the whole complexity of lifestyle variables at all levels of psychology and behaviour and at all stages of life. The type is a gestalt, an organizational equilibrium, a structure of mathematical factors, each of which itself synthesizes a large number of survey responses.

A lifestyles profile type is consequently the simplest and most synthetic expression of the greatest complexity that practical psychology is currently able to collect and process statistically in order to observe individuals and society. A socio-style is therefore at one and the same time the most versatile variable available today and an item of data that both considerably reduces the complexities of personalities and synthesizes the various stages of life. It is therefore particularly important to take great care with interpretation.

A dynamic principle

Finally the socio-styles system generates a classification which in contrast to other systems accepts the ephemeral, subscribes to cultural history, takes into account the evolution of the social environment and its effects on personal attitudes and behaviour. People are defined by their current lifestyle and capacity for change, their potential attitudes, their desire for innovation, their ideal life in the future; in other words, the balance or imbalance of various trends. The socio-styles typology is re-examined regularly and may be restructured completely in the light of the most recent studies. It is then correlated with the earlier classification to find identical models and discover which ones have appeared or disappeared.

Statistically a socio-style is mobile and ephemeral, since it is a complex of trends and influences linking personality and society, the inertia of habit and aspirations for change. Like every gestalt it is an unstable equilibrium which can be altered or destroyed by modifying a single component, only to be recreated in another synthetic model.

A gestalt variable

A socio-style is a variable made up of complex inter-relationships organized in a systematic rather than a structured way. This means that it has to be considered not so much as a structure (which suggests either a fixed organization or a closed process such as a mechanism), but as an open system which in principle cannot be fixed.

Nevertheless, socio-styles measurement, though looking to the future, is a photograph of stable and moving phenomena at a particular instant. The socio-style should therefore be seen as a gestalt variable capturing at a given moment a large proportion of social life which will already be overtaken by events the following day. The social dynamics which make a lifestyle into an unstable equilibrium, a gestalt, unfold at two levels which need to be taken into consideration in the organization of research.

❑ Firstly, there is the dynamic of the individual personality, its own desires and psychological motivations, and the stimuli of its encounters with the outside world: the private dynamics of the psychological imagination.
❑ Secondly, there is the dynamic of the collective reality, the truly social movement which results from encounters between all the different dynamics of individuals in a social context which imposes its own constraints.

In socio-styles studies we attempt to capture the psychological dynamic through what are called 'projective' questions, developed on the basis of qualitative studies of fantasies and desires, which offer ideal concepts in several domains to understand the ideal situation and its corresponding desires and motivations. To take account of the second social dynamic, socio-styles studies are repeated in order to survey the social indicators of change; and periodically all the social typology is reviewed by a widespread general poll.

In this way socio-styles are a true gestalt variable, the complete picture of equilibrium in a moving process taken at a given moment.

A DIALECTIC VISION

The major original feature of the lifestyles concept is that it places individuals at the crossroads of their personality and their social conditions, instead of compromising between social life and personal desires in trying to understand how a person becomes a social being and how society is made human through its culture.

A lifestyle is not an individual personality but a social character. The individual personality is infinitely richer and more complex. By looking at the range of cultural values and socio-styles, each person feels intuitively at what point personality is multi-dimensional (both conservative and innovative, rational and emotional, moral and libertarian). Once it reaches maturity this inner personality remains virtually stable.

A socio-style is the way in which a personality adapts to the social environment by understating some aspects of its potential, emphasizing others, balancing its characteristics.

What the socio-styles system offers is an analysis not of personalities but of how individuals are socialized and assimilated into cultural groups; not in effect profound, subconscious personalities but the forces which shape the social, commercial, political and cultural lives of a civilization.

An existential principle

The inner personality of 250 million Europeans or 600,000 West Indians has no social existence. Even if such knowledge were obtainable it would be of no use to any administrator or manager. Social stereotypes (such as workers or 15–24-year-olds) have no independent existence and to believe so is a dangerous and unproductive illusion.

The socio-styles system defines the methods by which personalities come to have a social existence.

What is a socio-style? Projecting an individual psychology into the socio-cultural framework is a way of injecting some of the energy of an individual's desires into the conditions and conditioning of the physical, social and political environment.

It is where the desire emerges, in the form of 'being there' between 'being no more' and 'being more' (J P Grard).

Motivation research only looks at an individual's basic impulses and driving forces without considering what physical form they take in practice. Opinion polls and market research only bring out superficial demonstrations of opinions, behaviour and social integration without knowing their origins, their foundation or what need they fulfil. The socio-styles system attempts to describe and explain the social being (that is, the person and the personality in one) through the dialectic of motivation and behaviour. In other words, a lifestyle is located not in purely private psychology nor in sociology, but at the meeting point of individual psychology and the external conditions of life. What we call a socio-style is one of the possible results of this dialectic between the inner personality and the sociological register; no one can be classified according to sociometric living conditions alone.

The lifestyle studies how individuals come into existence, the crystallization of the social personality between two opposing forces. And it is really there that the marketing negotiation takes place. An element of psychology (motivation) enters into all behavior, as does an element of living conditions (age, environment, etc). We have to explain how these two types of variables combine and balance out into a gestalt of existence. A socio-style is useful in practice precisely because it defines the individual in dynamic equilibrium.

A principle of assimilation

The socio-styles system is an attempt to understand and measure the ways of integrating individual psychologies into the material, technological, economic and political environment.

A socio-style is a model of assimilation, a plan of psychological, behavioural, factual, verbal, rational and symbolic ways of entering society. It is also a dynamic step by which an individual becomes civilized. In other words, at one and the same time an individual submits to the stereotypes and collective values; conforms and is moulded; is integrated and comes into social existence, with its influences and obligations, language and relationships.

The objective, therefore, is to analyze the structure, diversity and mobility of models of socio-cultural integration by which scattered individuals escape entropy and form a collective civilization which at the same time confines and transcends them. Analysis of these lifestyles reveals the living culture in which they are symptomatic of uniformity or diversity, of rigour or weakness, of stability or mobility. They are the place and the moment where society and culture are formed and continually re-formed.

'Culture' originates from the fact that a group of individuals launch themselves into an environment and create a language in order to adapt to it — a language for objects, an ideological language, a collective way of grasping reality, an economic language for relationships. Culture is this language, a collective gesture to take hold of reality. The research project is not limited to studying the lifestyles of individuals but looks beyond them to understand how culture is continually being reconstituted and recreated.

The aim is to use the lifestyles to follow how a system of values crystallizes at a given moment; how plans of behaviour are formulated; how the individuals who make up society communicate reality, make sense of things and confer status and roles on themselves. A socio-style could be likened to a suit which is a compromise between expressing the personality of its wearer and meeting the needs of the environment, climate or fashion. Analyzing the suit enables us to grasp both how an individual is socialized and how society evolves in its models and fashions.

A lifestyle represents at one and the same time the process by which individuals are socialized and the process by which culture or society is created and recreated through the involvement of individuals.

A principle of dynamic disequilibrium

The socio-styles system studies the unstable equilibrium as an individual adapts to constant variation in a changing environment. The socio-style is the most structured side of the set-up; the socio-waves are the most dynamic variable at the individual level; the socio-map is the visual representation of the interaction beween the forces of change and instability.

Compared to the preconceived theories and explanatory models of socio-logical ideology, the socio-styles system pictures this unstable system in the most empirical way possible without recourse to dogma or an overriding hypothesis. Socio-styles research provides a photograph, a series of social snapshots which over the years becomes a filmstrip. Socio-cultural analysis consists of researching the continually renewing cultural structure and identifying the forces for disequilibrium that generate dynamic trends.

The methodological principle is to research and measure these forces for disequilibrium in people's lives and everyday psychology, in their daily efforts at socialization. We therefore offer a view of the future in an additional variable of social dynamics seen across cultural values and from the viewpoint of individuals, not in structures, great collective acts or general averages.

Another principle of the socio-styles system is to observe how these trends are structured into a mosaic or typology of individuals which results from these forces and the permanent disequilibrium, and which places individuals in this structure and reveals in which groups people are more or less active, which types are reinforced and which profiles weakened.

At any given moment the socio-styles barometer manages the balance sheet of society, of the predominant and least influential models, of the most attractive and least attractive plans, of the images coming to the fore or retreating, of the types in which economic and political power reside.

CHAPTER 2
CONCEPTS OF THE SOCIO-STYLES SYSTEM

This chapter describes the principal working tools that the method offers to users:

- ❏ a socio-styles typology to classify populations;
- ❏ a socio-wave compass to identify the prevailing trends;
- ❏ a socio-map to position people and objects in alliance and in competition;
- ❏ socio-targets to segment markets.

These are represented in figure 2.1.

THE GENERAL SOCIO-STYLES TYPOLOGY

The socio-styles typology is the basic instrument for lifestyle studies in the international and multi-sectorial methodology of the socio-styles system. It offers a unique reference system to researchers and decision makers in different sectors in segmenting their population, public, audience, readership or customer base. This is the most synthetic reference system there is, since the classification into socio-styles is based on hundreds of responses, behavioural as much as psychological, and emotional as well as rational, at all stages of life, in all sectors of social and economic activity. It is a synthetic typology which attempts to describe the general equilibrium of the life of a group of individuals throughout their fields of activity.

The socio-styles typology is produced by a complex process applied to a voluminous databank. The typological process is carried out on factorial scores that summarize and structure the whole databank according to behaviour and habits, motivations and feelings about private and family life, objectives in life, social participation, political opinions, leisure patterns, cultural tastes and practices, consumer motivation and behaviour with regard to food, house decoration and household equipment, car, clothing, beauty and hygiene. Around 3,500 variables are used when embarking on a foundation study in a new country. When a databank exists which is regularly updated, the quantitative source of data processed can reach 12,000 items. This amount of information, requiring a considerable investment in research, and in particular the diversity of this databank, makes the socio-styles typology a new criterion for synthesis.

These four complementary types of information are drawn from the same data bank, derived from the same study or series of surveys. They form the main basis on which marketing decisions are made.

Socio-structure in the form of a socio-map
A structured sociological landscape based upon the main traits of different mentalities. *Can be used to understand positioning on the socio-chessboard.*

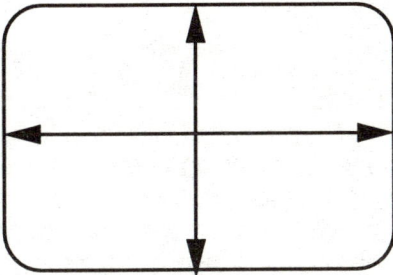

Socio-waves and cultural flows
Developing trends in the values and ideas which dominate public opinion. *Can be used to detect social trends and what is fashionable.*

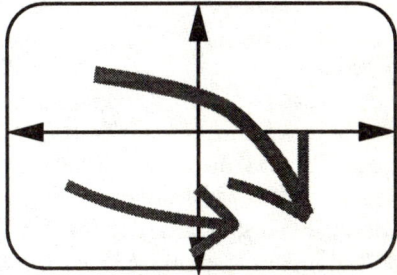

Real-life socio-styles
A gallery of portraits illustrating the typological diversity of the population, taken from data collected in multi-sectoral surveys. *Can be used as a new classification system for developing a consumer segmentation strategy.*

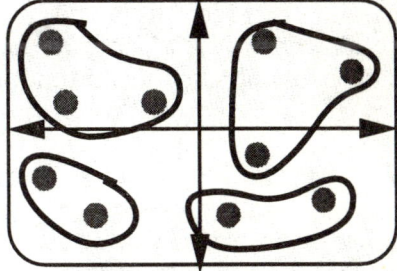

Sectoral socio-targets
Market segments showing how socio-styles are grouped by subject in a particular sector, in relation to their composition and motivators. *Can be used to define target audiences.*

Figure 2.1   The four key concepts of the socio-styles system

The socio-styles typology currently offers the only standard of reference that at one and the same time takes account of six levels of variable:

- ❏ from psychology to individual behaviour;
- ❏ the individual personality — from conditions of demographic and economic life to subconscious emotional feelings;
- ❏ social life — from politics to commerce;
- ❏ communication — from culture to advertising;
- ❏ consumption — from household goods to perfume;
- ❏ commerce — from hypermarkets to franchised shops.

It is intended as a tool for understanding, applicable to any subject in any sector, able to relocate it in the general equilibrium of thought processes, preoccupations and motivations, habits in private, family or professional life for each population segment. The socio-styles analysis says more about the human context in which an act, the forming of an opinion or the purchase of a product takes place.

The life of an individual is an enigma: at one and the same time a member of society, a parent, a television viewer, a customer, a worker, a target for advertisers, etc. The socio-styles system offers a portrait of each segment of the population from all angles at the same time. Through an improved understanding of the whole enigma that a lifestyle represents, we can better comprehend the importance of the function of each of the components and the part that a commercial product, the media or some social activity can play.

It is the only methodology to offer a synthetic segmentation that is also generalist, non-specialized and multi-sectorial. Indeed, each demographic criterion constitutes a general system of classification applied indifferently to all sectors of activity and to all markets, thus enabling us to juxtapose them for the purposes of comparison. Too often they are used as analytical and not synthetic criteria: first, classification by age, then by sex, by income and by habitat. They function separately as distinct, uncorrelated criteria and not as a synthetic typology.

Socio-styles typology integrates all these demographic criteria with other psychological and behavioural criteria. Attaching an individual to a socio-style type is sensitive enough (within the scientific limits of any study) to synthesize all the variables defining this individual in all sectors and at all levels of activity.

Socio-styles typology is thus the only tool which enables direct comparison of all sectors of activity for which information is available, whether in the existing socio-bank or in any new sector-based study using socio-style classification as a supplementary criterion for identifying interviewees (from a small range of specific indicators).

The multiple activities of marketing and communication, and beyond that both society and private life, represent a mosaic of fields of action. Each company and organization occupies only a limited territory which requires all its attention, focuses its energy, but also limits its field of vision. Socio-styles research is a method by which managers can understand their sector better by standing back and comparing it with adjacent sectors, where they can find more explanatory variables, striking analogies, strong trends that are useful to their own specialized activity. In practical terms only socio-styles typology enables us to answer the question 'What group of the population consumes less of product X on average, although they prefer natural products and shop regularly for food at hypermarkets; which newspapers do these people read and what kind of advertising do they respond to?'

In particular, this typology is an interface between the worlds of communication and marketing. Market analyses can describe consumer segments according to their buying behaviour or their psychological preferences; classical media audience studies can describe the profiles of readers and television viewers; but only demographic criteria serve as a bridge between the two worlds. The typology enables us to define directly which medium best reaches the socio-target identified as the target consumer for a product; or conversely define which distribution outlets best suit the habits of the socio-styles identified as the main audience for a particular medium.

Finally, the socio-styles method aims to be a source of intelligence about action in the socio-cultural context. Basic sociological studies at universities probably offer more profound views of social mechanisms, but they are often too theoretical and detached from the practical requirements of decision makers. In contrast, social opinion polls — like classical market studies — only provide partial visions of a fragmented society which are focused on micro-subjects and too obsessed with measuring details. Under the pretext of immediate realism they do not provide a context or extend the angle of sight; their view is not explanatory but descriptive, and they are too specialized to outline any general structure of understanding. Analysis by socio-styles offers at one and the same time:

❑ a general sociological vision as a backcloth to understanding the dynamics of public opinion, the range of social diversity and the dialectic of influence that is set up between them;
❑ a detailed point by point analysis which allows each subject and population to be relocated in a more general explanatory context.

The principle and aim of lifestyles studies are to stimulate researchers and decision makers into standing back and widening their field of vision to achieve a better understanding of the position their specialized activity and particular offering has come to occupy in the more general social landscape and in individual lifestyles.

This first objective of the socio-styles system facilitates the search for a general multi-thematic and multi-sectorial synthetic variable. This variable is complex: its aim is not to obtain the best predictive mathematical correlation with simple (and simplistic) variables but rather the best correlation with patterns of behaviour and thought, which are themselves complex. In other words, the socio-styles typology is a synthetic variable designed to explain clusters of attitudes or behaviour (economic or social). For this reason this variable cannot be compared with detailed demographic or economic variables, but is more synthetic and its value is explanatory and complementary.

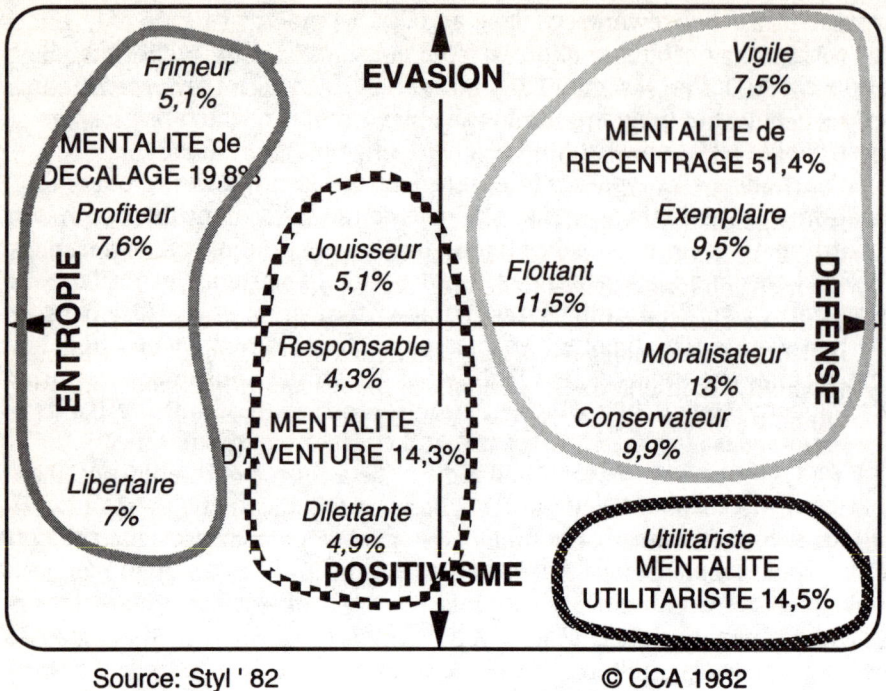

Source: Styl ' 82   © CCA 1982

Figure 2.2   A typology: 4 socio-mentalities and 12 socio-styles in France
in 1982

A social mosaic

The first objective is to observe and measure at a given moment the social
diversity of life and thinking styles among the population and to trace the
evolution of this socio-cultural mosaic over the years. In the CCA studies in
France from 1972 to 1984, for example, the typology identified between 10
and 14 different socio-style portraits depending on the year. Figure 2.2 gives
an example for 1982.

The socio-styles system provides a socio-cultural typology which goes
beyond the 'average French person' type of statistics of traditional sociological data (eg 1.8 children), undifferentiated bi-polarizations (eg 40 per cent
for, 60 per cent against), classical opinion or election polls, exaggerated
stereotypes (the young, dynamic middle manager, the housewife). It even
goes beyond socio-objective classification by age, sex, profession and living
conditions, not to deny their worth, but to supplement and enhance them
with shades of difference.

The socio-styles typology is a practical instrument for analysis and action
(social, cultural or commercial):

❑ to observe specifically and closely who does what: Who votes for whom?
   Who consumes what? Who reads which journal? Who prefers which TV
   presenter? Who holds which opinion? Who is swayed by which adver-

tisements or arguments? This involves getting away from excessively generalised statements;

❑ to envisage strategic choices for future actions: Who else should be informed? Who should we sell more to? Which social groups should we target? We no longer need to rely on intuition;

❑ to analyze the compatibility and coherence of these strategic opportunities for action against the various socio-style groups: Does the same message or advertisement, newspaper or TV programme, product or distribution outlet apply to the various target groups? The same advertisement no longer needs to be used across the board;

❑ to define clearly and precisely one or more well-demarcated target populations. This enables us to make informed choices about what to offer, through which channels, with what type of communication and using which media.

The second objective is to measure and describe each socio-cultural group that comprises the social mosaic using their specific characteristics which call for special treatment. Studying lifestyles offers two practical instruments for analysis and planning: detailed portraits of lifestyles and mentalities.

Socio-styles are practical portraits of lifestyles. They describe groups of individuals, whose statistical weighting can normally vary between 3 and 15 per cent. They are grouped mathematically because their responses to surveys show that they share to a significant extent practical ideas and ways of behaviour that are very similar in the majority of lifestyle stages (eg income, consumption).

Mentalities, also called micro-cultures, are practical portraits of value systems and patterns of adaptation to the environment which describe generally broader families of individuals and group together several socio-styles sharing the same basic beliefs, the same perceptions of the world, the same reactions and the same strong evolutionary trends.

Socio-styles and socio-mentalities are typological population classification systems which exist at two different levels:

❑ Mentalities offer a more restricted typology (3 to 6 groups) of the more important social groups (15 to 50 per cent of the population) defined in more cultural terms of patterns and general mechanisms of personal adaptation to the environment and social life. This instrument is better suited to macro-social strategic analyses of positioning, image, innovation and social activity.

❑ Socio-styles offer a more precise typology of between 9 and 17 smaller groups comprising 3 to 15 per cent of individuals. They are defined in more commonplace and pragmatic terms of behaviour and everyday attitudes in private, social, economic and cultural life. This tool is more suitable for tactical analyses of social practices (eg consumption, contact with the media, voting, commercial contacts) as well as immediate and concrete reality (eg attitudes towards pacifism, the impact of an advertising campaign, the popularity of a personality).

A centre of gravity

A socio-style does not represent the whole lifestyle of individuals but their centre of gravity and their collective reference point. Mathematically speaking it is the largest common denominator of X per cent of individuals, defining their dominant model of thought and behaviour. Statistically it is possible to define each interviewee by a probability coefficient applicable to all types in the typology. In practice every individual in the sample is allocated to his or her dominant socio-style for reasons of operational effectiveness.

This implies that certain attitudes and behaviour can be separated from an individual's socio-style type. Depending on the type of study, the survey and processing methods, the socio-style type explains 80 to 90 per cent of a person's responses to a questionnaire. The pattern of responses comes very close to a theoretical socio-style model, but 10 to 20 per cent of views belong to other, adjacent models.

A family tree of social variety

Similarly, a mentality is a much larger common denominator at a lower level of typological differentiation between various socio-styles and the individuals linked to them. The socio-styles present a correlation between them superior to any other correlation with a type.

A mentality is a main branch which supports and groups together several socio-styles in a typological family tree (see figure 2.3).

An unstable equilibrium

A socio-style is a dynamic equilibrium. A lifestyle must not be understood and used as a simple addition to the characteristics of life and thought. It is a synthesis of living conditions, aspirations and dreams, behaviour and thoughts which can converge or conflict. The incoherences and paradoxes form part of the useful information in this portrait. Certain profiles can display more or less coherence between effective forms of behaviour, opinions and psychological aspirations. In the same way we can speak of 'consistency' between the current lifestyle and the desired scenarios for the future (see figure 2.4).

By its nature socio-style is unstable. The fact that in the course of updating studies socio-styles appear and disappear or, more simply, change their statistical weighting over the years, does not mean that society has experienced a revolution or that individuals' lives have been overturned. It means that certain methods of adapting to certain environmental stimuli have changed. In practice, some of the factors that define the type mathematically in the typological family tree have changed in nature or weighting and as a consequence the general synthetic equilibrium of the gestalt has changed significantly: the model of adapting to the world has changed in nature.

This change generally comes about quietly, almost imperceptibly for individuals and their circle with no great break in the social continuum. But these discreet changes in balance are signs of cultural mutations as much as spectacular revolutions, perhaps more so. These socio-style remodellings constitute more of a change than a comprehensive shift in public

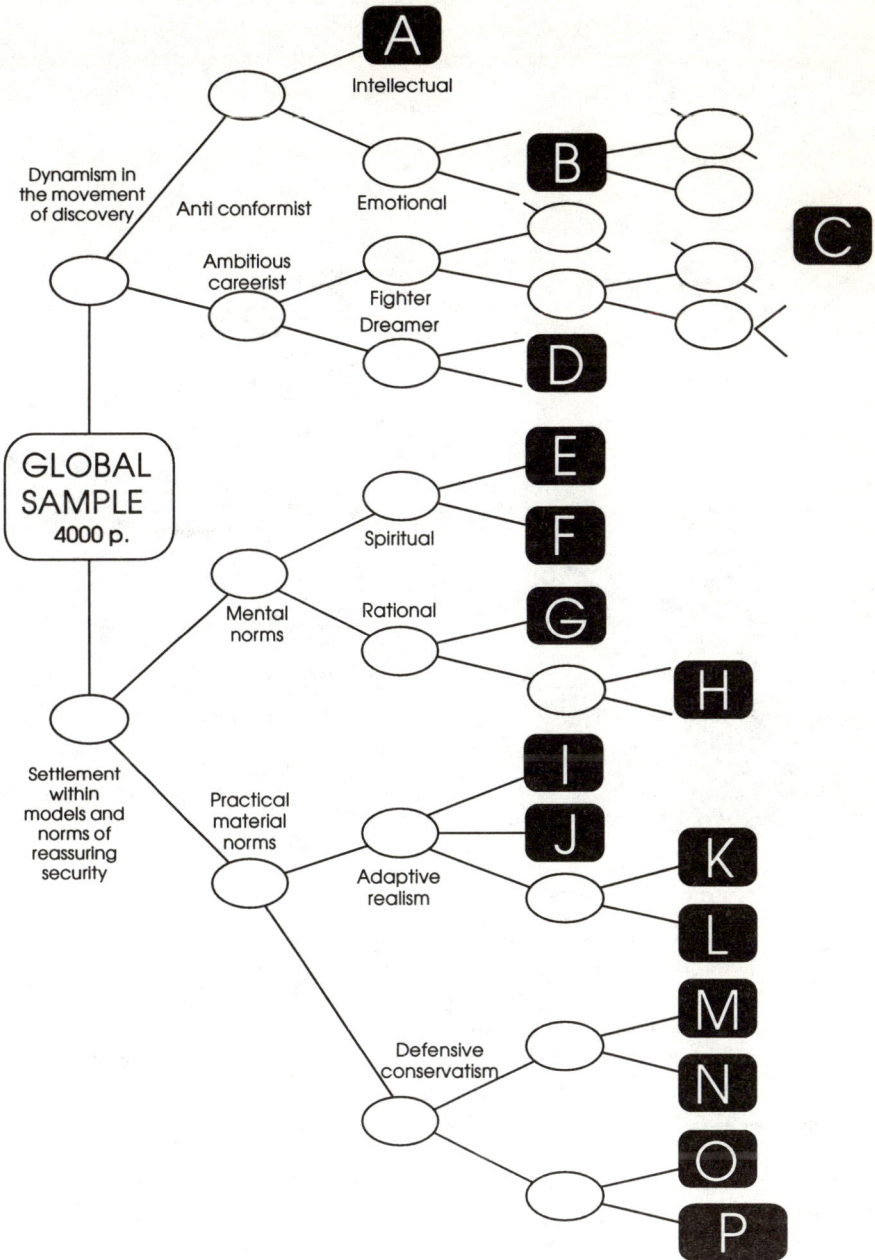

Source: Euro-Socio-Styles. Copyright CCA/EUROPANEL 1989

Figure 2.3 Typological family tree of socio-styles (the 16 European socio-styles)

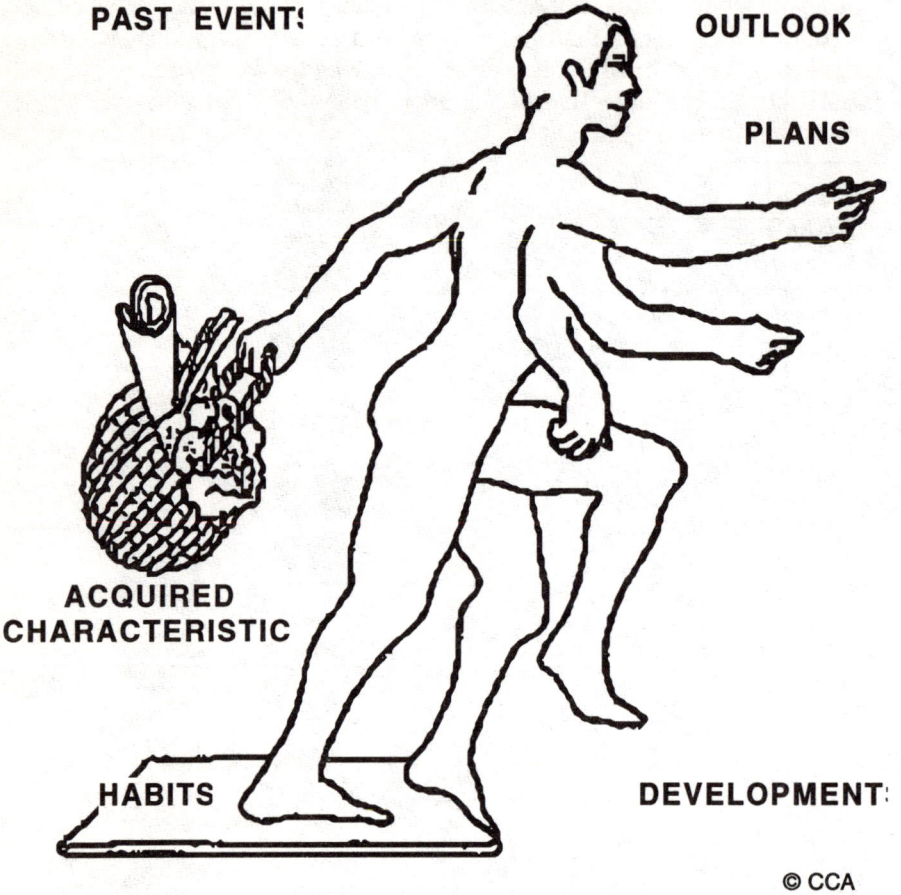

PAST EVENTS

OUTLOOK

PLANS

ACQUIRED
CHARACTERISTIC

HABITS

DEVELOPMENT

© CCA

Figure 2.4   Socio-style: A model of life in unstable equilibrium between
psychological and behavioural weighting and the dynamics of desire and novelty

opinion, a slow and progressive change affecting a particular cultural trend, because they are changes to real life and not simply changes in collective forms of thinking.

The objective of the socio-styles system in its recurrent surveys is to observe what models of change are dominant at a given time and how their changes in nature and socio-structure in the maps are indicative of undercurrents of change in society. For example, during the period 1974 to 1980 in France the disappearance (in terms of a significant statistical model) of the 'ambitious' socio-style model and the development of the 'dilettante' type reveal a social shift where the enterprise spirit declines in favour of job satisfaction, and where status is progressively replaced by motivation at work.

A socio-style is also a dialectic equilibrium. A type is a model of change relative to others with which it is allied or to which it is opposed in the general structure. The objective of the socio-barometer is to observe which families dominate the current social dialectic and to understand the evolution of these alliances. Figure 2.5 gives an example of an internal dialectic.

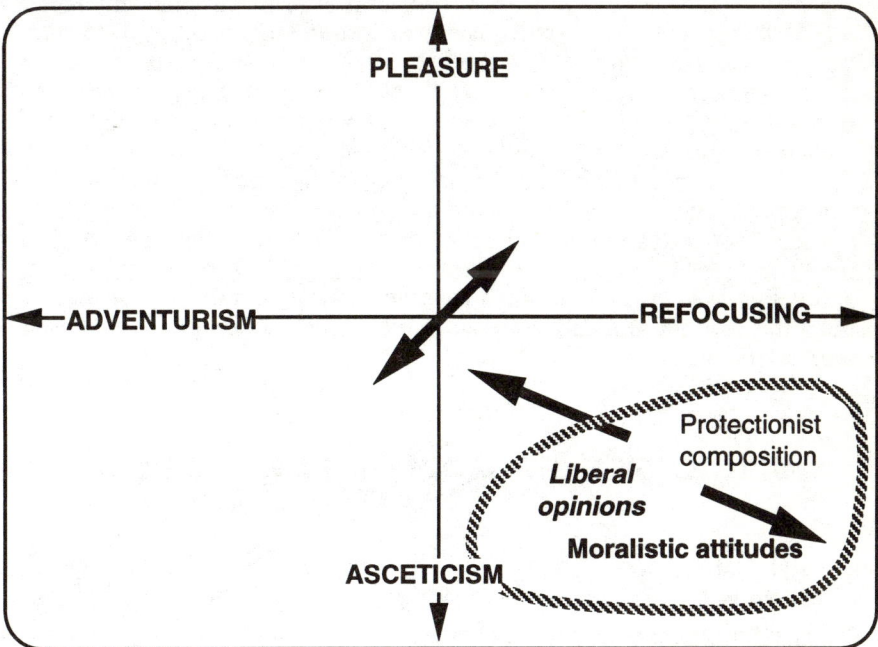

Source: Etude France 1987   © CCA 1987

Figure 2.5   Internal dialectic in a socio-style (France 1987). The socio-styles of a 'Rigorist' mentality are characterized by an apparent incoherence between nationalistic, xenophobic, protectionist and isolationist behaviour on one hand and opinions that favour economic liberalism on the other. This internal contradiction plays an integral part in people's life equilibrium and defines a way of adapting to reality. The positioning of the socio-styles on the map resulting from the stances taken at every stage of their lives reveals, however, that 'protectionism' generally gets the better of liberalism.

Example 1:
In 1984 in France the linking of the 'responsible' socio-style to a 'recentring' mentality and the slide of the 'dilettante' towards the 'marginal' micro-culture signify a profound change in the factors of social integration and professional movement. It is a sign of an 'adventurous' life model almost disappearing, which is characteristic of an industrial society; not the disappearance of individuals who had been labelled 'adventurous' up to then, but of a model of adaptation, culturally valued and statistically significant.

Example 2:
In socio-styles studies by CCA in France a new mentality appeared called 'marginal'. This new socio-cultural family was placed at the edge of the socio-map closest to the 'adventurous' pole and the majority were attracted by the 'pleasure' pole on the second axis. From the beginning it comprised a population of young graduates living in towns, students or young executives in the service sector and leading industries. At first measurement this mentality represented 18 per cent of the French population, to the detriment of the former 'adventurous' mentality. In 'marginal' types personal escapism replaces investment in society, playing a role replaces uncompromising self-expression, the imaginary takes precedence over the rational. Even if the number of 'marginal' types is not statistically very different from the 'adventurous' types in their consumer habits and the newspapers they read, their values and methods of socio-cultural integration are radically different. The appearance of these new socio-styles was emphasized and described in the CCA's general report on French lifestyles, distributed to all decision makers, forums, media, advertising agencies, political and governmental organizations. For each of them this new social family represented a challenge: a new group to be won over (see figure 2.6).

SOCIO-STYLES: COMPLETE LIFESTYLE PORTRAITS

Socio-styles are generally represented by a code name and sometimes by a graphic symbol, which experience has found useful. It goes without saying that these names should not be given a positive or a pejorative connotation; they do not encapsulate all the information, nor do they define a character.

Each type of family is given a dynamic synthetic interpretation, necessarily summarized into between 12 and 20 themes. This reduces the complexity of the data to a schematic model suitable for memorization and everyday use.

In addition to this interpretation, the socio-style variable can be analyzed in detail by its operational variables and throughout all stages of the socio-bank.

Figures 2.7 to 2.9 give examples of socio-styles portraits.

EVASIVENESS

DEFENSIVENESS

WITHDRAWAL

Sensualist

Responsible

ADVENTUROUS
MENTALITY
15%

Dabbler

POSITIVISM

The enterprising and innovative type underwent years of development. The expansion of this adventurous attitude slowed down and then receded.

EVASIVENESS

DEFENSIVENESS

WITHDRAWAL

Actor

INTERMEDIATE
ATTITUDE
22%

Profiteer

Libertarian

Stemming from the modernist, dynamic values of adventurism, this new mentality scorns these values and escapes from society

POSITIVISM

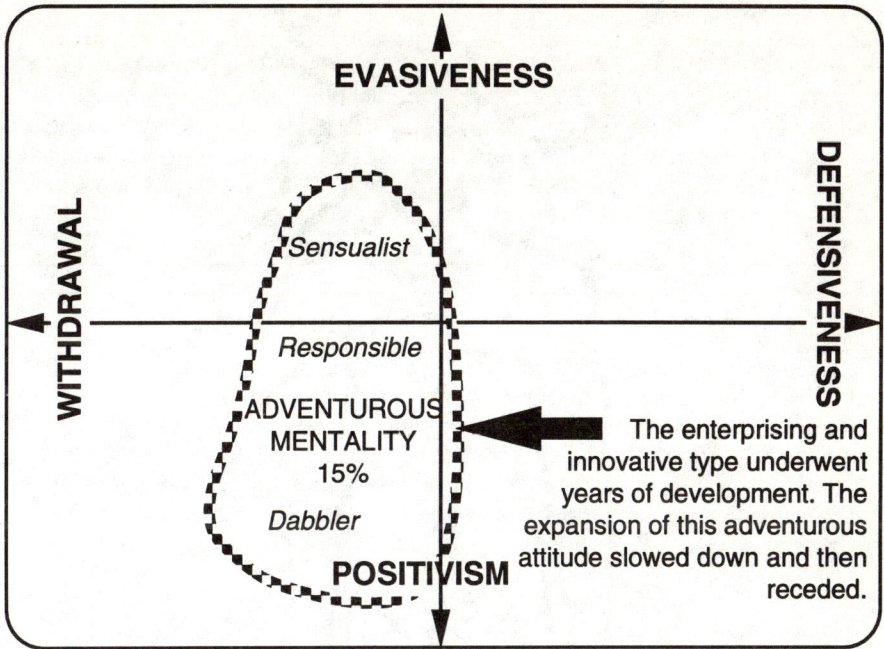

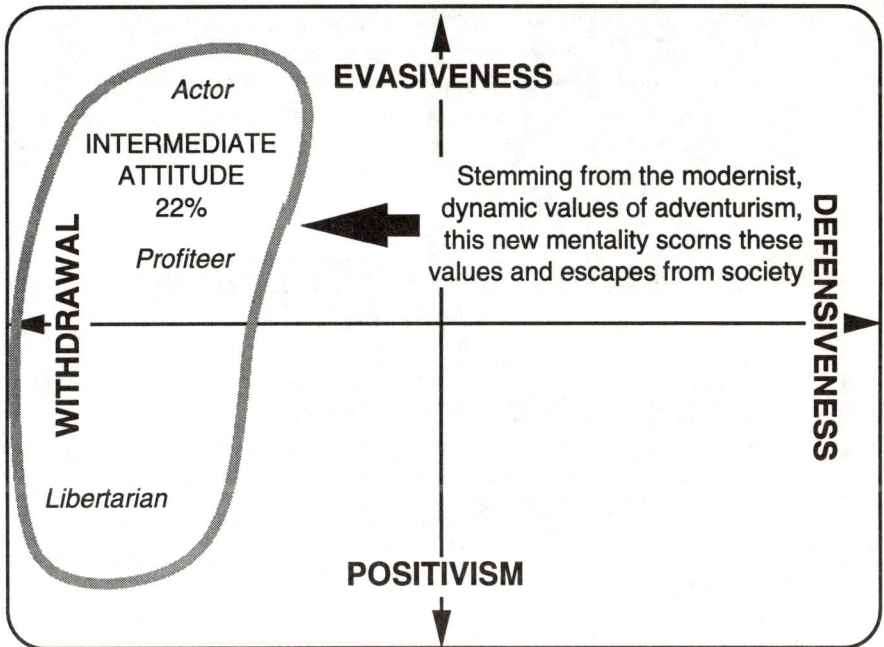

Source: Etude Styles de Vie France   © CCA 1980

Figure 2.6   The birth and decline of a mentality and socio-style, France 1980

© CCA

Figure 2.7 A socio-style: A complete lifestyle portrait: psychology and behaviour, reason and emotion, habits and choice

EXEMPLE OF SYNTHESIS PORTRAIT OF SPECIFICITIES OF A SOCIO-STYLE

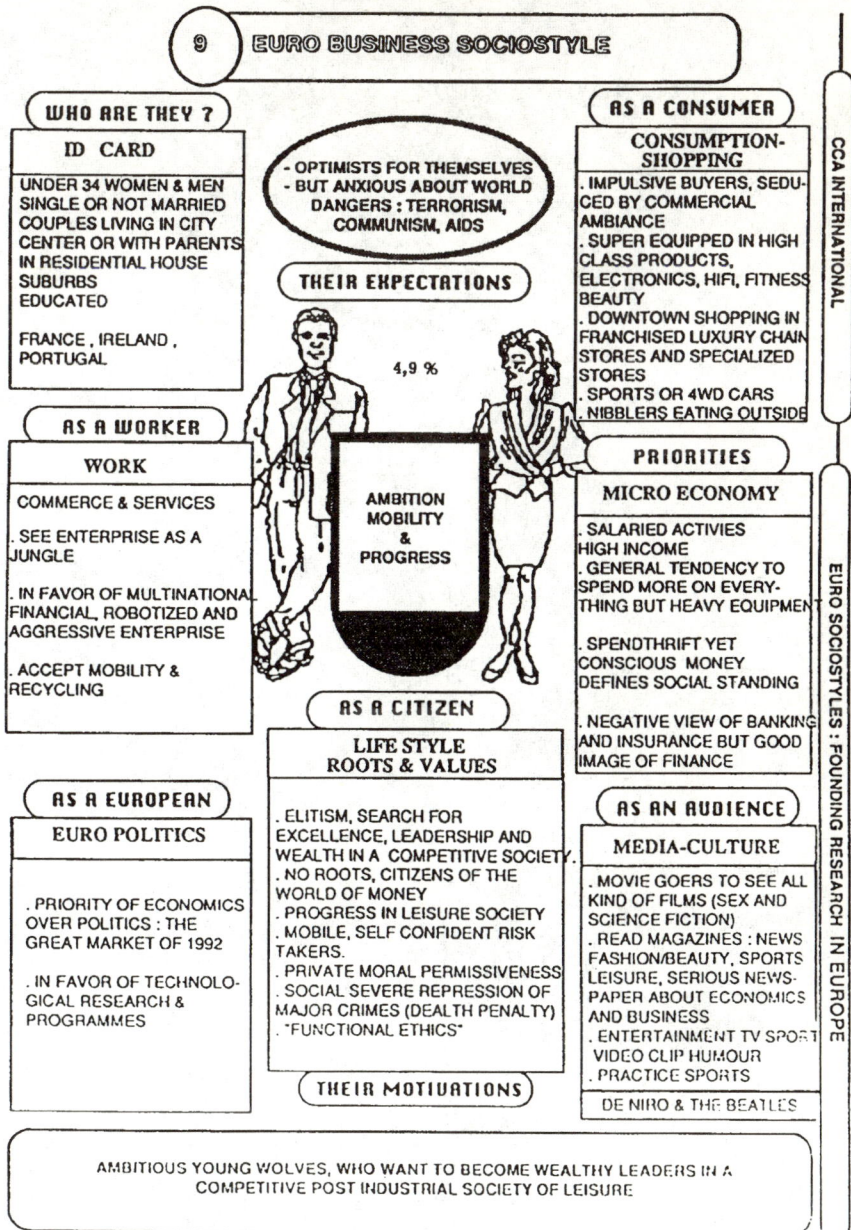

Figure 2.8   Synthethic portrait showing the specific nature of a socio-style

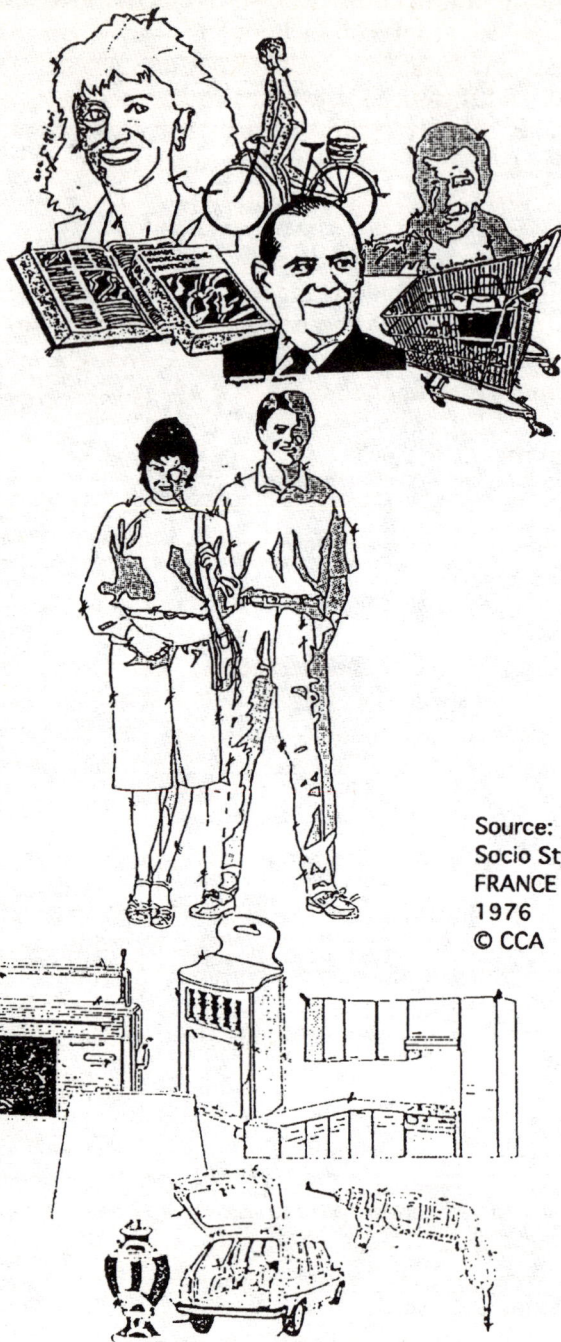

Source:
Socio Styles
FRANCE
1976
© CCA

Figure 2.9   Specific lifestyle and consumer habits of a socio-style

Living conditions

Socio-styles and mentalities describe the objective living conditions — physical, geographical, economic, sociological — which enable us to appreciate the thought and behaviour conditioning influencing a socio-cultural group. Analyzed and measured using classical demographic and economic principles (eg age, sex, profession), this information enables us to relate each socio-cultural type or family to the usual survey classifications into social and socio-professional classes. Figure 2.10 gives an illustration for the 'pioneer' socio-style.

This social identity card is completed by other data on such areas as geographical mobility, household arrangements or effective working conditions. The first dimension of the lifestyles typology is therefore linked directly to the factors which largely determine thought and action. This makes it a tool for market analysis.

Value systems

Socio-styles and mentalities also describe the value system of each population segment: religious and cultural beliefs, cultural values, myths and utopias, totems and sacred symbols which are ideological signs and predetermine how events are perceived and choices made. This allows campaigns (eg commercial advertising, political propaganda, social administrative information) to be analyzed and the impact of thematic content and symbolism assessed by reference to the ethics and philosophy of the target population, which define what is considered good or bad, shameful or glorious, beautiful or ugly, etc. Figure 2.11 offers an example of a portrait of a value system in Ireland.

Language

Socio-styles and mentalities also offer the opportunity to adapt the language of communication to a specific audience by analyzing linguistic sensitivity. Which words and types of address; which kinds of production and layouts; which pictures, photographs and designs; which colours and forms does each type of individual respond to spontaneously? What is their cultural language?

Information

Still in the area of communication, the portrait of each socio-style describes media and information support (eg press, local and national radio, magazines): whether they are watched, read or listened to regularly or occasionally, at what times and in what mental state, for information or for entertainment. The attractions of the new media forms (eg pay television, free papers) for each socio-style are also evaluated.

The socio-style is firstly an instrument of social analysis to enable those with cultural responsibilities to know what cultural influences each type of lifestyle is responsive to. Then for professionals in the media it is a tool for

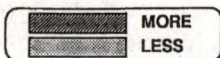

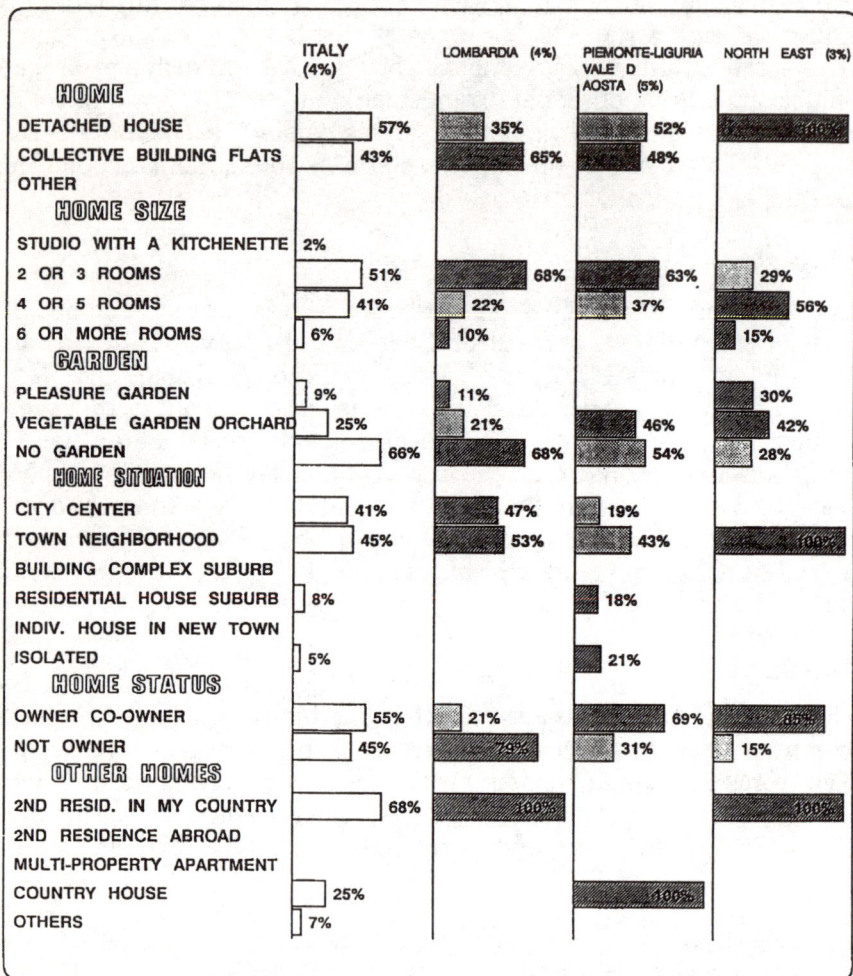

Figure 2.10 Regionalized analysis of the living conditions of a socio-type (Italy)

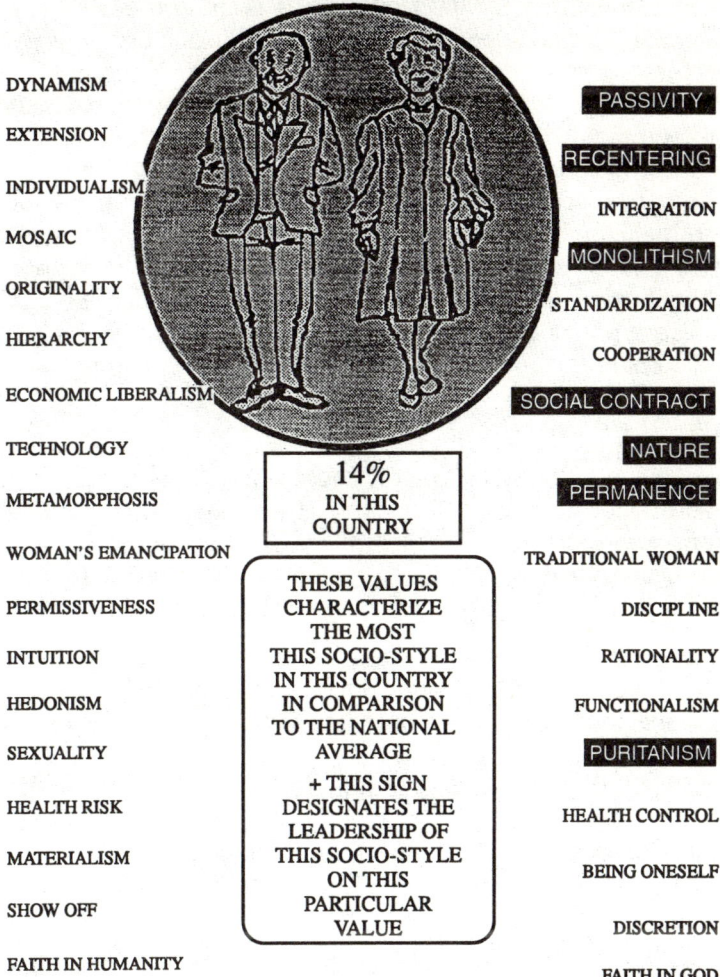

SOCIO-WAVES PORTRAIT IN IRELAND

SOCIO-STYLE : EURO'PRUDENT

DYNAMISM	PASSIVITY
EXTENSION	RECENTERING
INDIVIDUALISM	INTEGRATION
MOSAIC	MONOLITHISM
ORIGINALITY	STANDARDIZATION
HIERARCHY	COOPERATION
ECONOMIC LIBERALISM	SOCIAL CONTRACT
TECHNOLOGY	NATURE
METAMORPHOSIS	PERMANENCE
WOMAN'S EMANCIPATION	TRADITIONAL WOMAN
PERMISSIVENESS	DISCIPLINE
INTUITION	RATIONALITY
HEDONISM	FUNCTIONALISM
SEXUALITY	PURITANISM
HEALTH RISK	HEALTH CONTROL
MATERIALISM	BEING ONESELF
SHOW OFF	DISCRETION
FAITH IN HUMANITY	FAITH IN GOD

14%
IN THIS
COUNTRY

THESE VALUES
CHARACTERIZE
THE MOST
THIS SOCIO-STYLE
IN THIS COUNTRY
IN COMPARISON
TO THE NATIONAL
AVERAGE
+ THIS SIGN
DESIGNATES THE
LEADERSHIP OF
THIS SOCIO-STYLE
ON THIS
PARTICULAR
VALUE

Source: Euro Socio Styles   ©CCA 1989

Figure 2.11   Analysis of the value system of a socio-style

identifying the audience for each title or programme, the degree of saturation of each population, its subconscious and expressed preferences, and the competitive overlap between the different media forms. Finally, for those involved in advertising and public relations it is a media planning instrument enabling people to choose the most suitable support for getting the message over to the target audience.

Economic matters

At another, complementary level of analysis each socio-style or mentality draws a detailed, concrete portrait of economic life and consumption covering all sectors (eg savings, insurance, taxes, consumer spending).

It is a practical tool for economic analysis which in practice is differentiated from the main national indices because it emphasizes economic and financial behaviour which is sometimes contradictory and which statistical records do not report. It is a commercial marketing instrument for analyzing and influencing buying attitudes and behaviour, and also for organizing the distribution and sale of goods to potential consumers through analyzing which distribution outlets they use. Furthermore, by analyzing brand images lifestyle portraits offer professionals the opportunity to adjust advertising and communication to suit particular target populations.

Politics

If it is possible to talk of social marketing, or indeed political marketing (in the sense of a systematic analysis of the relationship between what institutions want and the aims or availability of various populations), the information about behaviour and psychology which is of use to commercial marketing is listed in the portrait of each socio-style and mentality:

❑ sensitivity toward positive or negative opinions about the institutional images of public services, political parties, public figures, etc;
❑ civic behaviour in different domains (eg voting, the black economy, finance);
❑ the acceptability of new regulations (eg for road safety) or legislative plans;
❑ opinions about methods of social communication and the conduct of political propaganda.

With a different procedure and different objectives from commercial marketing, a socio-cultural analysis of different civic lifestyles is possible.

Work

Between civic and private life, a portrait of professional life represents one of the facets of each socio-style or mentality as an indicator for organizational and company management:

❑ Reactions to social laws, trade union behaviour, attitudes towards authority, the acceptability of new work schedules and conditions. The

lifestyles typology is an instrument for reflection and a formative tool for organizations concerned with working relationships and training.
❏ More generally, knowledge about motivation at work and attitudes towards recession or unemployment enables us to improve our understanding of the position of work in a person's life.

Private life

At the heart of all this information, a socio-style or a mentality offers a portrait of a person's private life. As well its practical application, this information constitutes the integral point of the lifestyle where all social and personal attitudes and behaviour, inertia and dynamism, conditioning and instability are linked together.

Life prospects

Finally, the most dynamic components of this socio-style model, future scenarios, possibilities for innovation, plans and projected behaviour, indicate the future not as it will be but the preferred direction on the compass of possibilities which reveals current dissatisfactions, short-term instabilities and future aspirations. These life prospects anticipate the form of potential changes.

How to read a socio-style portrait

For each item researchers have analyzed which socio-styles responded in a way significantly different from the general average of the sample. The portrait of each socio-style therefore comprises at each stage of the survey all the responses by which this group of individuals is differentiated from the others. The individual responses can be given by both high and low percentages of people; they always indicate an attitude, motivation or form of behaviour, a preference for a particular product or reading material, where 8 to 12 per cent of the individuals in the same category exhibit a way of thought or way of life in common.

Example 1:
When the report states, 'socio-style 3 is the biggest consumer of soft drinks and consumes less alcohol than average', this should be taken to mean: 'socio-style 3 purchases and consumes soft drinks more often, more regularly and in larger quantities than not merely the general average of the sample but also any other socio-style type; and consumes less alcohol than the general average of the sample'.

Example 2:
When the report states, 'Socio-style 8 reads the business press regularly and never watches soap operas on television', this does not mean:

❑ that all type 8 individuals always read the business press;
❑ that no individual of this type ever watches serials and soap opera;
❑ that type 8 individuals are the only ones to read the business press;
❑ that type 8 individuals are the only ones not to watch soap operas on television.

It means that people belonging to socio-style 8 read the business press in greater numbers and watch soap operas in smaller numbers than the average of the population and of the other socio-style types.

Reading and understanding socio-style portraits must always be relative: the portrait of the type characterizes mainly the differences and accentuates the special points. It is useful because it shows analysts and social and economic decision makers the topics, ideas and objects to which this socio-style reacts positively or negatively in a particularly original way.

Bearing these special psychological or behavioural characteristics in mind, a company or organization can adapt its products and services, its message and advertising, its brand image and promotions, its distribution system and public relations to the particular target group it wishes to reach. Even if the socio-method aims mainly to look beyond the mass of people in order to account for the different sub-system within a society, and even if the 'average person' is split into several types, we are all in the same boat. The social boat is susceptible to currents to which no one can remain indifferent, but which influence everyone in a different way according to his or her position in the social sea. For some a current is experienced as a counter-current against which they struggle; for others the same current is felt to be in harmony with their personal motivations and desires. These dynamic phenomena are known as cultural flows or socio-waves.

SOCIO-WAVES AND THEIR SOCIO-CULTURAL FLOWS: TRENDS AND MODELS

If the socio-style typology emphasizes social diversity, provides evidence of its variety and mixes psychological and behavioural polarities, it must not conceal that all these people over and above their differences live within the same civilization (local or international) whose basic values (basic culture) they share. They cannot escape entirely from the influences of the socio-cultural climate in which the whole of society is steeped. The familiar expression 'we are all in the same boat' can be applied literally to the socio-styles typology.

It is this socio-cultural boat that is analyzed by socio-waves which produce bi-polar pairs of cultural trends or flows opposed in an ideological, ethical or practical choice. This concept defines the system of values expressed in trends of ideas, images and stereotypes which incorporate the collective dynamism of the socio-culture in unstable equilibrium at a given moment.

Socio-waves are the result of the dialectic between individuals and the socio-cultural environment. They are the language of society by which the images and functions of objects, the missions and roles of institutions, personal relationships and status, fashion codes and norms are defined and valued, located and organized. The cultural flow is a fashion in the best sense of the word.

This concept analyzes collective psychology rather than behaviour and it constitutes the ideological watermark of the socio-structural map, representing its predominant and less influential cultures, how individuals come to adopt particular ways of life.

The concept of cultural flows in the socio-styles system — despite different methods of study and analysis — is similar to the socio-cultural currents which are the essential idea in the American obedience systems practised by Yankelovich. They share scope and limits and are both methods in the domain of ideas.

Socio-waves are more profound because they integrate behavioural and emotional dynamics beyond simple attitudes and opinions. They measure the forced choices between ethical, ideological and behavioural models that everyone must make, between attractive ideal trends and the constraints of reality. Figures 2.12 and 2.13 illustrate socio-waves.

Fashion: A simple stereotype

The socio-cultural flow is a condensing variable which encapsulates as much information as possible in a simple way. Despite its psychological nature it can be compared with socio-objective criteria. In the same way that age or sex is a simple variable artificially isolated from the complexity of an individual, the hedonism flow, for example, is a simplifying notion which reduces the mental complexity of a way of thinking to a single reference point.

It is dangerous for practical social action to reduce the individual to an analytical criterion or list of criteria. It is on this principle that our research into types of synthetic socio-styles is founded. On the other hand, it is legitimate to isolate simple flows or trends in the case of social stereotypes of ideas and cultural phenomena. These are images and advertising symbols, recurrent themes in the media, the conventional ideas of ordinary people; they are cultural products.

The hedonism flow is therefore not a complex psychology of pleasure, but a stereotype of 'priority to sensual pleasure' expressed at a given moment by the collective language of public opinion. It is a caricature, but a true caricature that mirrors the mental images exciting society at that time. The cultural flow is therefore an idea whose caricature-like simplicity is opposite to the complexity of the socio-style. The flow or trend can therefore on occasions seem to be more mathematically discriminative than classical marketing analyses; conversely, it offers less explanation of reality, being just one of the lifestyle factors.

© CCA

Figure 2.12 Flows and socio-waves: Fashionable ideas, ideas of the moment, dominant values, preferential scenarios

The French CCA studies have analyzed in detail 26 cultural values collected in 13 bi-polar flows. From now on, international socio-styles system studies measure 36 values in 18 bi-polar flows from the perspective of private life on the one hand and social life on the other. Figure 2.14 illustrates a comparison of flows in a macro and micro context.

Social winds: A dynamic variable

Dynamic sociology is interested in measuring how people find particular values attractive. To take a meteorological analogy, cultural flows are social winds that blow over the socio-map, while socio-styles are boats following effective routes influenced by these winds and the pressures towards social conformity that they represent. But a socio-style does not only obey the main forces of opinion. Like the path of a ship, its social adaptation is the

PSYCHOLOGICAL VALUES

Recessive Values   **Dynamic Values**

Technical ————————————▶ Natural
Science ————————————▶ Ecology
Robot ————————————▶ Man
Artificiality ————————————▶ Authenticity
Industry ————————————▶ Craftsmen
Complexity ————————————▶ Simplicity
Modernism ————————————▶ Rusticity
Superfluous ————————————▶ Essential

SOCIOLOGIC WEIGHT:

- In 1974 : 52% of the French
- In 1977 : 65.6% of the French

ACTUAL EMERGENCE: dynamic (2/3) and with the majority (+13.6%)

SOCIAL INFLUENCE (1977) OF THE NATURAL

The less responsive

* the men (60%)
* the 15/19 years old (50%)
* the managerial staff (51%)
* People of the North and (51%)
  from the Mediterranean (57%)
  area

The more responsive

* the women (70%)
* the over 65 years old (81%)
* heads of firms (72%)
* unemployed (75%)
* people from the West (72%)

THE NATURAL IN LIFE STYLES (1977)

The less responsive

* Enterprising types (58%)
* Dabblers/amateurs (30%)

The more responsive

* Peaceful (88%)
* Exemplary (80%)
* Ambitious (74%)

CORRELATION WITH THE FLOWS OF PASSIVITY AND REFOCUSING

Source: Sociostyles in France   COPYRIGHT CCA 1977

Figure 2.13   An example of socio-waves from the technical to the natural.
Momentary state of equilibrium between two values in socio-dynamic competition

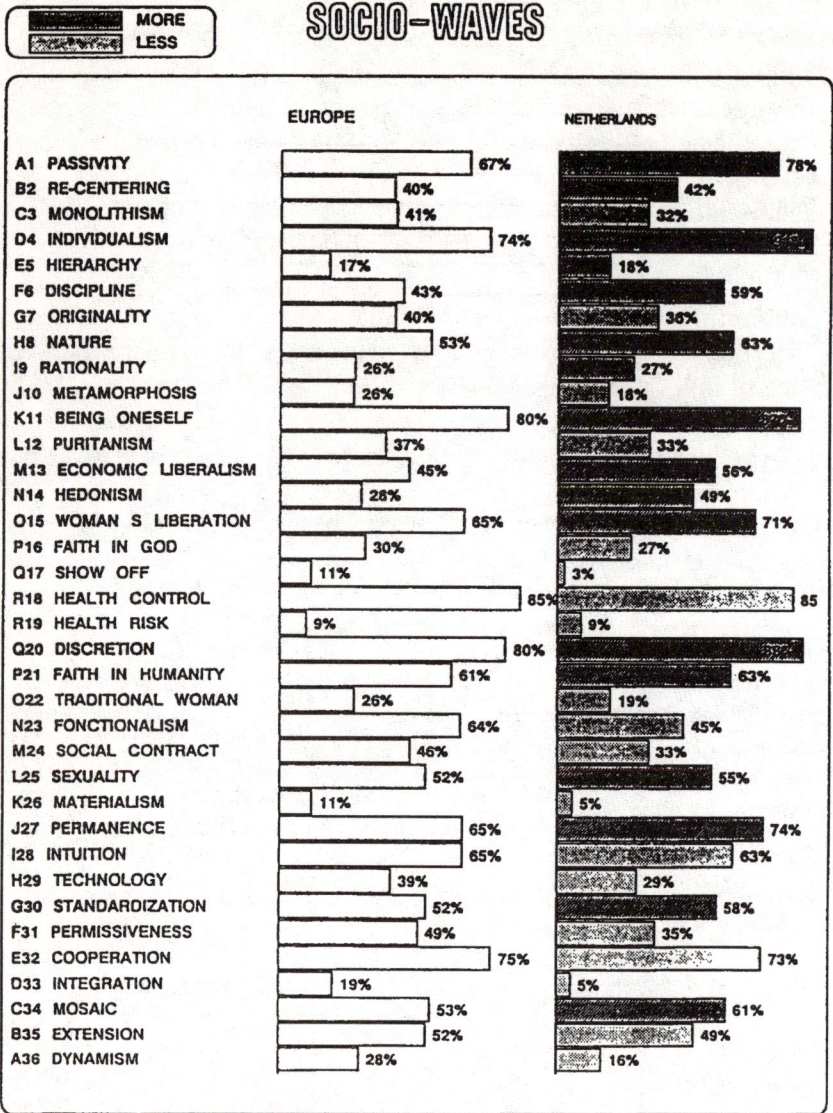

Figure 2.14   Comparative measurement of cultural flows in a macro-social zone (Europe) and a micro-social zone (one country)

result of its own structure and weight, its ambitions and plans, and its positioning and competitive strategy in relation to others. Social winds likewise are just one of the variables determining a way of life.

The potential importance of socio-cultural trends has to be qualified. They do not represent the future, but merely the social climate that favours certain values or images, certain languages and symbols, and they therefore influence the actual lifestyle — the socio-style — which is more complex and weighty.

A socio-cultural analysis by cultural flows alone would be dangerous, since it would give prominence to fashionable majority stereotypes and ignore different shades of opinion. It would also accentuate social change and underestimate the resistance of familiar habits and patterns of adaptation. The flow is often a simulation of change, mental imagery that takes the place of innovation and retains intentions, words and symbols. In this way the variable is particularly informative and relevant for advertising, propaganda, 'hot news', all of which are necessarily stereotyped, caricature-like in their brevity, need to make an impact and look to the future. But if flows are a tool for commercial communications, in the socio-styles system they are just one composite variable among others.

Social opinion: A psychological variable

Socio-waves are only one component in the multi-dimensional concept of the socio-styles system. They say nothing about behaviour or living conditions. As a consequence, the same current does not affect people with different ways of life in the same way. Socio-waves say nothing about a person's motivation and deep, subconscious, energizing aspirations; and as a consequence adherence to a trend does not involve the same enthusiasm for everyone.

Socio-waves are the third basic component of the socio-style: opinion socialized, made rational, relatively structured, stereotypical in language and reduced to symbols. Their boundaries are interesting to monitor and analyze since the flows indicate an individual's mental adherence to and verbal participation in a collective style of ideas, and therefore the acquisition of a cultural ideology. They are therefore an intermediate variable between behaviour and motivation, a form of verbal behaviour or psychology made concrete in social symbols.

The compass of cultural contrasts: A bi-polar variable

In contrast to the American methodological tradition of socio-cultural currents, socio-waves are bi-polar axes which oppose two implicitly antagonistic values in the current civilization. Each socio-wave is thus designated by this competing pair of social orientations. For example, the natural/technical flow analyzes an individual's relative preference for natural, ecological, rustic or craft imagery on the one hand, and scientific, technical, futuristic, automation imagery on the other.

The advantage of the bi-polar nature of the socio-wave is that it enables discrimination: the individual is analyzed through a cultural orientation rather than one opposing ideology or other. The social value system is analyzed in a competitive situation which is continually changing, abandoning some values and adopting others while negotiating between the attraction of fashionable ideas and the constraints of reality.

The values on each bi-polar axis are not philosophically opposed or logically or metaphorically incompatible; nor do they involve a moral judgement. They have appeared as actual cultural oppositions in our civilization and our time, and represent generally shared psychological choices of belief and social positioning. Thus there is no absolute opposition between the values of 'nature' and 'technology', but merely a broad axis of choices adapted over the long term.

These bi-polar oppositions have been defined and occasionally enhanced by motivation studies using the EPSY and CHORUM methods.

Another advantage of bi-polarity is tolerance. With single polar trends, which of necessity have to be oriented towards one thing, individuals are defined by a strong or weak rating on the axis. Since a weak rating is viewed negatively as a deficiency, there is a great risk of making value judgements with ethical or elitist connotations. Thus, if the trend is conceived as being towards progress, people are characterized as being ahead or behind.

With bi-polar socio-waves each individual is fully defined by a positive value system which is dynamic and equal to any other, even if the beliefs are not widely held at the time and are opposed to the concept of progress. When social trends are reversed the bi-polarity of values enables the change to be viewed against a balance of ideological choices. Figure 2.15 explains the impact of two competing values. In this national example the map shows what percentage of people and which people are receptive to each of the values and to the corresponding messages.

The meteorology of the socio-structure: A structural variable

In the socio-styles system socio-waves are used commercially for strategic communication analysis: advertising and the creation of new media forms to find a dynamic social style, brand images or images of organizations, etc.

However, the essential goal of this variable is to contribute to the structuring of the socio-map by analyzing conformity with socio-styles. In the organization of the social landscape of typological diversity and the game of social dialectic, the flows represent the dynamic component of social opinion while socio-styles represent a more static component of behavioural and mental change. The flows belong to the socio-map whose climate they define. They are active and explanatory variables of the socio-structure in the same way as socio-styles.

In particular, socio-waves can explain the positioning of passive variables on the socio-styles map by analyzing the proximity of a variable to one of

NETHERLANDS

Valuables pole

Dandy	Olvidados Vigilante
Rocky	
	Romantic Prudent
Squadra	Defensive
Business	
Movement pole	Settlement pole
	Moralist
Scout	Gentry
Protest	
Pioneer	Citizen Strict

Values pole

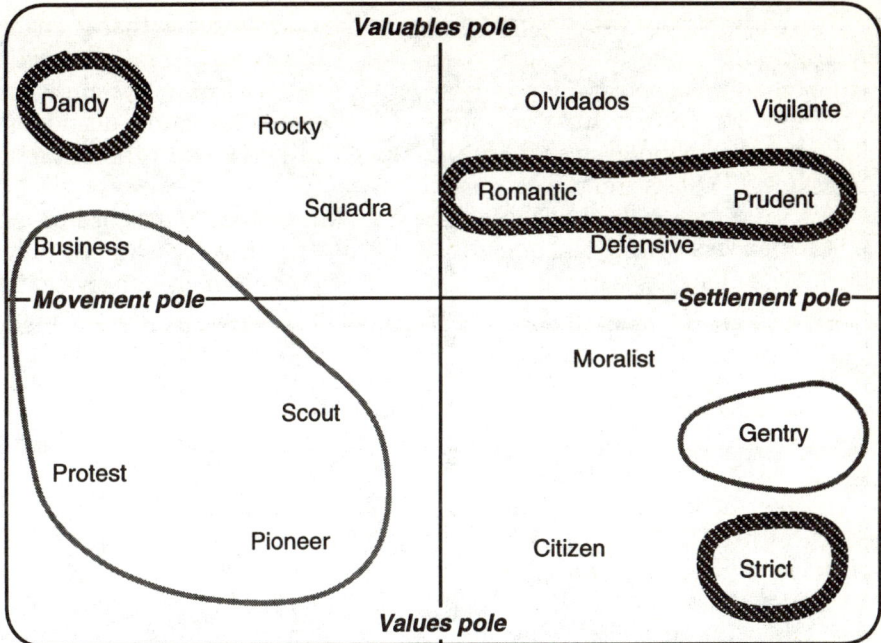

Source: EUROPANEL 1989   © CCA INTERNATIONAL

The ringed sociostyles are more sensitive to the corresponding type of message

DYNAMISM	PASSIVITY
- Struggle for life and will power	- Let's live peacefully and quietly
- Take risks	- Avoid conflicts and competition
- Accept challenges and competition	- Accept things as they are
- Be tonic	- Look for silence comfort and security
- Be resilient	- Quality price and no surprise
- You pay for what you get	

Figure 2.15   Analysis of the impact of two flows of a socio-wave with competing values in the socio-styles typology

the two flows that make up a socio-wave. When the statistical balance of the flows changes (because the proportion of those holding one of the values increases to the detriment of the other), the appearance of the socio-cultural map is affected, particularly in the definition of its axes.

When the relationship between a socio-style and certain flows changes (ie when one lifestyle type changes its opinions), the position of the socio-styles and flows on the socio-map is upset, since the position of one type (and therefore of all the others) on the map analyzing socio-structure connections depends directly on the values which it prefers in the flows.

Figure 2.16 is a socio-map of France in 1977.

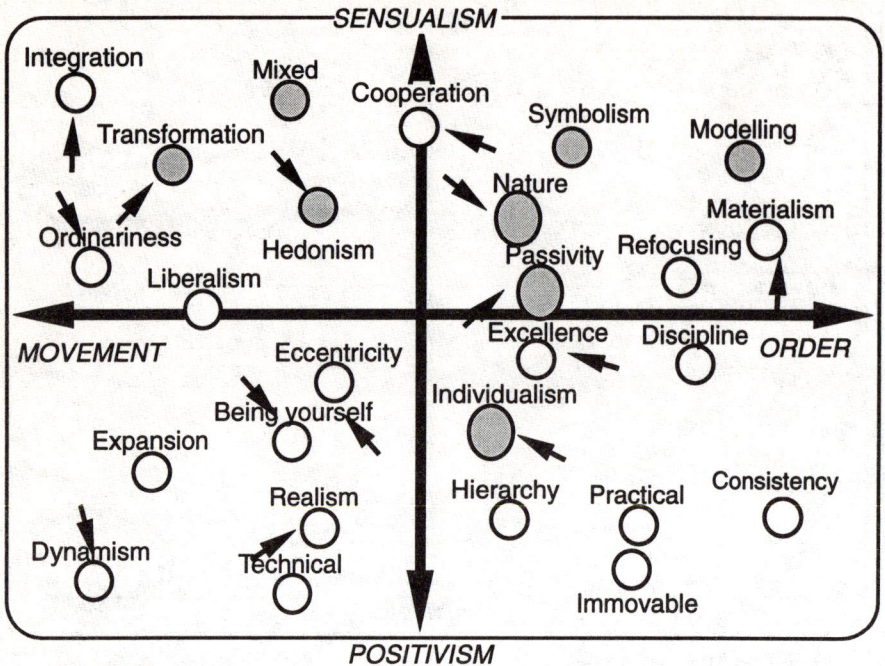

Figure 2.16 The organization and movement of all the flows on the socio-map. Socio-structure of France 1977

❑ Two flow-values comprise a socio-wave pair in opposition on the map (eg transformation and consistency).

❑ The hatching in the circles indicate the dominant pole for each pair of bi-polar flows which shows the meaning of the socio-wave. A concentration of these hatchings outline on the socio-map the region where the most 'fashionable' socio-styles are found.

❑ The circles symbolize the position of each flow-value on the map according to its correlation with socio-styles that were most favourably disposed to it in 1977.

❑ The arrows show any movement that took place since the earlier study in 1974.

Source: French study 1977

Strong trends: A constant variable

The explicit hypothesis of this method (which is the same as that of Anglo-Saxon socio-cultural currents) is that the flows are significant phenomena of the collective socio-psychology, pillars of the civilization, the expression of its simple and essential values — and not unstable equilibria arising from

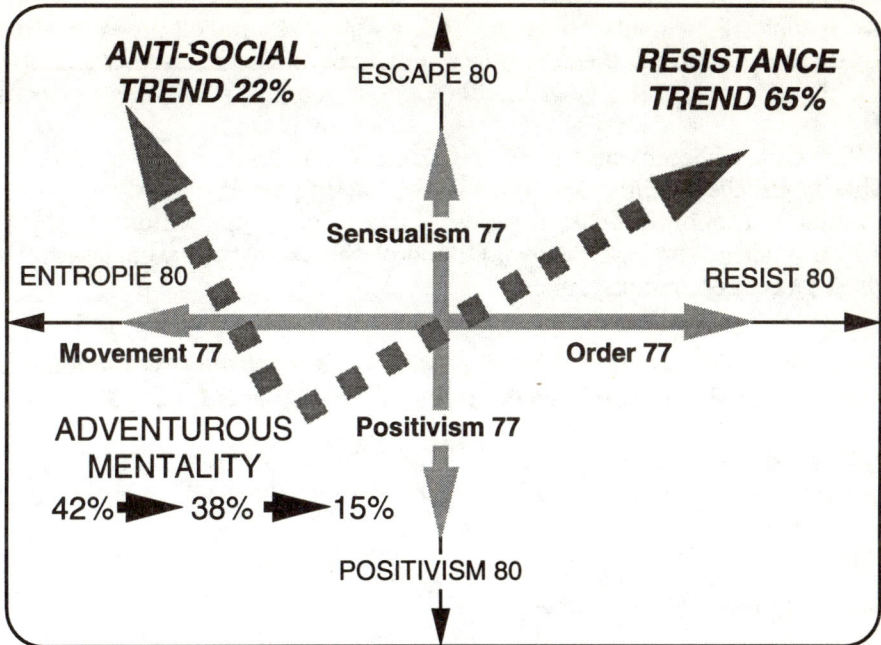

Figure 2.17   The measurement of strong socio-cultural trends through observation of the evolution of socio-waves and axes on the map

a combination of circumstances as socio-styles are. This seems to be made credible by the relative slowness with which flows and trends evolve — a few percentage points a year. This contrasts with the relatively faster changes among the equilibrium models represented by socio-styles. Figure 2.17 considers the development of socio-cultural trends in France between 1977 and 1980.

The simplicity of the values studied, stereotyped and caricature-like but almost conceptual, contributes to making the flows into a durable variable in the socio-structure. The socio-styles, on the other hand, are more transient and are therefore the circumstantial variable of the system.

How to read the socio-wave compass

The compass chart describes 9 axes and therefore 18 opposing poles starting with the three basic axes of the socio-map.

❑ The horizontal axis is the first basic socio-structure axis; the vertical axis is the second; and the third axis is represented by the circle at the centre of the compass.
❑ Six other diagonal axes indicate intermediate values which differentiate the socio-structure from axes 1 and 2.

This basic compass can be superimposed on any of the socio-style, socio-target or socio-niche maps. This is a practical way of reading off the motivating values and dominant themes in each quadrant of the socio-map and also enables the original trends of the socio-styles and socio-targets to be described.

Just as a navigator places a compass on a geographical map to discover what landscape or climate will be found by taking a particular direction, so a social or economic decision maker places a socio-compass on the socio-map to identify the psychology and kind of behaviour to be found within a given target population.

THE SOCIO-MAP: A MAP OF SOCIETY

All the socio-styles survey data converge on a socio-structural map which they help to define, and which in return explains the various socio-cultural positionings.

A synthetic structure

Two methods can be used in the socio-styles system to generate the central map.

Crossing socio-styles with socio-waves

A multi-factor correspondance analysis produces two active variables:

❏ socio-styles, models of a combination of factors that synthesize the 3,500 or so variables collected during the course of the foundation survey; and
❏ flows, synthetic indices structured as bi-polar socio-waves from dozens of standardized and repetitive replies, opinions and attitudes.

This formula produces a map which in its structural axes and the topographic distribution of socio-styles is strongly influenced by cultural flows. It is therefore a map which shows the position of the typology in relation to the values and ideas in vogue. The map is sociologically useful for describing the present, but it lacks stability over a period of time and is less effective for analyzing the positioning of behavioural phenomena.

Crossing socio-styles with factors

Another formula consists of choosing socio-styles typology and synthetic factors as active variables to generate the socio-map. The factors are those synthesizing the responses to the survey and resulting from earlier factor or canon analyses which created the typology. This procedure produces a map which is less susceptible to the effects of fashion and more durable in its basic socio-structure, since it is more influenced by behavioural variables, especially when canon analysis is used. It is therefore more readable as a marketing analysis. This is the technique that is currently being used by CCA for its international studies.

The socio-map is thus the result of a chain of synthetizing processes. It is the most refined structuring possible of the most characteristic elements of social variety (socio-styles), of cultural dynamics (flows) and also of the hard core which structures lifestyles (factors). In this respect it is very different from other maps obtained by directly crossing simple survey variables (responses to a questionnaire) where the axes are generally based on marginal and anecdotal responses and not on significant factors.

Present and future: A dynamic structure

The socio-map reveals a moment of equilibrium between familiar habits and the dynamic impulses of collective opinion. The equilibrium is temporary, so we need to update the map periodically.

This socio-structure, whether national or micro-social, reveals the state of a society in the lifestyles of its members at the crossroads of past adaptations established as realistic forms of behaviour and attractions to idealistic values. We can discern the movement by which familiar patterns of adaptation look towards new values or are reinforced by a return to former values, symbolizing social dynamics. It is also the movement by which ideas, the imaginary representation of change, materialize in a more realistic fashion as ways of thinking and lifestyles.

The axes: A multi-dimensional structure

Following correspondence analysis, the socio-map is organized into axes which are the main dimensions explaining the equilibrium of the socio-cultural system.

The axes with the greatest spread of socio-styles reveal the range of social diversity deconstructing society, and can be read as centrifugal horizons towards which individuals are dispersed.

The axes with the greatest homogeneity in socio-styles indicate cohesive values and define the basic cultural personality. They can be seen as centripetal axes of convergence and communion, over and above any differences.

Finally there are axes where types of lifestyles are in the greatest opposition, revealing the principal dialectics and dynamic choices in society and private life. These can be seen as sociological scales which reveal predominant or least influential cultures as well as majority or minority scenarios.

Normally correspondence analysis reveals two to four relevant axes. Only the first two axes are depicted; they usually explain more than 70 or 80 per cent of the variance. Nevertheless, the existence of a third axis is often important in reading the map to help differentiate socio-styles or variables paradoxically close in the two-dimensional structure, whose differences the first two axes do not manage to explain. Three-dimensional representation is possible but complicated to use; while more satisfying intellectually for the researcher it is less convenient for a professional user.

We hope that information technology will soon enable us to depict socio-structures on screen in three or four dimensions, enabling the user to choose by spatial rotation a succession of two-dimensional representations. All possible axis configurations can be examined two at a time before the most discriminating map reading for analyzing the problem is finally chosen.

The goal of the socio-map is first and foremost practical instruction. It offers a pattern of data organization which clarifies the analysis and is structured and synthetic. From a map we can expect a clear understanding of the data; correspondence analysis merely underlines an internal logic for the information which existed prior to the researcher's analysis and interpretation (ie all the responses from the survey sample). This logic is often complex and three- or four-dimensional, which inevitably means a loss of information in practice because we are not able to grasp it in sufficient depth.

We therefore do not hesitate to claim that the best map is not the most complex and complete one, but the most readable, since the independent logic of the information has to lend itself to practical interpretation.

The socio-structure axes are provided empirically by statistical correspondence analysis. They are neither chosen nor imposed, nor are they even predicted by the researcher prior to the analysis of the survey. The poles of the socio-map are objective in the sense that they emerge experimentally through pure mathematical logic from the whole process of synthesis and structuring of variables. They are an inner logic of the socio-bank suggested by the computer. We can maintain that socio-maps, like socio-styles, are experimental outcomes manipulated as little as possible by the producers of the study, if not by the choice of the statistical treatment to be used.

Yet this socio-structural map remains dumb; the statistical process is limited to revealing factorial dimensions, the most explanatory axes mathematically speaking for the spread and organization of replies to a survey or number of surveys. An internal logic which is more or less clear and simple (according to the number of axes and their explanatory power) informs the mass of data synthesized as socio-styles and flows. Summarized into dozens or hundreds of factors, this logic gives it a graphic, spatial shape which is nothing but a conventional structural visualization. The sense of the logic remains to be discovered.

This interpretation is the work of researchers who decipher the socio-structure and try to understand the dimensions of its axes according to the factors, socio-styles and flows that define them, grasp the polar oppositions and name them in a useful way without losing their complexity. The study thus becomes qualitative once more and the research team has to interpret the information in a relatively subjective way. The socio-map therefore consists of objective logic which can be interpreted by its users.

Figure 2.18 analyzes one axis of a socio-map.

Mentalities: A structure of interrelationships

Defined by two or three axes from the correspondence analysis, the active variables (socio-styles, factors, flows) are positioned within the socio-map according to their interrelationships judged by their correlation to the axes.

AXIS 1 opposes

Socio-styles...   *socio-styles*

Show-offs ◄──── within Egocentrism ────► Vigilantes

Profiteers and ◄──── Gap   R. materialist ───► Arduous/Utilitarian
dilletantes

Libertarian ◄──── Gap   R. rigorist ───► Responsible/*moralist*
values...   *values...*

(On the main values)

Being one self   *Individualism*
Personal egoistic   Social unity (family)
Beaming: private unity

Liberalism   *Discipline, order*
Anarchistic permissiveness   Repression, authoritarianism

Extension   *Withdraw, cocooning*
Exterior opening
Adventure, escape

Standardization   *Transcendency*
Without ideology   Religious spirit, faith

                        (and on)
Metamorphosis   (secondary values)   *Permanence*
Changing, evolution,   Traditionalism
ephemeral   Immobility

Originality   *Standardization*
Anticonformism   *Conformism*

Dynamism   *Passivity*
Spirit   Assistance
(Realism)   *(Monolithism)*

                        (interpreted as)

This life orientation   *... this life orientation*
asserts its anti-social autonomy   reinforces its social identity by
by rejecting norms and   adhering to the ideologies and
laws/ideologies and by escaping   immutable laws of protective
into the unknown   social groups

Source : Life Styles France   CCA 1984

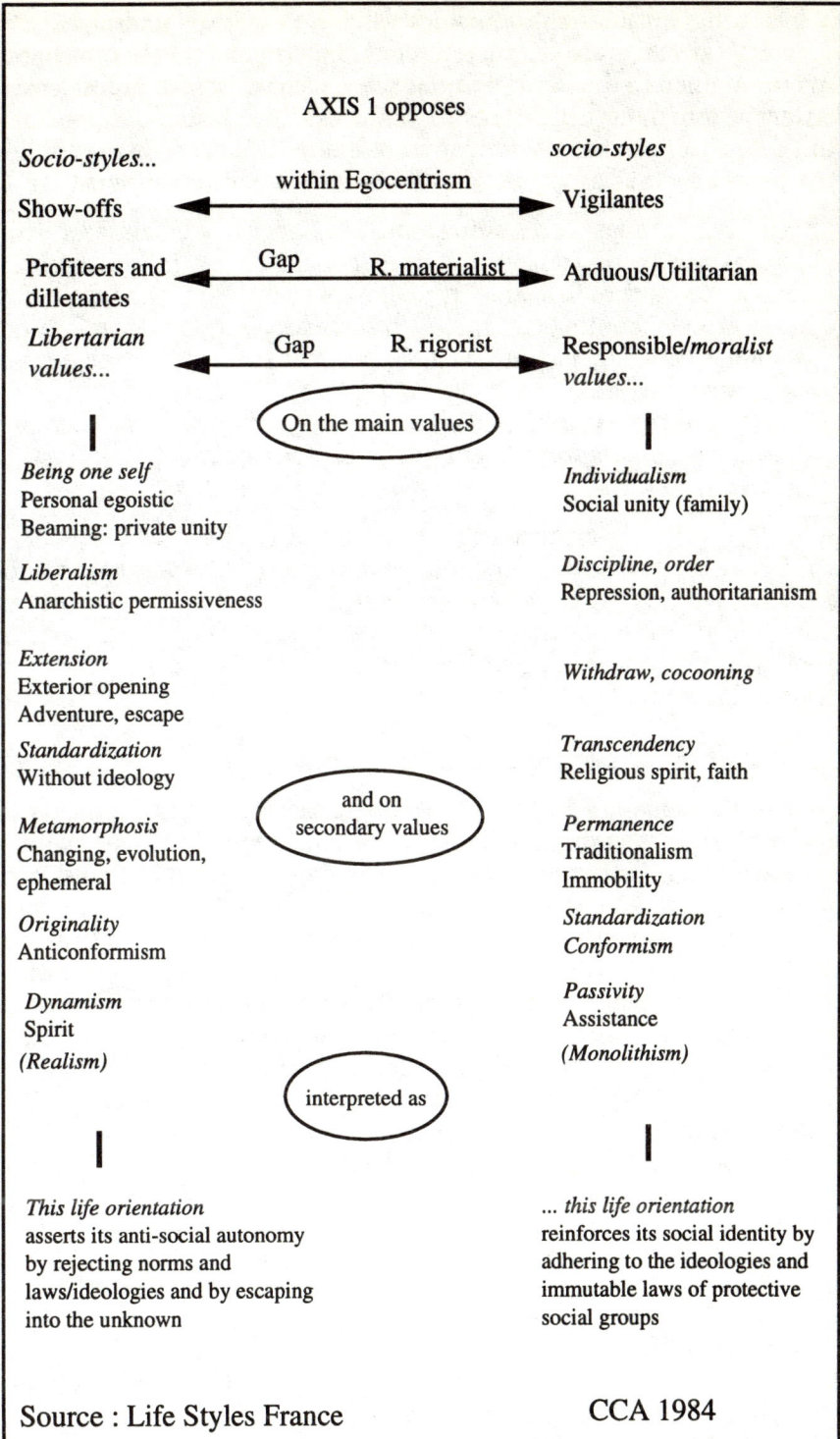

Figure 2.18   Analysis of a socio-map axis

This map can be read as a geographical landscape where the lifestyle types and ideological values are placed according to their proximity to or distance from one another. In this socio-cultural space each variable occupies a place relatively near to or far from the other variables.

In this way we can see the formation of groups which operate according to the same logic (in this system of two-, three- and four-dimensional axes):

❑ Socio-styles groups representing a meta-typology of mentalities, micro-cultures occupying competitive, predominant or less influential positions in the social dialectic. These groups come from the typological family tree, where they are the main branches. They are therefore not groupings in simple proximity on the two main axes but correlations of the group of factors.

❑ Flow groups representing syntheses of values, coherent cores, revealing ideological options for current social charges related to contrasting socio-waves.

The lifestyles map is a panorama of the social dialectic where we can observe how society is diversified into micro-cultures, which oppositions and alliances are taking shape between these two groups, which dimensions (axes) unite them or set them against each other, which value systems (flows) give them an ideological identity, and which factors give them a behavioural identity.

Socio-styles: A structure of groups

Groups of individuals, socio-styles, are organized in the geographic space which symbolizes the extension of the social field in four directions (if there are two axes) and six (if there are three). These types are not character portraits or uniform stereotypes, but likely models of ways of life and thought representing the largest common denominator of a group of individuals, explaining how it is integrated into and adapts to the social environment.

Socio-styles are not chains of conformity which restrict the individual to a limited and fixed range of behaviour, but dominant models which are the centre of gravity of the lifestyle, typical of a general system of adaptation and predictive of a large majority of ways of behaviour and attitudes.

This typology is different from segmentation where individuals are classified starting from a variable point of departure judged to be the most important for differentiating them. It differs from target filters where the number and order of variables separating out individuals are predetermined by particular hypotheses or objectives. Socio-styles are experimental and empirical groupings of people starting from the factorial organization of their responses into a synthetic pattern where no one lifestyle dimension is accorded priority.

The typology of the socio-styles system therefore does not classify the population from a hierarchy of responses but from a general range of data. This is why the socio-map is a general socio-structure valid for forecasting all aspects of behaviour, opinions and motivations at every stage of life.

On the socio-map we have to consider the focal point of each socio-style as the centre of gravity around which gathers at variable distances a cluster of people whose dominant life pattern it defines. By analogy, in the galaxy of the lifestyles map each socio-style is a star system. The individual planets gravitate around a sun which is the virtual centre in which they find their essential, though relative and variable, force of attraction.

This map serves as a basis for all other socio-bank maps. It is the general socio-structure, the reference chessboard, on which all maps resulting from these analyses can be superimposed.

Passive variables: Projecting a structure

The basic socio-map, which serves as an explanatory reference system, is one of the primary active variables in the socio-structure of the foundation study. It represents a structure of widespread ambitions intended to serve as an explanatory backcloth for the individual analysis of each of the passive variables, the socio-bank's thematic variables.

In socio-styles system reports the survey results are always presented in the form of maps. Maps are better than tables or histograms because they emphasize the typological variety of responses, oppositions or groupings, as well as the socio-cultural positioning of items on the general socio-map. Going beyond a simple, instructive, graphic representation, the cartography of lifestyles survey results is an intellectual principle and an interpretative discipline. It leads to a structured look over the data, going beyond basic analysis to find the dynamic, dialectic structure of responses on a subject. Reading the structural synthesis requires training, for the systematic data-map is an integral part of the method or way of thinking in socio-styles research. Experience shows that it is both practical in nature and valuable for enhancing strategic analyses.

Several types of map result from the detailed and operational analysis of items from the socio-bank. An item is one possible reply to a question and the smallest unit of information from the studies.

Analytical maps

Resulting from cross-referencing, these maps portray how far an item permeates the socio-styles typology. They replace the classical statistical table of cross-references. On the socio-map each socio-style is influenced by the number of responses about each item. A graphic representation of percentages, symbolizing their size and deviation from the average, is sometimes used to assist interpretation.

One map is required per item; so in the case of a question with 20 response items, 20 maps would be needed. This is the most detailed and differentiated way of understanding how replies are structured, but it is also the most cumbersome. Figures 2.19–2.20 are examples of analytical maps. The larger circles indicate which socio-styles were relatively larger than average in rejecting the product (figure 2.19) or reading the newspaper (figure 2.20.)

ITEM ANALYSIS MAP
* Among 100 people in this subarea 5% picked item
* Among 100 people of each Sociostyle which picked item

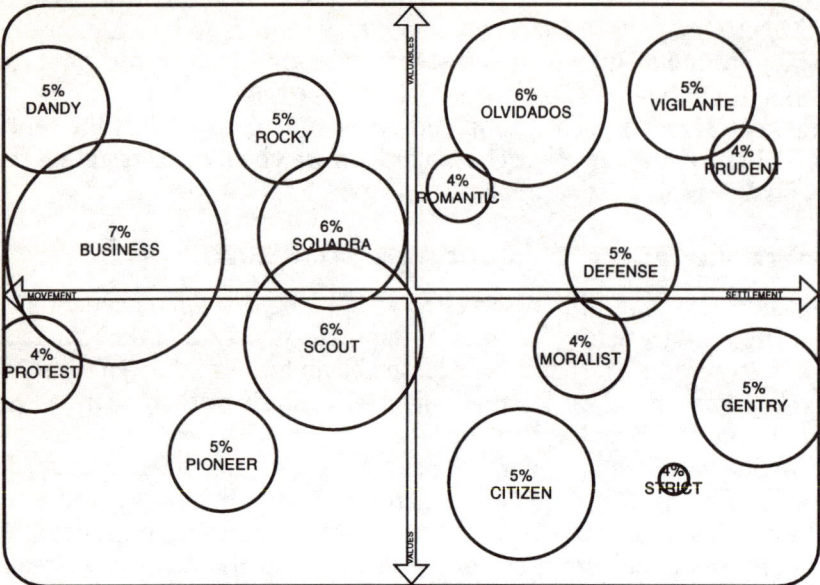

Figure 2.19 Analytical mini-map showing a commercial consumer target 'not interested' (ie with lower than average interest) in the concept of a four-wheel drive all-terrain vehicle

Equilibrium maps

These competitive or socio-comparison maps depict the average positioning of an item within the socio-structure. The item is projected onto the socio-map by correspondence analyzing as a passive variable and therefore not modifying the structure of the basic map. The position of the item can be seen simply as the point of equilibrium in the amount of attraction to different socio-styles, or as the centre of gravity for the cluster of responses spread over the map.

The point of equilibrium must be read and interpreted with caution in relation to the socio-styles in the immediate vicinity. It can effectively explain a group of responses concentrated on one or two types very near to each other on the map. However, it can also be placed halfway between two groups of contrasting responses on the map, in which case a dual positioning can be envisaged.

If a purely geographic reading is sometimes awkward, this equilibrium projection enhances the interpretation considerably since it reveals the central or marginal character of an item of data in the socio-structure.

Competitive maps

These depict the relative equilibrium positions of all terms from the same question (or thematically close questions) projected as passive variables.

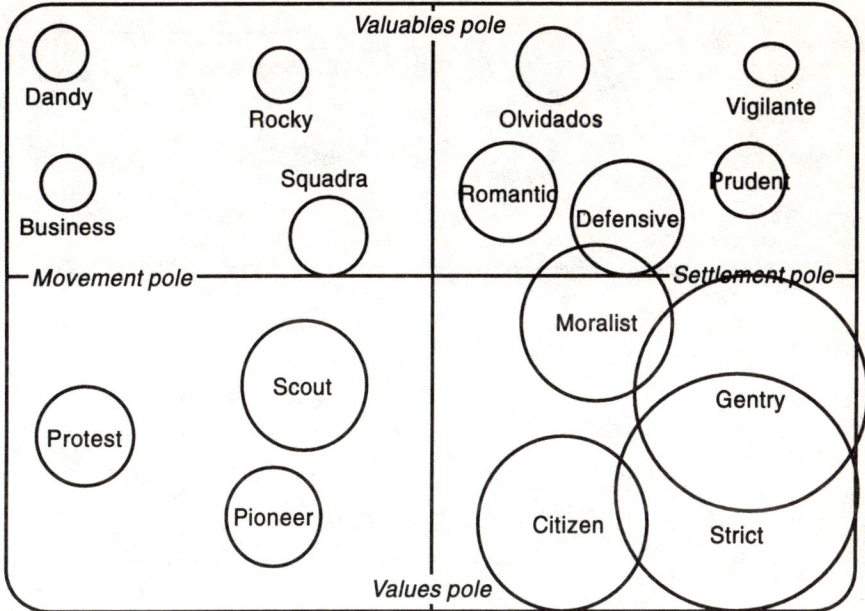

Source: Socio Styles FRANCE 1989   © CCA

Figure 2.20   Analytical mini-map: impact of a French newspaper in terms of its regular or occasional readership

The technique enables us to show simply the spread of responses on the same theme as socio-styles, as well as significant groups and radical opposi-tions. It is the basis for interpreting groups of responses, but care has to be taken with the interpretation mentioned above. Figure 2.21 illustrates this kind of map of news magazines in Italy.

Superimposed maps of analogies

These project passive variables of different kinds, such as opinions or behav-iour, or of diverse themes (eg culture, consumption) in order to attempt to observe significant convergences and oppositions in the typological variety of socio-styles as complex wholes.

The first precaution to be taken is never to regard as identical two vari-ables that are close graphically, since they are only linked in a secondary way through active variables. The second precaution is not to explain one passive variable by another, since only active variables have a structuring value on the map and therefore an explanatory value as well (socio-styles and factors or flows).

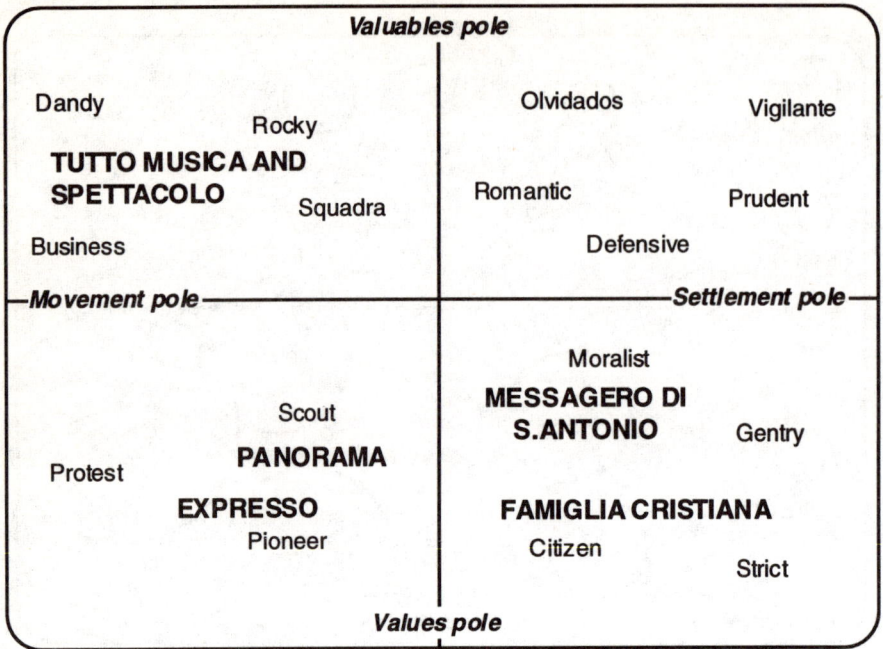

Figure 2.21   Competitive equilibrium map showing the position of news magazines in Italy

Thematic maps

It is equally possible to project any items as active variables crossed with socio-styles in correspondence analysis. In this case the graphic landscape of the map becomes deformed and reorganized by giving precedence to the responses concerned. This allows analysis of individual themes in life-styles. We can, in fact, observe how generally contrasted socio-styles can converge on a particular theme and how a mentality can splinter and become dissociated from a precise theme. Figure 2.22 gives an example of a thematic map.

How to read and interpret the socio-map

The socio-map is a graphic diagram with three main dimensions based uniquely on a socio-style survey. One map will serve to analyze all stages and topics. Its fundamental axes retain the same basic meaning, even if they are sometimes described in different terms according to the sector and market.

The position of a socio-style on the map and its axes is always the same whatever the sector or market being analyzed. Similarly, the position of psychological and behavioural factors that form the framework of the map remains constant. All maps derived from the socio-bank can be superimposed on one another.

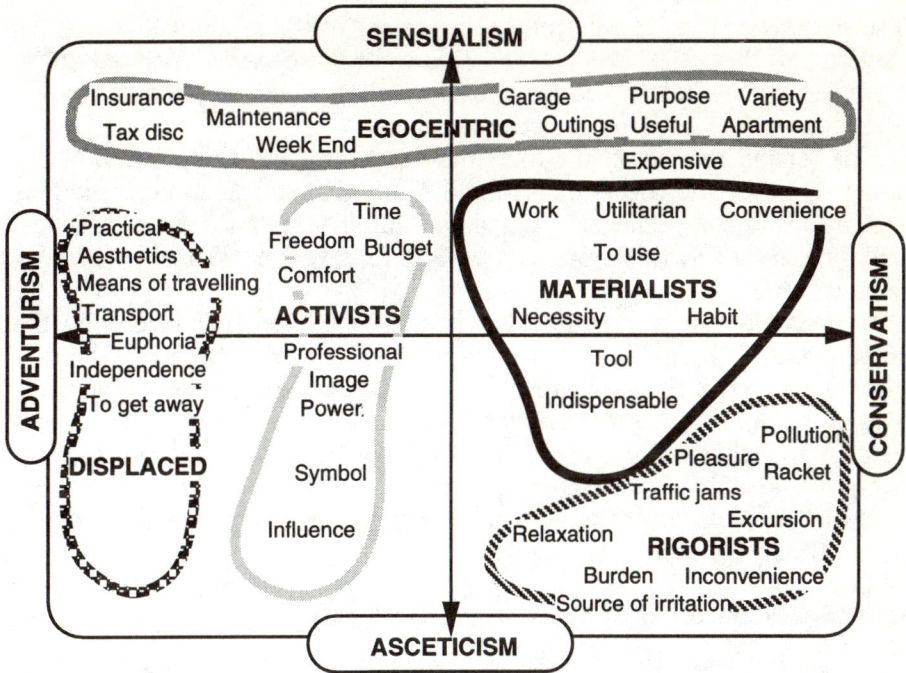

Figure 2.22   Thematic equilibrium map showing the motivations regarding cars of five socio-mentalities

Reading the basic socio-structure

The three axes that are mathematically most significant make up the basic three-dimensional socio-map. Each axis is a bi-polar dimension which depicts opposing socio-styles with contrasting values, attitudes and forms of behaviour. Each of these axes has to be understood as an opposition between two value systems. The most extreme factors, those nearest to one or the other pole of the axis, are the ones that give it its significance and according to which it is labelled.

The socio-map can be used as a geographical map or a mariner's chart:

❑ different regions can be distinguished by their climate: the clouds of psychological and behavioural factors describe the characteristics of the zone where they are positioned;

❑ the position of each socio-style can be charted by referring to the three main axes of the socio-structure which defines its ways of life and thought. Distances, oppositions and convergences between socio-styles can be measured. It is a means of identifying quickly and practically which types of people can be handled in the same way and which have to be tackled in a different way through different products, different retail outlets and different advertising methods.

The first step is to identify the axes in order of the amount of statistical explanation they offer: axis 1, 2 and 3. Each of these axes is analyzed not as a single variable but as a factorial axis which synthesizes a group of flows and socio-styles which are its active variables.

The second reading of the map involves identifying the position of the socio-styles in the three-dimensional space that has been created. This indicates in a comprehensive, visual way affinities, relationships, closeness and similarities in this system as well as relatively or radically opposing connections.

Socio-styles can be considered to be adjacent when they belong on the same plane of three-dimensional space. They can be considered relatively close or related if they are similarly positioned on one or two of the three axes, but significantly different on the second or third. They can be considered completely opposing when they are placed in opposite planes. In positioning the socio-styles and analyzing their differences, the axes can be imagined as scales which allow a two- or three-dimensional positioning, as with latitude and longitude on a map.

Reading the positions of items on the socio-map

There are two ways in which the socio-map can be used as a practical marketing instrument:

❑ Cluster readings involve drawing an area on the socio-map which encloses a particular section of the public (eg people who read *Time* more regularly than others, people who buy more from mail order catalogues than others, people who are less favourably disposed than others to the government's economic policies, or people who like witty advertising more than others. Each cluster forms a niche: this is a homogeneous population which comprises a segment of a commercial market, a category of voters or a particular audience. In general, the cluster identified on the socio-map groups together socio-styles which have given more positive answers than the sample average; but a cluster may also designate the group of socio-styles that has responded in a less significant way than the general average. This reading by clusters is more precise because it enables the spread or concentration of the socio-target to be seen visually and clearly as well as its heterogeneity or homogeneity.

❑ Barycentre readings involve placing each item (a socio-style or a variable) at the mathematical centre of gravity of its cluster. A competitive equilibrium map can then be drawn. This technique enables us to position a large number of items on the same socio-map in a comparative and competitive manner in order to observe their convergence or opposition. Cluster analysis, in contrast, only allows us to study one item per chart.

Reading mini-maps

This specific analysis enables the capacity of a concept to reach a small or large number of marginal and central socio-styles to be appreciated in more detail. This is done in a visual way which allows the bull's-eye of a potential target to be identified in concrete terms.

This map expresses the percentage penetration of the concept in the general population and in the sub-population of each of the socio-styles:

❑ in general X per cent have said they are interested in this new product concept;
❑ in comparison Y or Z per cent of the people in each of these socio-styles have said they are attracted by it.

These statistical results are usually presented in the form of a table with the item studied in rows and the socio-styles and the sample as a whole in columns. Here they are presented in map form. Each percentage is written on the map at the spot where its socio-style is positioned. The main aim of this presentation is to show:

❑ which percentages could easily be added together because they belong to adjacent socio-styles which could combine to form a unique consumer target;
❑ which percentages could never be combined because they belong to socio-styles which are distant on the map.

Bubbles maps

A new and exclusive graphic representation has been devised for CCA which makes this map easier to read and more useful. An item's penetration of each socio-style (ie the relative number of people in each socio-style accepting the concept) is represented by the size of the circle surrounding it (see figure 2.23).

❑ a small circle means that only a small percentage of consumers belonging to this socio-style are motivated by this concept; a large circle, in contrast, indicates that a large percentage of people in this socio-style support the concept;
❑ a thin circle means that the percentage of motivated consumers within this socio-style is lower than the percentage of people motivated in the whole of the European sample;
❑ a thick circle indicates a percentage of acceptance of the concept for this socio-style which is above the general average.

With this map we can identify at a glance which socio-styles are most motivated by this concept (thick circles). We can easily see whether they form a unique and relatively homogeneous consumer niche — adjacent socio-styles are shown by partly superimposed circles — or whether they are spread over the map in several remote or contradictory niches. Finally, by noting the percentages, we can measure whether a majority, a strong minority or only a slight majority are interested.

These mini-maps enable us to refine the analysis for each of the items studied in the survey and positioned on the synthetic map.

SOCIO-TARGETS: SEGMENTATION INTO LIFESTYLE PORTRAITS

The working principle of the socio-styles system is to present all the market and social sector analyses on the same socio-cultural map (the socio-map) and to describe their respective populations across the same typology of life

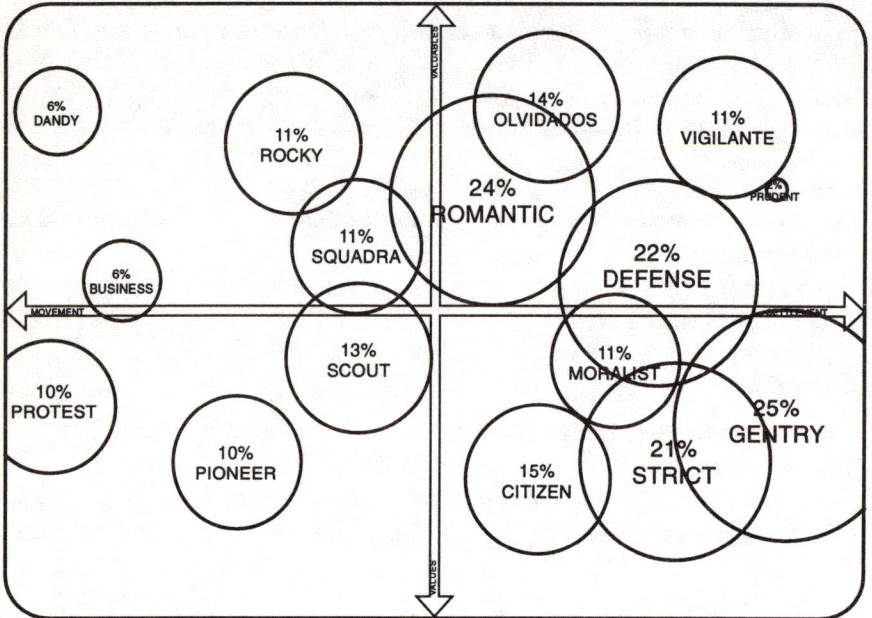

Source: Euro-Socio-Styles   Copyright CCA/EUROPANEL 1989

Figure 2.23   A bubble map

and thought styles (socio-styles). This is in order to create an interface between the different stages and facilitate moving from one sector to another. The generic typology and basic map (described earlier in this chapter) constitute a common reference, integration and synthesis of all the socio-bank data, a reflection of lifestyles at the most general level.

However, we need hypotheses for predicting variations in motivation, thought and habit depending on the sector. Socio-styles are not rigid chains but models of the main areas of convergence which accept that individuals are relatively mobile. For example, 'concept seeker', an American socio-style, may exhibit competitiveness in political matters and so converge with the 'show-off seeker'; yet this socio-style is harder to please as a consumer, highly original with regard to cars — like 'hedonism seekers' — and extremely traditional about food, like 'status seekers'.

The particular selection of attitudes and forms of behaviour that socio-styles typology assumes for each social subject or in each market takes two forms in the socio-styles system:

- ❏ sector-based socio-style portaits;
- ❏ socio-targets — the sector-based reorganization of the typology on the map to describe the segmentation of populations on a theme or around a consumer item.

Analysis into sector-based socio-style portraits

In each sector or market in the socio-bank the basic portrait of each socio-style can be specified, differentiated and enhanced with sector-based data by simple cross-reference. This sector-based picture is the most detailed method available for redefining the basic typological tool in order to adapt it to the requirements of a user from a particular sector, while preserving its multi-sector character.

For example, the basic portrait of the 'dilettante' (French typology 1986) describes 7.5 per cent of students or junior managers who are urbane, educated, well-to-do non-conformists as well as innovative, fashionable, mobile and socially diverse individualists. From the culture-media stage of the socio-bank we can paint a more precise portrait of this sector:

- ❏ motivations and culture receptiveness — by selecting at random various kinds of entertainment for stimulation;
- ❏ their tastes — from the most intellectual to the most prosaic;
- ❏ their learning and consumer styles;
- ❏ their visits to the theatre, the cinema, to museums;
- ❏ their favourite radio stations and television programmes;
- ❏ the magazines and newspapers they read;
- ❏ their favourite styles of communication;
- ❏ their favourite presenters;
- ❏ their attitude to advertising, etc.

The portrait can be used for marketing. From the section of the socio-bank on cars or household goods a complete consumer portrait can be produced for this product for each socio-style and mentality.

Take as an example the 'executive' type (France 1988) and the beauty aids market:

- ❏ portrait of motivations, needs and desires (to preserve health and good looks by taking precautions against illness, self-discipline);
- ❏ image of brands liked and disliked;
- ❏ product use and consumer habits (ritual use, loyalty, perseverance);
- ❏ shops used (chemists and perfumeries);
- ❏ buying behaviour (regular, deliberate, loyal, never on impulse);

❏ buying intentions (tendency to spend more for proven quality);
❏ advertising preferred and disliked;
❏ attraction to certain types of packaging or product presentation (clean, sober lines without flourishes, white);
❏ knowledge of a product's technical characteristics (great importance attached to raw material, rare natural extracts);
❏ product, brand or shop loyalty (pronounced);
❏ openness to innovation, amenability to new products and tendency to change behaviour (weak without performance tests, greater acceptance of a traditional brand).

This portrait can be developed over 200 to 300 variables. It is intended at the same time for manufacturers, businesspeople and advertisers. This sector-based socio-styles portrait provides more information than the usual studies. Just as in market studies, each element of brand image or consumer behaviour is analyzed according to the usual socio-descriptive criteria. In addition, however, the sector-based report provides consumer portraits which offer more in-depth understanding of consumers.

The same portrait can be analyzed in the specific sectors of distribution, business, merchandising and promotion. For example, the 'security seeker' socio-style (US socio-bank 1987) and a description of shopping behaviour:

❏ frequency, regularity, means of transport, type of shopping (periodic trips to the supermarket for large family purchases; purchase through mail order catalogues);
❏ brand images of different competing names (good image for Sears);
❏ preferences with regard to product presentation (clarity, cleanliness, range, hierarchy of price);
❏ profile of preferred salesperson (mature, experienced, calm, reassuring), method of automatic vending or distance selling;
❏ receptiveness to persuasion (demonstration, ease of use, guarantee);
❏ demand for complementary supplier or business services, after-sales service, installation (very pronounced);
❏ demand for information, documentation and advice (detailed instructions regarding use and maintenance);
❏ interest in mail order, direct marketing (pronounced, growing for specialist catalogues);
❏ relative attraction of the distributor's brand-name (weak);
❏ preferred type of in-store advertising (promotion weeks);
❏ impact of games and competitions (rejected), special offers, sets of products (accepted), cut-out shopping coupons and loyalty vouchers (highly motivating);
❏ impact of all promotional techniques and general purchasing attitudes (prudence, loyalty, being considered as a family).

This commercial portrait has many facets which are often studied in isolation in different market studies. The characteristic feature and advantage of the socio-styles system is to combine them in one survey and, in particular, to synthesize them. In this way we can draw up a complete portrait of a consumer personality that is multi-dimensional and dynamic — a living portrait of a commercial target.

Synthetic sector-based segmentation into socio-targets

The same multi-sector socio-bank enables us to determine mathematically a general multi-sector synthesis for the socio-styles and also to focus the analysis on each of the sectors studied to define a specific segmentation.

The socio-target represents the way in which general socio-styles in a particular sector (of social, business or commercial life) are grouped together into families representing kinds of behaviour or similar psychologies. The sectorial grouping defines a more or less precise segmentation of useful target populations in this particular sector, though generally simplified by comparison with the detailed socio-styles typology. Socio-styles are therefore not grouped in the same way for each activity and market.

For example, in the French typology of 1984 the 'profiteers' share the same psychological and behavioural characteristics as the 'show-offs' in the fashion market, yet converge in the information sector with the 'libertarians' and 'dilettantes' in their use of media.

Thus every socio-style study offers a dual reading:

❏ a general socio-cultural view of the diversity and organization of social dynamics, in the form of a multi-sectorial typology on a socio-map — this is intended for a global understanding of the social chessboard and the relative position occupied by each product, population and sector of activity;

❏ a micro-sectorial view focused on a particular market or field of information, using only the information from this sector but in more depth — segmentation into socio-targets which directly define the target populations to seek answers to particular problems.

Classification by socio-targets stems directly from socio-styles typology:

❏ It is simple. Experience shows that between 10 and 16 socio-styles are generally necessary to define the multi-sectorial sociological diversity of a population (9 socio-styles in metropolitan France in 1972 and 14 in 1987; 11 American socio-styles in 1986; 11 socio-styles in the West Indies in 1986; 16 types in Europe in 1988); and 4 to 7 socio-targets are generally sufficient to define the main population or consumer segments, each of which comprises a number of socio-styles.

❏ It is precise. The descriptions of socio-targets allow greater detail about behaviour, attitudes, judgements about image, sensitivity to presentation, preference for presentation, basic motivations peculiar to one sector, its products, its messages, its leaders and brands. A socio-target is a detailed sectorial portrait of the behaviour and psychology of a particular homogeneous and unique population which can be conveniently handled in this way.

However, segmentation by sectorial socio-targets remains part of the general logic of the socio-styles system. They appear as socio-style groupings on the same general socio-cultural map.

The wealth of multi-sectorial content and general sociological information contained in socio-style portraits is therefore available implicitly in portraits of socio-targets. It is easy to move from the sector-based market analysis offered by the descriptive portrait of a socio-target to the broader socio-cultural interpretation offered by the socio-styles which it comprises. All the possibilities for interfaces between different sectors and markets are also available in the study of socio-targets. It is easy to compare the nature of one of these segments in the car sector, for instance, with the nature of a television audience or advertising population by comparing the respective component socio-styles.

The complete psychological and cultural dimension is therefore achieved by using socio-styles. Each behavioural or consumer socio-target is cross-referenced with the general synthetic typology, providing an explanatory socio-cultural portrait.

Socio-styles represent the context and significance of consumer behaviour. They serve as a reference point for investigating the motivational roots of buying behaviour, the cultural roots of media consumer behaviour, the psycho-economic roots of consumer choice, the socio-economic roots of distribution outlets. Here the socio-styles variable fulfils its role as a synthetic variable providing general socio-cultural interpretations for sector-based analytical variables — socio-targets by market sector.

Depending on the sector, these commercial, cultural or socio-political portraits translate the general socio-styles from the foundation study into more concrete, practical and readily useful terms for a firm or organization:

❑ Each portrait describes how to change the technical composition, performance, packaging, use and advertising of a product to turn a socio-target into a purchaser.

❑ Each portrait describes the business organization, the type of promotion, the architecture of the retail outlet, the sales atmosphere and window displays which would turn this type into a regular and loyal customer.

❑ Each portrait describes the policies, kind of propaganda and language, image and personality profile of the leader which a political party would need to convince voters from this socio-style group.

❑ Each portrait describes the kind of newspaper, layout, content, tone and style of illustration which would turn this socio-target into a newspaper reader. In the same way it describes the type of radio or television programme, tone, style of presenter which would result in loyal listeners and viewers.

These market or sector segmentations defined from a small number of basic questions on psychology and behaviour in the foundation study can then be thoroughly investigated, completed and their evolution traced by sector-based studies (maxi-scan):

❑ social and political investigations into major problems in collective and personal life — mainly intended for governments, administrations, party officials, associations and lobbyists;

❑ cultural surveys of art, culture, the media, language and advertising — mainly intended for film company executives, radio and television networks, advertising agencies, media professionals and the public relations departments of large firms;

❑ in particular, market investigations into all the major consumer sectors — tools offered to manufacturers, importers, distributors, mail order companies, direct marketing firms, advertisers, recruitment and sales training companies.

Figure 2.24 gives an example of segmentation into socio-targets in the food sector.

How to read sector-based socio-styles studies

In each market and sector of study socio-targets are presented as a practical working tool for decision makers. Different items of information are included following the same standard model:

❑ *The socio-target map.* In the general socio-map of socio-styles population segments appear as groups of socio-styles combined into a homogeneous target. This is not an exact point on the map but a group of individuals belonging to one of several socio-styles within a zone or cluster. Sometimes several socio-styles overlap: this means that one socio-style shares the behaviour and psychology of two different socio-targets.

❑ *The socio-niche map.* On a general socio-map the mathematical centre of gravity identities the main psychological and behavioural variables and factors regarding products, brands, sector-based themes and concepts arising from the survey questionnaire. On the general socio-cultural chessboard of the socio-map and in each sector or market:
   — the socio-target map positions population/audience/consumer segments;
   — the socio-niche map positions products and services, advertising and brand images, ways of behaviour and characteristic motivations, innovations, etc.

❑ *The sector trend compass.* This compass chart defines the principal axes of the socio-map in terms of the sector or market being studied. It describes the whole range of motivating themes, attractive images and positive characteristics concerning a product or service as well as value-enhancing personalities for the leaders in this sector. This plan represents the range of all possible strategic choices for a decision maker to orientate an innovation, define a brand image or adapt to the way customers are developing.

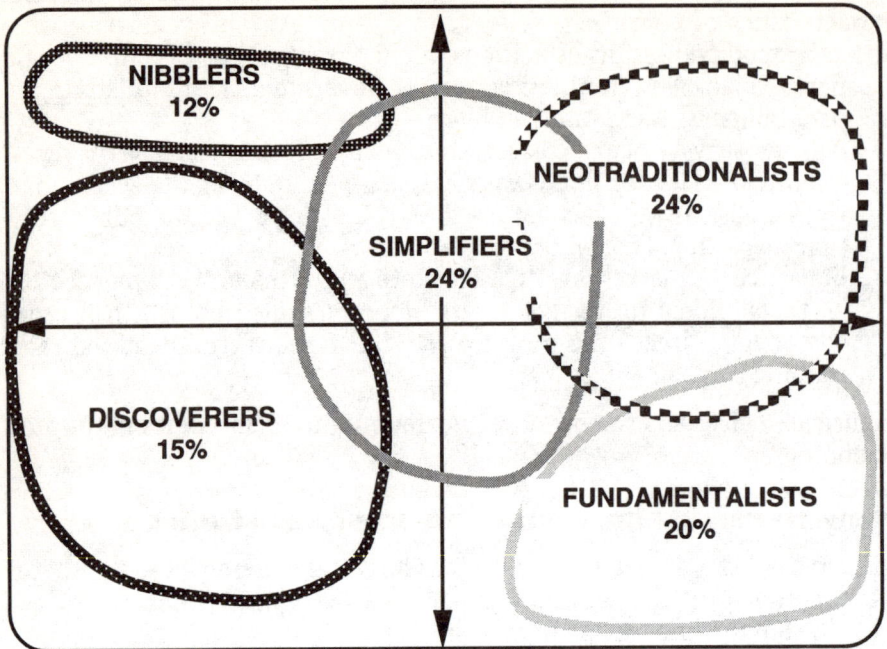

Source: Food Styl ' 84   © CCA 1984

Figure 2.24   Consumer segmentation into synthetic socio-targets.
In 1984 in France the 14 general socio-styles were grouped into five socio-targets in
the food sector

❑   *The sector hit parade*. This is the general analysis of the strongest and
    weakest replies in percentage terms revealed by the survey across all
    sector-based questions. It is therefore a hierarchical classification of
    values and motivations, images, products, ways of behaviour, majority
    and minority attitudes, as well as being a general snapshot of the state
    of public opinion across the population with every socio-style and every
    social class combined. It is a practical tool for identifying topics on
    which the majority agrees or disagrees.

❑   *The portrait of socio-targets*. Each of the targets identified on the map
    is analyzed and described in detail in terms of:
    — its component socio-styles;
    — its demographic and economic identity;
    — the actual ways of behaviour and habits in the sector surveyed;
    — its attitudes and opinions in this sector;
    — its motivations and future ambitions on this subject. It is a
      synthesis of all the useful variables studied positioned on a niche
      map.

Moreover, the portrait of each socio-target can be completed by adding characteristics of buyer behaviour, patronage of distribution and business outlets, responsiveness to advertising and merchandising tastes, exposure to the media ... all taken from the general socio-style portraits that make up each socio-target.

LIFE PROSPECTIVES

One of the objectives of the socio-styles system is to identify how the social mosaic is structured at a given moment in a given geo-cultural zone. This is what the concepts and tools, the socio-map and the socio-styles typology, are intended to define.

With the same objective the socio-target concept and technique offer a sector-based view of this segmentation. However, in order to move from static photography to moving pictures the concept of life prospectives must be introduced. In social and business studies predictions must not be too ambitious to prevent the danger of confusing the analysis of a movement, its direction and its energy with knowing in advance when and where it will occur.

It must be emphasized that nobody today can predict the cultural or commercial future in terms of precise lifestyles. However, describing the social future is possible. It is here that the term 'prospective' has a meaning — an attempt to predict possible future developments (B de Jouvenel) and their effects based on what has happened in the recent past (retrospective) together with current trends for change.

In a society where innovation is accelerating, as is the case with all industrial societies today, one of the principal conditions for success is that institutions and companies are able to adapt their products and services according to the ways their customers are changing. This adaptation takes the form of:

- ❑ new products, either at the level of basic technology or merely with regard to external appearance and handling;
- ❑ new sales methods;
- ❑ new social or professional structures and organizations;
- ❑ new media, languages, words and images.

It often takes the form of superficial change: a new brand image, a change in packaging, new advertising methods. This is a declaration of impotence on the part of a firm or institution which is incapable of adapting its real offering to the needs and habits of its customers.

An instrument for detecting social as well as commercial and cultural trends is therefore indispensable for all decision makers, whatever their sector of activity and whatever type of organization they lead. After all, they have to renew on a continuous basis their technical, business, cultural or ideological offerings.

Opinion polls and classical market studies do not meet this objective. Indeed, their technique is to measure ways of behaviour and stereotyped opinions in existence at the time of the survey without considering the past or the future. Only opinion or consumer panels enable evolution to be tracked through repeated studies of the same population. But this is merely retrospective and its conclusions often arrive too late, after the trend has become widely established.

The principle of permanent socio-cultural panel studies in the socio-styles system also traces the evolution and retrospective evaluation of change. However, the very nature of the socio-scanner questionnaire enables us to go further — to be at the start of new trends and even to anticipate them.

Retrospectives

The first way of detecting the trends that carry potential innovations in a sector-based socio-style study is the retrospective. As in opinion and consumer panels, we try through regularly updating the sector-based lifestyle surveys to measure objectively the volume and rhythm of change in public behaviour, opinions and perceptions concerning a product, communication or topic.

The sector-based socio-style survey should therefore not be a one-off survey but a databank continually fed with new information and regularly updated by asking the same questions of the same sample (or a similarly constituted sample). In this way the progress of a family of products with common characteristics can be observed over the years. This shows the prevailing trend of innovations whose central driving theme is the common characteristic of all products under development.

For example, in the sector-based surveys of food and drink consumption conducted in France between 1975 and 1985 we could see significant progress in the consumption of drinks, like Coca-Cola, Schweppes and Gini, and food products, like Nutella, Mars bars and large chocolate ices, at the same time as we measured the brand images of these products gaining in prestige. This indicates in this particular country and in these food sectors a clear, established trend among consumers starting from one main point in common to all these products: sweet flavours.

Trends can be observed in a similar way in the media, advertising and culture. There is one quite spectacular example of this. In the lifestyles surveys in France between 1972 and 1977 we observed a mathematically greater score for the impact of large-scale Hollywood-type advertising; progress in the sales of magazines like *Paris Match*, *VSD* and illustrated weekend supplements; the great success of television entertainment programmes. This indicated a recurring trend and a point in common to these media and advertising successes has to be sought to explain it. This is the image — spectacular and emotional, poetic and fantastic — that addresses the heart rather than the mind; a trend that reached its peak at the start of the 1980s.

After the identification of this trend by CCA new media forms could be created successfully, and French advertisers adopted a correspondingly imaginative and spectacular type of communication. In the same way in socio-political sector-based studies the establishment of new values and forceful themes could be observed across all areas that the socio-scanner questionnaire measured repeatedly over months and years.

However, this study of trends is only retrospective. By the time a poll can measure a phenomenon and find it in different areas of activity, the trend is no longer innovative but already well-established.

❑ This is positive because it guarantees that from now on this trend will represent a significant population and a sufficiently large market.

❑ But it is also inconvenient for those who want to be first and need to prepare their innovations far ahead. Indeed, it is often too late for them by the time the definite establishment of a new trend can be observed after several years and months of retrospective studies. It is therefore necessary to have access in addition to a diagnosis which forecasts sector-based trends for lifestyles.

Prospectives

A second way of revealing the main developmental trends in a sector-based study involves analyzing opposing current forms of behaviour and satisfaction or dissatisfaction with them. A lack of coherence between a form of behaviour and its actual or imaginary psychological experience is most often symptomatic of growing instability in a formerly entrenched attitude in a socio-target which no longer responds to current motivations and feelings, but has not found a satisfactory form of behaviour with which to replace it. In such a case an apparently well-adjusted and positive mode of behaviour co-exists in a sector-based lifestyle with often subconscious, negative mental images that contradict its usefulness.

❑ The lack of coherence may be evident (eg the purchase and regular use of a model of car and a negative psychological opinion of the product and brand image).
❑ The lack of coherence may be hidden (eg the purchase and regular use of a model of car and a positive, rational opinion of its qualities set against the dream of a completely opposite ideal car).

All these cases centre on an uncomfortable co-existence between a former model of behaviour that is old and outdated and new motivations with no outlet. If this lack of coherence between behaviour and psychology is observed and measured in defined socio-targets in a significant and systematic way, a new hollow socio-target can be discovered — a population defined by its lack of satisfying lifestyle patterns rather than by a particular need.

Within this population and its lack of satisfaction are potential desires which will soon generate a new trend of re-adjustment. By surveying this population of unsatisfied socio-styles regularly we can see the start of this trend defined through a new ideal product. There are two ways to watch this socio-target in which a trend is emerging:

❑ We can use a specific quantitative survey by polling the panel in a rapidly repeated sequence which enables us to obtain an objective statistical measure of the phenomenon.

❑ We can also try to uncover the trend at an earlier stage in the collective unconscious psychology of this socio-target before it becomes statistically measurable. This is possible using projective qualitative methods in group dynamics such as EPSY and QUORUM.

It is at this stage that predicting trends is most difficult. However, it is also here that a prospective can be most successful, since it enables us to identify the prevailing trend at the very moment that it originates in a very precise population, whose socio-styles we know, to replace a former model of thought and behaviour that will become outdated and unsatisfying.

In the sector-based questionnaires of the socio-styles system there are numerous projective questions which suggest new, imaginary, ideal, radical and crazy product concepts in the form of prospective science fiction scenarios. These scenarios can be about new products, new media, new types of business, new social organizations, new laws, new organizations in people's private lives. They enable us to grasp the directions in which the people of a socio-style dissatisfied with their current way of life are turning subconsciously, even before they are rationally conscious of their changing needs and which new product corresponds to them.

The socio-styles system has used proven projective techniques for years for qualitative study of in-depth psychology. Only this questioning technique enables us to uncover a still subconscious collective trend and to measure statistically its potential importance by identifying clearly on the socio-map the socio-styles in question.

In this way the sector-based survey enables us to measure at the same time:

❑ the behavioural socio-target: the population that consumes, possesses, acts, votes, reads, watches television, etc;

❑ the psychological socio-target where the lack of coherence between adapted behaviour and unsatisfied psychology becomes evident: the socio-styles that judge the product they use negatively, the television viewers who have a poor opinion of a programme they watch regularly, the voters who dislike the candidate for whom they vote;

❑ the trend socio-target: the socio-styles that dream subconsciously about a radically new way of life, consumption, culture or social life.

If these three population segments are superimposed on the same socio-styles we can define a population, its percentage volume and its socio-demographic identity. We know its point of departure (eg the products currently consumed), the current psychological journey (the current mental dissatisfaction) and the direction of the prospective trend (the ideal concept of a new product). This is a very important item of strategic information for social decision makers who can in this way predict the demise of a product and the necessary creation of a replacement. Figure 2.25 illustrates the definition of innovation niches in the French car sector.

Measurement by repeated panel surveys of this target population then enables us to verify the motivating value of the trend, to observe the moment when it moves from being an unconscious, idealized trend to a rational, conscious demand, and to measure mathematically its growth in intensity, urgency and potential population volume.

Tests

Another way of identifying prospective sector-based trends is to ask questions in thematic maxi-scans about the acceptability of new products. We can ask the panel about effective behaviour with regard to the testing, regular use and definitive adoption of new products which have recently appeared. It may be a question (depending on the sector) about new technology in professional life or household tasks, or new consumer products related to food or beauty, or even new forms of social life. All have the characteristic of upsetting the usual way of life which preceded them.

This enables us to detect in particular socio-targets for innovation and also to identify which future trends would motivate them. For example, we see certain socio-styles motivated by a 'natural state' trend which leads them to test and adopt new products in different areas of their lives which are characteristically more ecological, simple and natural. We can also see other socio-styles driven by a 'conviviality' trend which leads them to new forms of social, cultural, political or business behaviour, all of which have as their starting point new, richer interpersonal relationships.

We can therefore identify a prevailing trend and measure its importance in population percentages at the same time as we reveal which socio-styles are affected by it. As with the previous technique, we measure in a similar way fashion trends that are already happening and established in people's lives.

Through these methods the socio-styles-systems provides decision makers in all sectors with reliable, evaluated hypotheses on new trends which are already starting to modify behaviour and also on those that are emerging to meet dissatisfaction. Innovation socio-targets are not certain forecasts and even less certain predictions, but rather prospective hypotheses defining possibilities which are not speculative but represent motivating and driving psychological realities among certain populations with known profiles and social statistical weightings.

Socio-trends observatory

Completely different yet complementary to these statistical methods CCA International has developed a more advanced diagnostic system for detecting growing international socio-cultural trends.

We no longer need to describe a typology of current socio-styles or measure the strength of a concept in current public consciousness (socio-waves). We are trying to uncover socio-cultural forces for change still in the

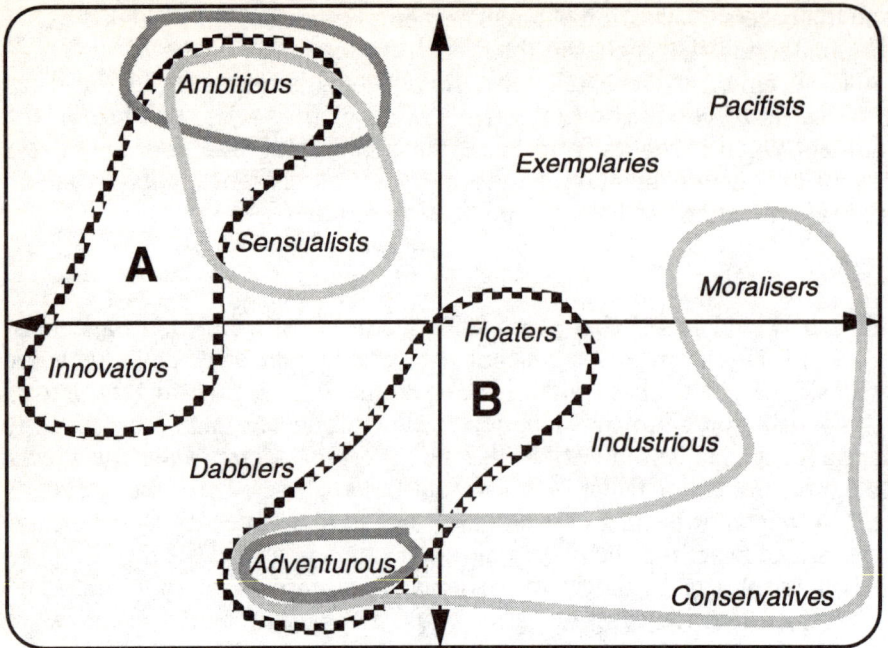

The chart shows the integration of 3 complementary analyses.

	Objectives of well-off drivers owning cars at the top end of the scale
	Objectives of drivers dissatisfied with the cars of today
	Objectives of drivers interested in new models of cars
A	Concept of the small, powerful town car
B	Concept of the 'mobile home', habitable and comfortable 'monospace'

This analysis predicts the potentialities of two new generations of cars – the small, compact, sporty cars such as 'GTI' and 'Turbo', and the 'monocorps' such as 'l'espace'.

Source: Auto Styl' France   © CCA 1975

Figure 2.25   Defining innovation niches (car sector, France 1975)

collective subconscious, several years before their effects can be measured. The method does not rely on polls but on social observation, on ethnological study of minorities and the avant-garde, on analysing the content of the media, on the interpretation of events, on the projections of experts.

The difficulty lies in distinguishing incidental anecdotes from the prevailing strong and marginal trends, the precursors. For this reason socio-waves and socio-styles are then measured to validate and assess these hypotheses.

CHAPTER 3

THE SOCIO-STYLES SYSTEM IN THE CONTEXT OF LIFESTYLE THEORIES

SUMMARY

The socio-styles system is not the only method which has claimed to take a new psychosociological approach to social and business phenomena, particularly during the last 20 years. Indeed, a number of procedures have been developed since the 1960s with the common ambition of extending analysis of individuals as consumers, audiences and citizens by taking more account of the complexity of lifestyles and ways of thinking, thus going beyond the narrow set of themes which justifies direct market studies and opinion polls. This widening of the field of vision is accompanied by an extension in time: greater attention is given to past and future attitudes and behaviour to depict how the subject studied develops.

What have been called 'socio-cultural approaches' can be summarized as follows: we will understand the motoring habits of consumers if we analyze more broadly the rest of their way of life; we will grasp the opportunities they represent better if we fit their current behavior into the general development of motoring habits and lifestyles; and we will be better able to measure the relative interest of this type of client if we place them in the context of their social mosaic. This indicates the implicit and partial application of a new paradigm of complexity which is likely to revolutionize the design of scientific and professional approaches to social phenomena.

However, beyond this brief definition of intent roughly common to all socio-cultural approaches, the methods and especially the attitudes of this approach diverge considerably. The preferred variables to be studied, their concept and treatment and which social phenomena they explain are very specific to each approach.

In a fertile period for research at the end of the 1960s and beginning of the 1970s, numerous paths were followed both in the United States and Europe. Today only a few have stood the test of time and particularly practical application. As often happens in applied research, the need for confidentiality limits access to methods and results; and when the results are

unveiled presentations are by no means exempt from a competitive element. As a result the presentations use everyday language, which distorts
their scientific rigour and makes it difficult to analyze critically the different methods available at present.

The purpose of this book is to shed light on one of these socio-cultural
methods: the socio-styles system. We will refrain from criticizing other
'competing' approaches and arguments and confine ourselves to the sphere
of practical applications, leaving it to others to make an inventory of other,
purely academic concepts.

In the context of more theoretical conclusions we will limit ourselves to
sketching out and positioning the principal methodological approaches and
their epistemological foundation:

- in order to connect the 'lifestyle' notion (of which the socio-style is a
  particular concept) to its many roots in the human and social sciences;
- and to indicate how a choice of socio-cultural research technique is also
  by implication a fundamental epistemological choice.

ORIGINS OF THE LIFESTYLE

Before considering how it has developed, it is convenient to recall the origin
of the key lifestyle concept. The idea stands at the meeting point of different
scientific disciplines and of studies of the individual and society.

The lifestyle concept appears in modern human sciences both as a sociological concept with Max Weber and as a concept relevant to individual psychology in the work of Alfred Adler. Weber conceives the lifestyle as a mark
of status, enabling a person to be recognized as belonging to a group. It is
therefore a concept of socially instituted conformity, where its function is
tribal integration. With Adler, in contrast, the same term is applied much
more to the individual, expressing the existential effort of personality adapting to environment. Adler thus reintroduces the social fact in opposition to
inner psychology, making the lifestyle the dynamic mechanism of an individual's movement towards society. The point common to these two views is
an individual's socialization, one with a sociological viewpoint, the other
more psychological.

From these two points of departure various applications have been developed which make the lifestyle either a reflection of the personality and its
motivating values, or a sign of social stereotyping. However, the lifestyle
concept remained significantly on the fringe of the social sciences until the
1960s, perhaps because its multi-disciplinary nature ran counter to the traditionally very specialized procedures of basic and academic research.

The application of this concept has come from another direction: applied
market research. This may be because the practice of consumer studies
accustoms researchers to the individual's multi-dimensionality and because
their realistic concern for effectiveness makes them more open to and tolerant of a new way of understanding and explaining behaviour. Indeed, the
real applications of the lifestyle concept have originated with professionals

concerned with surveys and polls with a professional or commercial aim (eg consumer studies, social marketing, etc). Marketing's interest in this socio-cultural approach came about through dissatisfaction with methods previously used to classify populations and individuals. The principles of these methods can be summarized in four points:

❑ specialist studies focused exclusively on a social, cultural or commercial subject in a specific market;
❑ separate collection and processing of psychological and behavioural data;
❑ one-off studies of individuals, particularly their psychology;
❑ exclusive descriptions of populations classified by their socio-demographic and economic identity (ie sex, age, income, etc).

The socio-styles concept seemed to offer a richer methodological alternative to this fragmented, atomised view of the individual, since it aimed to understand in a more global way a more complex individual in interaction with the environment. In particular it has pushed this conceptual opportunity furthest by inverting these principles:

❑ by combining in the same survey and databank information about different sectors and topics;
❑ by coordinating in a synthetic portrait (socio-style) multi-dimensional data on behaviour and rational psychology about attitudes and subconscious motivations;
❑ by systematically following the development of attitudes and value systems using a type of trend barometer;
❑ by proposing a socio-styles typology as variables complementary to classical socio-demographic criteria for identifying and describing populations.

The various operational applications of lifestyle concepts, including socio-styles, have developed from marketing needs. They represent a conceptual and methodological break with the traditional practices of surveys and polls, and perhaps even a cultural revolution which would explain the violence of certain reactions and reservations.

In the industrialized, developed world living conditions have changed in such a way that socio-demographic variables have lost a good deal of their relevance because of individual mobility, changing lifecycles, the dissolution of the traditional family unit, and the explosion in information and consumer goods. These disturb the traditional stratification into social classes narrowly determined by age, educational level or income. In these countries during the second half of the 1960s the most obvious profound social changes and cultural revolutions also occurred, illustrating the desperate search for new rules and new models in a disorganized society which could no longer be handled by traditional institutions and social classes.

Lifestyle studies were developed in this context of an extremely complex society in the process of change, first in the United States during the course of the 1960s and then in Europe, particularly France, from the beginning of the 1970s.

Various forms of experimentation developed almost simultaneously without mutual exchange of information and often in different directions, because of a pressing need at the time. This need manifested itself first among professionals who every day had to select people from the general population, define and understand them in order to provide them with suitable products and services. In this way marketing professionals found themselves experimenting and breaking new ground for the sole reason that their daily operational requirements made them more sensitive to the new social climate than were academics.

In order to humanize the portrait of consumers beyond their sociological identity, Ernst Dichter introduced his psychological motivation studies into marketing in the 1950s. Later, at the beginning of the 1960s, Sydney Levy developed the notion of a symbolic function for consumer goods, a concept later developed on a different basis, notably by the sociologist Jean Baudrillard and the anthropologist Mary Douglas. But it was William Lazer who in 1963 introduced the lifestyle concept into the world of marketing by formalizing the idea that a systematic relationship exists between the consumption styles and lifestyles of a social group.

Practical research and experimentation on the lifestyle concept flourished, often in opposing directions without finding a satisfactory common definition. Although the common aim expressed by all these research teams was to understand the dynamics of the way consumers adapt to the socio-cultural environment beyond simple socio-demographic and economic determinants, the practical lifestyle concepts diverged.

After 20 years of diverse experiments, a small number of methodologies have stood the test of time and professional application in the market economy. An even smaller number are able to be used on an international basis and meet the requirements of sociology and modern marketing. Yet it is true that experimentation and application have always preceded theory, methodology applied to the theory of method, blurring the outline of the lifestyle concept.

The objective of this book is to shed light on one of these methods, the socio-styles system, considering its fundamental concepts, methodological principles and techniques and also — more modestly — the theory behind it. However, in the sphere of international socio-cultural research we can also see four other main schools, all of which draw on the basic lifestyles concept to some degree, but defining it implicitly and applying it in a different way. Thus there are today five competing lifestyles on offer to the researcher and the professional user; and behind these methodologies are five competing concepts of people and society.

THE PANORAMA OF INTERNATIONAL LIFESTYLE STUDIES

Our purpose is not to embark on an exhaustive description of the different techniques available and even less a critical analysis of them. On the one hand, our point of view might not be objective because of the competition between these methods; and on the other the secrecy which traditionally (and naturally) surrounds the methods and results of these commercial studies makes it difficult to give a well-informed account. We will try above all to open the debate and distinguish the broad approaches which are suggested and compete in the general field of socio-cultural and lifestyle studies. We can currently distinguish five, including the socio-styles system.

In this attempt at classification we will include a certain number of methods and techniques, either because they are among the most notable and widespread or because they are or have been particularly typical. A brief description (not a critique) will be given based on information available to the author. In order not to betray any confidential information, we do not include any plans and the examples mentioned are incomplete and taken from published material.

The abundance of empirical information in socio-cultural and lifestyles studies since the end of the 1960s can be attributed to several causes. The 1960s was the decade of acute awareness of social chaos, the disintegration of status and roles, a disturbance in influence and authority, calling for a new view of society more receptive to diversity, mobility and permanent change.

In business and marketing particularly this was a time when the growing segmentation of populations was recognized, not totally explained by traditional social classes and socio-demographic criteria. A new system of population classification became necessary. The many experiments in lifestyle studies therefore responded to a market and social desire for new tools, new representations or explanations of society, and marketing methods adapted to this new diversity.

But the divergence that can be seen in these experiments is also partly a reflection of a whole range of contradictory and competing scientific schools in social and human sciences. Later we will describe the different scientific schools implicitly present behind the variety of lifestyle approaches.

However, it is convenient first to attempt to organize this diversity of experiences and intellectual and commercial offerings. We will try to summarize the five main trends, taking account of seven principal criteria:

❑ the object of the study: individuals and their personalities, the social being, the 'man-machine' or 'homo economicus', which refer to different concepts and schools of social sciences;
❑ the level of data collection: motivations, beliefs and values, attitudes and judgements, forms of behaviour or living conditions, which define the complete or partial character of the research;
❑ the field of investigation: thematic or sector-based, multi-sectorial, socio-cultural;

❑ the method and techniques for collecting data, which reflect earlier choices;
❑ the guiding concepts for interpretation: a pre-existing theoretical model for verification, measurement or experimentation;
❑ the analytical approach: static and fixed, historic and retrospective, or prospective and dynamic;
❑ the final structure of the end data, the 'product' offered to users: analytical, synthetic, typological or cartographic, etc.

Psychographic approaches — The lifestyle as a personality style

The first step in the study of lifestyles which was taken at the beginning of the 1960s was the psychographic approach, in the tradition of applied motivational studies following Dichter. Such was its pre-eminence that for a long time the terms lifestyles and psychographics were interchangeable.

The object of this type of study is clearly an individual and his or her original personality studied on a semi-conscious level in an imprecise way looking at the combination of character and personality, motivations and cultural values. However, psychology is clearly predominant in this approach, implicity defining the lifestyle as a fundamental and durable category of character and personality, and neglecting behaviour, living conditions and even attitudes, opinions and judgements as too superficial. Psychographic studies are therefore very individualized: precedence is given to the individual over the group and society itself, to the personality rather than its relations with the external environment. The social and cultural dimensions of consumption are neglected, as are its function in role playing and status, its stereotyped adherence to a collective model, its socio-economic determinants and the importance of established habits.

This psychological approach was also taken in the pure motivation studies in the 1960s which at that time represented radical progress. It has sometimes been criticized for lack of correlation between its analyses and the actual behaviour of citizens and consumers, giving rise to doubts about the explanatory and predictive value of its data. This is the reason that psychographic research has developed which is increasingly open to other, more rational variables that are more easily measured and more reassuring to users (eg judgements, opinions, attitudes and interests, as in the AIO method). Other research has felt the need to bring a socio-graphic design to psychographic analysis, including in the surveys a summary of individuals' conscious beliefs and values (the Rokeach method). In this way the purely psychological studies at the beginning of the psychographic trend were profoundly transformed and extended during the 1970s. This may have come about because pure psychology was fashionable during the 1960s but became less so afterwards.

The central motivation concept was therefore progressively transformed into one derived from values and conceived as a sort of cultural guide to individual behaviour, a demonstration of individual psychology's attraction to 'collective motivations' peculiar to civilization. Rokeach has defined them as types of beliefs about ideal objects and stereotyped models of behaviour. Following Lovejoy (1950) he distinguishes two value systems: instrumental, referring more to individuals and their personality; and terminal, referring to society and a person's place in social life. This notion is in between the motivation concept of pure psychology and the attitude concept of socio-graphy. The individual's value system is supposed to describe with a small number of key ideals what determines every thought and action in every cognitive, affective and behavioural domain.

However, as heir to a North American scientific and professional tradition the psychographic approach has stayed faithful to a positivist process. Although it refers almost exclusively to psychological variables that are most often subconscious, its method is no less obsessed with the measure-ment and accumulation of statistical data. The search for mathematical correlations often seems to be an obsession with these psychologists. The purpose of this technical rigour may be to compensate for the supposed fragi-lity of psychological concepts. If these methods are heirs to motivation studies, psychographic study methods have over the years come closer to classical sociographic attitude, opinion and interest surveys.

In the psychographic tradition, the approach is more analytical than synthetic, resting on general rather than thematic or sector-based socio-cultural data and searching for motivation models likely to define people. It is only through the evolution towards the sociography of values (the VALS and Rokeach methods) that psychography has established its own models.

Some practical lifestyle studies

Pure psychographic procedures can be identified in the work of Emmanuel Demby (MPI method) and William Wells of Chicago University. With them the radically psychological orientation of the procedure is most pronounced, being placed at the outer fringe of lifestyles studies. The term psychography is defined as 'a type of design segmenting the market according to the pro-pensity of homogeneous groups to buy a given product'. Being therefore considered as empirical and sector-based research from the viewpoint of desires and wishes but aiming to extract types which can be generally applied to a population in order to define potential consumers, these studies form a bridge between Dichter's motivation studies and the properly called socio-cultural studies of the 1970s.

Demby's MPI system

Emmanuel Demby defines psychography as 'a type of design segmenting the market according to the propensity of homogeneous groups to buy a given product'. The variables studied are concentrated mainly on consumer psy-chology from the point of view of the 'advantages of the product considered desirable, the personal concepts of potential consumers, *vis à vis* the envi-ronment and the process of decision making'.

Marking an evolution from Dichter's pure motivation, the central notion of MPI is therefore a sort of general psychological orientation, whose roots are deep personal motivations, but whose applications are translated into predispositions to types of behaviour. We see here the outline of a concept which will be progressively taken up in the notions of value (the culturalist approach) and attitude (the sociographic approach). It is an attempt to find in psychology, in some degree of depth, a driving mechanism for selecting and orientating behaviour patterns.

IPSOS psychographic profiles
Although not calling itself lifestyle study, this system deserves mention as a good example of methodology coming from the psychographic tradition but more oriented towards defining psychological profiles, seen as personal filters used by individuals to choose or reject from an immense series of ideological and commercial information.

Presented at the end of the 1970s as sector-based or operational studies intended particularly for products with a strong psychological implication, these studies defined six principal psychological types from a range of 64 questions. For example:

❏ Type 1 — family oriented, altruistic, seeking a loving environment, susceptible to frustration, escaping into romantic dreams;
❏ Type 4 — seductive and mobile, imaginative and curious, innovative, more responsive to form than things;
❏ Type 6 — introverted and dreamy, withdrawn and isolated, preoccupied with the inner life rather than with immediate and concrete action.

These types appear as characters or temperaments, and the terminology is differentiated into sub-types, leaving room for a more evolved combination, and which take account of the real complexity of personalities. A given individual is never 100 per cent rigid traditional or seductive mobile. This reflects the psychologist's concern not to lose sight of the profound individuality of every person, which goes beyond the classification and terminology necessary for social analysis and action.

Although it has not enjoyed extensive practical or commercial use, the general psychographic approach has had a considerable influence on all other procedures (with the exception, however, of pure mechanistic-behavioural methods). Notably, we can place on the frontiers of psychography:

❏ study techniques which attempt to combine taste and sensitivity variables with behavioural variables (eg AIO);
❏ sociographic studies which have done little but evolve from the analysis of individual psychologies towards collective motivations and values (eg the VALS system, the Rokeach method).

Culturalist approaches — The lifestyle as a value system

Culturalist procedures evolved from psychographic lifestyle studies, seeking to be seen as less speculative, more legitimate by using a definite, pre-established conceptual framework and a supposedly more objective measurement of variables.

Their central concept is that of 'value', an idealized collective model of thinking and behaviour which is abstract, general and supposedly universal. It replaces the concept of personal motivations and needs which is more contingent, anecdotal, subjective and best represented physically by projections on an immediate object (a relatively vague concept peculiar to the psychographic approach). Whereas motivation is the projection into the external world of an individual drive finding its source in the inner history of the person, value is rather the introjection by the person of an ideal norm whose source is manifestly external and to which the individual adheres and submits.

The notion of value introduces a split between the psychographic and culturalist approaches. The former considers the lifestyle implicitly as an expression of individual personality (which makes any typology or collective terminology more difficult). The latter sees in the lifestyle a process of socialization by rallying individuals to collective norms of civilization, which guarantees them integration into a group at the expense of reducing and normalizing their personality into the ideological framework of a collective system of values.

It is thus the ideological person who is the subject of sociographic studies. What is measured is a person's degree of adherence to a system of collective values which is macro-social (civilization) or micro-social (the tribe, the group). Culturalist studies can therefore be considered as studies in socialization, the normalization of individuals with reference to a pre-established model of civilization.

This is the reason that sociographic approaches are always founded on a pre-existing model supposed to define a matrix of stable, limited and stereotyped references, with which the individuals studied are confronted in order to measure their degree of participation and adherence.

❏ This model can be a collection of values defined *a priori* as key ideas in the social body being studied, or even as fundamental values of humanity itself (Rokeach).

❏ It can also be a portrait gallery of stereotyped ways of life embodying socially valued ideal 'moulds' (VALS system).

The culturalist approach is not presented as an exploratory study intended to discover the social structure, its current models of reference and how they take concrete form as ways of life, but rather as an *a posteriori* verification of the current adherence of a population to ideological values and pre-existing life models which are general and 'eternal'. Sociographic studies are therefore less socio-dynamic surveys of adaptation and change in society, more a barometer for evaluating the popularity of a supposedly intangible model of civilization.

The first advantage of this process is that it provides a definite and stable conceptual framework fed later by sociological theories, serving as a starting hypothesis for surveys according to the best scientific traditions.

However, this preliminary terminology of values or lifestyles also imposes a theory with no other experimental foundation than an academic's intuition and the rigidity of a terminology that is closed and limited as much in the number as in the nature of its concepts.

A second advantage is that the process offers a stable and codified methodology whose concepts and tools hardly vary over time. By reference to the same survey items we can measure the same quasi-eternal basic values or lifestyles. But this stability is also a weakness: its methods are less able to grasp change and take note of new ways of thought and life not previously included in the model. The culturalist approach measures the extent to which people today adhere to a group of norms and values with which theoreticians defined yesterday's civilization.

The culturalist study of values aims to be more generalist, socio-cultural and multi-sectorial than psychographic approaches. Indeed, value defines an ideal objective of thought and behaviour towards which all an individual's acts would gravitate at all stages of life and at all levels of thought and behaviour. Value would therefore be a principle for mobilizing energy (just like individual motivation) and a lifestyle organizer, impelling the individual to normalize thoughts and actions in order to approach an ideal type.

This concept presumes that individual drives and motivations (studied in psychography) are reformulated without variation on entering the stereotyped and pre-established moulds of values — collective motivations. It also presumes that the attitudes and judgements of rational psychology and especially behaviour are the direct expression of these beliefs and this adherence to ideal values. It is an ethical and ideological person who is being studied according to the hypothesis that: 'one does what one believes in and resembles those whom one admires'. This culturalist approach therefore gives precedence to a mass measurement of individual beliefs as normalized and stereotyped collective values, to the detriment of more per-sonal character traits and more rational attitudes and judgements, and above all to the detriment of conduct and behaviour.

Finally, a specific characteristic of the culturalist school is its eminently intra-cultural character. Indeed, the method does not explore but verifies, and presupposes a group of conceptual hypotheses about key values and key lifestyles which define a basic theoretical model. This can only be done by reference to a particular civilization in a given place: eg a tribe, a very structured social class, a country or region with a pronounced culture. It is almost impossible to undertake a multi-national extension to the research, except to postulate a fundamental humanity or universal civilization whose values and rules of behaviour are eternal and omnipresent. This may explain why lifestyle studies of the culturalist school are difficult to export from their country of origin to other societies which cannot recognize themselves in the terminology of values and lifestyles.

In fact, the originality of culturalist approaches is expressed more by the value concept (individual belief in an ideal projected by the group) and by the stance of *a posteriori* verification and measurement of a group of values or types previously defined ideologically or theoretically as reference models. The method hardly differs from polling techniques that use judgement scales — a technique inherited from American psychosociology — which are also the principal tool for collecting information from another 'sociographic' school.

The working tool intended for users is not determined in the culturalist approach, unless by its continual reference to previous theoretical models. We also find analytical formalization of data (Rokeach) and typological presentation (VALS).

By their very fundamental socio-cultural dimension as regards concept if not method, culturalist approaches are also furthest removed from commercial and cultural marketing. They are concerned with analyzing the participation in civilization of individuals whose nature as an operational tool for analyzing behaviour and attitudes is merely secondary. This may also help to explain why these techniques have fewer professional applications than others.

Some practical research methods

Rokeach's 'values survey'

At the end of the 1960s in the USA an interest developed in value system studies which went beyond psychographic research. The pragmatic objective was to analyze consumer attitudes and behaviour.

Unlike sociographic studies which later formed an amalgam between opinion, attitude and value, Milton Rokeach's procedures give a specific and significant place to values in determining forms of individual conduct, behaviour and thought: 'values not only represent an opinion as to what is preferred but also a preference for what has been chosen'. For Rokeach, therefore, values are an individual's beliefs about ideals such as truth, beauty, purity, justice and equality. These values are assumed to be more fundamental, durable and explanatory than attitudes, of which they are the main determinants. Attitudes then serve as relays towards opinions, judgements and behaviour. Although an individual can exhibit from day to day thousands of different opinions and judgements founded on hundreds of different attitudes, these are only based on a small number of fundamental values which set the direction of these mental and behavioural mechanisms.

Returning to a distinction established by Lovejoy in 1950, Rokeach defines two systems of values:

❑ eighteen terminal values orienting the individual towards ideas of personal integration and social organization (eg harmony, true friendship, family security, freedom);
❑ eighteen instrumental values orienting an individual's personal development (eg courage, purity, self-control, honesty, logic).

We can see the ethical character of these values (ie what differentiates them radically from a system of attitudes). They are ideas that have been expressed by society at a given moment, whose degree of acceptance by each person can be measured.

The psychological and the social are equally taken into account in the culturalist works of Rokeach across these two internal and external, narcissistic and social value systems. However, they are juxtaposed without really establishing any correlation, interaction or, even less, any dialectic between them.

The VALS system (values and lifestyles)

This methodology, developed by the Stanford Research Institute in the USA at the end of the 1970s, is also inspired by the central notion of values applying a culturalist lifestyle concept. But the way of processing data is noticeably different, seeking to group individuals into profile types according to their value system.

The terminology of values studied is established *a priori* founded on the theoretical concepts of Riesman and particularly on Maslow's hierarchy of needs. The particular feature of VALS is that it has developed an *a priori* typology of nine American lifestyles. This typology can be interpreted as a classification of individuals according to their level of 'self-achievement' and the method or route of this personal development.

❏ This is a hierarchical typology where we can distinguish at the bottom of the scale lifestyles that are oriented purely towards the satisfaction of fundamental needs (need-drives); further up the 'belongers'; and then the successful lifestyles at the top of the pyramid.

❏ We can also distinguish segmentation according to two main routes to success: conformity, according to which success comes about through accepting collective rules and integrating into groups (outer-directed); and more marginal promotion through the system by self-made people (inner-directed).

This *a priori* typology is obviously ideological. It measures the method and degree of individual ambition and success according to norms peculiar to American society. The theoretical nature of this approach and the conceptual clarity of a stable typology (points common to all culturalist approaches) make the study into an *a posteriori* verification of *a priori* hypotheses. However, these hypotheses clearly express a pre-established theory. The research does not aim to find out the forces behind social action or individual methods of integration, but to verify the success of certain stereotyped models of success. Perhaps one of the difficulties of the VALS system in becoming established outside the United States is due to the typically American character of its *a priori* theoretical typology.

The LOV system

More recently a simplified system of values has been put forward by L R Kalhe, who estimates it is possible to summarize Rokeach's thirty-six values into nine, including warm relationships, self-respect, security, enthusiasm, fun and pleasure. The method involves getting interviewees to classify these topics in order of importance.

A study carried out in two countries on two generations which supports this technique indicates, for example, that a feeling of belonging stands in first place for German adults and in second place for their children; however, it is only a very secondary value for American adults and next to last for their children. (The study samples were very small: between 43 and 150 people.)

Sociographic approaches — The lifestyle as a fashionable way of thinking

The study techniques of sociographic lifestyles have a similar methodology to culturalist approaches (based on measuring acceptance of judgements on attitude scales) but a noticeably different attitude, and they therefore represent a more empirical alternative which is also more circumstantial and pragmatic. This may explain their significant international development at the end of the 1970s and the beginning of the 1980s.

If the subject studied in the culturalist school is the ideological person of cultural anthropology, in the sociographic approach it is more the social person, the atom of public opinion.

However, in both cases the lifestyle is investigated and defined at the level of conscious psychology. This is at a slightly more general and profound level of beliefs and ideals in culturalist studies, and at a more superficial, circumstantial anecdotal level of opinions and attitudes in sociographic studies. The study of sensitivities, tastes, emotions and drives which make up the subsconscious individual personality is neglected even more in sociographic than in culturalist studies. Precedence is given in both approaches to conscious and rational psychology above the study of behaviour. The subject of study is therefore conscious and rational attitudes and opinions expressed as general rules on lifestyles (not far removed from value studies) or formulated more concretely by reference to everyday life, the present, objects and institutions. If the basic definition of an attitude is a general tendency to orientate judgements and behaviour in a certain direction, nevertheless it is intended to be a less fundamental concept than values. It is no longer a mobilizing and organizing ideology of observed lifestyles, but merely a group of assertions whose correlations seem to define an individual's preferred mental tendencies. Sets of attitudes classify individuals.

The specific concept originated by sociographic approaches at the beginning of the 1970s was that of the socio-cultural current. This is understood as a set of opinions and attitudes converging in the same direction (a more or less actualized, circumstantial value) whose evolution is studied over a period. Breaking with the earlier psychographic and culturalist approaches, the sociographic lifestyle studies introduced a study method concerned with historical development. Socio-cultural study became dynamic, analyzing and measuring the position of individuals against a group of evolving trends, themselves defining a changing society.

By means of repeated studies over the years we can see the rise and fall of a socio-cultural current through its average penetration of the general population; and we can position each individual on this axis of change in relation to the population average.

Socio-cultural currents are defined in most sociographic studies as single-polar axes indicating the theme of progress. For example, the 'self achievement' socio-cultural current means that in society there is a trend towards this attitude; and individuals are judged to be 'in advance' or 'behind' according to whether they accept this idea more strongly or more weakly than the general average.

We can see clearly how in this type of approach the social variable completely dominates individual variables in the lifestyle concept (in radical antithesis to the psychographic approach). Social individuals are 'judged' or 'evaluated' not according to the internal logic of their own lifestyle, not according to their personal dynamics, but by reference to a linear concept of social progress defined purely quantitatively in terms of socio-mass.

This concept of a single-polar socio-cultural current presents several problems:

❏ confusion between an attitude or a set of attitudes being accepted by the majority and the notion of a social norm. By assimilating one with the other, we run the risk of identifying society by a quantitative assessment of public opinion;

❏ confusion, too, between the statistical progression of an attitude in public opinion (in terms of socio-mass) and the notion of social progress. This is to forget rather quickly that 'fashion' in ideas, attitudes and values is subject to cycles which sooner or later are reversed, like a pendulum.

By persevering with the measurement of a single-polar socio-cultural current, we run the risk of focusing the attention of researchers and users on the opposing pair of values on one pole currently in vogue and not being sufficiently sensitive to the other pole which tomorrow may be in the ascendancy. (This is the reason why the socio-styles system has chosen to study socio-cultural trends from the point of view of bi-polar cultural flows or socio-waves.)

Defining lifestyle portraits almost exclusively by a series of indices 'in advance' or 'behind' leads to a definition of individuals as leaders of fashion. The definition is therefore extensive for types 'in advance', but we end up with a negative, hollow definition for people who are 'behind' in the group of trends. To us it seems dangerous that the lifestyle studies introduce (implicitly and probably involuntarily) the notion of the 'full' individual and the 'empty' individual. We find again in sociographic approaches the tendency of the culturalist school to consider individuals as social objects defined solely by their relation to a norm which is totally external. This can too often lead to social groups being devalued if they are outside the norm, minorities, 'behind' and marginal, while forgetting that their motivations, attitudes and conduct are nevertheless quite abundant, positive and dynamic in their own eyes. Out of respect for these people and social groups as well as to work with them effectively it is necessary to qualify positively individuals in their lifestyle and system of values and attitudes by reference to the concepts and models which motivate them, even if these are not fashionable, held by the majority or developing.

The different sociographic approaches differ sharply from culturalist studies by being more empirical. The list of socio-cultural currents studied and the ranges of attitudes that it is based on do not come from any dogmatic sociological theory. They are supposed to be the fruit of experience — empirical experience of discovering socially dominant attitudes which is, however, likely to be modified and extended over the years. The terminology for socio-cultural currents has thus increased from 25 to 35 themes over 10 years, although the list of socio-cultural currents has not been profoundly modified during 20 years of investigation. It is still structured according to the same terminology studied by Yankelovich in the USA at the end of the 1960s; people seem to have proceeded by accumulation rather than by selection and replacement; and no concept or process of reconsidering these socio-cultural currents appears to be followed except at random.

We can talk of *a priori* empiricism to the extent that the list of socio-cultural currents for study is finite, predetermined, based on past experience and not continuing study. Like culturalist studies, sociographic surveys are not exploratory research but polls that verify a previously defined model (theoretical for the culturalists, empirical for the sociographists) and are supposed to take account of all socio-cultural reality. These studies are presented as 'monitors' or barometers, and are intended to measure phenomena already known through repetition rather than to discover new phenomena.

This empiricism, however, has certain limitations when these studies take on an international dimension. Yankelovich's first, American-based list of socio-cultural currents remains the pillar of international surveys, such as those imported into France in the 1970s. There is an ambiguity about the very nature of the studies. Are they concerned with measuring the penetration of an American system of attitudes and values throughout the world? Are they concerned with measuring a country's specific socio-culture (although is it really possible to ensure that three-quarters of the socio-cultural currents are shared)? Or is it a question of measuring common international denominators of public thinking (in which case the socio-cultural currents would not be a 'whole' lifestyle, but merely a group of shared stereotypes carried by the media and everyday culture)? The socio-styles system has clearly chosen this third concept in its study of socio-waves which are considered a partial and superficial component of the lifestyle.

The processing of data in the original sociographic studies is analytical: each socio-cultural current is measured for its social penetration; the population of the sample is distributed in quartiles according to four classes of response from the most to the least favourably disposed towards an attitude (a literal translation of the interrogation technique using a scale of support). Each individual is placed in one or other of these quartiles, from the most advanced to the most behind. The lifestyle definition of a social individual as atom of public opinion results in the juxtaposition of 25 or 35 scores 'in advance' or 'behind' collected in a complete list of socio-cultural currents.

The fundamental philosophy of this sociographic school is analytical in the tradition of positivism, a direct inheritance from opinion polls. It is only recently that certain study organizations have become preccupied with presenting their results in a more synthetic way, which could take two forms:

❏ a map of socio-cultural currents obtained by direct correspondence analysis;
❏ a portrait gallery obtained by a cluster technique (a group of individuals making up a cluster of proximity, if the whole sample is projected on to the previous analytical map).

Other practical research methods

Yankelovich's Monitor

The pioneer of this approach was Yankelovich's Monitor in the USA in the late 1960s. It defines a list of 26 socio-cultural currents measured by scales of attitude and judgement. This is still the backbone of many international applications which are directly influenced by it, showing the extent of American socio-cultural influence.

Yankelovich's concept of socio-cultural currents is that of a trend in collective psychology orientating forms of thought and behaviour in a certain direction. He cites the lifestyle of the Alfonsins, a 50-year-old couple who decided to have a smaller apartment with fewer household appliances, to change their car for a model lower down the range, to have more simple frozen meals, to use the extra time available for leisure and cultural activities. Here Yankelovich sees the lifestyle as the manifestation of a trend towards 'the simplification of life' which impels individuals to turn their backs on everything complicated and sophisticated and to buy pre-cooked food and automatic equipment. In this way the concept of the socio-cultural current is defined, not unlike the attitude concept, as a psychological tendency to prefer certain values systematically in every kind of behaviour.

For Yankelovich the aim of research is less the lifestyles themselves (variables to be explained) and more the socio-cultural currents (strong collective trends). Individuals are defined by their degree of receptiveness to a group of socio-cultural currents. Thirty-one socio-cultural currents were studied from the point of view of opinions and attitudes by Yankelovich's Monitor in the United States at the beginning of the 1970s. The currents included introspection, personal creativity, confidence in science and technology, sexual liberalism, tolerance regarding physical stimulants and drugs.

Five main sets of currents summarize this range of trends:

❏ the psychology of abundance, seeking the satisfaction of psychological needs, basic utilitarian needs having been satisfied;
❏ a trend towards sensory stimulation, against the boring routine of everyday life, seeking escape in the imagination;

❑ a trend towards simplification, against the excessively complex and restrictive modern life;
❑ values of tolerance and permissiveness against the former Puritanism;
❑ the rejection of authority and order.

This list of socio-cultural currents is established first of all from long-term social observation and measured across indicators of attitudes and standardized opinions. Repeated measurement (Monitor) results in the identification of a trend towards or against each of these separate currents.

COFREMCA'S '3 SC'

This method was developed in France at the beginning of the 1970s by COFREMCA using Yankelovich's Monitor. The list of socio-cultural currents was adapted to suit France from previous experience of qualitative studies. The list was first reduce to 26 currents, then progressively extended by integrating new information about collective attitudes and opinions over a period. Some currents are defined as specific, such as self-manipulation, concern for appearance, rejection of manipulation. However, the majority of the currents are identical to the *a priori* models of American attitudes: eg self-expression, marginal differentiation, hedonism, polysensualism, nature.

These studies prompt a general question about international socio-cultural currents: is there a danger of measuring how much North American attitudes penetrate the world or do these lists of currents really reflect the existence of a civilization with international values and ways of thinking?

Basically, all individuals are rated according to their degree of adherence to each of these currents, by reference to the general distribution of opinions on this attitude. They are considered 'advanced' if they are in the first quartile and 'behind' is they are in the last quartile (the people least favourable towards this attitude); and there are two intermediate positions (corresponding to the 50 per cent who are moderately favourable and moderately unfavourable).

This approach produces socio-cultural profiles which define, for example, 'behind the times' (8 per cent of the population according to COFREMCA), 'country-dwellers' (14 per cent), 'do-it-yourselfers' (8 per cent) or 'anti-establishment pioneers' (8 per cent).

More recently a map has been drawn of the distribution of socio-cultural currents in a multi-dimensional space though correspondence analysis.

Other experiments with socio-cultural currents

An application of socio-cultural studies was also developed in Italy in the mid-1970s following Yankelovich's attitude Monitor. It set itself the objective of representing in each framework of cultural references the population, its social and consumer values. Here we find 30 socio-cultural currents grouped into three cultural models, such as authority (53 per cent in 1976), effort (3 per cent), religiosity (30 per cent) belonging to an 'ancient culture', romanticism (4 per cent), repression (57 per cent), permissiveness

(18 per cent), nature (27 per cent), anarchy (28 per cent) and anti-consumption (43 per cent).

Another quite similar national application of this approach was developed by the Taylor Nelson Group in Great Britain.

The Risc Network
In Europe during the 1980s the Risc Network brought together various market research and polling organizations. Their national sociographic studies following the same procedure can be synthesized from time to time by the use of a common list of socio-cultural currents adapted from Yankelovich's American Monitor.

Aesop's barometer
We can also link the work of Aesop in France with this general sociographic approach. However, this has less to do with studying a general socio-cultural pattern, showing ways of thinking defined by sets of basic attitudes; it is more concerned with classifying individuals by current themes as models of perception, judgement and reaction. Conducted by a public sector organization and large firms whose activities depend closely on public acceptability, these surveys aim to analyze social risk in terms of acceptance or exaggeration of major problems or plans at the time, and also to follow up opinions about these themes. They are to some extent studies of the kinds of circumstantial views held by the individual as citizen.

Mechanistic approaches — The lifestyle as a condition of existence and a manner of being

The above approaches, while manifestly different in stance, are nevertheless all preoccupied with studying individuals' lifestyles from the perspective of psychology. These three schools are distributed along a continuum from the individual psychology of subconscious drives (psychography) to the most rational public opinions (sociography); from an endogenous concept of a lifestyle determined by personality (psychography) to exogenous concepts defining a lifestyle as a means of adherence to a group system of values (culturalism) or a method of adaptation by adopting stereotyped, fashionable, collective opinions. All these studies bear witness to the major trend of psychological research inherited from the 1960s in both social and business sciences.

A fourth approach to lifestyle study takes a radically contrasting research stance whose inspiration is purely behaviourist and positivist. The object of its study is the existential person seen entirely in the context of living conditions, environmental determinants, social, professional and family status, equipment and possessions, and behavioural habits. The subjective experience of this mode of existence, motives and motivations, possible dissatisfactions, dreams and plans are not taken into account.

We find implicitly in these studies a purely materialistic concept of the social individual, able to be classified and explained totally by demographic, economic and physical criteria. The individual is a machine reduced to a group of external mechanistic determinants without mental energies of any sort (or at least these are not taken into account).

Of all the families of studies of the individual in society this approach is the least theoretical and conceptual. It is not a school of thought or an organized method, but rather a vast field of practice in the human, social and commercial sciences inherited from the scientific positivism of the end of the 19th century.

Individuals are studied just as physicists study an object in a laboratory, only accepting as 'scientific fact' what is measurable and tangible. This practice had almost completely invaded the social and commercial science until the arrival of the new psychographic, culturalist and sociographic research into lifestyles in the 1960s. It is interesting to note the consensus that until then united extremely diverse categories of practice in this concept of the objective person:

❑ general social census studies (eg INSEE in France);
❑ general social and economic observations and planning (eg CREDOC in France);
❑ consumer panel studies (eg SECODIP, Nielsen, GFK, NFO, Market-Facts, Home Testing);
❑ all the commercial market studies (despite a small proportion progressively won over to attitude questions since the 1950s).

The research stance for these studies is founded on a lack of confidence in the individual interviewee. Attempts are made:

❑ to reduce the variables collected to facts, because of distrust of the subject's subjectivity;
❑ to verify what interviewees say by checking questions, because of distrust of their 'lies' or illusions;
❑ to reduce the questions asked to the simplest possible single-word ideas, because of lack of confidence in the researcher's ability to interpret a multi-dimensional response;
❑ as often as possible to replace the interview with a summary of facts by a researcher or even by a machine, pure observation avoiding any subjective expression of experience;
❑ to standardize as much as possible the collection and processing of data, as if to ensure them a life of their own independent of the people they qualify.

The processing of this information is purely quantitative atomistic and analytical. Each simple one-word variable is studied separately as a primary unit of a way of life, in terms of socio-mass. General population averages, medians and modes are calculated and each individual assessed against group norms. It is only very recently that procedures for structuring data, synthesizing variables and segmenting individuals have been introduced (first of all in commercial market studies, then very slowly in studies of general social interest).

This behaviourist and mechanistic approach applied to the measurement of living conditions and behaviour takes the same scientific stance as the sociographic approaches later applied to opinion variables: the collection of simple data processed in an analytical manner, analyzing the position of each individual with reference to a general average in place of a norm, in order to define lifestyles as having a 'normal' or 'marginal' position in relation to this external model: the 'majority' or the 'average'.

Here the lifestyle idea is reduced to its simplest expression, the way of life. And commercial market studies have again offered the most widespread version in what are called 'usage and attitude' studies, taking some account of psychological data on satisfaction, brand image and intended image, acceptability or rejection, preference, etc.

The main quality of these mechanistic and behavioural approaches is their concern for objectivity in variables and for procedural rigour in the collection and processing of information.

In the human and social sciences the individual's psychological dimension opens up an uncertain territory of subjective variables, unstable over time, where words do not mean the same thing, and difficult to measure in financial terms. But to abandon totally study of this psychological dimension out of concern, however commendable, to avoid any distortion in collection or interpretation, is to abandon any hope of completely understanding the lifestyle.

In fact the research which for decades has generated 'official statistics' is derived from a retrograde movement by researchers and their financial backers for nearly a decade away from the psychological dimension of social facts and individual ways of life. This fear became institutionalized in an approach whose bias and lack of completeness had been forgotten over the decades. It was out of recognition of the reductive nature of this approach that various attempts were made to introduce more structuring and synthesis of and classification of individuals.

The concern for objectivity led to the categorization of individuals according to supposedly 'socio-objective' concepts which it is hoped are easily identifiable in any form of investigation, from factual observations of simple interrogations, avoiding all distortion. The best examples of this are the socio-demographic and economic classifications. These classifications, by sex, age, income, profession, level of education, family size and type, location and type of habitat, have become the identity card of every individual studied and the 'necessary and sufficient' system of analytical criteria. The value of these criteria in isolation is not in doubt, but the limitations of the system are evident:

❏ none of the variables offers information about the person's psychology and subjective experience;
❏ their analytical use (separated and juxtaposed) does not give any synthetic portrait of the person;
❏ above all these conventional classifications lose their theoretical

objectivity when they are used over a long period. For example, can the notion of executive have the same meaning in 1988 as in 1958? And can the notion of a farmer be seen in the same light when agriculture has been transformed over 30 years? The same is true when we try to study the classifications in international surveys. For example, a secondary school diploma does not have the same meaning in the different countries of Europe. Habit, the diffusion of these criteria into all sectors of activity and the quasi-official status accorded to the major state social and economic survey organizations have all obscured the fact that these allegedly objective variables are only conventions, and as such should be periodically reviewed.

Realization of the limits of these socio-demographic variables has led to the need for more qualitative classifications of people into thinking styles to supplement living conditions, and has opened the way for psychographic, sociographic and culturalist studies.

Different experiences

Some very different studies illustrate the attempts to create a bridge between socio-mass surveys and the lifestyles idea reduced to behaviour.

The AIO System

This concept and methodology, developed at the end of the 1970s in the United States by Yoram Wind, is the most direct heir to the philosophy and practices of marketing studies.

The AIO system reflects the need felt by motivation specialists to integrate the variables of rational and concrete psychology (intention) with behavioural data for a more universal understanding of the individual. In addition AIO represents the concern to leave a role for psychology in behavioural studies. AIO (meaning 'attitude, interest, opinion') is uniquely placed in its basic intent at the crossroads of behavioural psychological approaches.

However, when putting these applications into practice the AIO system quickly diverted towards behaviourist inspired studies, mainly oriented towards summarizing purchasing behaviour and possessions, and only secondarily enlightened by rational judgements and opinions about behaviour, supplemented by a summary of declared interests and ideal preferences.

What seems generally to emerge from applications of the AIO system is therefore a behaviourist and mechanistic model. Here the individual is not considered from the point of view of a demanding, active psychology; rather models of behaviour and preference (behavioural psychology) are observed which originate in social conformity. These lifestyles are externally based moulds: this approach aims to delineate the activities and attitudes of an individual rather than his degree of support for cultural values and behavioural norms. Empirical intention and pragmatic ambition are clearly formulated.

Applications of AIO have been developed mainly in a sector-based way and no general socio-cultural vision has been published.

After a broad starting definition which combines psychology and behaviour to describe lifestyles profile types across their daily lives, their work and leisure habits, and the image they have of themselves and the world, practice is often limited to summarizing behaviour and the most immediate inclinations for action (in the form of a summary of interests and purchasing intentions). In these applications the AIO system shows itself to be the most classic and static kind of market study which underestimates the importance of psychological variables, particularly subconscious ones, in favour of a more superficial measurement of declarations of intent on action and behaviour, without only synthetic structuring. This is why we think we can classify this methodology as a mechanistic and behaviourist approach and as the nearest to the sociographic intention.

The CREDOC studies

In France during the 1970s Victor Scardigli at CREDOC developed annual analyses of French living conditions and ambitions. These multi-sector studies stress behaviour, habit and actual living conditions as well as the rational psychology of opinions and judgements applied to these living conditions.

Some strong trends emerged from the quantitative measurement of these variables, such as 'the collapse of religion, the development of an enjoyment morality, an increase in time spent watching television, a reduction in expenditure on clothing and eating at home' (CREDOC 1974).

From these analyses prospective scenarios of society are elaborated, such as a 'society in disarray' scenario predicting weak and irregular growth; a multiplication of conflicts; young people spontaneously leaving school; revolutionary actions by minority groups; a marked differentiation in income, lifestyle and consumption between very unequal social groups; and considerable pockets of poverty.

The intention of these studies is to offer social prospectives based on the use of traditional sociological data combined with economic and demographic variables as well as variables related to general living conditions and attitudes. This work reaches the frontiers of socio-economic and commercial applications of lifestyles studies and basic, often academic, sociological research.

One of the main interests of CREDOC's work is to place itself at the meeting point of the two spheres of thought, method and application.

The Pryzm system

This system was developed in the mid 1970s by Claritas in the United States to offer a practical geo-social typology of groups of consumers with similar purchasing power and ways of consumption, clearly intended for marketing (mail order marketing, in particular).

Five main types of active variables are taken into consideration: wealth and social status, standard of living, ethnic roots and allegiances, mobility and place of residence, as well as general socio-demographic data. Using typological procedures the data is processed to define profiles which are portraits both of ways of life and of urban areas with similar characteristics.

At the beginning of the 1980s 10 principal clusters were defined, subdivided into 40 sub-groups. Cluster S2, for instance, describes a profile of individuals who are well educated, influential, elitist, white and house owners in comfortable, green, residential suburbs. This cluster is divided into four sub-categories, such as swimming pool owners or station wagon owners.

Cluster R2 is a mixture of poor whites, blacks, Hispanics and Indians living in the poorest rural areas. It is divided into five sub-categories such as 'Marlboro country residents' or those who have to 'scrabble hard'.

Another type is U1, single, well-educated people living in lively districts close to universities or artistic centres. They are subdivided into 'sunbelt singles', 'bohemians', etc.

This type of classification (which has an equivalent in France) appears to be one of the most behaviouralist, since it defines a lifestyle as a group of signs of social status embodied in possessions (and generally those most visible by simple external observation). This approach is effective mainly in the United States where the social habitat normally groups together individuals of a similar socio-demographic, ethnic, financial and cultural profile. This is less the case in Europe where town districts and suburbs are more mixed and do not tend to become ghettos of a certain social class.

Other behavioural lifestyle studies

All the commercial market studies and a good number of social studies depend on a mechanistic, associationist and behaviourist philosophy and method. Examples of those that have tried to broaden their analysis to a more general portrait of ways of life are:

❑ the Leo Burnett Advertising Agency studies carried out at the end of the 1970s, mainly in the USA, Great Britain and France. Similar to the AIO system, it involves mainly sector-based 'usage and attitude' surveys for a particular market, which gather behavioural data on centres of interest, intention or satisfaction (rational psychology). The aim is to define thematic consumer typologies;

❑ the studies by Sydney Levy, which could be termed 'symbolic kit' analyses. At the beginning of the 1960s Levy took the view that consumers buy things not only for their utilitarian function but also for the symbols they represent. Every product consumed is thus a sign of self-expression, of lifestyle. A lifestyle is defined from the general range of purchases made by an individual as well as his of her choice of brands and supplemented by more general behaviour and social attitudes;

❑ the studies by L Albert and R Gelty at the end of the 1960s took the same starting point, introducing the use of factor analysis to improve the structuring of information. Thus 16 basic ranges of life-styles (ie styles of consumption) were defined from a survey of 5,000 people and 80 products and services. For example, drinkers of brand X are described as heavy drinkers with a fondness for the open-air life, whereas consumers of brand Y are described as travellers, car fanatics and cocktail drinkers;

❑ System W, tested in France in the 1980s, uses a purely behaviourist typology, is radically (and even violently) opposed to sociographic and psychosociological approaches. The declared aim is to eliminate 'ambiguity and bias' which every psychological variable introduces into lifestyle studies. Nine families of behavour are described and grouped into three categories.

These few examples illustrate the muddled awareness in the marketing world of the need to define individual consumer profiles in as complete and extensive a way as possible. At the same time they demonstrate the inertia and conservatism which frequently draw the concept we want to develop of the individual back to mere behaviour and mere declarations of intent.

We have no doubt that the range of products and brands used has great symbolic meaning in a consumer society such as our own. And these variables deserve to be included in the indicators making up a lifestyle portrait. However, is it necessary to confine the portrait to this range? Is it necessary to describe individuals' profiles only by the static juxtaposition of products consumed? It seems to us that this limits the lifestyle too much to consumption and denies its capacity to be adapted, only seeing in it socio-commercial conformity coming from the collective pressure of public opinion or the influence of advertising.

The socio-styles system: A synthetic approach

The founders of the socio-styles system methodology began their research at the beginning of the 1970s, when the psychographic, culturalist, sociographic and mechanistic schools had already outlined their concepts and developed some experiments, notably in the United States. Our research was based on the information acquired from these preliminary studies and aimed to construct a more extensive methodology, if possible.

We decided to orient our research first to a critical analysis of these four methodological schools. Each approach seemed to be scientifically based and technically reliable but remained within the relatively narrow limits of its *a priori* concepts and its survey and data processing conventions. None of these methods seemed to us sufficiently comprehensive to meet the basic goal of a lifestyle study: to broaden the view of individuals in society in order to better understand the mechanisms of their lifestyles and act more respectfully and effectively towards them.

A desire for synthesis has dominated the establishment, experimentation and application of the socio-styles system since 1972:

❑ From the psychographic approach we have retained the importance of the most profound psychological variables, motivations related to character and personality traits, the motivating role of the unconscious, the deciding value of mental images, desires, imaginary pictures and dreams. And from their psychological study techniques we have kept non-verbal questions, projective tests and multi-scenic variables. However, we do not accept that individual character is the only typological factor defining a lifestyle.

❏ From the culturalist approach we have retained in the socio-styles system the concepts of values, beliefs, the motivating character of certain
idealized representations of an idea, scenario, product or self-image.
However, we have refused to limit our research to the simple repetitive
measurement of a list of values or a predetermined typological classification. In our view this would be to reproduce a pre-existing theoretical
model and to miss an opportunity to see the appearance of new profiles
of individuals or new forms of belief as society evolves. The socio-styles
system's approach to values therefore aims to be emperical.

❏ From the sociographic approach we have retained the notions of attitudes, opinions and judgements — and especially the concept of the
socio-cultural current (cultural flow or socio-wave in our terminology)
as a coherent set of fashionable ways of thinking in socio-dynamic evolution. However, the socio-styles system refuses to define *a priori* the
direction of history or progress, avoiding any pejorative classification of
individuals as 'advanced' or 'backward'. Our bi-polar definition of socio-
waves meets this requirement to anticipate changes of direction and to
define a person's mentality positively at every moment, whether it is in
the current direction of fashion or the opposite. From sociographic survey techniques the socio-styles system has retained Likert and Osgood's
attitude scales, but we have not made them our exclusive measuring
tool since they are too rational; they are supplemented in our surveys
by many other interrogation techniques. Basically, the socio-styles system refuses to define lifestyles solely from the point of view of attitudes
and opinions. We need to define the complete person, from the most
profound motivations to the most factual behaviour, moving through
judgements and attitudes. From the sociographic school the socio-
styles system has also kept the necessary but insufficient study of 'social
winds' (currents of conceptual opinions) and added lifestyle typologies
which define how these currents of opinion influence behaviour.

❏ From the mechanistic behaviouralist we have obviously retained the
importance of behaviour, habits and living conditions and the need to
make them active variables in defining lifestyles profiles (in contrast to
all the above approaches). However, we refuse to accord exclusivity or
pride of place to behaviour as market studies and sociological research
have done for 30 years. The socio-styles system wishes to balance the
definition of a lifestyle between the realism of behaviour and the subjectivity of psychology.

Right from the outset the ambition of the socio-styles system has been to
achieve a synthesis without denying or calling into question the respective
values and intrinsic techniques of these different schools:

❏ a synthesis of concepts to define the lifestyle in a multi-dimensional
way as the gestalt (and not only the sum) of variables about living conditions, behaviour, judgements and rational opinions, irrational attitudes and values, emotions and tastes, more profound motivations,
unconscious dreams;

❏ a synthesis of information in studies generating multi-sector databanks to define the lifestyle both from the point of view of private and social, political and cultural life, as well as from that of the economy and consumption, communications, the media and advertising;

❏ a synthesis of survey techniques combining on the scanner questionnaires a large variety of interrogation methods likely to collect behavioural and psychological, rational and emotional data;

❏ a synthesis of data-processing techniques according to a systematic process (Galaxy);

❏ a synthesis of results putting forward two complementary views and two kinds of operational information for different uses: on the one hand, dynamic socio-cultural currents (socio-waves), which measure at a given moment the competitive equilibrium of fashionable topics and ideas and the evolution of mentalities and values over a period of time; and on the other, the socio-styles typology, a classification of individuals which outlines at a given moment the segmentation of the population and indicates the evolution of customs over a period;

❏ a theoretical synthesis which resolutely places the lifestyle at the crossroads of psychology and sociology but in a dynamic way through opposition, attempting to approximate the way in which the individual personality becomes socialized and collective models are individualized in the socio-style.

Figure 3.1 is a comparative analysis of these five approaches, and figure 3.2 explains how they are brought together in the socio-styles system.

COMPARATIVE ANALYSIS OF 5 APPROACHES

	Psychographic	Culturalistic	Sociographic	Mechanistic	SOCIO-STYLES SYSTEM
LEADING CONCEPT	MOTIVATIONS Personality Character	System of VALUES	SOCIO-CULTURAL TRENDS	LIVING CONDITIONS	SOCIO-STYLES OF LIFE AND SOCIO-WAVES with tendencies
Scientific REFERENCE	Psychology PSYCHO-ANALYSIS	CULTURAL ANTHROPOLOGY Groups Dynamism	PSYCHO-SOCIAL Opinions	POSITIVISM BEHAVIOURISM Associationism Psycho-experimental	Attempt to integrate all the traditions of human sciences
OBJECT OF STUDY	THE WISHING PERSONALITY	THE CULTURAL MAN Ethical and ideological	THE SOCIAL MAN The atom of public opinion	L'HOMO ECONOMICUS The machine man	INTERACTIVE MULTI-DIMENSIONAL MAN
LEVEL OF STUDY	Convergent Unconscious Individual PSYCHOLOGIES	Subconscious Collective PSYCHOLOGY	Conscientious Collective PSYCHOLOGY	Bodily HABITS AND CONDITIONS of life	Multi-dimensional study Subconscious PSYCHOLOGY Rational PSYCHOLOGY Declared BEHAVIOUR
FIELD OF STUDY	How a personality expresses itself towards its environment Styles of Personality	How a person integrates himself into common ideals Styles of Acculturation	How a person reacts to fashions of the time Styles of Fashion	How the physical home-life is organised Style of materiality	How the individual personality and the social norms balance Three styles of balance
VARIABLES OF STUDY	MOTIVATIONS	BELIEFS PRINCIPLES ATTITUDES	ATTITUDES JUDGEMENTS OPINIONS	Living conditions BEHAVIOURS Equipment Preferences	Motivations Behaviours and equipment
ORIGIN OF VARIABLES	Uni-dimensional EMPIRICAL THEMATICS	Uni-dimensional CULTURAL THEORETIC	Uni-dimensional steady empirical MULTI-SECTORIAL	SECTORIAL EMPIRICAL Uni-dimensional	MULTI-THEMATIC EMPIRICAL MULTI-DIMENSIONAL
MODEL OF ANALYSIS	ANALYTIC Interpretative	ANALYTIC Theorized structural	ANALYTIC ASSOCIATIONIST Clusters	ANALYTIC ASSOCIATIONIST Segmentations Variations with the average	TYPOLOGICAL STRUCTURAL SOCIO-DYNAMIC
WAY OF STUDY	QUESTIONNAIRE	SCALE OF ATTITUDES	SCALE OF ATTITUDES	Statement of life Conditions and behaviours Scales of preferences	'Heavy' questionnaire Multi-thematic Multi-dimensional

Figure 3.1   Comparative analysis of five lifestyle study approaches

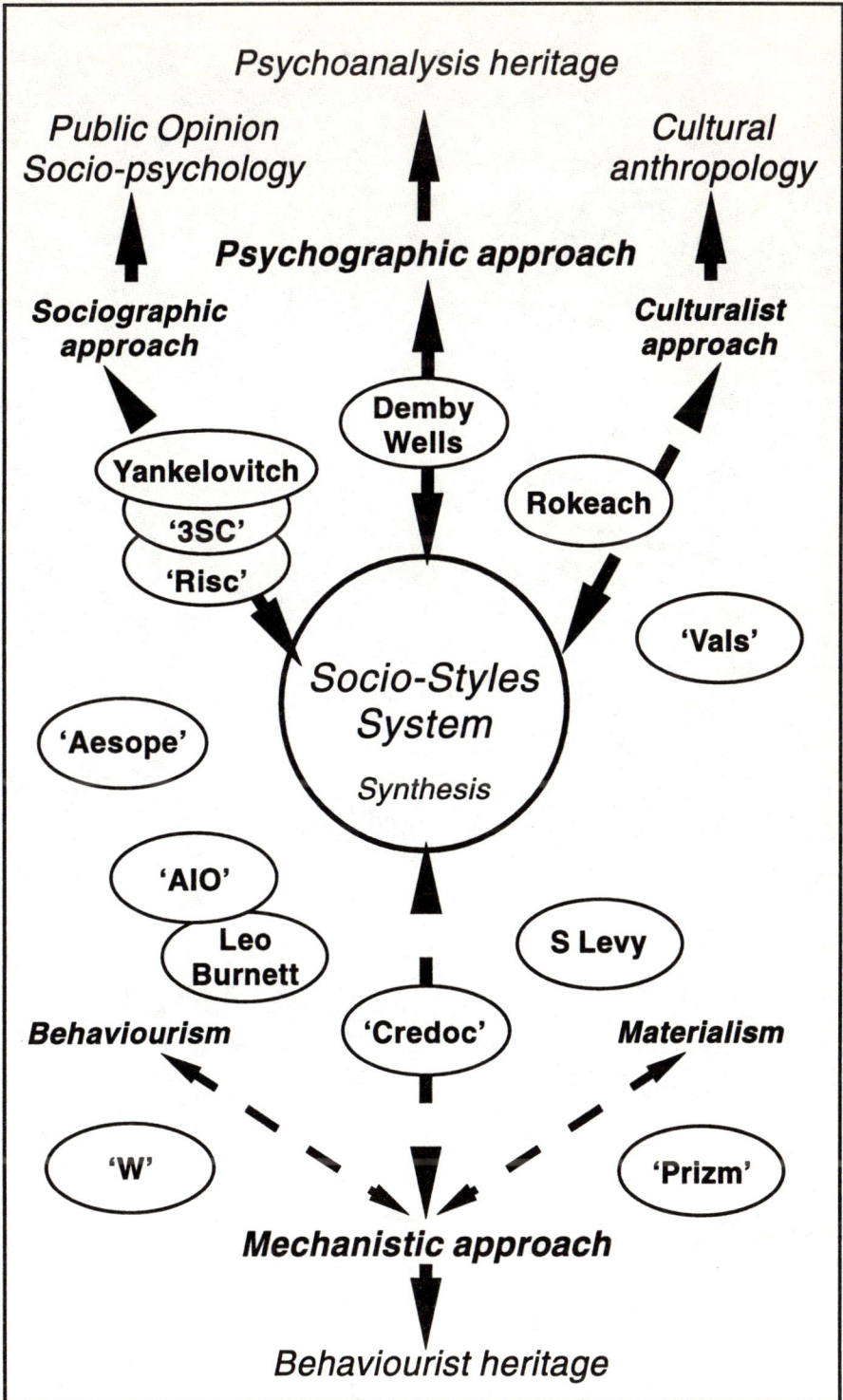

Figure 3.2   Overview of methodological approaches in lifestyle studies

PART TWO

WHERE DO SOCIO-STYLES COME FROM?

The use of any knowledge reaches into three areas of the mind: the search for truth, the skill of forecasting, and the gift to imagine a future different from the present. There will never be clear-cut rules of procedures. The best we can hope for is to sort out the different strands and look for regularities as they are combined into cords. The more we succeed the more energy and freedom will be left for the creative and innovating element indispensable in all utilization. (Lazarfeld and Reitz, *Toward a Theory of Applied Sociology*, 1970.)

SUMMARY

Complementary qualitative and quantitative studies

Whatever the objectives, the geographical areas, the macro- or micro-social character, socio-styles studies follow a common methodological process which combines complementary techniques. Their specific nature lies in the process more than in the techniques.

The amount of information collected on lifestyles through field surveys is very great, because of repetition and also because the variables are multi-thematic and multi-dimensional. The foundation study from the socio-bank comprises both qualitative exploratory studies and extensive polling.

Qualitative studies have an essentially methodological function: to supply the survey questionnaires (socio-scanner) with hypotheses for new questions or new ways of expressing particular items.

Many original techniques, created by the socio-styles system team and their partners and applied in different sectors on different populations, combine for this preparatory work: observation of life (Ethno); analysis of the thematic content of the media and cultural productions; analysis of social discourse (by the socio-check-board); projective interviews (Dip); creative and projective groups (EPSY); dialectic and consensus groups (Quorum).

Although the statistical surveys which feed the socio-bank are most visible to users, the qualitative observation of lifestyles is an essential component. Qualitative study methods are also often used to investigate more thoroughly the psychology or behaviour of one or more socio-styles or socio-targets previously statistically defined.

Systematic quantitative surveys have a dual aim:

❑   to explore at a given stage of life the ways of thinking, judgements, behaviour, feelings and ambitions of a population, analyzing this data first against the socio-styles typology. This is the micro-thematic use of the study;

❑ to feed the socio-bank where all the variables merge and are synthesized, producing the socio-styles typology and mentalities. This is the multi-thematic use of the same study.

Progressive construction

When a new socio-bank of socio-styles has to be created in a new geo-cultural zone, it is progressively built up from exploratory qualitative studies:

❑ first by a foundation study which defines the basic conceptual tools (eg socio-map, socio-styles, socio-compass);
❑ then by an extension study which analyzes the results both by region and by sector and refines the measurements over a larger and more structured sample;
❑ finally by a maxi-scan (thematic study) specializing in sectors or markets.

An initial foundation study is carried out on a representative sample of the population with socio-scanner 1, a lengthy multi-dimensional and multi-thematic questionnaire dealing with psychologies and behaviour at all stages of life and in all sectors of social, cultural, commercial and economic life.

This considerable volume of information is processed statistically by the Galaxy information process, enabling us to define in three stages the socio-styles typology and the socio-map, a graphic representation of the lifestyles socio-structure. The study also formulates hypotheses on socio-targets which represent target consumers and their psychological and behavioural characteristics. This basic research enables us to make an initial statistical evaluation of the size of the population for each of these sector-based socio-targets and of the social importance of the trend socio-waves.

Finally the foundation study defines a range of key questions taken from the basic questionnaire, which are a simple, economical and practical tool for identifying which socio-styles the interviewees belong to in any new survey.

The socio-bank is created from this foundation study, offering decision makers basic information on the profiles of populations, the positioning of images and products and the motivating themes in all sectors and on all subjects. It also offers a practical working tool for a more thorough analysis of markets and public opinion.

A second extension study is then carried out to check and regionalize the socio-styles on a much larger sample of the population which is representative of different regions and social, ethnic and cultural sub-groups, different age ranges and different socio-professional classes.

This second study is carried out using a simple, short, basic questionnaire made up solely of mathematical key questions about socio-styles. This quantifying study enables us to take a second statistical measurement of the socio-styles' penetration of the whole population, both national and regional, with a higher validity coefficient. Above all it enables us to measure the volume of general socio-styles and sector-based socio-targets as well as the importance of socio-waves in each region and population sub-group. This is a tool for regional marketing and specialized marketing among social classes. The survey is often used as the basis for a thematic study questionnaire to enrich the socio-bank; it is an operational extension study.

Using this dual study to define and measure the socio-styles on the socio-map and socio-waves, the socio-styles system is a practical working tool for social, commercial and cultural decision makers.

The socio-bank and socio-styles can then be extended and considered in detail with specialist sector-based thematic studies carried out for an organization, firm or association. These surveys can be carried out on a panel, by interrogating the same sample or a new sample mathematically merged with that of the foundation study. These sector-based market, social or media studies apply the same multi-dimensional study principles focused on a single subject (eg motoring, international politics and defence, television audiences). In this way a databank can be progressively built up with sector-based studies, which enables us to carry out increasingly detailed statistical processes on increasingly precise subject areas.

CHAPTER 4

QUANTITATIVE SOCIO-STYLE SURVEYS

Qualitative studies and expertise are indispensable to the socio-styles system to which they bring more material about both inner motivations and models of behaviour than polls and market studies normally contain. Yet the socio-styles system is fundamentally a quantitative process for structuring this qualitative data. A great deal of data, interviews and repetitive surveys are essential to ensure the success of the synthetic process and the subsequent structuring.

The methodology of the socio-styles system is therefore weighty and complex, a long and onerous technique — at least during the foundation study and its periodic revisions (see figure 4.1).

Contrary to the generally accepted idea that quantity does not produce quality, it does not seem possible to carry out a reliable professional lifestyle study economically — at least not according to our criteria. A small questionnaire administered on a minimal sample and processed in one step will reveal neither a rich socio-structure nor an extensive typology. While investment in quantity has no value in itself and does not automatically guarantee quality or, above all, understanding, it is necessary. For this reason socio-styles system studies are without doubt the most complex currently available and require considerable organization.

SAMPLING

The general principle of the socio-styles system is to carry out an inventory of the different lifestyle models in a population and to measure the trends which drive them. This involves surveying a representative sample of the total population of a geo-cultural zone, as large as possible and as significant as possible in each of its component sub-populations.

Since their inception lifestyle studies have dealt with individuals, but a family lifestyle study is planned for the future.

Sample size

Socio-style study is typological, aiming to segment a general population into a mosaic of types, the expression of a whole variety of ways of life and thought which differentiate the individuals in this population beyond the

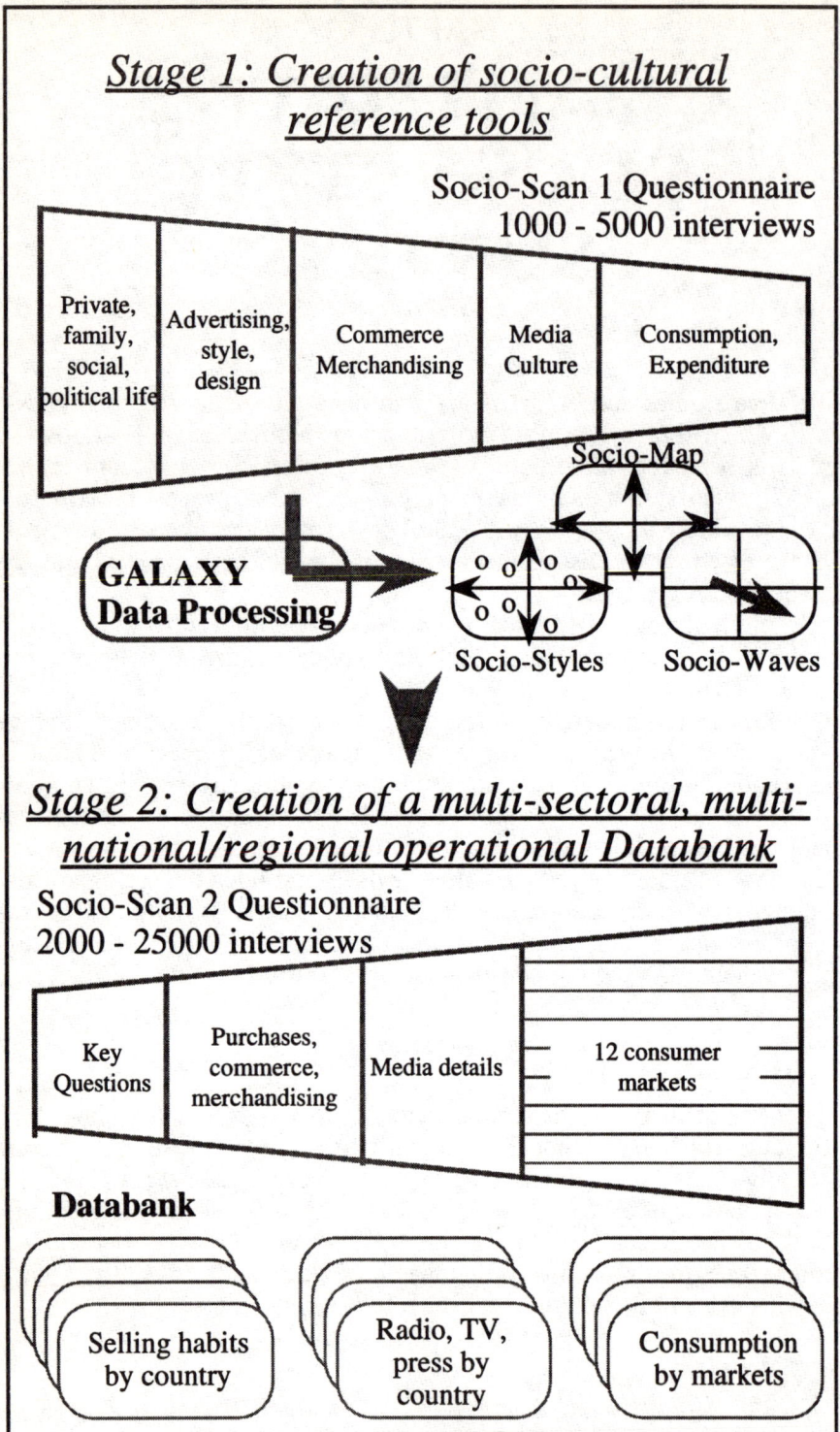

Stage 1: Creation of socio-cultural reference tools

Socio-Scan 1 Questionnaire
1000 - 5000 interviews

| Private, family, social, political life | Advertising, style, design | Commerce Merchandising | Media Culture | Consumption, Expenditure |

GALAXY Data Processing

Socio-Map

Socio-Styles   Socio-Waves

Stage 2: Creation of a multi-sectoral, multi-national/regional operational Databank

Socio-Scan 2 Questionnaire
2000 - 25000 interviews

| Key Questions | Purchases, commerce, merchandising | Media details | 12 consumer markets |

Databank

Selling habits by country   Radio, TV, press by country   Consumption by markets

Figure 4.1   Two-stage creation of a tool and a databank

usual limited classification by age, sex, profession and income. Experience of socio-styles system studies shows that usually between 8 and 17 different socio-styles can be defined in a mathematically valid manner in the analysis of western industrial societies.

The typological method requires as extensive a sample as possible. The larger the sample, the more the segmentation can be trusted and the more the validity of each of the types is mathematically reliable. For example, a sample of 800 people (the size of sample often used for opinion polls or surveys of voting intentions in medium-sized countries such as France) is much less trustworthy for a typology of 12 to 14 socio-styles than a sample of 4,000. Indeed, segmentation of the 800-person sample into a dozen socio-styles runs the risk of producing one or more types comprising 4–5 per cent, ie less than 40 people representing one socio-style. If we then have to segment these 40 people further into six age categories or eight socio-professional categories in order to describe this type, there is not enough mathematical reliability and the probable margin of error becomes too great. In contrast, a sample of 4,000 people under the same conditions enables us to have available a sub-sample of 200 individuals, which makes analysis of a small socio-styles sub-sample of 5 percent more valid.

However, another feature of the socio-styles system is the use of very full questionnaires, both general and sector-based, to collect the largest number of multi-thematic and multi-dimensional variables possible on each subject (see below). This methodological choice of a long questionnaire makes it more difficult and above all more expensive to use a large sample in the survey.

Professional practice has led us to discover by trial and error the best possible compromise between the ideal of a very large representative sample and the technical and economic necessity of a long and full questionnaire.

For the foundation study of the socio-typology and the socio-map it is essential to have available a broad sample which allows for in-depth and regionalized of analysis of socio-styles and socio-waves. The best procedure established by our team in various countries involves two successive waves of research with complementary aims:

❏ The first survey, called Scanner 1, is carried out on a sample of the general population representative of the diversity of social classes, regions and main ethnic, religious and cultural communities. For example, we have successfully carried out polls on around 1,500 people in a country like France; between 2,000 and 2,500 people in a large diversified country such as the USA; and between 3,000 and 4,000 for a multi-national continent such as Europe. A complete multi-thematic, multi-sectorial and multi-dimensional socio-scanner questionnaire is administered to the basic sample and then analyzed by the Galaxy statistical process to generate the socio-map and socio-styles typology (see chapter 5). The questionnaire contains 3,000 variables on average and the interview takes around 2½ hours.

❏ A second survey, called Extension Scanner 2, can then be carried out on a larger representative sample in each region and sub-group, with further samples of small but important populations. For example, the Scanner 2 sample can be in the order of 4,000 people in a medium-sized country such as France; 8,000 to 10,000 in the USA; and 15,000 to 20,000 for the 15 countries of western Europe. A simplified mini-questionnaire is administered to this broader sample, consisting mainly of key questions that define mathematically an individual's adherence to the socio-styles typology with a great degree of probability. Normally this 3- to 5-page questionnaire contains 80 to 150 variables and the interview lasts 5 to 10 minutes.

This is at first a quantification questionnaire. It is possible to add to the Scanner 2 questionnaire some specific questions that will make regional or micro-cultural socio-styles typologies possible at a later date. It then becomes a regionalization questionnaire.

This investigation can also support a major operational questionnaire for multi-market or multi-sector studies, thus it is valuable as a practical extension study.

In the socio-styles system the purpose of the foundation study is to structure data into a typology and map for which a representative sample is sufficient. The purpose of Scanner 2 — the quantification, extension and regionalization survey — is as follows:

❑ firstly, to measure more precisely the weighting of each of the socio-styles in each of the sub-groups, even the smallest;
❑ then to measure the proportion of each of the social sub-categories by age, profession, educational level, ethnic or religious affinity in each of the socio-styles;
❑ finally, to measure precisely the intensity of the socio-waves in each of the social sub-categories.

These two stages can sometimes be combined into a single survey if the sample is large in relation to the total local population. For example, the socio-styles study in Guadeloupe and Martinique was carried out in just one stage on 1,200 people out of a resident population of less than a million.

From this foundation study to structure (stage one) and measure (stage two), the range of key questions can be used to construct a permanent panel from the Scanner 2 survey respondents or to investigate a pre-existing panel by socio-style criteria.

For surveys with sector-based or thematic applications (eg market studies, socio-political studies, audience surveys) a sample corresponding to the needs of the survey yet representative of the whole population can be taken either from existing panels or at random by using the key questions (socio-style indicators).

Figure 4.2 describes a sample from the European socio-styles study. In the right hand column the two figures indicate two samples (the Scanner 1 and Scanner 2 surveys) after correction.

EUROPEAN MULTINATIONAL SAMPLE				
AREA	CODE	POPULATION	Regions	SAMPLES IN SURVEY 1 IN SURVEY 2
EUROPE		349 240 000	80	4 000 + 20 000
AUSTRIA	02	7 500 000	5	200 + 1 000
BELGIUM	03	9 860 000	5	300 + 1 600
DENMARK	04	5 100 000	5	150 + 800
FRANCE	06	55 500 000	8	500 + 2 800
GERMANY	01	61 000 000	5	500 + 2 300
GREAT BRITAIN	07	56 850 000	9	500 + 2 300
GREECE	08	10 100 000	3	100 + 700
IRELAND	09	3 600 000	4	100 + 700
ITALY	10	57 400 000	7	350 + 1 600
NETHERLANDS	12	14 500 000	5	300 + 1 600
NORWAY	11	4 200 000	6	100 + 800
PORTUGAL	13	10 300 000	4	100 + 700
SPAIN	05	38 500 000	6	300 + 1 600
SWEDEN	14	8 330 000	4	200 + 1 000
SWITZERLAND	15	6 500 000	4	300 + 1 000
SOURCE EURO STYLES		© CCA/EUROPANEL 1989		

Figure 4.2   Sample from the Euro-socio-styles study

Composition of the sample

The feature of a lifestyles survey sample is that it is mathematically representative of the whole population and of each of the sub-groups regarded as important in this population.

Socio-cultural studies in particular have to pay great attention to sub-groups that are usually neglected, such as the very young or very old, minority religious communities, ethnic and cultural minorities, immigrant populations. Similarly the greatest importance must be given to populations in the sample that are leaders in socio-economic, technological and fashion terms, whose statistical weighting among the general public is weak but whose influence on the population is very strong. These populations are often small in number: in a sample by quota which adheres strictly to the respective weighting of each category in the general population they are in danger of being too few for a significant analysis of their life and thought to be carried out. For this reason it may be necessary to oversample these small, innovative social groups, so as to have available a sufficient number of individuals to carry out particular statistical procedures.

In every case and despite every precaution the survey sample is not always precisely representative of the ideal statistical population model. Before starting the statistical process it is therefore necessary to make a statistical correction of the sample. This is intended to increase the theoretical statistical weighting of those population categories which are effectively under-represented, and conversely to reduce the statistical weighting of sub-populations that are effectively over-represented. In cases of oversampling (or in time the undersampling of populations that are difficult to interview materially or culturally) this statistical correction is indispensable in restoring the effective undersampling to the theoretical weighting of its representation within the population. The mathematical process for sampling correction involves multiplying an actual individual and his or her responses by a coefficient (of 1.2 or 0.85, for example) which increases or reduces their relative weighting in the general sample. Thus a person's responses will be his or her relative weighting in the general sample counted as the responses of 1.2 or 0.85 people.

However, polling techniques are by no means perfect. A certain number of population categories are not reached by opinion and behavioural surveys (eg enclosed communities, the military, monks and nuns who live in social isolation). Other populations are very difficult to interview because they exist on the fringes of society or culture (eg tramps with no fixed abode, cultural minorities who are poorly assimilated and do not speak the national language). Finally, the very small number of high-level political, economic and cultural executives usually elude this kind of survey.

The social photograph taken by the socio-styles system is therefore relative to the population that can be reached by quantitative survey techniques. The 95 per cent who are integrated socially and economically are normally represented in a satisfactory way. But it is useful to bear in mind that extreme minorities, the most powerful as well as the most disadvantaged, are not sufficiently represented, despite the fact that these social sub-groups can in certain circumstances have a considerable influence on the future of society. This holds true of all mass survey systems.

Regulation and administration of the sample

One of the basic principles of the socio-styles system is the establishment of a multi-thematic and multi-sectorial databank which accumulates numerous items of information on varied subjects that cannot be studied completely in a single survey.

A second important feature is the repetitive nature of studies in order to measure evolutions in behaviour and mentality. The socio-bank from the foundation study is a reservoir of information which is regularly updated and enhanced by new surveys.

Ad hoc samples

First of all, it is possible to carry out each new study with a new sample. The main advantage of this is the 'mental freshness' of the people interviewed who have not been influenced by previous surveys of the same type. However, there are three drawbacks which make this solution difficult:

❏ firstly, it requires a range of indicators to be added to each new study questionnaire which enables each new interviewee to be attributed to one of the socio-styles from the typology of the foundation study;
❏ secondly, it is a long and expensive solution which is not economically practical;
❏ finally, and most importantly, it is a procedure that does not enable comparisons of responses over a period, or their relation to questions derived from different surveys, since the respondents are not the same.

We therefore have to merge samples mathematically. Each individual in the survey is assimilated mathematically to another individual in another survey, who in turn is assimilated to a third person in a third survey. Each fusion of a sample is a complex and difficult mathematical process; and above all there is a danger of losing a part of the information and weakening the universal validity of the sample after the fifth or sixth fusion.

In our experience the most realistic and trustworthy solution for adding to the socio-bank, in terms of both technical reliability and economy, seems to be a panel.

Panel samples

A panel is a permanent population sample whose members are interrogated repeatedly. This enables their responses to be related to different surveys directly and simply in a single and unique databank. Panels have the following advantages:

❏ the economic and technical advantages of a unique selection of samples which can be much more painstaking and therefore keeps statistical correction to a minimum;

❏ more reliable opportunities for studying the evolution of attitudes and ways of behaviour by comparing the responses of the same individuals to the same questions on different dates;

❏ opportunities for statistical cross-referencing between the variables resulting from different surveys at different periods and on different topics but with the same sample of people;

❏ standardization of particular oversamplings of populations which are small but important, and their automatic statistical correction;

❏ economy of information: it is no longer necessary for each new survey to determine the complete socio-graphic or socio-economic identification of the interviewee, nor to identify the socio-style by the range of typological indicators.

However, the panel method also has a certain number of drawbacks:

❏ The very principle of setting a panel up assumes that its members agree to reply to several surveys over a period of 8 to 16 months, and sometimes longer; and that they are available both physically and psychologically during this time. This makes the sampling of certain population categories more difficult, eg those who are particularly mobile for family or professional reasons, and certain socio-style profiles who live for the present and do not wish to commit themselves for the medium term, such as the French 'marginals'.

❏ However, the main inconvenience may be the panel effect. After several surveys the responses from panel members sometimes become less spontaneous and unaffected. Familiarity with the variety of questions, with the different forms of response, with the forms of projective question, with all the specific characteristics of the socio-scanner, is a positive factor for the quality of the replies. But at the same time a certain mental conditioning may emerge after a large number of surveys. The panel member is therefore in danger of becoming a professional interviewee who is no longer completely representative of the average population, particularly with regard to questions on opinions and attitudes.

❏ Also, varying dependent on the country and population group, the reward offered to the respondents by the survey company (either in the form of a gift or a small sum of money) can play a positive role of encouragement for the effort the questionnaire represents, but also a negative role of artificial stimulation to the detriment of the quality of response.

From the experience of socio-styles system studies in different countries since 1972, the formation of a sample population panel seems the best solution as much from the economic point of view as from that of the quality of data available in the socio-bank. It is the device which will now be used in Europe.

To offset the drawbacks of the panel effect and also spontaneous desertion by some panel members, the sample has to be renewed regularly. It is desirable to limit participation by a person or household to a maximum period of 16 months or a maximum number of 8 interviews.

Ideally the membership of a panel is renewed by looking for the statistical twin of the retiring member. One the one hand we look for an identical individual according to the main demographic, geographic, economic and cultural criteria; on the other a new member must belong to the same socio-style as the departing member according to responses to a range of typological indicators.

For each new sector-based socio-style survey it is necessary to interrogate, in addition to the general sample survey of existing panel members, a supplementary sample intended to select new volunteers to take the place of the old ones.

This statistical twinning is clearly imperfect at the personality level, but it seems completely effective as far as the identification of socio-style types is concerned. Mathematically it is the same statistical individual who survives on the panel when one human being takes the place of another. In the same way over the years individual 1158, for instance, stays constant whereas he or she has been embodied by seven people in succession over ten years, all with the same identity profile. For example, male, aged 25 to 35, single, senior manager, annual income 300,000 to 400,000 francs, living in an apartment in the centre of a very large city, working in the service sector, graduate level education, belonging to the 'dilettante' socio-style (French example, 1984).

All the surveys carried out over the last ten years are attributed to this index number and all their responses are considered as coming from the same individual. All the replies can therefore be compared either to observe the evolution of responses to each question year by year or to carry out statistical cross-referencing to research the correlations of factor analyses between them.

Of course, these successive approximations from person to person around a theoretical statistical model progressively modify the general profile of the sample. For this reason, about every ten surveys we need to redefine a new general sample profile and merge the past socio-bank sample with this new sample, with the necessary statistical correction.

This panel can be managed by creating a new permanent sample taken from the whole of the population or by extracting a specific sample for socio-style studies from a broader panel already in existence. This formula has been used in the USA (where a foundation survey sub-panel was extracted from market facts panels) and in Europe (where the samples of two Euro-socio-styles surveys were almost all sub-panels extracted from jury panels in 15 different countries).

The major advantage in carrying out socio-styles studies with consumer panels (or a jury) already in existence is benefiting from all the knowledge available about purchasing behaviour, general economic attitudes, responsiveness to advertising and the media, and the evolution of commercial behaviour. Following the foundation study these consumer panels can be analyzed immediately by the new qualitative socio-styles variable. The consumer panel's databank immediately becomes an operational instrument for analyzing the market enhanced by the socio-styles system. The same advantage could exist if there were permanent sociological or socio-political study panels.

However, the use of pre-existing consumer panels for lifestyle studies also has a number of disadvantages:

❑ These panels are generally samples of households or housewives and not representative of all individuals within the population. Women are generally over-represented, single and young people under-represented; old people are frequently over-represented, as are residents of small towns. The task of replying each week to long, precise and somewhat boring consumer questionnaires centred on daily utilitarian spending induces a more pronounced panel effect than the socio-style surveys themselves.

❑ From another point of view, consumer panel members are mentally accustomed to behavioural surveys concerned with small factual details related to the purchase of products. They are less used to replying to psychological questions, illustrated projective questions or complex questions in the form of scenarios. Familiarity with the scanner questionnaire is therefore necessary. Experience of consumer panels shows that we can use them in a valid way for socio-cultural studies under the following conditions:

— by using on every possible occasion 'consumer jury' panels (permanent survey panels used for blanket multi-thematic surveys of both behaviour and attitudes) in preference to specialist consumer panels;

— by using panel members as interviewees-respondents every time they correspond to the sampling criteria and asking them to have the questionnaire filled in by a member of their family or circle who corresponds to a precise socio-demographic and professional profile every time people other than housewives or heads of household have to be interviewed. In this way general representativeness can be obtained with limited statistical correction;

— by devising a self-administered questionnaire which is sent out and returned by post and completed by the interviewees themselves. The first pages contain simple instructions on how to answer the questions in the socio-scanner questionnaires.

Finally, it should be noted that experience in the USA and Europe has shown that panel members receive these surveys very positively because of their psychological character and their game-like presentation. The panel members generally responded more conscientiously and more punctually than randomly selected samples. Rates of return of useable questionnaires are currently of the order of 70 or 80 per cent despite their considerable length.

Experience has demonstrated the manageability, economy and quality of information from panels with regard to the objectives and operational constraints of the socio-styles system.

THE SURVEY QUESTIONNAIRE

The socio-scanner: An exclusive concept

The questionnaire is one of the essential components in the socio-styles system methodology. Its structure and form reveal the basic principles:

❑ a multi-sectorial study: the questionnaire for a foundation study or general updating tackles all areas of life from politics to consumption, from philosophical and religious values to the receptivity of new ideas, from the media to private life;

❑ a multi-thematic study: the questionnaire tackles each subject studied from different socio-cultural, civic, political, economic and symbolic angles;

❑ a multi-dimensional study: the scanner questionnaire for all studies and subjects combines questions of behaviour and actual living conditions; questions about opinions, attitudes and rational judgements; vivid or symbolic projective questions, questions about taste and emotional and imaginary choices; and questions about ambitions and motivations for change.

Following methodological principle, the socio-scanner questionnaire is long and multi-form. It is therefore necessary to place very great importance on its physical presentation in order to obtain a consistent quality of response throughout the interview and stimulate the respondent by giving values to the different questions and themes.

Also following methodological principle, the lifestyles questionnaire includes a number of conceptual questions, multi-word scenarios and abstract propositions that have to be understood equally by all interviewees whatever their level of education and knowledge.

To meet these essential objectives of the socio-styles system a totally original type of questionnaire has been devised.

Design

Considerable attention is paid to the layout, clarity and convenience of reading and using this questionnaire to improve the motivation of respondents, reduce their fatigue and retain their interest in the contents of the questions. This readability doubles the physical size of the scanner questionnaire compared with normal questionnaires used for market studies or opinion polls. However, the experience of socio-styles studies in different countries shows that this investment is worthwhile because:

❑ it improves the proportion of questionnaires that are correctly filled in and returned (rates of 70 to 80 percent are obtained both in Europe and the USA);

❑ improving the quality of questioning improves the quality of replies.

A socio-styles questionnaire is designed to communicate with an audience of respondents. The scanner questionnaire is a magazine that should interest the interviewee and not be seen as a bind or a punishment.

As a consequence the graphics and layout are entrusted to an art director whose task it is to optimize the relationship between the interviewees and the questionnaire, especially in the case of self-administered questionnaires. The objective is that without influencing the replies the questionnaire should create a climate of confidence between the institutional interviewer and the private interviewee which improves the frankness and spontaneity of the replies even for complex or relatively indiscreet questions.

Illustration

Another original aspect of the scanner questionnaire is the abundance of illustration:

❑ The first function of illustration is realism. It is linked to the multi-dimensional principle of the survey. Unless we show elements of language and symbols in a concrete graphic form:
— we cannot analyze aesthetic tastes regarding the shapes of objects or the colours of clothes, or study receptiveness to advertising images;
— we cannot study the credibility and sympathy engendered by the look of a leader or television presenter, the brand image generated by a set of initials or logo, the attraction exerted by the atmosphere and decoration of a shop, or the personality evoked by the layout of a magazine cover.

For this reason a significant part of the scanner questionnaire is devoted to pages illustrated with photographs and pictures where interviewees are asked to choose between who or what they like or dislike, who or what inspires scorn, who or what attracts and repels them.

❑ The second function of illustration is to facilitate the understanding of complex verbal questions or sometimes to replace words with pictures to test concepts. It is educational.

In general more than a quarter of the pages of a foundation study questionnaire are essentially devoted to graphic items, half of which are presented as colour photographs. A sector-based, thematic or market survey follows roughly the same proportions. However, certain specialized studies in communication and advertising (such as the 'Pub Style' study conducted by CCA in France) can be devoted entirely to testing the reactions of interviewees to pictures, photographs, logos, typestyles and layouts in magazines, cinema posters and record sleeves, with more than 1,000 full colour pictures in a fully illustrated questionnaire.

Questions

The variety of interrogation methods is another original facet of the socio-scanner questionnaire. Different forms of questions and answers alternate regularly in order to tackle each problem in a multi-dimensional way at the level of subconscious psychology, current behaviour, subtle judgements or incisive sensitivities.

Variety in subjects
Questions can be related to:

❑ living conditions (How do you live?);
❑ behaviour (What do you do, where and when do you do it?);
❑ opinions and attitudes (What do you think? What do you agree with?);
❑ judgement (What is your view on ... ?);
❑ taste and emotional sensitivity (What do you like or dislike spontaneously? What are you fond of?);
❑ the imagination (How do you imagine yourself symbolically?);
❑ psychological priorities and urgency (What is the most important, the most essential, the ideal?);
❑ motivations and desires (What do you dream of?);
❑ prospects or prediction (What do you predict for the future? What do you desire or fear from the future?).

In this way the same theme (eg unemployment or electrical household equipment) can be studied at the level of facts and concrete gestures (behaviour), rational declarations of principle (opinions), irrational subconscious emotions (motivations, sensitivity), and dreams and fears for the future. The objective of the variety of forms for questions and responses is to avoid the systematic methodological bias associated with each type of interrogation. We know, for instance, that yes/no type questions lead to opinions being caricatured while attitude scales (ie not at all, not much, hardly, average, a little, a lot, completely) result in centralised average opinions. We also know that one-word questions result in responses with rational attitudes while multi-word formulations lead to projective, impressionistic responses.

It is therefore dangerous to base a questionnaire on one type of question, as opinion polls and market studies usually do, and so lifestyles surveys aim for the greatest variety of interrogation methods.

Variety in the formulation of questions
The questionnaire may require:

❑ one-word verbal questions (ie an item is expressed by one word which is a concept, object, event or person);
❑ multi-word semantic questions (ie an item takes the form of a complete sentence or a scenario of several components);
❑ objective graphic questions (ie an item is represented by a photograph or descriptive drawing, generally uncaptioned);
❑ symbolic graphic questions (ie the item is represented by a drawing or photograph, captioned or uncaptioned, evoking a concept, feeling or idea);
❑ illustrated questions (ie a multi-word or one-word item is illustrated by an explanatory drawing);

- ❑ schematic questions (ie the group of items is represented in the form of a graphic diagram to which the interviewee has to express his response: for example, a clock on which the respondent has to note down the time when he is at work).

Variety of forms of response

- ❑ bi-polar questions (ie the respondent has to choose between just two possible and opposing answers: eg yes or no; true or false; sentence A or sentence B; near or far);
- ❑ scaled questions, where the relative positions are differentiated (eg in agreement; not at all; a little; a lot; completely);
- ❑ attributive questions (eg In which of these ten shops would you like to buy these ten products? Which of these five political leaders would you trust to solve the problem?);
- ❑ limited and unlimited multiple choice questions (eg Which of the following 16 things? Which 3 of the following 16?);
- ❑ choices and rejections (eg Of the following 20 things which 3 do you like and which 3 do you detest? Which 3 are real and which 3 false? Which 3 are most important and which 3 least important?);
- ❑ identifying questions (eg Which caricature applies to which leader? Which adjective applies to which brand?);
- ❑ ranking questions (eg Classify in order of importance).

The same variety of techniques is used:

- ❑ to summarize ways of behaviour, particularly in analytical cross-questions (eg What do you buy and where? How do you take your vacations and when?) and in 'chains of behaviour' (Holidays: yes/no — when — how long — where — how — with whom — to do what?);
- ❑ to study motivations and sensitivity, when considering brand images, with the aim of summarizing irrational, or at least non-rationalized, data whose dominant characteristic is emotional or imaginary. Questions derived from the 'projective methods' of psychology are largely relied on, ie role play (If you were prime minister what priority would you give to ... ?), 'portrait games' (What or for which of these people would you ... ?) and also 'projective images' (spontaneous preference for drawings, photographs or collages without captions that have been devised and tested from previous qualitative psychological studies).

Projective techniques are also used to capture both dynamic and conservative trends in attitudes and behaviour, confronting the interviewee not with a theoretical idea of progress, but with acceptance or refusal of a change or a new way of life. They involve questions on the effectiveness of recent innovations, 'innovatory propositions' (Would you be prepared to ... ?) and 'prospective scenarios' concerning lifestyles, organization or technology. These reponses regarding the future clearly have no direct predictive value, but reveal a current trend towards possibilities or future actions.

In this way the socio-styles system varies questions according to the three criteria of the subject, the way items are expressed and the form of replies.

We generally require more illustrated and graphic questions when we have to interrogate populations with different educational levels (in order not to penalize populations whose spoken and written culture is less developed) or populations with different cultures and languages (although graphic techniques make it possible to some extent to transcend linguistic barriers). But graphic techniques are also used to interrogate populations and people with a high level of education precisely in order to cross the intellectual barrier of words and seek out more spontaneous, emotional and motivational responses. We normally find that considerable variety in the presentation of questions makes a long questionnaire session easier for the interviewees.

Technique

The size of the sample influences the interview technique in these extensive studies. What are called closed questionnaires are always used, laying out systematically the number, order and formulation of standard questions as well as suggesting predetermined answers. Although it has a smaller capacity for deep psychological analysis, this technique offer the advantages of standardization which alone enables us to use statistical structuring procedures to reveal the lifestyles typology.

Figures 4.3–4.9 illustrate different questions and ways of measuring responses.

Which types of films do you prefer to see at the cinema?

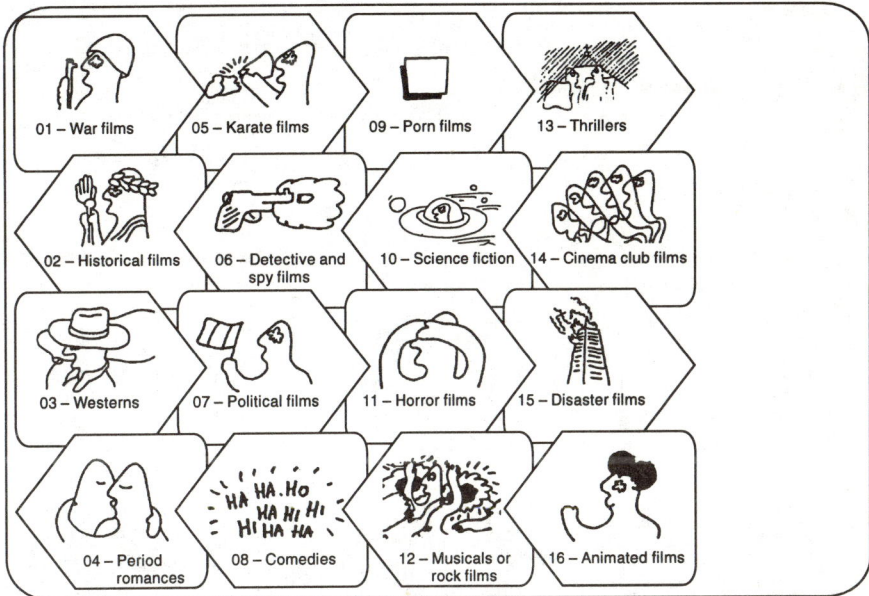

01 – War films	05 – Karate films	09 – Porn films	13 – Thrillers
02 – Historical films	06 – Detective and spy films	10 – Science fiction	14 – Cinema club films
03 – Westerns	07 – Political films	11 – Horror films	15 – Disaster films
04 – Period romances	08 – Comedies	12 – Musicals or rock films	16 – Animated films

Symbolic illustrations of themes especially created for a study about young people.

Source: Styles de Vie des Jeunes   Copyright CCA – 1978

Figure 4.3   Illustration for a question on subjects of interest

In an ideal world, and without considering any other circumstances, which type of clothing would you like to wear?

The clothes shown here don't exist in reality. The drawings express concepts of style, issued both from previous qualitative studies of motivations and from the work of designers. The question is non-verbal and unlimited.

Source: Tex Styl' and Styl' 86

Figure 4.4   Question about motivation towards fashion concepts

Which perfume bottle do you prefer?

Source: US Socio-Styles   Copyright CCA - 1986

Figure 4.5   Non-verbal, multiple-choice question about taste in graphic design or packaging

How often do you use these modes of transport?   What do you use them for?

	All the time	Several times a week	Several times a month	From time to time	Never	For getting to work	For leisure pursuits, holidays	For short trips or journeys
7. Moped	1	2	3	4	5	6	7	8
8. Motorbike	1	2	3	4	5	6	7	8
9. Car	1	2	3	4	5	6	7	8
10. Aeroplane	1	2	3	4	5	6	7	8
11. Bicycle	1	2	3	4	5	6	7	8

Source: Auto-styl   Copyright: CCA – 1982

Figure 4.6   Question on product usage: frequency and purpose (vehicles)

How often and why do you shop in the following places?

	OUTDOOR MARKET	DOWN TOWN SHOPPING AREA	WAREHOUSE WHOLE-SALERS	MAIL-ORDER CATALOGUE SALES	SUPER-MARKETS	DEPARTMENT STORES	SHOPPING CENTRE OR MALL	LARGE SPECIALITY SHOP	SMALL LOCAL SHOP	FLEA MARKET
I go at weekends. It's a place to go to relax and look around.	1	1	1	1	1	1	1	1	1	1
I go every day for one thing or another.	2	2	2	2	2	2	2	2	2	2
I go occasionally to window shop or just see what's new.	3	3	3	3	3	3	3	3	3	3
I do almost all my shopping there.	4	4	4	4	4	4	4	4	4	4
I only go there for the out-of-the-ordinary purchase.	5	5	5	5	5	5	5	5	5	5
I only go there when there's nowhere else to go.	6	6	6	6	6	6	6	6	6	6
Almost never, I don't care for this sort of shopping.	7	7	7	7	7	7	7	7	7	7
I can't do this sort of shopping because it doesn't exist where I live.	8	8	8	8	8	8	8	8	8	8

Source: Euro-Socio-Styles   Copyright: CCA – 1988

Figure 4.7   Question on buying behaviour

What do you consider important when buying household appliances, furniture and fixtures?

	BUYING 2 answers only	DISPLAY AND PRESENTATION 2 answers only	ADVERTISING 2 answers only	SHOP AMBIENCE 2 answers only
	Ease of access: near my home 1	Products organized around a central theme in specialized sections 1	Information given over loudspeakers in the store 1	Sign board, shop name 1
	Information available about the products 2	A large selection, variety 2	Games, prizes, drawings, lotteries 2	Decoration 2
	Animation, amusement, fun 3	A limited selection 3	Special promotional offers 3	Organization, counter setup, checkout 3
	Sales personnel, demonstrators 4	Special offers and pro-motions clearly displayed at the head of counters 4	Posters outside the store 4	Markings, indication, floorplan 4
	Rest area, cafeteria 5	Huge quantities piled high on display 5	Window decorations 5	Store announcer, atmosphere 5
	After-sales service, repairs 6	Labels indicating the price clearly and allowing the shopper to compare 6	Tasting/trying out or free samples 6	Lighting 6
	Parking lot 7	Bulk display of merchandise which can be searched through 7	A salesperson or demon-strator who explains about the product 7	Information 7
	Restrooms 8	Pre-packaged products (cellophane cover, can or box) 8		Availability of shop baskets, caddies, trollies 8
	Home delivery, installation 9	Products in protective showcases 9		Cleanliness 9

cd11   25   26   27   28

Source: Euro-Socio-Styles   Copyright CCA – 1988

Figure 4.8   Step-by-step multiple-choice question on preferences in promotion and merchandising

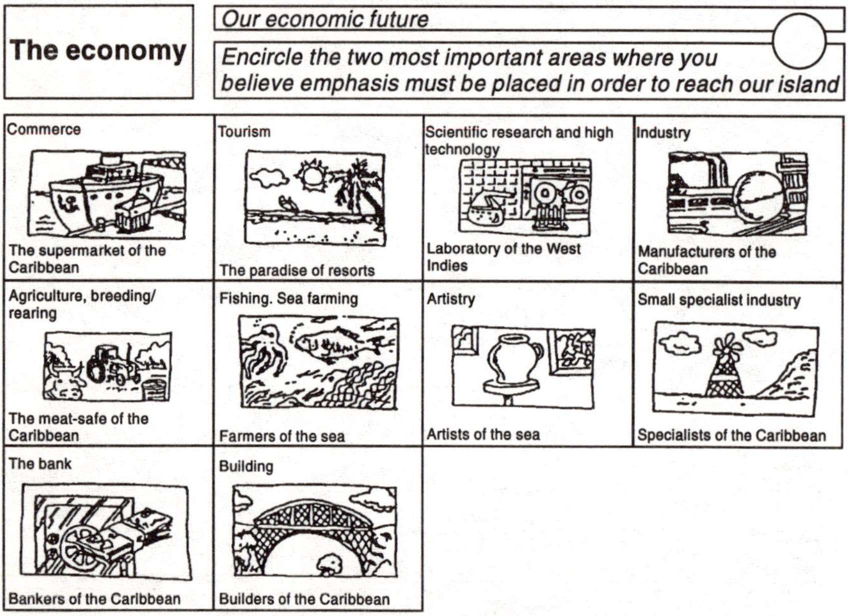

The economy   *Our economic future*

Encircle the two most important areas where you believe emphasis must be placed in order to reach our island

Commerce	Tourism	Scientific research and high technology	Industry
The supermarket of the Caribbean	The paradise of resorts	Laboratory of the West Indies	Manufacturers of the Caribbean
Agriculture, breeding/rearing	Fishing. Sea farming	Artistry	Small specialist industry
The meat-safe of the Caribbean	Farmers of the sea	Artists of the sea	Specialists of the Caribbean
The bank	Building		
Bankers of the Caribbean	Builders of the Caribbean		

Each item represents a scenario of future economic development in particular sectors or areas of activity. Each one is illustrated by an 'advertising' slogan or a symbolic drawing to be comprehensible to all groups.

Source: West-Indian socio-styles   Copyright CCA/M Consultants 1985

Figure 4.9   Projective question in the form of conceptual prospective scenarios

A range of questionnaires

Structure of the socio-scanner 1 foundation study questionnaire

A foundation study is a general update, the purpose of which is to generate or revise the socio-styles typology and the socio-map. It is often divided into two surveys:

❑ firstly the intensive Scanner 1, where a precise representative sample is interrogated using a long multi-thematic and multi-dimensional questionnaire in order to analyze the behavioural and psychological structure of lifestyles;

❑ secondly Scanner 2, an extensive survey over a much wider sample, using a short questionnaire with the sole aim of measuring the weighting of socio-styles and socio-waves in all the population sub-layers and in all social regions (see chapter 3).

The Scanner 1 foundation survey questionnaire is generally structured into seven main stages which scan all areas of social life and all stages of a person's private life in a multi-sectorial and multi-thematic manner:

❑ the first stage is private life: the household and the family, the home; personal morality and relationships within the family and friends; spiritual ideas and beliefs; routine, leisure, pursuits; household equipment;

❑ the second stage is professional life: the firm; relationships with colleagues; income; employment and promotion prospects;

❑ the third stage is social life: social leaders and heroes; social institutions; involvement in important problems; attitudes towards foreigners; problems of law and order, morality and justice, education and social information; roots and feelings of belonging; participation in associations and militancy;

❑ the fourth stage is politics: leaders; political parties; electoral practices; ideologies and political convictions; national policy, foreign policy and defence; economic policies; the image of one's own country and its role in the world; national identity and patriotism; images of other countries and relations with them;

❑ the fifth stage is culture and information: cultural tastes and practices; reading the press; going to the cinema; listening to the radio and watching television; favourite programmes and presenters; languages and styles of communication; words and images; preferred layouts and productions; advertising;

❑ the sixth stage is household business and finance: shopping at different shops and retail outlets; shopping areas and purchasing methods for different products and services; commercial priorities and consumer decisions; favourite types of promotions and merchandising; the role of the salesperson, of games and competitions, of packaging, of advertising at the shopping outlet and in the media, of décor, of labelling, of brand logos; general consumer psychology; the image and use of money; purchasing motives;

❏ finally, the seventh stage (which can be very long) is the consumption of products and services in the main markets: cars, household equipment, household furnishings, gardening and do-it-yourself, holidays, leisure and sport, everyday clothing and high fashion, personal hygiene, body and beauty care, food and drink, financial services, cleaning materials.

The Scanner 1 questionnaire for a foundation study is divided into three roughly equal parts: around one-third is devoted to consumer marketing problems in different markets, business, merchandising and promotion; one-third to advertising and information in the media; and one-third to private social, political and cultural life.

The Scanner 1 questionnaire expresses the basic principle of the socio-styles system in concrete form: to consolidate in the same survey research into private ways of life, socio-cultural and cultural opinion studies, media audience analyses and advertising trials, and commercial market studies.

Structure of the Scanner 2 extension study questionnaire

This complementary survey comprises the basic questionnaire made up of key questions (socio-indicators) and additional extension modules.

The basic Scanner 2 socio-indicator questionnaire is much simplified. Questions are selected that discriminate mathematically between different socio-styles: the typological key questions (socio-indicators). The questions (usually less than 150 variables spread over 10 questions) are chosen because the socio-styles typology becomes most obvious in this set of questions (not through reading the replies but in mathematical modelling, see below).

The basic Scanner 2 questionnaire does not usually exceed five pages and a seven- to eight-minute interview. The questions are chosen so that they can be used in practically any form of interview — over the phone, pen and paper, with a researcher or self-administered, in the street or at home.

However, this questionnaire is frequently combined with a thematic or multi-sector consumer or media survey questionnaire. A second survey with a large sample helps to enrich the practical data in the socio-bank.

Sector-based thematic questionnaires

Thematic questionnaires for sector-based studies can deal either with a sector of social life (eg cultural practices and contact with the media), with a particular consumer market or with a socio-political subject (eg foreign affairs, defence, education).

A thematic Scanner questionnaire is obviously more homogeneous in content, but is also structured according to the multi-dimensional principle. The questionnaire has to scan systematically:

❏ the living conditions and actual behaviour of the subject studied (eg What do you own? What do you do ... where, when, how?);
❏ opinions, attitudes and judgements about the subject (Is this good or bad, fashionable or out of date, beautiful or ugly, for you or not for you?);

❏ tastes and emotional sensitivity about representations of the subject or object studied (Which kinds of advertising, words and pictures, personalities and symbols are liked or disliked?);
❏ opportunities for innovation or evolution of new products, ideas or organization (What novelties, scenarios for the future, fantastic dreams of science fiction or new concepts frighten or attract?).

THE INTERVIEW

The search for a variety of data

With socio-styles studies a new generation of polling questionnaires came into being. Experience has shown that it is possible to sustain the interest of interviewees of all ages and profiles for 2½ to 3 hours, and also to use a self-administered questionnaire on several occasions, provided a considerable effort is made to structure the questionnaire into logical questions for the interviewee, with a clear formulation, adopting clear and well-spaced layouts, explaining how to respond with illustrations that explain the questions or replies, and making the questionnaires more human.

Extending the length of the interview without an excessive loss of quality in the answers is essential, since it enables us to tackle a subject from many dimensions with questions on living conditions as well as ways of behaviour, opinions, feelings, motivations and thoughts about the future.

The collection of quantitative data is intended to enable factor analysis (which requires a large quantity of primary variables) and also to compensate for the rigidity of the closed questions in the poll. Experience has led us to use more multiple-choice questions offering a wide selection of replies. The interviewee feels less restricted by the caricatured choice, can differentiate the reply better, even display contradictions, and is less inclined to rationalize than when confronted with a logical scale of responses.

Another way of attempting psychological realism is to have a number of items in the socio-styles questionnaire which are polysemic, ie one response involving a combination of several pieces of data, such as a scenario. The question is more difficult to interpret at first sight; but factor analysis is enhanced by these complex variables and in turn enables them to be interpreted. But the main justification for this technique is its realism: choices between life and thinking styles are never simple, social rewards are always complex, people often choose the same option for different reasons; and it is essential for the lifestyle questionnaries to accept and integrate this diversity.

With the same concern to include in the surveys the often complex reality of psychologies (and not to be restricted to simply measuring opinion that has been artificially simplified and experimentally rationalized, as in classic polls) extensive use is made of projective questions and graphic items. Recent experience has shown that an entire questionnaire can be based on illustrated projective questions. This technique is particularly effective when interviewing young children or culturally marginal populations (those whose command of the language is insufficient or whose cultural logic is very different and who are disoriented by classical opinion polls).

The search for a wealth of responses

The objective of the socio-styles system's research methodology has therefore been, and remains, the psychological enhancement of the poll questionnaire. A new type of interview has emerged from 17 years of experience in socio-cultural studies (see chapter 3).

The search for interviewee involvement

In research of this kind the goodwill and interest of the respondent is crucial because of the length of the questionnaire and the openness expected. For this reason the questionnaire and survey technique in the socio-styles system are designed to give the interviewee the most comfortable conditions. Based on these original models of Scanner questionnaires for sector-based foundation studies, several types of survey can be carried out:

❑ *Interview with a researcher*. This is normally face to face. The respondent reads and completes the questionnaire in the presence of the interviewer who acts principally as a guide. This lengthy, uneconomical technique is used mainly to interview populations who would not respond by themselves and need permanent stimulus. However, there is a danger that the presence of an interviewer may make the replies less spontaneous than they would be with a self-administered test, especially if the researcher has a socio-cultural background obviously different from that of the respondent.

❑ *Completely self-administered interview*. The questionnaire is sent by post, completed by respondents at their own pace and returned after a set period. This is the most economical and practical technique for interviewing pre-existing panels whose members are already used to replying to self-administered questionnaires by post. The technique requires great care with formulation and illustration so that the questions are perfectly clear and the replies can be interpreted without confusion. The drawback to this technique is the lower return rate of questionnaires which are correctly filled in and useable (although the most recent studies in the USA and Europe achieved a response rate of 70 to 85 per cent, which is much higher than the norm). Above all there is a comparative risk that respondents may be influenced by their family or friends when they answer the questions, which is virtually impossible to control.

❑ A mixed solution involves letting the interviewer select the sample randomly. He or she calls on respondents at home and explains the questionnaire and how to answer it, gets the respondent to reply to a few questions by way of example, and deals with the particularly difficult questions. Then the questionnaire is left with the respondent for about a week, during which time it is completed. Finally the interviewer, after a telephone call, returns to collect the questionnaire, checks that it has been filled in fully and correctly and perhaps completes questions with the interviewee that have been difficult to understand or answer. This solution is the most comprehensive since it combines assistance and stimulus from the interviewer with comfort and time for reflection on the self-administered test by the respondent. However, it is time-consuming and difficult to administer to large samples.

From the methodological point of view we have to remember that socio-styles system surveys, like all other forms of polling or sociological qualitative studies, are scientific experiments in a real environment. This means that we can never have total or perfect control over factors which can influence, orientate and even distort the respondent's replies. It also means that the interviewees are not all in the same physical and psychological contexts or in the same experimental conditions.

Laboratory studies are impossible in quantitative sociological or business research. The value of socio-style studies is therefore relative to the rigour of the conditions of their administration, study and statistical processing. The innovative nature of the socio-scanner certainly plays a part in the quality of answers from respondents, and experience shows this part to be a positive one.

A characteristic of the socio-styles system is the particular attention and very pronounced investment devoted to improving the data collection tool to guarantee that information is not manipulated by researchers themselves and to increase opportunities for answers on the same subjects from different angles. This is without doubt what can be called 'objectivity' in the social and human sciences.

The search for objectivity

One of the essential features of the socio-styles system is empiricism, which excludes any prior hypothesis by researchers or their clients about the nature of typologies, the socio-structure of the map and the organization of socio-cultural trends.

The axes of the socio-map are defined empirically by analyzing the connections between the factors or socio-waves on one hand and the socio-styles typology on the other. The typology itself originates empirically from a mathematical analysis of factors which themselves came from empirical factor analysis. All precautions are therefore taken at the level of the Galaxy statistical process so that the data for typological and cartographic synthesis reflect as faithfully as possible the structure of responses to the questionnaires by the public opinion sample. (see chapter 5).

The socio-scanner questionnaire itself must therefore offer the best guarantee of objectivity.

In the human sciences we know that the possible results of a survey depend on the potential of the questionnaire, the questions and the forms of response. At the end of a poll using closed questions we only get out what has been put in at the beginning.

For this reason our principle is to ask more questions; tackle each subject from different and complementary angles making cross-checking possible; and to increase the forms of responses to the same question. This guarantees that no researcher can limit the choice of possible answers to one point of view and neglect others.

A socio-styles system questionnaire has to be devised by a very broad, multi-disciplinary team made up of a group of people as varied as possible in professional and intellectual experience so that it reflects a wide variety of points of view and not a specific or biased standpoint.

UPDATING AND MONITORING SOCIO-STYLES

The objective of socio-styles studies is to attempt at a given moment to take an instant snapshot of a socio-cultural reality in permanent evolution; and if the photo is a little blurred, we can see the evolutionary movement of lifestyles and mentalities. The object of the study — at least in part — is change.

Theoretically, therefore, the ideal would be to repeat frequently the basic research that reveals empirically the socio-structure and the socio-styles typology of the time. This purist solution, however, is unrealistic:

❑ in economic terms, because investment in the socio-styles foundation study is considerable (around 10 million French francs for a European or American-sized study) and cannot be made frequently;

❑ in operational terms, because the map, the socio-styles portraits and the cultural flows are permanent working instruments for firms and organizations; to change them too often would make it impossible to set them up as a system of reference in a firm that needs sufficiently stable tools.

The socio-styles system in its professional use has adopted a compromise solution validated by experience:

❑ The foundation study, which is very large and time-consuming, is carried out with a view to defining a reference tool (the socio-map, the socio-styles typology, socio-waves) and creating a multi-sector databank of the significant basic variables of each market which is structured into consumer segments and marketing niches (socio-targets).

❑ An annual updating of socio-styles and socio-waves is undertaken as verification.

❑ Periodically new specialist studies come along which enrich one or other sector of the databank and supplement the general portrait of socio-styles and socio-cultural trends.

❑ Throughout this period the tool remains stable. The socio-map axes, the denomination and nature of socio-styles, as well as the nature of the socio-waves, do not change. It is just their statistical weighting and socio-demographic profile that are corrected regularly.

❑ It is only when the socio-styles typology loses its coherence and mathematical consistency and becomes less discriminating in practical statistical analyses that the decision is taken to embark on a fundamental updating. This involves embarking on a complete new foundation study to verify the hypotheses inherited from the experience of recent years. A completely new typology and map may eventually come out of this.

The experience of the socio-styles system in France since 1972 seems to show that a five-year cycle of using the stabilized socio-styles typology between two foundation studies is professionally effective and scientifically prudent. At the international level we must wait for a decade of experience to verify this.

Updating the socio-styles tool

The most frequent task of socio-bank managers is to organize regularly (generally every year) a new measurement of socio-styles and socio-waves. Socio-waves (socio-cultural trends) are not modified in terms of number, concept or question format but simply measured again to observe the evolution of their value in social motivation.

The socio-styles typology is not modified either in terms of number or definition (and denomination) of types. The updating survey only measures the weighting of each of the socio-styles in the general population, as well as the socio-demographic profile of these people. It brings out the quantitative social importance as well as the sociological profile of each of the socio-styles.

The socio-map is not affected by this update. All the results are presented on the same basic diagram defined by the foundation study.

Measurement in the socio-styles update involves reattributing the interview sample to the parent typology. The methodological problem is to find the simplest, quickest and most economic method possible of recognizing a pre-existing typology in a new population which has been defined from the 3,500 variables of the foundation study.

This update takes the form of a survey carried out on a representative sample (new panel or sample) by a mini-questionnaire made up only of key questions (socio-indicators). This is a selection of a small number of the most discriminating questions (around 80 to 150 variables) taken from the typological foundation study questionnaire.

Typological indicators of socio-styles

Socio-styles are established based on the collection and analysis of a considerable number of questions to interviewees about the 3,500 basic study variables. The ideal solution would be to ask these 3,500 questions again in order to reattribute all new respondents to the socio-style which describes them the best. There are obvious economic constraints on this.

The problem is to determine the smallest number of questions to enable this reattribution to take place, thereby accepting a certain loss of information. Thanks to a thorough knowledge of our analytical techniques and their limits, both practical and theoretical, we know the right number of questions between the ideal of the researcher and the pragmatism of the marketing man (see chapter 5).

Enrichment of the socio-styles databank

The foundation study has the following objectives:

❑ to establish the socio-styles typology and map from a broad range of questions covering private, social, cultural and political lifestyles;
❑ to establish a basic multi-sector socio-bank where all activity and market sectors are represented, each by a small number of motivating and behavioural variables judged to be fundamental and giving a lasting structure. For each market the databank segments consumers into socio-targets, defines the principal market trends, describes the range of possible communication themes for the targets, as well as the positioning of main existing product categories or new product concepts. However, it is obviously not an exhaustive and detailed market study.

The databank can therefore be extended in each market or sector with new, more detailed, circumstantial information.

To update the socio-bank in a logical way, complementary sector-based studies are organized on a representative sample of the parent population (or another new sample defined as socio-styles by using the key question mini-questionnaire). These polling surveys consist of a thematic and sector-based scanner questionnaire of between 60 and 150 pages devoted exclusively to motivations, attitudes and behaviour in a particular sector or on a particular topic (see above). It therefore becomes possible to examine in greater detail different products and competing brands, and to integrate all the constituent elements of a 'usage and attitude' market study into the framework of a sector-based lifestyle study.

From these specialized sector-based studies we can define mathematically a sector-based consumer typology correlated to the general socio-styles typology and positioned on the basic socio-map. This contributes to improving not only the specific knowledge of a market but also the general understanding of socio-style portraits. It also serves as a landmark for evaluating the operational effectiveness of the basic typology over the years and detecting the need for updating.

Connections between the socio-styles system and other databanks

The socio-styles system is not a closed system. Socio-styles typology in a given geo-cultural zone is a multi-sector interface which enables us to combine different types of information, provided we are able to qualify the individuals in the sample in terms of socio-styles. This typology enables us to establish a bridge between databanks of different surveys.

The range of typological key questions (socio-indicators) can be used quickly, simply and economically within the framework of any other polling survey. It can be applied to consumer watchdog panels (permanent samples) or media audiences as well as to special *ad hoc* study samples of all kinds.

All the responses provided by this new sample (after one-off or repetitive study within the framework of a panel) can be compared with the results of any other study whose interviews can be qualified in terms of socio-styles. The original databank can therefore be enriched by connecting it with other one-off surveys or other permanent databanks.

Panels

One application involves connecting the general socio-styles databank with permanent panel consumer study databases on products and the media. In particular in Europe the Euro-socio-styles databank and its typology are connected to all the databanks resulting from consumer studies by panel and all the polling institutes belonging to the Europanel network in 15 western European countries. This enables socio-styles system users to have access to a very large quantity of extremely detailed information without having to bear the cost of *ad hoc* specialist studies.

Ad hoc studies

Another application involves using the socio-styles typology as an analytical criterion for any form of *ad hoc* study carried out usually for a particular company: a market study of a sub-segement, a brand image study, pre-testing and post-testing of advertising, testing a new product or concept, a pre-launch market test study. In this case the results of a special private study can be illuminated by the synthetic view provided by socio-styles. When a particular consumer target has been chosen from this one-off study, the whole basic socio-styles system databank is accessible. Access is by defining the target in terms of socio-styles which then offers information on distribution, promotion, publicity, the media and merchandising in general, as well as research into the explanatory variables in the basic socio-cultural stage.

Qualitative extensions to socio-style studies

Finally the lifestyles typology, considered as a multi-sector interface between different kinds of studies, can also be useful for combining detailed qualitative samples according to socio-styles criteria, or more crudely according to mentalities criteria, in order then to refer to the general databank to analyse their motivations or attitudes more thoroughly.

To summarize,the socio-styles system typology must be considered as an interface tool whose objective is to offer a standard of classification of populations and customers which can be applied to studies of different kinds, at different times and in different places. It enables us to compare and combine the results due to a unique definition of interviewees that is more extensive than their simple economic and demographic identity.

CHAPTER 5

GALAXY: A STATISTICAL PROCESS FOR SOCIO-STYLES

SUMMARY

The general problem

Classification into lifestyles is difficult because of the requirement to solve simultaneously two conflicting problems:

❑ *The need to be exhaustive*. The ideal aim is to explain the behaviour and attitudes of consumers and ordinary people in all areas of their activity. This ideal implies the need to take an infinite number of measurements in order to cover the whole field of variables that describe an individual's relationship to the world.
❑ *The need to be economical*. To be practical the system must not be too complex on two levels:
— the number of classes must not be too high to remain compatible with our capacity to produce effective marketing plans;
— the number of questions asked to enable new consumers to be allocated to lifestyle classes must not be too large to be integrated into a questionnaire of acceptable length.

Data preparation

Exhaustivity

Of course, it is not possible to be totally exhaustive. Two characteristics work towards this end:

❑ the experience accumulated by CCA over years of studying developing lifestyles has given us access to a vast amount of items which have been found to be structuring and explanatory;
❑ more superfically, the large number of questions in the questionnaire provides a significant amount of information.

Data reduction

This is an important matter when we consider the large number of variables involved. It can be divided into three main stages:

Classification of variables

The variables in the questionnaire are classified into two main categories. The implicit model used for this classification is (as is normally the case in marketing) a model of attitudes with their three conventional components: cognitive, affective and conative. We can distinguish:

❑ variables which describe the cognitive components of interviewees' attitudes: opinions and perceptions about the different subjects covered in the questionnaire. All these variables can be said to represent their 'view of the world and themselves';

❑ variables which describe the affective and conative components: behaviour, behavioural intentions or universal preferences, particularly for brands and products.

Factor analysis

In each of the two groups the variables are grouped by topics and each topic is submitted to factor analysis. The method used is a classical one: the extraction of eigen values and eigen vectors. The Kaiser criterion is used (unity on the diagonal of the matrix and eigen values above) and also Varimax rotation. It must be noted that Varimax rotations have no influence on the results of later calculations; they are used to make an intermediate interpretation of the results (which may lead to the elimination of certain variables, although this is rare).

Factorial scores are calculated for each individual by regressing the variables on the factors.

Canon analysis

The previous analysis results in a large number of factors, some relative to cognitive components, the others to affective and conative components.

We then conduct a large canon analysis for which the variables on the left (called 'explanatory' for simplicity) are opinions and perceptions, while the variables on the right ('explained') are behaviour, purchasing intentions, brand preferences, etc. The logic behind this analysis is that what interests us most (and perhaps exclusively) in the questionnaire is:

❑ for the explanatory variables, the elements of opinions and perceptions which translate into behaviour (and not those that translate into group conformity, the need for self-actualization, etc);

❑ for the explained variables, the elements of behaviour determined by the knowledge of consumers (and not by the chances of distribution, nearness to points of sale, etc).

Canon analysis will reveal this information which forms the intersection between the two planes of explanatory and explained variables. The individual scores on the canonical variables are calculated by regressing the explanatory variables on the canonical axes. These are the scores which are taken forward to the next typology.

The search for typological cores

This is the most decisive stage in the process of establishing types of lifestyles. We know that using empirical methods to develop classifications with no reference to an existing system can produce misleading results if the variables introduced into the system are not chosen with great care, particularly with regard to their relevance to the problem being studied.

To solve this difficulty a series of iterations is carried out between the calculation stage and interpretation of the results until a satisfactory classification is obtained.

Calculation stage

For this we use a divisive hierarchical algorithm; ie at first every individual is classified in the same group. A dichotomy is obtained consisting of two groups as unrelated as possible (although the lambda used is easier and quicker to calculate than Wilk's lambda). The group with the strongest internal spread is then divided again, and so on until the desired number of groups is reached. The distances used are Euclidian and the programme orthogonalizes the variables by the Cholesky method (although in our case the information is already orthogonal).

It should be noted that in our opinion the method used plays a relatively limited role, in view of the permanent exchange set up between calculation and reflection.

Interpretation stage

Analysis of the results enables us to judge the quality of the variables used based on a group of criteria which are not completely formalized but which follow certain principles:

❑ psycho-sociological prevalence: types determined too strongly by a socio-demographic characteristic (sex, age, income, etc) have to be avoided. We do not see the point of measuring sex when the determinant variable can be observed easily!

❑ conceptual homogeneity: all types must have the same degree of generality. For example, we do not want types that are too specific and linked to an over-represented field in the questionnaire (eg an amateur sports person and an amateur team player).

A new calculation stage results from this interpretation with at least one discriminating axis or a new canon analysis, after eliminating any disruptive factors. The number of cycles necessary to obtain a balanced result varies between 10 and 20.

The operational phase

This stage has a dual function: to reduce the number of variables necessary to classify an individual and to stabilize the results on the basis of retained variables.

Location of indicators

The choice of variables retained for use as questionnaire variables is made step by step by a long series of analyses. The principle is simple: we distribute the original variables (not the factorial scores which we have worked on up to now) and we look through them for those which best distinguish the types and consequently best classify new individuals in the existing typology.

The number of variables which have to be examined causes difficulty. The programs available are incapable of taking account of them simultaneously. We carry out a series of discriminative analyses which serve as successive eliminators until the retained variables can be combined in one run of the program to proceed to the final elimination. This procedure is not entirely satisfactory, and we are therefore investigating the possibility of writing a program for which the number of variables is not limited (but the number of retained variables is).

Final stabilization

We now arrive at a definitive result. The principle is to use the retained, definitive variables in a dynamic cluster classification program, taking the types obtained during the previous stage as initial pivots.

The sequence of calculations is as follows:

❏ we calculate the probability of each individual belonging to each type in the preceding typology;
❏ all individuals are allocated to the type for which they obtain maximum probability;
❏ new groups are formed in this way which serve in turn as a pivot for a new iteration and so on in succession until there is no change in group. This occurs very quickly, generally in between three and ten iterations.

Probability failure

The final questionnaire consists of several pages with questions in different parts of the questionnaire and presented in quite different contexts.

In the initial questionnaire these variations can cause a variation in the probability of individual responses and consequently the probability of their belonging to a particular type. We have perfected a probability adjustment procedure which enables us to compensate for this with a final questionnaire adjusted after the first survey has been carried out.

Figure 5.1 illustrates the Galaxy process.

A DATA STRUCTURING PROBLEM

The raw product of a survey can be imagined (and could be physically realized) as a large, two-dimensional statistical table (or general matrix) comprising as many rows as there are individuals interrogated and as many columns as there are possible responses. Each cell in the table identifies by

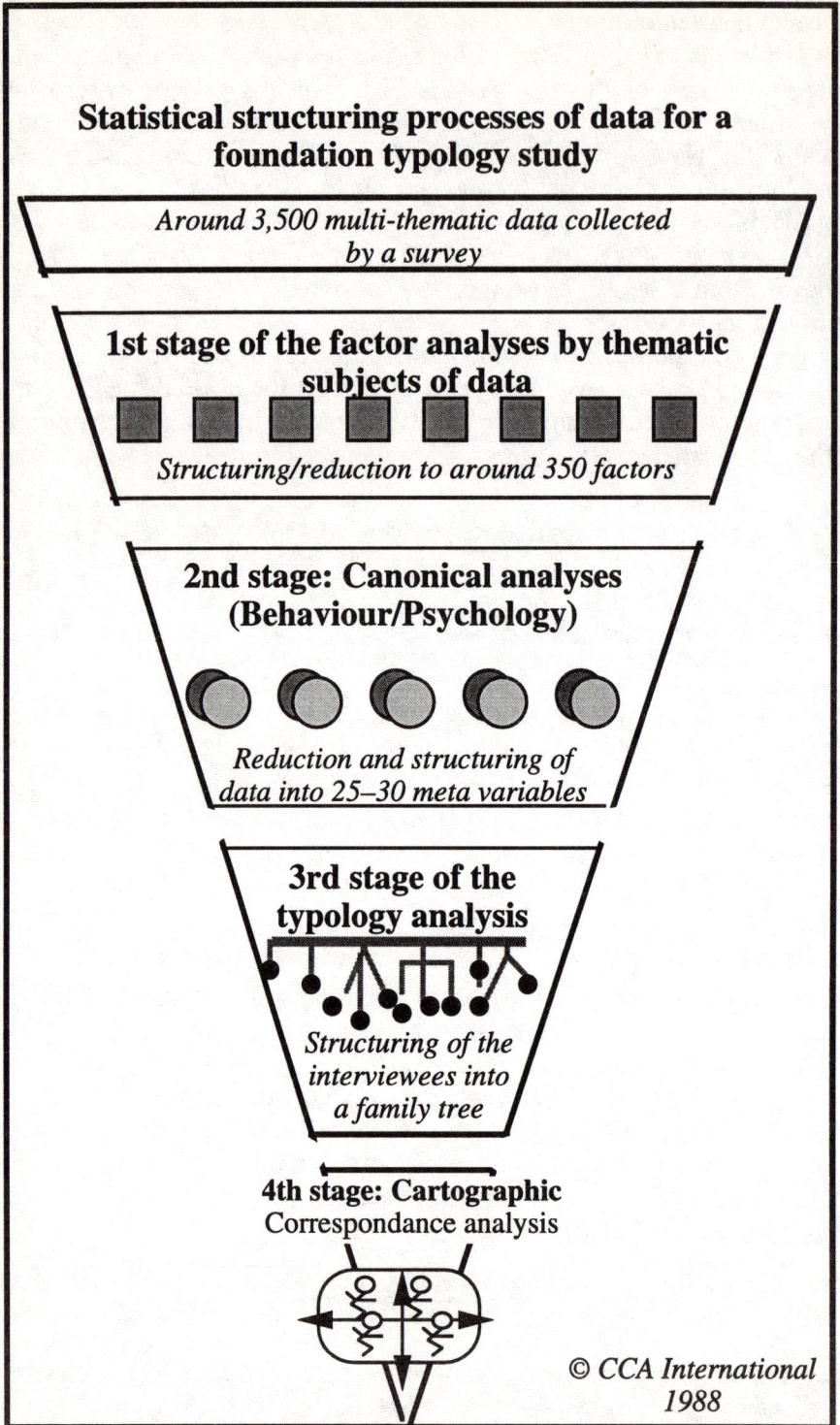

Statistical structuring processes of data for a foundation typology study

Around 3,500 multi-thematic data collected by a survey

1st stage of the factor analyses by thematic subjects of data

Structuring/reduction to around 350 factors

2nd stage: Canonical analyses (Behaviour/Psychology)

Reduction and structuring of data into 25–30 meta variables

3rd stage of the typology analysis

Structuring of the interviewees into a family tree

4th stage: Cartographic
Correspondance analysis

*© CCA International
1988*

Figure 5.1   Galaxy statistical process (Euro-socio-styles)

a code (boolean or numeric) the value of a particular person's response to a particular question.

For example, the general matrix of the Euro-socio-styles foundation study (socio-scanner 1) was made up of 4,000 rows/individuals and some 3,500 columns/responses; that of the extension study (socio-scanner 2) 20,000 rows and 3,800 columns.

In the socio-styles system this matrix is heterogeneous, multi-thematic and multi-dimensional. The columns represent items of different kinds (psychological, behavioural, products or concepts) measured in different ways (eg yes/no, multiple choice) and on different subjects (eg private life) (see chapters 1 and 4).

This general matrix contains all the available information. It constitutes the databank on which all the analyses and interpretations are based.

In theory it is the most complete description of the reality pictured by the survey, and any other representation of the results would be necessarily less extensive. But this matrix is too much for the human mind to understand, especially in very large and varied surveys like socio-styles polls. Moreover the raw matrix is non-intelligent, being disorganized, unstructured, without any logic.

All forms of statistical analysis tend to:

❑ reduce the amount of information to make it more accessible;
❑ organize data so that it is easier to understand.

However, this selection of facts involves a loss of information. The 'art' of statistical analysis involves choosing the (quantitative) reduction process and the (qualitative) structuring of raw data which is best able to organize the largest possible quantity of information into the most synthetic model possible. It is this balance between loss of quantity and simplification of knowledge that defines the quality of a statistical process (not to be confused with the 'truth' of the results).

Statistical data processing is therefore just a tool to assist human thinking. Its role is to make an enormous databank manageable and comprehensible. This process does run the risk of loss of and even distortion of the original information. However, this is the price the researcher has to pay to rise above the role of simple collector and guardian of facts to achieve the practical function of interpretation and advice.

No databank will be useful for understanding or action if it has not been organized and made intelligible by data structuring.

A choice of information

Mathematical procedures are all objective. Researchers have the responsibility of deciding which procedure to adopt, however, and this involves a conscious choice of a certain way of understanding phenomena from a particular view of reality.

Pure calculation is a myth. No analysis of data can escape intellectual risk-taking by the researcher, whether this is in the preliminary formulation of hypotheses that guide the drafting of survey questions, in the final interpretation, or in the human contribution to the statistical process. And a refusal to think in terms of statistical analysis is itself a choice reflecting a particular form of subjectivity.

Methodological arguments are not usually technical discussions, but philosophical and ideological conflicts. Individual subjectivity plays a role, like the force of habit and culture. Anglo-Saxon sociology and marketing, for example, prefer analytical procedures; researchers from the Latin countries of Europe prefer synthetic structuring methods.

For this reason we talk of the treatment process and not just statistical techniques. The choice of an overall procedure linking various data reduction and structuring techniques, alternating stages of statistical, empirical calculation with stages of human analysis, interpretation and choice, characterizes the Galaxy process in the socio-styles system.

An inductive or deductive process

Two procedures distinguish the statistical work on the collected survey results. They are complementary processes which correspond to two methodologically opposed schools.

An *analytical procedure* involves processing information into simple, similar sub-groups to avoid getting too bogged down in data (the iterative approach). A limited thematic analysis organizes the material (eg a 'hit parade' of opinions on the subject, or the observation that well-off youth is more likely to show behaviour X than the elderly poor). The database is analyzed by a gradual, question-by-question process (the associationist approach).

Descriptive statistical methods can then be applied to this partial data. No overall synthetic view results from this analysis apart from a subsequent speculative interpretation which subjectively weaves links between scattered, partial results (eg the opinion polls that are regularly published and commented on in the press).

Alternatively a synthetic view may already exist which is ideological, theoretical and the product of earlier experience. Analysis is then restricted to measuring the occurence of known phenomena (eg the lifestyle studies of the culturalist and sociographic schools).

A *synthetic procedure*, in contrast, processes all the data in the database even it is about different subjects or of different kinds or forms of response (as is the case with socio-styles system research). This is an integrative approach which requires computers and software with considerable calculating capacity, and more especially research ambition.

We apply inductive statistical methods to the general data matrix resulting from one or more surveys but considered as a whole. This uses algorithms that simultaneously take into account relationships between more than two items of data in the search for a systematic organization of the whole.

Three inductive methods are applied to reach this goal:

❏ the first tries to establish and measure statistical similarities between variables in the general data matrix;

❏ the second tries to establish and measure by segmentation and typology similarities between the individuals interviewed on the same matrix;
❏ a third method asks the sample to define similarities between the objects studied and then processes these judgements by multi-dimensional analyses of similarities or preferences.

The aim is to present evidence of the possible existence and nature of logical phenomena underlying the observed facts which are general trends guiding the various responses, the architecture of observed behaviour and attitudes (structuring research). Nothing is decided in advance (the inductive empirical approach).

The Galaxy process has chosen a primarily synthetic approach for research into the socio-structure of responses to a lifestyle survey. It puts together the structuring of variables into synthetic factors and of individuals into a typology.

FACTOR RESEARCH

The principle of socio-styles system surveys is to collect a large quantity and wide variety of anecdotal and detailed information on ways of thinking and everyday life.

The principle of statistical processing involves structuring a considerable amount of data by finding the implicit logic which organizes the responses of everybody in the sample, without using preconceived ideas.

This logic is culture. It is made up of values and norms, models and stereotypes, which are a way of seeing and thinking, acting and communicating by all members of society. It defines laws which fix the limits of normality or marginality (eg good taste, mental health); it fixes norms which constitute other internal barriers between social classes, ethnic or religious communities, status and roles (eg financial, intellectual).

No individual is completely aware of these complex rules of communal life which set laws of thought and behaviour. While we see them as natural and universal they are actually arbitrary local and transient conventions.

Socio-styles system studies try to understand the mechanisms of social regulation, the similarity of public opinion and the diversity of lifestyles, personal status and roles. They also try to understand the rules of apprenticeship and influence, normalization and marginalization. Social decision makers have to organize their strategy around the mechanisms of social management or else their programmes, ideas and products will be considered dangerously antisocial. The great variety and detail of scanner survey questions are intended to spot the symptoms of these rules of the socio-cultural game in all areas of life and all dimensions of the lifestyle. The mathematical processing methods aim to find collective core responses which indicate norms and models of common thinking and behaviour.

This is the role of factor analysis methods: empirical research into collective models of belief, thought and behaviour, the implicit architecture of the many detailed responses to the survey.

Factor analysis in the socio-styles system

Factor analysis is the first step in the Galaxy process of analyzing the large database resulting from the foundation study on lifestyles.

The 3,000 to 4,000 multi-dimensional responses collected on a wide variety of subjects are too much for the capacity of the human mind to grasp, which guarantees that the data will not be greatly manipulated. The search for an organizing structure for these responses is the first step towards the search for people offering these responses, and finally the search for an organizing map for the general system of responses.

This first step uses factor analysis techniques to reduce and structure thousands of items of data into 300 to 400 psychological or behavioural factors, comprising meta-variables which define each individual in a more synthetic way through a smaller number of more significant variables. At the conclusion of this research, for example, the general matrix of data for the Euro-socio-styles study was reduced from 3,500 columns/variables and 4,000 rows/individuals to a more manageable table of 350 columns/meta-variables and 4,000 rows/individuals.

META-VARIABLE RESEARCH

The factor analyses carried out in the first phase of data structuring in the Galaxy process are carried out on homogeneous groups of variables on the same theme (eg method/motivation, media/future scenarios). Overall the psychological and behavioural factors are therefore separated but at the same hierarchical level.

If we carry out typological analysis on this group of heterogeneous factors, the resulting typology is more heterogeneous. Some socio-styles are defined by both psychological and behavioural factors, but others are dominated by one or the other. The difference between types can therefore only be psychological with a behavioural character, or vice versa. This procedure gives a typology that is very sensitive to the individual's psycho-behavioural duality and very fertile for sociological interpretation. But it may also be less discriminating for the statistical analysis of actual facts, notably in purchasing studies.

This is why the methodological evolution of the socio-styles system has led us to introduce a supplementary phase for reducing and structuring data between factor and typology analysis. It involves researching by canon analysis mixed factors linking a model of thought and a model of behaviour into a logical plan of conduct. By crossing psychological and behavioural factors in a new matrix of relationships, we obtain a smaller number of psycho-behavioural meta-factors.

This technique is also a way of structuring the data, aimed at reducing it to a smaller number of meta-variables which might also exist in databases of different kinds and themes.

Canon analysis in the socio-styles system

This is the second stage of data structuring in the Galaxy process and follows factor analyses. It focuses on the factors extracted earlier to draw from them meta-variables that are even more synthetic but fewer in number. Through these two complementary stages of progressive structuring of the raw survey data (factor and canon), each interviewee who was defined at the outset by some 3,000 to 4,000 primary variables is defined by some 300 to 400 secondary factorial scores after factor analyses, and then by 20 to 40 canonical scores which summarize all the responses by connecting them with one of the basic response models.

The data matrix in our example has thus been transformed from a table containing 4,000 rows/individuals and 3,500 columns/responses (14 million cells) to a simplified table of 4,000 rows with 20 to 40 columns/meta-variables (120,000 cells).

The recent introduction of canon analysis into the Galaxy process has brought improvements: a reduction in the number of variables to be managed in the subsequent typology, and in particular the multi-dimensional character of these meta-variables (behaviour and psychology) which meets the real objective of the socio-styles system.

Apart from the mixed character of these canonical factors, the advantage of this technique is to provide a smaller number of active variables for typological analysis which are even more synthetic. By moving away from the raw survey data the risk of basing the typology on anecdotes diminishes, and we build a classification of very structured response models verified on the plane of both ideas and facts. It is therefore a more solid typology.

We must also recognize that the resulting typology, while generally more successful for the statistical analysis of behavioural studies, is less sensitive to minority or marginal phenomena that only appear at the psychological level without translating into behaviour.

The result is a smaller number of meta-factors directly used to structure a typology that we hope is more consistent, realistic and discriminating of behaviour.

TYPOLOGICAL RESEARCH

The second major stage of the Galaxy process consists of segmentation of the general sample according to the diversity of individuals' responses to arrive at a typology which reveals the social mosaic empirically and without preconceived ideas.

This stage of the Galaxy process is essential. The socio-styles system is the only lifestyle study method to put forward a truly empirical typology, a reflection without any *a priori* hypothesis of the variety of survey responses, reduced and structured into synthetic factors.

Typological research is distinguished from segmentation by the absence of *a priori* hypotheses. In segmentation we seek out which variables best explain the phenomenon that is to be explained (eg a vote for a party, a purchase) by

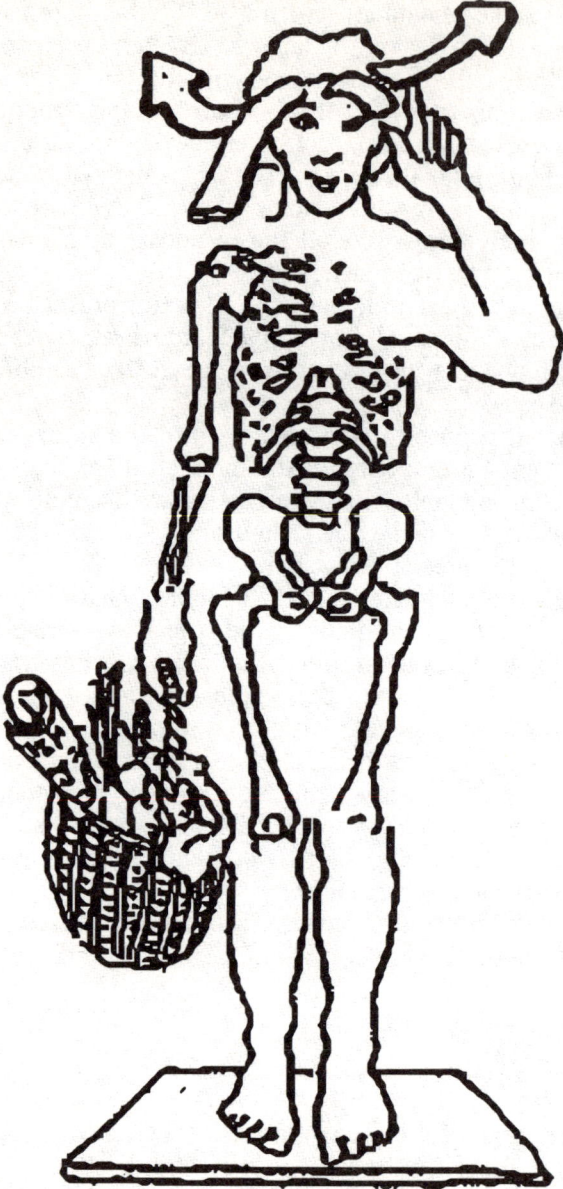

© CCA

Figure 5.2   The search for a socio-styles typology

classifying the population according to those criteria. Segmentation is a classification technique based on a subject. Typology, in contrast, looks for the main models of responses represented in the sample with all variables combined, without giving precedence to any of them and with no hypothesis other than that of diversity.

Although these terms are frequently used as synonyms, they cover two very different research techniques. Socio-styles result from a typological analysis; socio-targets or *ad hoc* sector-based typologies result from segmentation.

This structuring method does not rely on similarities between the variables studied (the study themes) as the previous factorial and canon analyses do, but on similarities between individuals (subjects studied). The aim is not to structure the observation or survey data but to classify the information sources (people interviewed or objects observed) by reducing the original sample to a smaller number of groups representing synthetic models or families.

Procedure

Typological analysis tries to form groups of individuals from the general body of their characteristics:

❑ the sample of individuals can be made up of people observed or interviewed, objects analyzed, information sources used;

❑ the body of characteristics can be made up from their responses to surveys, their behaviour or equipment, their qualities and any form of indices associated with each individual source.

In socio-styles system studies, typological analysis aims to create group-types of human beings from a sample of people who have responded to foundation survey polls, using their responses about behaviour, attitudes or motivations in the various stages of life.

Typological analysis proceeds empirically without prior hypothesis and without giving preference to one type or characteristic, so that the types produced are as different as possible from each other and the individuals within each group are as similar as possible.

A type is a group of individuals who by reference to a defined body of their characteristics are more similar to the model (group centre of gravity) than to any other model-types. Although not completely identical, the individuals define a model-type (family) whose basic profile can be described — a group of characteristics differentiating this family of individuals from the average of the sample and from each of the other model-types.

In practice typological analysis is based on measuring the similarity between individuals, consisting of calculating the distance between each pair of individuals in terms of the intensity with which they identify or contrast with each of the characteristics studied.

We may imagine the sample as a cluster of individuals at the heart of which are families of responses (which each factor analysis detects on a limited sub-sample of characteristics and which the graphic representation of the factorial axis can depict). Each typological procedure takes into account all these characteristics (possibly synthesized into factors) to distribute this cluster into families and recognize constellations within it.

Typological analysis in the socio-styles system

During two decades of experimentation various typological approaches have been tried out, resulting in the conclusion that the choice of technique is less important than its implementation on a matrix of synthetic variables reduced and structured in advance. However, the choice quickly focused on aggregative hierarchical methods which correspond best to our lifestyles philosophy of observing the way in which individuals resemble one another in social models.

Today this has become the Galaxy process, a complex procedure of canonical typology according to a five-stage data-structuring process:

❑ factor analyses into sub-groups of homogeneous variables (which distinguish particularly psychological and behavioural factors in the case of socio-style studies);
❑ canon analysis crossing these two types of synthetic factors to give each individual a score on an even smaller number of more synthetic and multi-dimensional meta-variables (for the socio-styles system mixed psycho-behavioural canonical variables);
❑ hierarchical typological analysis dealing with the whole sample and on the limited number of canonical meta-variables, in order to identify the model-types and their genealogical organization in a differential family tree;
❑ these types are evaluated, analyzed and described by descriptive cross-reference with all the psychological and behavioural factors and with all the original variables from the database in order to build up a more detailed and concrete portrait;
❑ correspondence analysis between types and active variables provides a graphic representation of the typological space from the position of each constituent type and each explanatory factor.

In this way typological analysis, while it takes up much of the time of research to reveal the cultural socio-structure and provide a practical segmentation tool, is just one constituent element of a complex statistical process.

From experience this procedure ensures more differentiated types and is more discriminating in the analysis of behaviour and psychology, more stable over time and less sensitive to survey bias and sampling errors.

Typological choice

The procedure for defining socio-styles typology in the socio-styles system takes all the precautions necessary to guarantee an experimental and empirical typology without prior conclusions by researchers or operations determined by any hypotheses. However, we must remember that in methodological terms a population typology constructed from the responses of many people to many variables is merely a relative picture of these people. There is no absolutely true typology, and no typology expresses social reality totally. Any typological construction of socio-styles is merely a reasoned and scientifically experimental approach to social reality, the best account possible of the information available on the sample studied.

Figures 5.3 illustrates a typology in the form of a family tree.

From a theoretical model ...

The implicit model for typology programs assumes that the objects studied are distributed in the area of the variables by being grouped in cores separated by spaces which are empty or at least much less dense.

Computer programs therefore only have to isolate these cores to reveal them to the user, who knows nevertheless that this model remains an approximate representation of an approximate reality, and not reality itself:

> Most people using the typological method employ it probably in a spirit of exploration, but sometimes with an excessive tendency to regard as gospel whatever the computer delivers. To take mechanically produced figures to be reality is risky both in typological analysis and factorial processes.

(Michael R Anderberg, *Cluster Analysis for Applications*, 1973)

... to an optimum equilibrium

While it is often the rule, in practice accepting the results of programs automatically is dangerous. Indeed, the supposed distribution of data in the theoretical model described above never occurs when we work with psychosocial data: the individuals interrogated generally form a unique cluster more or less multi-normal in shape.

In this context all typology programs make up groups of homogenous individuals by putting separating cordons between groups in the areas of lowest density, sometimes as a result of sampling errors. The same program will often obtain typologies that are quite different for two samples of the same population.

The results of an analysis should therefore be examined with great caution. In their most sophisticated form typological analyses are an aid to thinking by putting forward a hypothesis for data analysis. This approach, used to determine the final socio-styles, alternates processing and interpretation procedures until a 'balanced typology' is obtained, where all types have the same level of generality.

Although there is no such thing as an ideal typology, the optimal lifestyles typology is one which offers the best mathematical explanation of the structural organization of the largest number of variables on the largest number of individuals, and also the best instrumental qualities of clarity, manageability, experimental reproductibility and practical applicability.

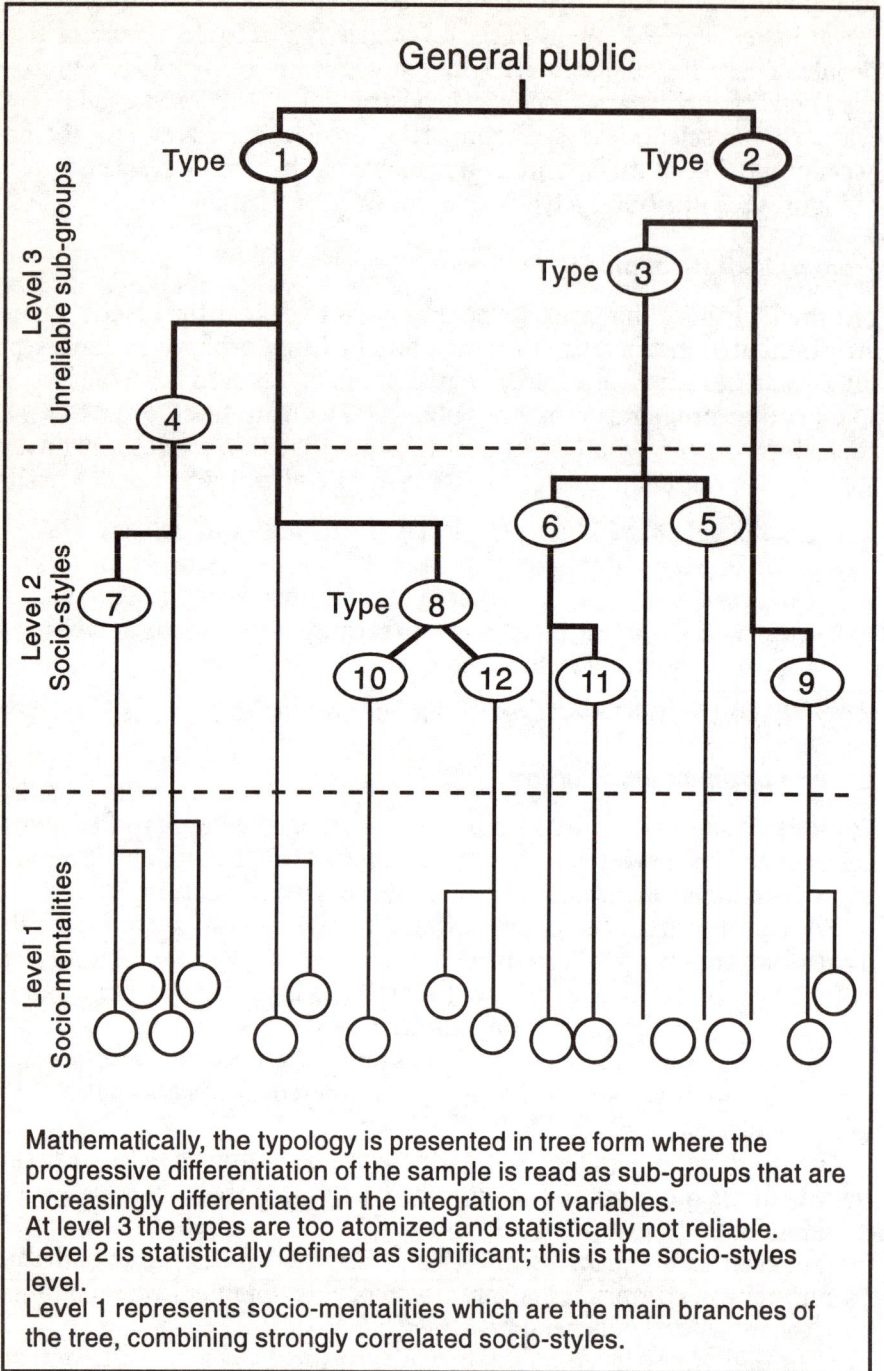

Figure 5.3   Typological family tree

Primarily the socio-styles system is an analytical tool for commercial and social situations, to detect risks and opportunities in the prevailing trends of collective psycho-sociology, and for operational decision making. It is intended for decision makers in social, commercial, cultural, economic or political spheres.

The research plan and the ambition of general socio-cultural analysis are affirmed in our principles and practice. But the objective of this research is action: the creators and developers of the socio-styles system intended it to be first and foremost applied research to improve long-term, strategic decision making as well as immediate, tactical decision making. For this reason priority is given to the ease of operation and use of this practical tool.

If there is any conflict the socio-styles system gives preference to a typology which is perfectly explanatory from the mathematical point of view, but more understandable and practical for effective everyday professional use, over another more theoretically perfect typology which is of less practical use. The principle of the system's methodological realism is that it is better to have an imperfect but productive tool than ideal knowledge which cannot be applied.

Analyzing the survey data with the Galaxy process aims to obtain the typology which is both most scientifically valid and practically effective.

Several typologies can be generated in theory and in practice from the raw data of the socio-styles foundation study, depending on the number and nature of the factors selected and their treatment. We often try out several typologies. When we work in two stages, during the first stage priority is given to the explanatory mathematical value of the structuring typology; during the second stage we look for the most practical related typologies. These typological trials are carried out using the same software and statistical method and are not far apart, but they can vary slightly in the number and size of types and in the definition of certain types on certain factors.

Several criteria of practical usefulness, besides those of statistical validity, can help researchers choose a better typology:

❑ *The number of types* is a reality which expresses social diversity; but it is also a mathematical socio-structure of sub-groups of the population which has to remain statistically credible. Above all as a segmentation tool it has to remain manageable. The size of the sample itself allows us to research in a statistically valid manner a more or less segmented typology. This would be no more than between 4 and 7 types for a sample of around 600 people, and up to 17 to 20 types for a sample of around 3,000. But in particular the typological tool must find a balance between an intellectual interest in many types that express the full diversity of the population and the difficulty of remembering and using too many types differentiated by very slight distinctions.

❑ *The size of a socio-style*: the practical interest of the typology is in distinguishing types that are sufficiently important in statistical terms to constitute target populations which are small enough to offer effective segmentation units. Without wanting to impose an ideal size for types, experience shows that socio-styles of between 6 and 14 per cent are the most useful. Very small ones of less than 5 per cent are both dangerous because they are statistically unreliable and difficult to use because they represent consumers or target populations that are too small for general social, commercial or cultural strategies. The definitions of very large types (more than 18 per cent) are often commonplace and represent market or population segments that are too small for a mass campaign and too large for a very selective campaign.

Faced with types that are too small or too large, researchers may sometimes combine several small types that are strongly correlated on important factors of the typological structure; they may also split an excessively large group into a sub-typology using the secondary factors in the typological structure. In international studies it may happen that a medium-sized type of macro-social dimensions is very small or very large in a particular country or region. A local reorganization of the typology may therefore be necessary.

❑ *The multi-dimensionality of types*: the general typologies of socio-styles and socio-mentalities have to be as explanatory as possible for all stages of life and sectors of social activity at the level of behaviour, opinions, attitudes and inner motivations. A typology which is excellent for analyzing socio-political phenomena but unsuccessful in analyzing consumption is not a good socio-styles typology. Moreover, a typology which is successful in describing the variety of behaviour in all sectors and mediocre in describing the variety of psychologies and motivations is not a good socio-styles typology. The optimal typology sought by the socio-styles system is one which offers mathematical analytical performance which is practically sufficient in all the sectors of activity studied to understand the variety of behaviour and psychologies. For this reason the balance between the different types of factors used for typological research is important. We have to avoid a marked predominance of behavioural factors over psychological ones, or commercial factors over social ones, for instance, so as to obtain a real multi-thematic, multi-dimensional typology. We have to watch out for this right from the creation of the questionnaire and the composition of groups of variables for factor analyses and then canon analyses.

CARTOGRAPHIC RESEARCH

Socio-styles typology measures how individuals vary. The range of trend socio-waves, which measure changing public values and opinions in the population, all the factors that summarize and assess the main logic of lifestyles survey responses make up the socio-map which synthesizes the socio-
structural architecture of the social system and offers a practical tool for analysis and decision making.

The socio-map organizes individuals who are brought together or set apart according to their degree of attraction to socio-waves and psychological and behavioural factors obtained by correspondence analysis. This last stage of empirical structuring of the lifestyles data in the Galaxy process is essential for two reasons: it offers a structural view of the typology and not merely an atomistic one, opening the door to interpretation. Moreover it influences the practical value of the socio-styles tool by putting forward a graphic representation of the systemic organization of types of lifestyles and socio-cultural values at a given time and in a given place.

The correspondence analysis process enables this structural analysis and its graphic representation to be done in a space with several hierarchical dimensions, crossing 'active variables' in a frequency matrix of their correlations to the general sample.

Although known for 20 years this technique has only slowly taken its place in sociological and commercial analytical tools. Socio-styles system researchers were among the first to use it systematically, and it is even less common in, for example, the USA and Germany. This may be because it puts forwards a completely new view of data: the classical statistical table is replaced by a map, a landscape on which data items are positioned in relation to one another. The analytical map of correspondences puts its user in an active position of exploration and interpretation which is more elaborate but also more intimidating.

Correspondence analysis in the socio-styles system

This is the final stage of the Galaxy process. It enables us to visualize the organization of the socio-structure of responses in a landscape map (a socio-map) which will later serve as a base for analyzing positionings and targets. It is also used to project passive variables onto the socio-map without changing its structure, its axes or the positioning of socio-styles. In addition it can be used in *ad hoc* sector-based studies to generate an original map (with new axes) from a selection of thematic variables and the typology.

Several qualitative criteria are taken into account in selecting the optimal socio-map, apart from mathematical indices which indicate the explanatory coefficient of the variance by different cartographic axes:

❑ *The logic of the axes.* The socio-map is first of all a compass with which the user can seek out the main lifestyle choices of individuals, citizens, consumers or audiences — strategic choices about image positioning, preferred product quality, tone, added value for advertising or a service. The first evaluation of an outline of the socio-styles map is carried out firstly as a mathematical value explaining the main axes and their qualitative explanatory value. It is particularly necessary for users that the two main axes of the map clearly contrast value and behaviour systems that correspond to the main ways forward for today's society.

❑ *The distribution of explanatory variables.* The landscape of the map is composed essentially of dozens of socio-cultural factors and values connected with socio-styles typology. A map is useful when these analytical variables are distributed in a balanced way in all zones of the map and define in each of them a dominant social climate, a clear mentality and comprehensible models of behaviour. A map is difficult to use when its active variables are too concentrated in the centre, which indicates that it lacks sensitivity to the variety of lifestyles. On the other hand, too great a distribution of all the active variables at the extreme edge of the map indicates a map which exaggerates their differences and neglects their common characteristics.

❏ *The distribution of socio-styles and mentalities on the socio-map.* The optimal map for operational use is one where the different types are distributed evenly across all quadrants and geographical zones. The beauty of this cultural landscape is not a gratuitous aim; professional users have to have before them a map which clearly illustrates the similarities and differences between different socio-styles populations. Rotating the axes shows that sometimes the most useful map for understanding a market is not the one depicted by the axis 1/axis 2 combination.

How the socio-map is represented graphically

The correspondence analysis process sketches a two-dimensional space formed by crossing two axes. These axes result empirically from the process without prior hypotheses about their meaning or the values they oppose. Their hierarchy and explanatory value are equally experimental, reflecting the way socio-styles types are distributed according to the logic of individuals' responses to questions grouped by factors.

The social geographic space put forward by the socio-styles map is itself an empirical socio-structure which expresses the variety of individuals and their responses:

❏ neighbouring or related types whose responses to the lifestyles scanner questionnaire are 80 per cent the same; these appear close to each other in the same area of the n-dimensional map;
❏ socio-styles that are alien to one another, whose responses to the same lifestyles questions are 90 per cent dissimilar; these are found in diametrically opposed parts of this mathematical space;
❏ two socio-styles, 50 per cent of whose responses are similar to one another for certain questions, and 50 per cent diametrically opposed; these are positioned on the same pole of one axis which defines their similarly and on the two opposite poles of another axis which reveals their difference.

The most important factor for understanding and using this map is the structure of respective socio-styles positionings, active analytical variables which define and summarize all their thoughts and behaviour, and the positioning of all other survey data that can be projected on the map. The originality of this analytical tool for social and commercial decision making lies in the structure of the typological similarities and oppositions it outlines. It is an ordnance survey map.

The first two axes, chosen after their significance and mathematical weighting have been analysed, make up a graphic space easily and readily perceived by all users. As on a geographical map or a chessboard the respective position of socio-styles and variables can be read directly and appreciated. When it is necessary to take into account a statistically important third axis, the graphic representation is more complex to express practically and informatively. In effect, we have to express the similarities which may exist in a third dimension between socio-styles that are opposed elsewhere on the first two axes; in the same way as we have to express the distances which may exist between two socio-styles or two neighbouring variables in two-dimensional space. Figure 5.4 analyses the meaning of an axis.

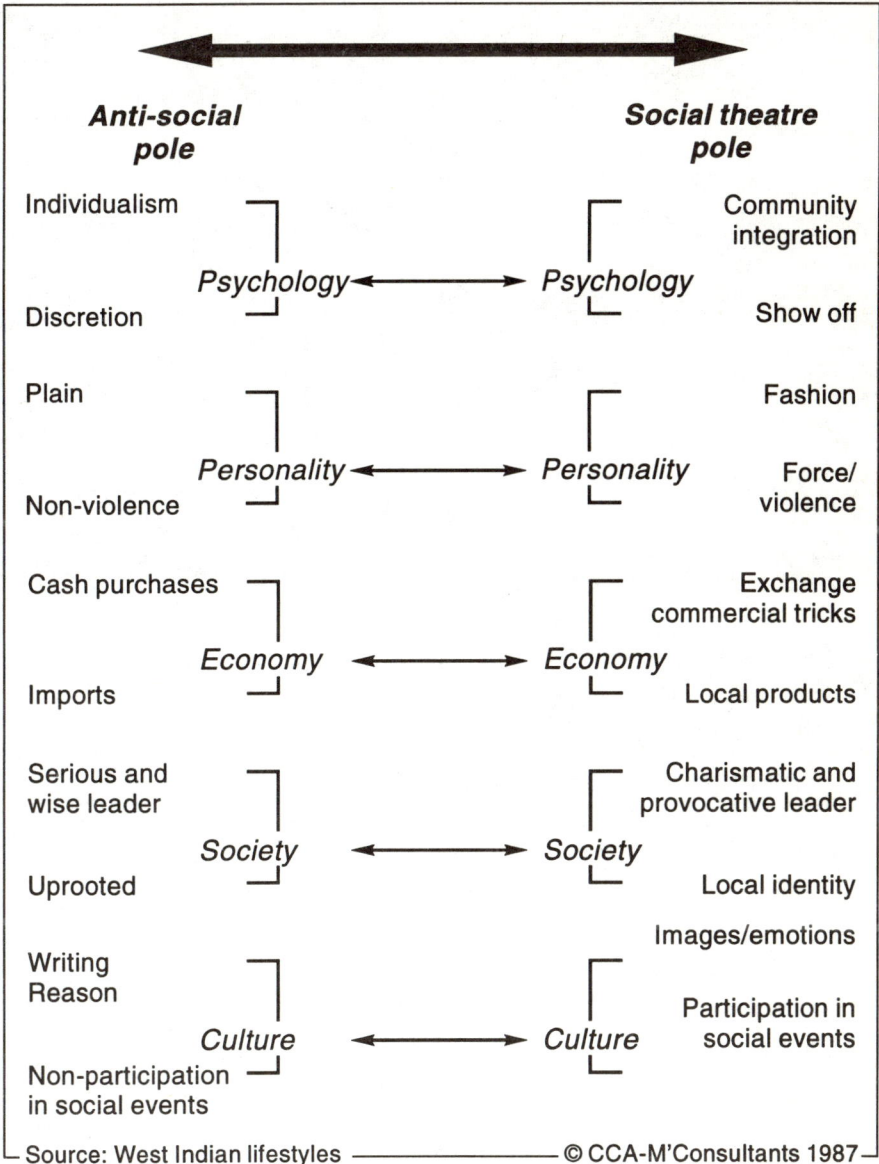

Figure 5.4   Analysis of the meaning of an axis

CHAPTER 6

READING THE SOCIO-STYLES MAP

HOW TO INTERPRET THE SOCIO-MAP

The socio-structure is produced empirically by the Galaxy statistical process from a group of variables, first of all using factor analysis, then typological analysis, and finally correspondence analysis. It is presented in the form of a socio-map which synthesizes all the significant variables.

Analysis of this raw data calls for the map and its active variables to be interpreted in several successive exploratory stages. Figures 6.1 to 6.7 summarize the six stages of this analytical and interpretative process which leads to a definition of the axes of the socio-map, the significance of the zones in this socio-cultural landscape, and the position of the socio-styles in the sociological mosaic.

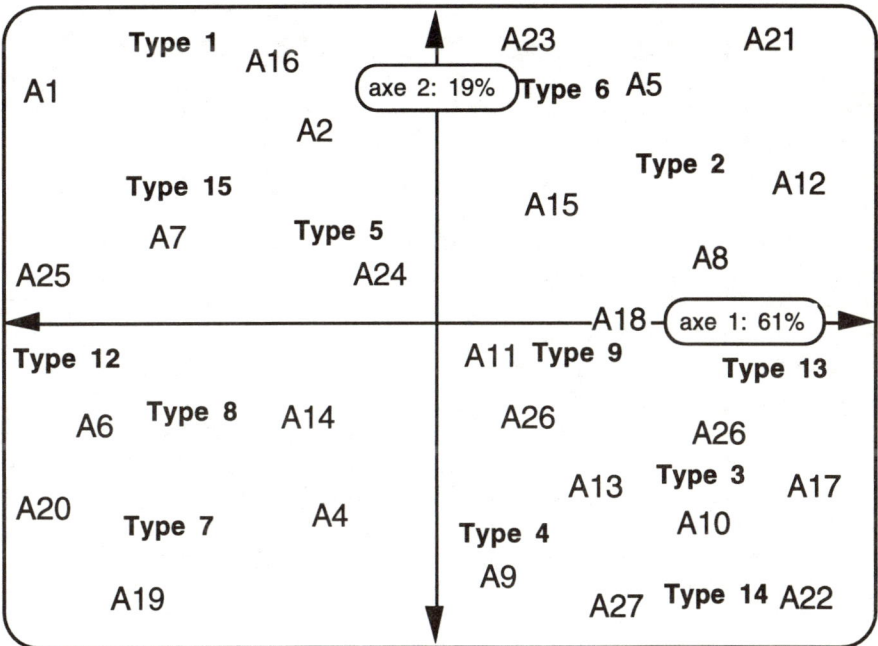

Figure 6.1 First stage: Starting point of the socio-map
This map depicts the correspondences according to the two most explanatory axes whose percentage expresses the explanatory coefficient of the variance.

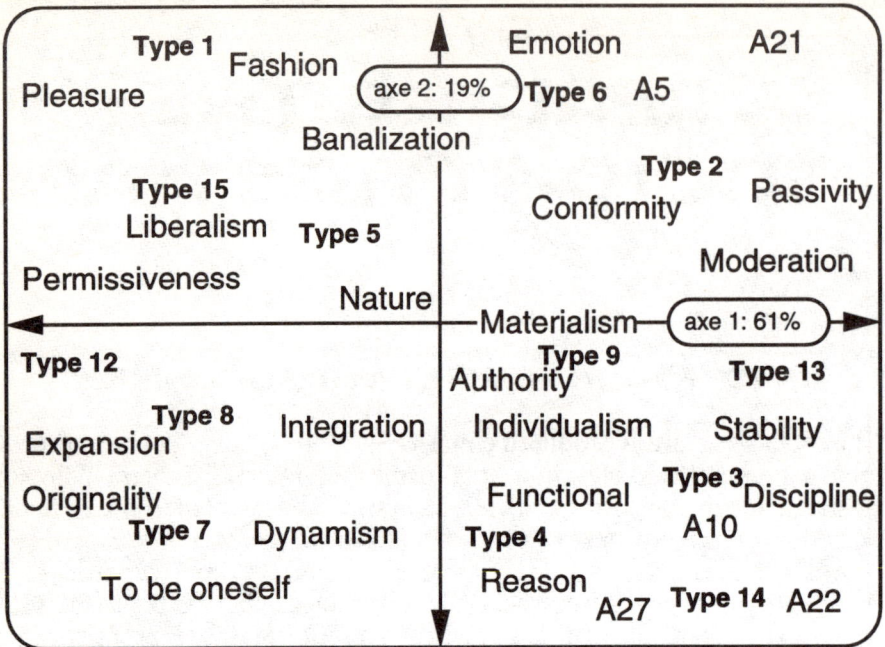

Correspondence analysis between the most explanatory types of socio styles and canonical factors

Figure 6.2   First analytical stage: Starting point of the socio-map

HOW TO READ SOCIO-STYLES MAPS

On every map the types which are furthest away from the centre have to be interpreted as antagonistic and radically opposed lifestyles, 90 per cent of their responses being opposed. On the other hand, when two types are extremely close on the map, it means that over all the themes studied their survey responses are extremely close and only differ in detail. They are off-spring of the same parent mentality.

Two types can also be close in one dimension and very far apart in the other. For example, they may both be situated in the extreme south of the map but one in the extreme south-west and the other in the extreme south-east. This means that they share a particular essential dimension of mentality and behaviour on this subject but differ profoundly on another. For example, two types are both extremely serious and responsible with regard to the household budget, but one is a traditional saver relying on sound financial values, while the other has more business-oriented investment habits and uses modern fiscal and financial information on the international stockmarkets. They are close in their seriousness but also different, one being a technocrat and the other traditionally conservative (see Figure 6.8).

The socio-checking map presents in the same space various items suggested as passive variables by their point of equilibrium on the socio-map. The same reading can be applied to the variables subjected to correspondence

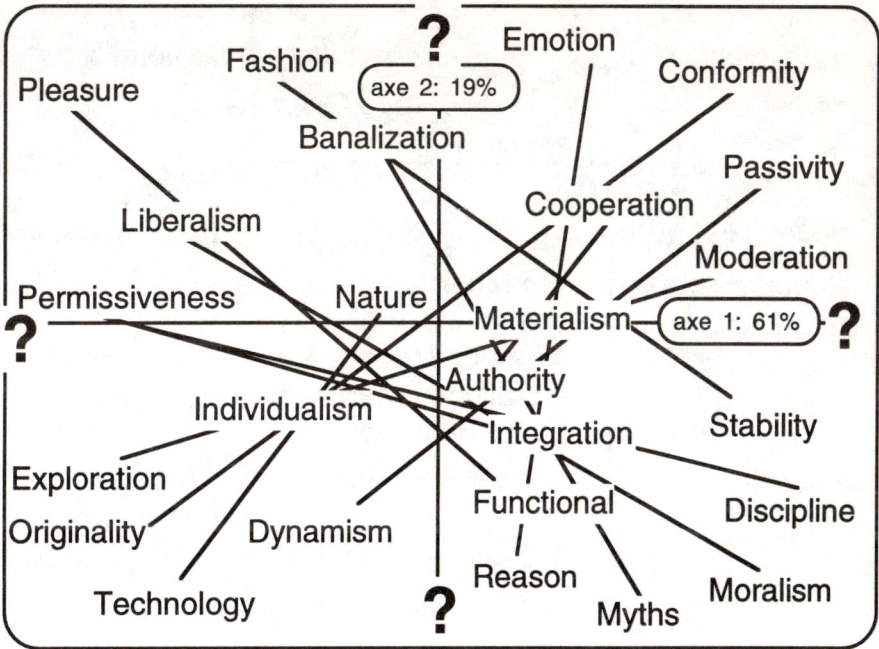

Figure 6.3   Second analytical stage: Exploration of the axes

Analysis of the significance of the active variable factors enables us to see a group of bi-polar oppositions whose axes are the result of synthesis.

We see at this stage various sets of oppositions emerging according to the two axes:

1. permissiveness/discipline, exploration/recentring and individualism/social integration on the horizontal axis;

2. emotion/reason and banalization/myths on the vertical axis;

3. pleasure/morality, nature/technology and passivity/dynamism on both axis 1 and 2.

analysis, either between variables and population sub-groups or between two kinds of variables.

Variables that are opposite one another in the mathematical space of the map can be considered to be antagonistic, with populations having completely opposite lifestyles. These variables symbolize contradictory choices of socio-cultural values in personal and social life.

In contrast neighbouring variables on the map, whatever their differences in origin, composition, seniority or apparent prestige, can be considered as belonging to the same market niche or social register. They apply to the same populations and symbolize the same types of civilization in the same niche.

The socio-styles system generally gives precedence to representing results in the form of maps as well as databanks, computerized expert systems or written reports. We think that they offer a more immediate, sensitive and synthetic perception of the environment. Visual thinking favours interpretation, scenarios and decision making.

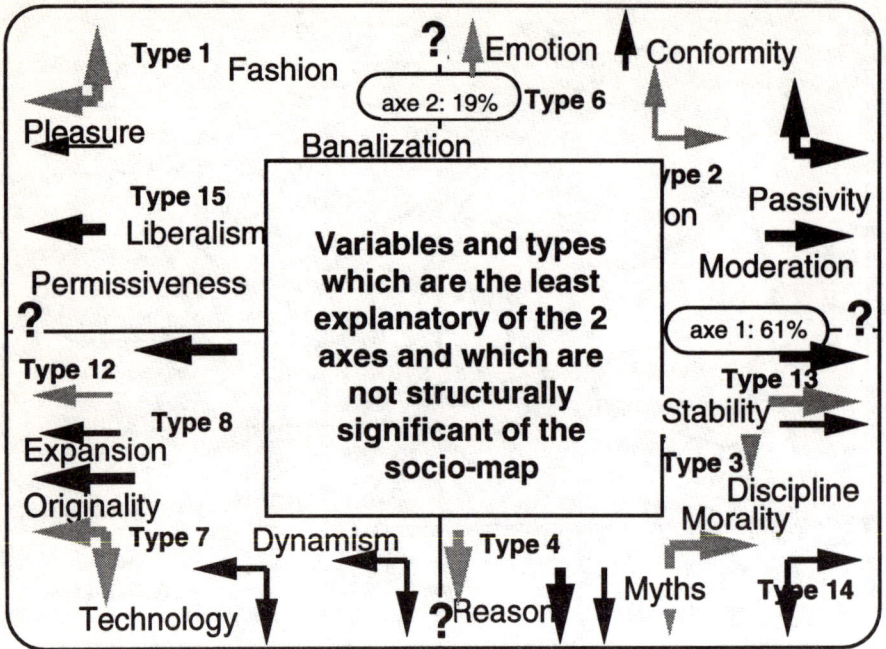

Figure 6.4   Third analytical stage: Interpretation of the axes

The positions of active variables on the map express their degree of explanatory value. The variables at the centre of the map are the least significant for these two axes (but could be significant for axes 3 and 4) and are not taken into account in seeking a definition for axes 1 and 2. The most marginal variables on the map are mathematically the most significant for interpretation.

The arrows on the map symbolize which variables contribute to the explanation of which pole on which axis. The size of the arrow expresses its intensity; black arrows represent variables-factors; grey ones, types).

Beyond the synthetic maps already prepared, this process offers decision makers a practical working tool — an ordnance survey map for their field of decision where the problems and populations being considered are placed, like a chess problem on which we can simulate possible strategies and choose the best.

This type of map is the most synthetic information that the socio-styles system can offer decision makers to help them:

❑ understand the main axes that organize lifestyles on a given subject and the main poles of attraction which divide the population;

❑ adjust the compass chart of all the motivating themes offered for strategic choices in a given sector, to communicate an image through advertising or to decide on the dominant technical characteristics of a new product;

❑ analyze the variety of different homogeneous population groups on this theme, measure their statistical weighting, describe their socio-demo-

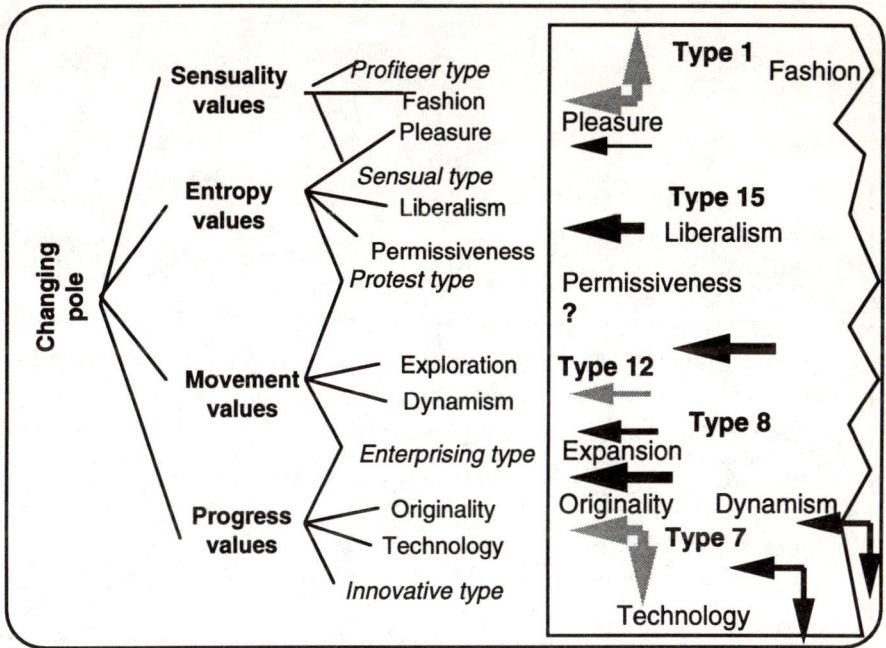

Figure 6.5   Fourth stage: Interpretation of each pole

Each pole of each axis is defined and named by means of the work of researchers. Account is
taken of all the active variables that are correlated with it, as well as their intensity and their
correlation with other variables of close significance.

graphic and economic identity and build up a detailed portrait of their
attitude and way of life;

❑   place motivating themes in relation to this social mosaic and on this
chessboard (eg brand images, products and services, advertising
messages, leaders, corporate images).

All this information is given on the same basic socio-cultural map — the
socio-map. All the information that is of use to a decision maker can be
summarized on a single unique strategic map. This working tool is the
equivalent of a detailed military ordnance survey map where the strategist
decision maker can synthesize all the available forces and opportunities for
conquest. The directions to be taken, distances to be covered and means to
be taken to develop the territory can be evaluated.

This presentation is used systematically in socio-styles reports to synthesize thematic analysis for one of the following purposes:

❑   to present all the forms of response concerning an item (eg I buy this
product regularly, sometimes, rarely, never);

❑   to present in competition different items chosen by interviewees (eg
different consumer products);

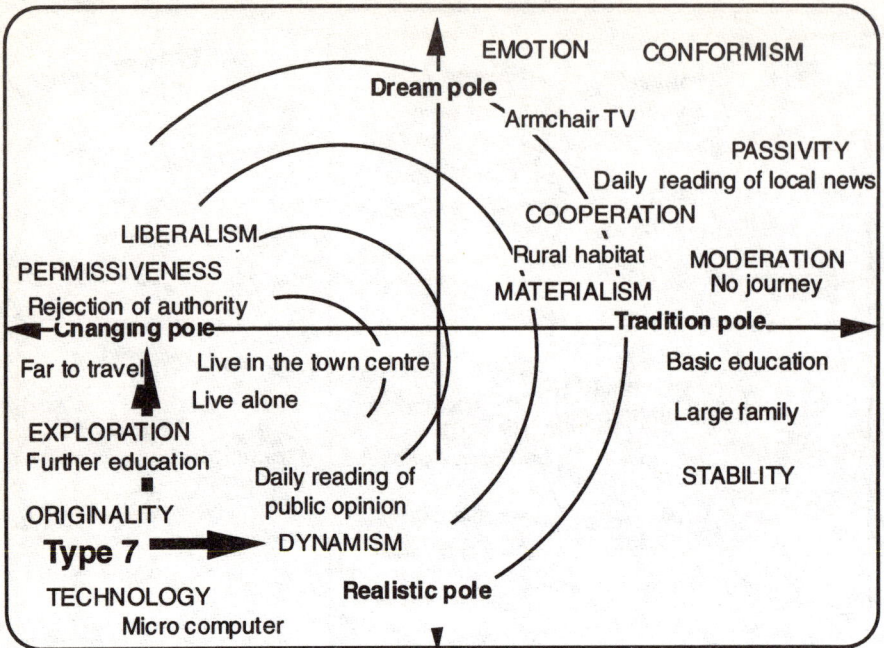

Figure 6.6   Fifth stage: Position analysis of socio-styles

Each socio-style may be analyzed by reference to active variables-factors which are close to it on the map, and also to other factors projected on the map as passive variables to enrich the field of interpretation.

Socio styles must also be analyzed by 'negative' reference to the variables that are most remote from them on the map. This interpretation provides an indication of the position of the socio-style in the socio-structure. The complete portrait of the type must be established from the group of cross-references.

❑   to observe correlations between items of a different nature with the same consumers (eg products bought regularly).

These competitive synthetic maps do not require percentages. We can refer to a mini-map or a statistical table to analyze the weighting of each item. Figure 6.9 offers an example.

Precautions to be taken in reading and interpretation

The average positioning of a product, a brand or an item in isolation is always less precise than the detailed statistical analysis of its distribution over 16 socio-styles. It is always prudent to refer to the mini-map for this item or to the statistical reference table, if a subject needs to be analysed precisely. Indeed, the precision and significance of the centre of gravity of an item's average positioning depends on the size of the total sample from which it has been chosen and on the relative weight of each socio-style:

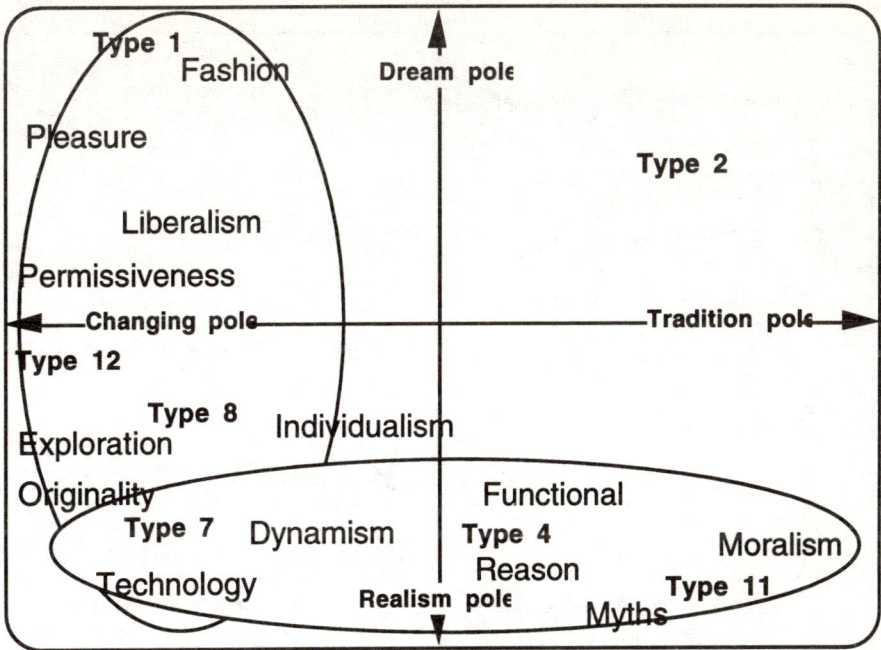

Figure 6.7   Sixth stage: Comparative analysis of types

Each socio-style may be analyzed by reference to other types with which it shares certain values or to which it is radically opposed. In this example socio-style 7 is compared with others on the map. It shares with types 1 and 12 the modernist, hedonistic and innovative values of the *change* pole: these socio-styles are positioned together in the west of the map; but type 7, which is attached to the technological innovation values of the *realist* south pole, is radically opposed to type 1, which is more attracted by sensualist values. Socio-style 7 also shares the values of realism with types 4 and 11 which are also in the south of the map. But this very modernist profile in the west is opposed to types 4 and particularly type 11, both of which are more conservative and in the east. In the whole typology type 8 comes closest to socio-style 7. However, it is less radical, a little less modern and realistic. Type 2 is the most remote, being interested in values that are always radically contradictory.

❏   If an item is chosen by a large number of people in the sample (more than 80 or 90 per cent) its average positioning on the map is not scientific. The centre of gravity has a tendency to be at the centre of the map and the origin of the axes. In this case a visual reading could be misleading. These items are marked with a plus sign (+).

❏   If an item has been chosen by a very small number of people (less than 5 or 10 per cent of the reference sample) its average positioning can be imprecise. These items are marked on the maps in the report with a degree sign (°) or a minus sign (−).

❏   If an item is chosen by socio-styles whose positions are extremely distant or even opposite on the map, the theoretical mathematical centre of gravity could be positioned half-way between these two core populations.

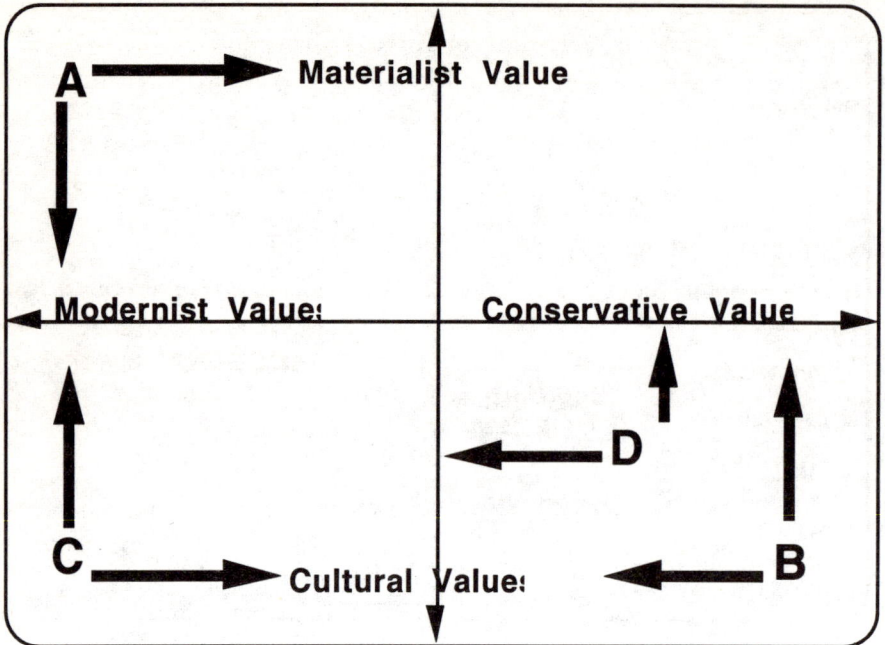

Figure 6.8 How to read the position of socio-styles on the socio-map

Types A and B are radically opposed in the lifestyle (90 per cent).
Types B and D are close; they share 80 per cent of each other's attitudes and behaviour.
Types B and C are similar with regard to half their way of life and thought (defined by the
south pole of the map) but are radically opposed for the other half (defined by the east-west
polar opposition).

In such a case the visual reading could be misleading and particularly
conceal a dual population or customer base for this item. In order to
make the map easier to interpret, a dual positioning of an item is
generally depicted by writing its name twice as close as possible to the
two over-represented socio-styles families. The dual positionings are
indicated by the name of the item being underlined; the name written in
capitals indicates the main positioning and the one in lower-case letters
a secondary positioning whose over-penetration in socio-styles is of less
significance in terms of value.

❑ If an item is the overwhelming choice of one socio-style but not of those
immediately adjacent, we use an arrow to designate it on the map (➔).

Generally if these map-reading precautions are taken, these synthetic competitive maps can enable us to identify visually which profiles of populations
(a group of socio-styles on the basic map) are attracted more than average
by which groups of concepts, attitudes, behaviour, products or brands.

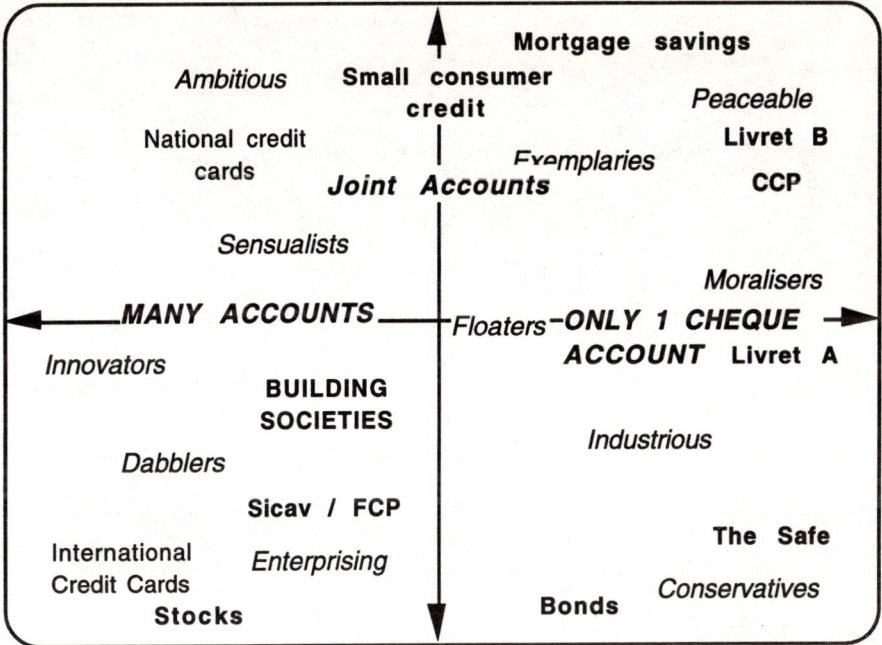

Source: Socio Styles France   © CCA 1976

Figure 6.9   Map showing the penetration of products and services

Positioning of passive variables: here different financial products are positioned according to the socio-styles and their customers.
CCP (Post Office) and Livret B (the Savings Bank) are adjacent: their clients are the same; CCP (Post Office) and Stocks are radically opposed: their clients are radically different. The owners of Stocks and Bonds are similar in their serious management outlook (south pole) but are opposed in axis 1 which is modernist/conservative.

PART THREE

PRACTICAL APPLICATIONS OF THE SOCIO-STYLES SYSTEM FOR PROFESSIONAL DECISION MAKING

Defining profiles of target consumers is an essential part of modern marketing, whether commercial, social or political. Strategically it affects the capacity of a product brand to differentiate itself from its competitors by attracting the loyalty of a customer base which becomes its own territory; tactically it affects the specific character and coherence of the commercial offering to these customers.

The first objective of the socio-styles system is to improve targeting techniques by:

❑ setting out a standard, international, multi-market segmentation tool using the socio-styles typology;
❑ providing a more detailed portrait of consumers which goes beyond their sociographic and economic characteristics to include ways of thinking and behaving in all areas of social, cultural and commercial life;
❑ placing this mosaic of populations in the evolutionary dynamic of socio-cultural trends;
❑ making this typology the multi-sector interface which enables us to move from market studies to sociological analysis to increase understanding, and to commercial and advertising methods to take more effective action.

We can describe the main applications of the socio-styles system according to two major orientations upstream and downstream from this targeting.

Upstream the application is strategic. The socio-styles databank enables us to define the best target population (or hierarchy of target population) by one of two methods:

❑ *a strategy of innovation*: defining a target customer base for a new product or service by analyzing current dissatisfactions, changing needs and prospective socio-cultural trends; and choosing the most influential customer segment according to the objectives of the firm;

❏ *a competitive positioning strategy*: defining a target to attract the loyalty of or to win over, and a target of leaders to influence as opinion formers. This results from an analysis of consumer niches already occupied by different competitors or still virgin territory, according to the evolution of their statistical importance, their economic profile and their way of life.

Downstream the application is tactical. When a target customer base has previously been defined in terms of socio-styles, the databank enables us to set out a commercial and promotional action plan by selecting the most effective contact networks and methods of influence for this population:

❏ distribution and sales channels;
❏ methods of promotion;
❏ profiles of salespeople and service providers;
❏ product design and packaging or presentation;
❏ brand image styling;
❏ advertising style;
❏ advertising media and support.

For this the user of the socio-styles system has available a multi-sectorial, multi-thematic databank:

❏ upstream from market analysis a report and a socio-cultural databank which describe the general variables of the social climate, the way of life, the population segmentation and typology weighting by country and by region which are likely to influence all markets — a sort of cultural meteorology;
❏ downstream a group of reports and databanks on distribution, promotional merchandising, communication and advertising, design and packaging, and the media. These are practical tools for use on different lifestyle profiles — a sort of marketing tool kit.

These upstream evaluation tools and downstream weapons for action are valuable for all users of the system, pivoting on the analysis of their own sectors.

In each of these market sector databanks the user will find not only a detailed analysis of all the available items but also four synthetic forms which represent four different views of the market, all presented on the chessboard of the socio-map:

❏ a synthesis of motivations, behaviour, attractive innovatory concepts, consumer attitudes, etc. This cross-check is mainly of interest for innovation strategies;
❏ a positioning analysis of product categories, brands, designs and ways of presentation, forms of service. This cross-check of commercial offerings is essential for applying the socio-styles system to product repositioning strategies;

❏ a sectorial compass of communication themes, image positioning and their dominant trends. This cross-check of concepts is essential for image and advertising strategies;

❏ socio-targets: segmentation into a limited number of consumer types peculiar to this market and giving a detailed portrait of them. This information is a priority for market reports and defining universal strategies for action.

Strategic applications are more fundamental and less frequent in the life of a firm, but of greater importance. They are mainly based on the two information stages in the socio-styles databank:

❏ the market study of the sector under consideration: analysis of motivations, behaviour, innovation needs, economic and psychological trends, consumer sensitivity; analysis of current customer bases for different products brands, position of competitors, brand images;

❏ the socio-cultural environment report which provides information about the weightings of different socio-styles by region or country; about the nature and intensity of socio-cultural trends; and about influences on lifestyle.

Tactical applications are more everyday matters and more subject to circumstances, but they must be based on a previous strategic definition of the target. They use mainly the marketing tool box — specific stages on marketing, distribution, advertising and the media analyzed in terms of socio-styles.

Figure III.1 describes how to use the databank.

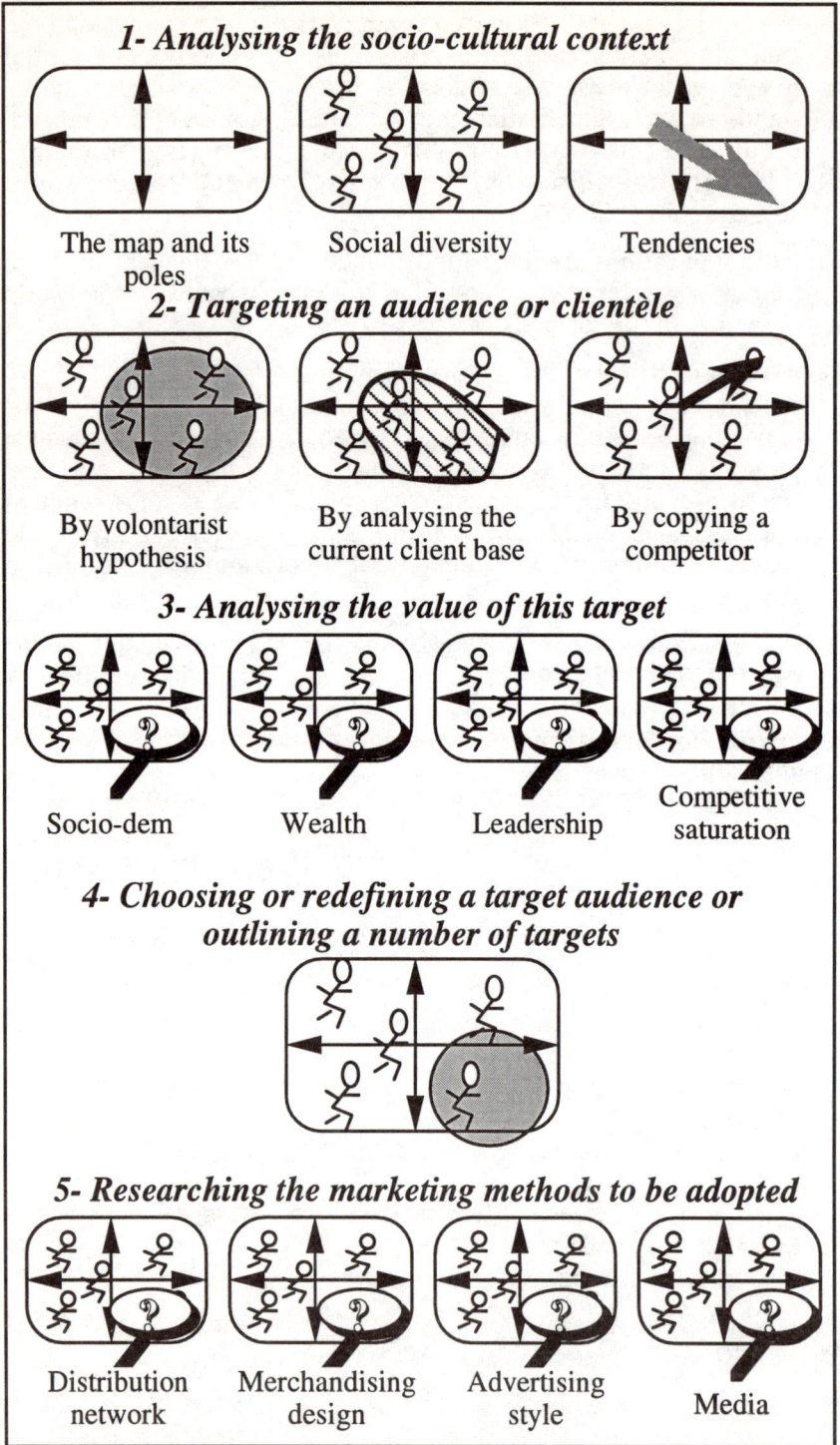

1- Analysing the socio-cultural context

The map and its poles | Social diversity | Tendencies

2- Targeting an audience or clientèle

By volontarist hypothesis | By analysing the current client base | By copying a competitor

3- Analysing the value of this target

Socio-dem | Wealth | Leadership | Competitive saturation

4- Choosing or redefining a target audience or outlining a number of targets

5- Researching the marketing methods to be adopted

Distribution network | Merchandising design | Advertising style | Media

Figure III.1　How to use the socio-styles databank in a general socio-cultural environment

CHAPTER 7

WHAT IS THE SOCIO-STYLES SYSTEM FOR?

The socio-styles system offers decision makers in all sectors and markets a practical instrument for analysis and decisions making in three areas:

❑ Conducting a sociological check-up:
— to identify your public, the readership of your newspaper or consumer of your product within the socio-styles typology;
— to identify the publics and customers of your main competitors and compare their typological profile with your customers;
— to locate on a socio-map the niches occupied by all competitors in the market or sector;
— to position on this map your brand image or company image.

❑ Describing opportunities:
— to identify and measure the prevailing socio-waves in the sector;
— to detect and describe precisely the socio-styles of newly developing populations;
— to understand the major choices for responding to demand across the socio-contrasts of the sector;
— to uncover unexploited market niches for conquest and to define their unsatisfied needs;
— to measure the 'hit parade' of dominant values and motivating communication themes on the sector-based compass.

❑ Choosing a method of action:
— to choose the target public you wish to reach from the socio-targets of your market and socio-styles typology;
— to adapt your products, services and proposals to the needs of this socio-target;
— to choose the retail outlets and distributors that this socio-target patronizes;
— to choose advertising, promotions, marketing and public relations to which this socio-target will respond;
— to select the best media to communicate with this population.

The socio-styles-system offers a comprehensive tool. On the socio-map every decision maker can:

❑ work out the balance of competitive positions in a particular sector;
❑ identify the prevailing trends which represent opportunities for development and conquest;

❑ choose the products, presentation and communication forms adapted to the chosen target populations.

The socio-styles-system is intended to be a multi-professional tool. It was devised by and has always been led by a multi-disciplinary team of researchers and consultants:

❑ sociologists who do basic research into society and civilization;
❑ market research advisers;
❑ specialists in audience and media studies;
❑ psychologists who study inner motivations;
❑ advertisers and communication advisers;
❑ creators and designers.

All these professionals used their own methods for their own activity in their own sectors, and none of them used instruments to analyze and understand influence outside their own sectors. The intention of the socio-styles-system method is to open up the field of reflection and provide each of the specialists with a more comprehensive view of all the variables that influence their customers both within their sectors and outside them.

Right from the outset in 1972 the first experiments wanted to make this an open method, both multi-disciplinary and multi-sectorial, which would produce a multi-thematic bank of information that would be useful to all professions and trades involved directly or indirectly with population behaviour and psychology. In other words, all social decision makers from all institutions in all sectors.

THE SOCIO-STYLES SYSTEM ASSISTING COMMERCIAL MARKETING

This method of studying consumer life styles offers marketing directors a complete range of information covering all needs of strategic and tactical marketing.

A new complementary qualitative criterion

In addition to the classical 'skeleton' criteria of demographic, economic and professional identity, we offer a supplementary criterion for qualifying a survey population. This is the socio-styles profile which synthesizes and summarizes the general logic of forms of behaviour, attitudes and motivations throughout life.

Cross-tabulating the socio-styles typology with any of the variables in a market, consumer or image survey enhances the analysis. It goes beyond variables of the socio-objective conditions of life to measure the impact of psychological and lifestyle factors on the lives of consumers.

This socio-styles criterion should be used to complement economic and demographic criteria. Socio-styles often seem the most discriminative and explanatory variable for studying novel and segment-specific products. For popular or mass-market products socio-styles typology is more valuable for finding explanations complementary to demographic and economic analysis, which explains quite well basic influences on their consumption.

Enhanced segmentation

Secondly and most importantly, the socio-styles system offers market researchers an opportunity to segment their consumers into homogeneous groups not only by age, sex and income, but also according to their psychology, buying behaviour, responsiveness to advertising and exposure to the media.

For every market, sector and subject socio-targets are defined by all the socio-cultural criteria of the socio-styles, and further by all the criteria specific to the products and markets studied. These types enable us to choose for a product or brand image a particular customer segment whose motivations, commercial behaviour, current consumption and taste in media and advertising are known.

This segmentation into socio-targets for each market offers all the advantages of a sector-based consumer typology associated with the advantages of the general socio-cultural databank, which draws the most complete portrait of a population in terms of its behaviour and psychology, its tastes and feelings (see examples in chapters 11 and 12). Figure 7.1 gives an example of a commercial analysis, and figure 7.2 considers distribution networks.

A competitive chessboard of products

Thirdly, the socio-styles system offers a matrix for analyzing competitive positionings in each market. By this we mean the respective positionings of brand images, products or product specialities; competitive positionings for packaging, promotion techniques, distribution and publicity campaigns; and in politics, ideas, people and symbols.

The general socio-map shows a landscape where the different socio-cultural regions are inhabited by the socio-targets of different customer bases. In this landscape we can see which products are consumed, which images are preferred and which commercial technique is desired, as well as which ones are known or not known by different customer groups.

Thus marketing specialists have at their disposal a competitive chessboard on which they can easily locate their own territory and competing territories to be conquered, and also analyze the distances between them and the directions to be taken to reach them (see chapters 11 and 12).

A meteorology of trends

The fourth item of information that the socio-styles system brings to marketing is socio-waves analysis. To explain the changing trends on the map of the market and to understand the social currents which influence the different

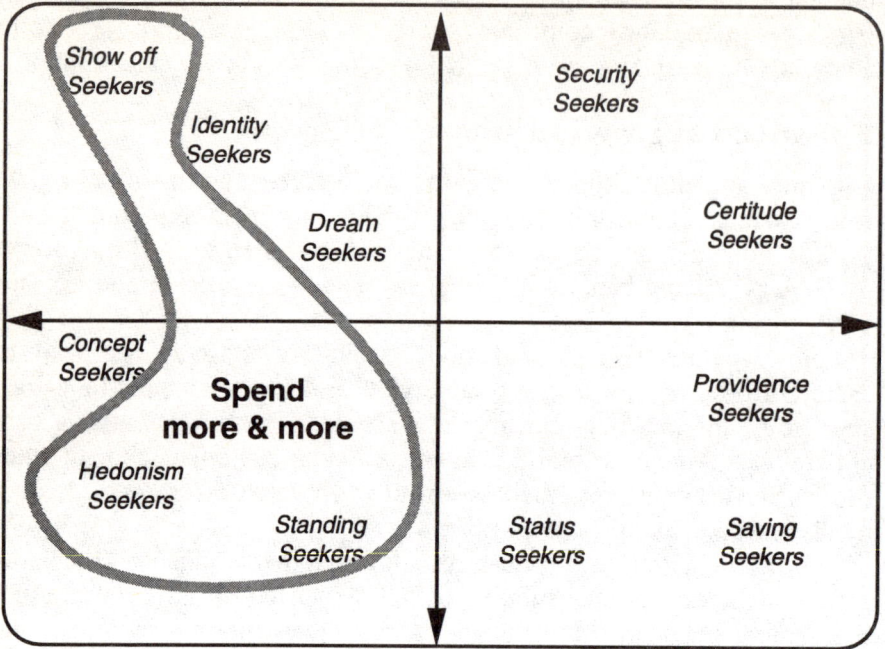

TOBACCO

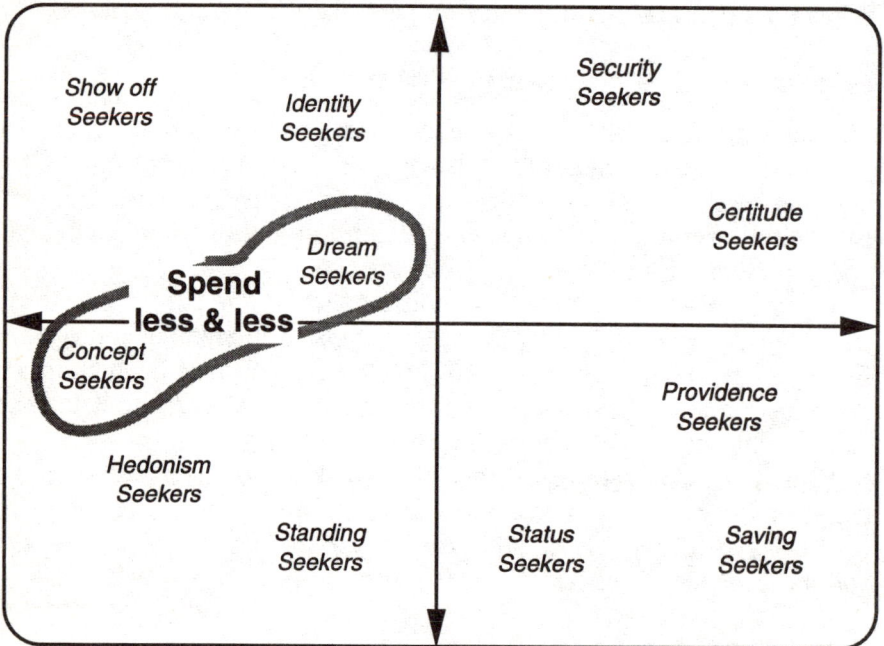

Source: U.S.Socio-Styles   © US Mapping 1988

Figure 7.1   Commercial analysis: Definition of tobacco consumers and
expenditure trends

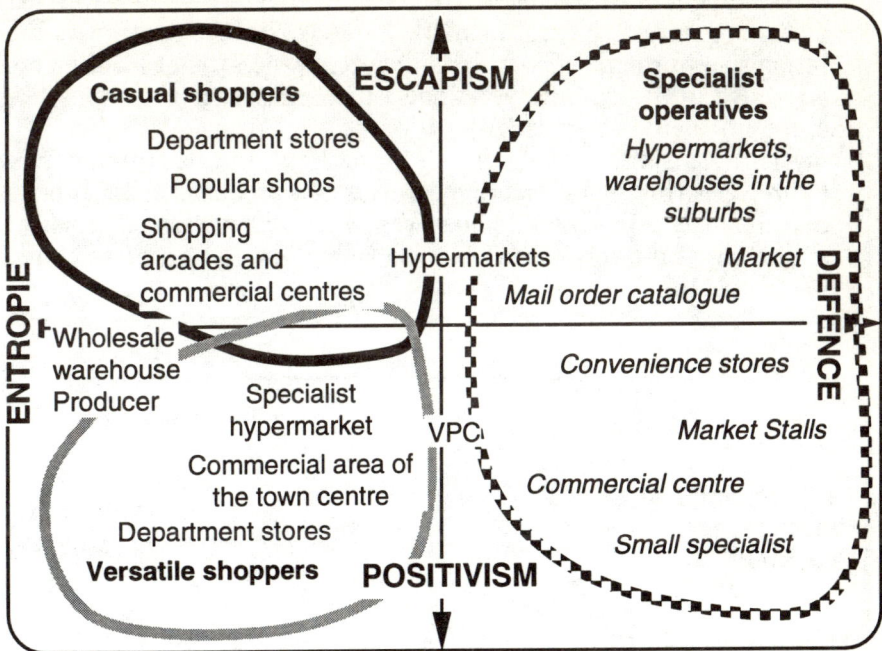

Source: Styl ' 82   © CCA 1982

Figure 7.2   Analysis of distribution networks that reach different socio-targets
according to products purchased

customer segments, the method draws the compass chart of dominant values
and socio-contrast diagrams for each market.

This analyzes the main themes which are attractive and motivating, in
opposition and competition in the four corners of the lifestyles map and
influencing more or less all segments of the population. This compass chart
represents the range of all possible positioning choices for a brand image,
for advertising slogans and images, for value added by a product.

In order to choose from these possible strategies, the socio-bank shows
in each market which customer segment is influenced most by a particular
theme and what sociological weighting is currently given to each socio-
waves (see example in chapter 10).

Paths of innovation

Fifthly and finally, the socio-styles system diagnoses prospective market
developments. This takes several forms:

❑   the diagnosis of socio-targets undergoing expansion or regression,
    becoming older or younger, poorer or richer;
❑   ongoing market observation which updates sector-based studies;
❑   detection of new customer bases right from their inception and descrip-
    tion of the new socio-style, its specific consumption patterns and
    purchasing motivation;

❑ measurement of the changing trends of the different socio-waves, diagnosis of the most important market trends and the consumers most responsive to them. This analysis indicates which themes will be most attractive in the coming years and which consumer socio-target will exemplify them in the market;

❑ measurement of the attraction of innovations and new products (see figure 7.3). This enables us to measure a new product's chances of success, to analyze the trend socio-waves which will sustain or penalize it, and to target the consumers who will be the first to buy it (see example in chapter 10).

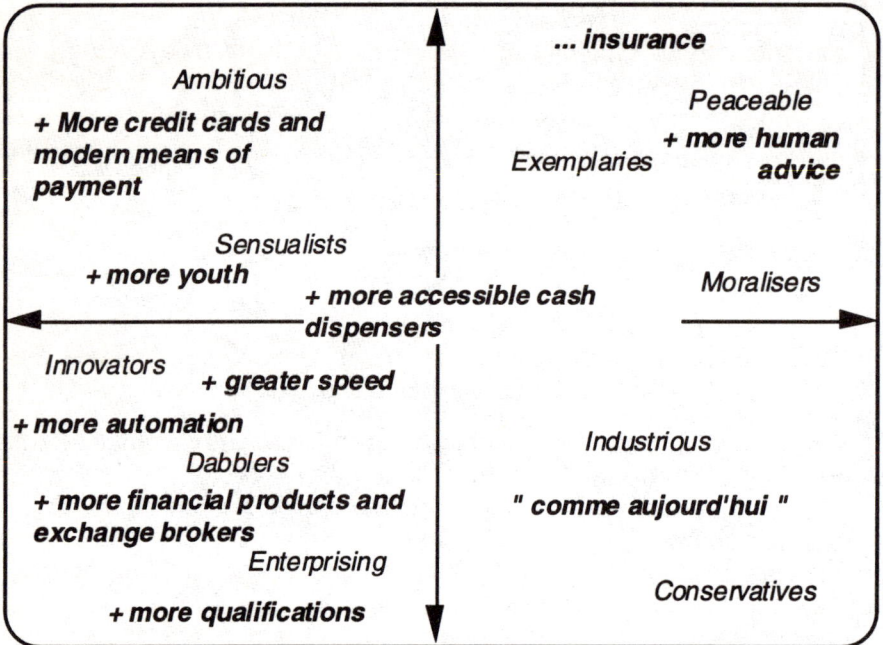

Source: Socio Styles France   © CCA 1976

Figure 7.3   Research into innovation cores in the finance sector

In short, the socio-styles system offers a range of tools for analysis and decision making that can be used in the marketing of goods and services:

❑ a socio-styles typology to analyze the market according to more qualitative criteria;

❑ a socio-target segmentation of customers and products specific to the market;

❑ a consumer map for positioning products and brands, business and advertising;

❑ a compass of dynamic socio-waves for choosing a strategy from all the motivating market themes;

❏   a socio-prospective diagnosis of new customer bases to identify new products and brand images.

HOW THE SOCIO-STYLES SYSTEM HELPS THE MEDIA

This methodology can offer the marketing departments of publishers, television and radio networks, and more broadly of all cultural products (eg films, art, the performing arts) the same service of analysis and strategic decision making.

A new criterion for audience identification

First, socio-styles typology is a tool for advertising media planning. It enables us to analyze the respective audiences for newspapers, magazines, radio and television programmes, as well as the profiles of cinema-goers and visitors to exhibitions and museums, according to a more qualitative additional criterion.

In fact, media studies intended for advertising media planning show very well that demographic, economic and professional identity variables are useful for describing differences in audiences for the major types of media (eg readers of news magazines and fashion journals), but are not as successful in explaining differences in audience personality within the same media group (eg between the audience for *L'Express* and *Point*, two French news magazines).

Since socio-styles are qualitative synthetic criteria which leave considerable room for psychology, value systems, cultural sensitivity and social and political opinions, it is natural that this typology should be particularly interesting for explaining differences in publics between media. It therefore offers marketing executives in the media the opportunity to draw both a qualitative and a statistical portrait of the audience for a publication or a television programme (see figure 7.4).

Consumer segmentation in the information market

Secondly, socio-targets are an editorial marketing tool: they are families of homogeneous publics that are defined by their information preferences and their consumption of different media forms. This segmentation enables us to identify different audience targets and to understand the position that each medium occupies in the multi-media mix. It also enables us to analyze the informative function (news or entertainment, escapism or education) that each media form fulfils in the lifestyle of this audience.

For press, radio and television advertising it is a tool for competitive marketing to improve the targeting of specific populations and increase the standing the product has with them.

MAP SHOWING PENETRATION IN THE AUDIENCE
* Among 100 people in this country 2% = Regular audience and 19% = Occasional audience
* Among 100 people of each Sociostyle which are Regular or Occasional audience

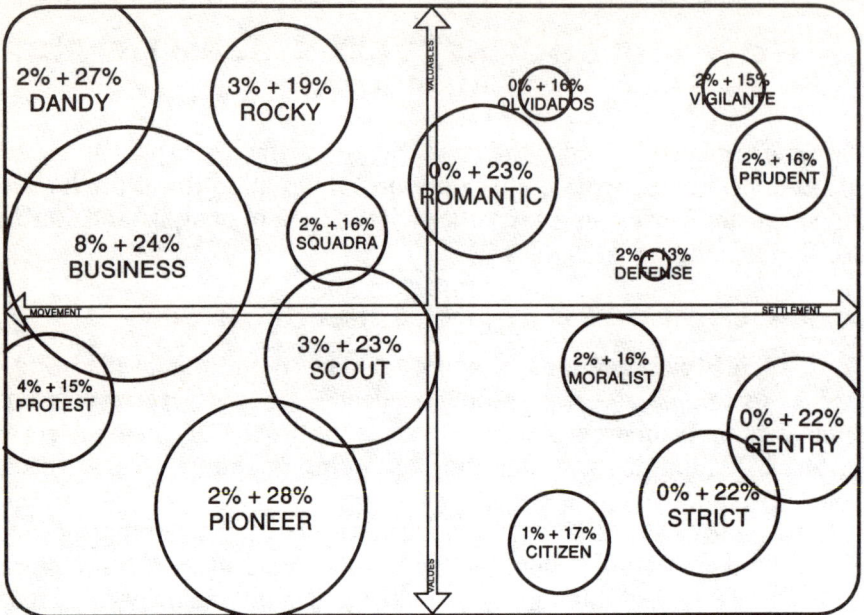

Source: Euro-Socio-Styles   Copyright CCA – 1989

Figure 7.4   Media studies (a daily sports newspaper in France)

A competitive media chessboard

Thirdly, the socio-bank positions competing media, publications and programmes according to their penetration of different audience socio-targets. Likewise the lifestyles maps enable us to observe the respective positioning of network images, channels and press titles.

Paths of innovation

Finally, the socio-styles system is a tool for innovation. It enables media marketing to diagnose and measure the prevailing socio-cultural trends which represent opportunities to create new media forms or transform existing newspapers or programmes. This can be done in a number of ways:

❑ observation over several years of the qualitative and quantitative evolution of multi-media socio-targets which shows the disappearance of certain audience profiles, the appearance of others, the impoverishment and ageing of certain publics in decline or the rejuvenation of others; the system also reveals developments in tastes and interests for each of these audience sectors;

❑ socio-cultural analysis of press, radio and television successes;

❑ measurement of motivations and aspirations about new media, new languages, new images and new styles of communication.

Briefly, the socio-styles system considers the world of culture, the media and information as a market where techniques for segmenting populations, positioning images and products and detecting innovation trends are available using lifestyle studies. Figures 7.5 and 7.6 give some examples.

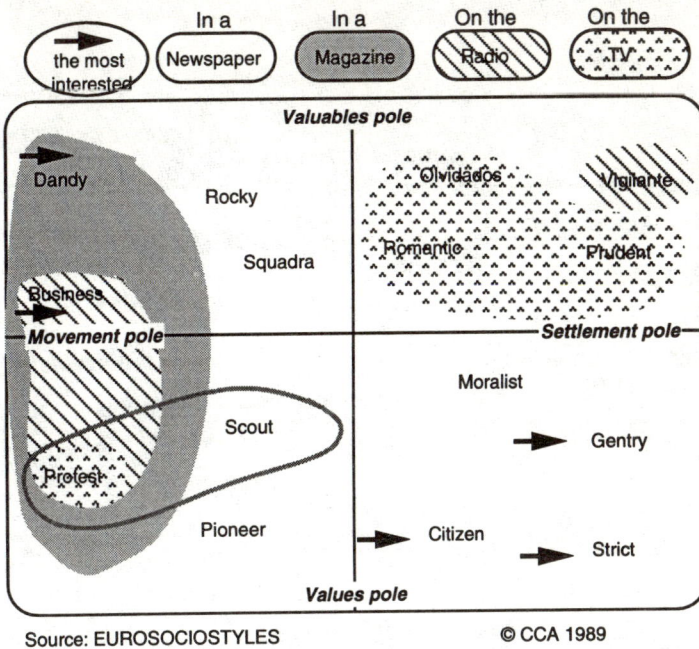

Figure 7.5   Segmentation of the information market by media in the Netherlands

HOW THE SOCIO-STYLES SYSTEM CAN ASSIST SOCIAL MANAGEMENT

State administrations, public services, foundations, political parties and the government have very different objectives to commercial manufacturers and distributors or large cultural networks.

The mission of social management is to be concerned with every citizen and not to give preference to a particular population segment. Social managers have to take long-term decisions for the public good, not satisfy immediate partisan needs. State institutions, laws and regulations have to unite all citizens in a consensus on the collective ground rules, not specialize in serving a small group. Finally, social management strategy represents a political and ethical desire for building a civilization in the long term and not a commercial tactic for immediate profit.

Yet there is a form of social and political marketing just as there is commercial and cultural marketing, and they both have to face up to the same socio-cultural conditions of public opinion. Political and social managers operate in the same society with the same population motivated by the same trends and in the same dialectic between communities.

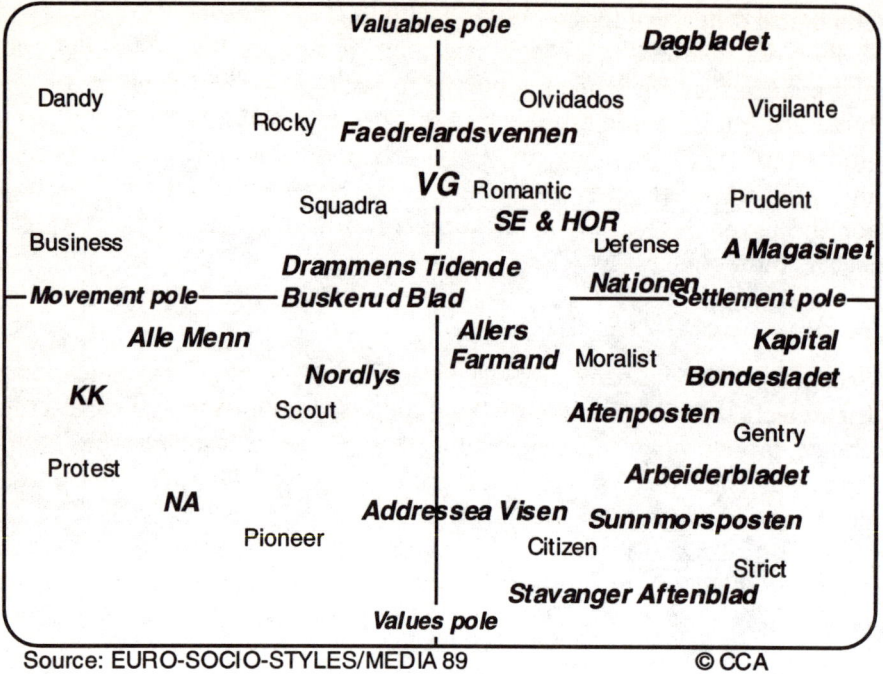

Figure 7.6   Analysis of competitive positioning of the media
(daily newspapers in Norway)

Socio-styles research is therefore just as necessary to help them understand the diversity of motivations and lifestyles in the population, measure the difference separating the different socio-styles, identify the evolutionary trends in attitudes and habits and identify the beginning of new population groups with new needs and sensitivities.

The socio-bank also provides political leaders, civil servants and managers of foundations with factors for analyzing society and precise socio-political information on the main topics of the day on which they have to react, communicate or legislate.

A new criterion for political analysis

First of all, the socio-styles typology is a criterion for analyzing the reaction of different populations to social problems and leading figures, which explains more than simple classification into demographic, economic and professional classes. In effect, the public's reactions to a political candidate and programme, to a campaign about pollution, to an army recruitment poster, to financial appeals from a charity, to a new law or regulation are not only determined by a person's age, family status, income or profession. Psychology, motivations and dreams play an important role in social and political choices. Socio-styles are the sole analytical variable which combines socio-objective criteria which influence everyday behaviour and psychological criteria which motivate the public.

By cross-referencing all social and political topics, all the leading figures and policy proposals studied regularly in socio-political studies can be analyzed according to socio-styles classes. This can help first to improve our understanding of the diversity of public opinion. Secondly it enables us to interpret reactions better by looking in the databank and lifestyle portraits for the psychological or behavioural variables that are likely to explain social policy choices.

A new social classification

Secondly, the socio-bank provides political leaders with a segmentation of their electorates into socio-targets for each of the subjects studied: electoral choice, foreign policy, domestic policy, the economy, law and order, education or defence. Each constitutes a group of people who are similar in their positive or negative motivations and driving forces on all subjects.

A political executive may not use this in the same way as a commercial manager. In commercial marketing the tendency is to place in front of each population segment a product that is specific to its needs. This also often happens in electoral marketing. However, real social and political marketing will tend to look for themes and proposals likely to unite the different socio-targets of electors and citizens.

A competitive chessboard of ideas, projects, institutions and leaders

Thirdly, we offer social and political managers a positioning map of figures and leaders, parties and organizations, programmes and law proposals, social facts and collective programmes in general. On this map we can easily see the uniting areas of consensus, both positive and negative, and also the minority and marginal topics that have been pushed to the edge of the socio-map. We can also discern the points of interest and the favourite leaders of each socio-target and each component socio-style.

It is therefore a chessboard of social problems, possible solutions and leaders who are credible in the eyes of different groups of people. Figure 7.7 gives an example of an analysis of electoral potential.

A meteorology of the prevailing themes of the age

Fourthly, the socio-bank produces a compass of social and political socio-waves. These are values and topics that compete on the social chessboard. The compass represents different strategies possible in the current environment for mobilizing a particular population segment. This socio-political compass chart summarizes the main choices in organizing a leader's public relations, promoting an idea, writing a political broadcast, making a new

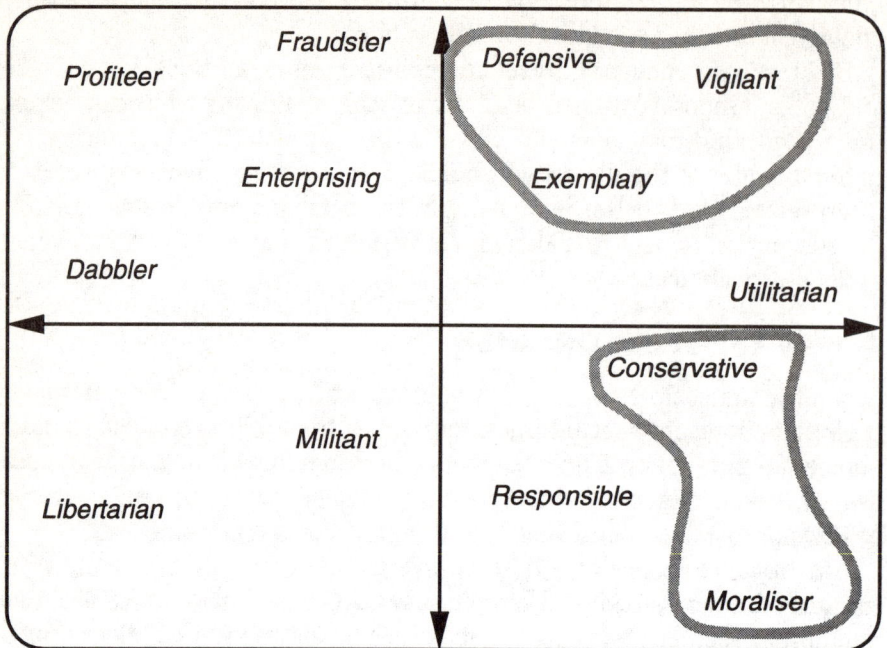

Source: Baromètre Social France   © CCA 1986

Figure 7.7   Analysis of electoral potential (National Front in France)

law acceptable to public opinion. It is a decision making instrument for political and social managers.

A diagnosis of expected reforms

Fifthly, it is a prospective compass. Socio-styles studies offer these managers a diagnosis of the development of attitudes and customs which require institutions to adopt their laws and regulations, to innovate and educate. This socio-cultural dynamic is analyzed in several ways:

❏ regular monitoring of the development of political socio-styles and socio-targets to see which ones are emerging or disappearing, which are ageing or becoming rejuvenated, which are more frustrated or content, which vote most often and which are disinterested in politics;

❏ regular monitoring of social indicators of satisfaction, motivation and future ambitions;

❏ most important of all, regularly repeated statistical measurement of the 36 socio-cultural trends which give information about the dominant values in public opinion to enable social and political initiatives to be judged.

In short, for social and political decision makers the socio-styles system offers a way of identifying in a new and more exploratory manner segments of the electorate whose motivations and ways of life we have come to know better. It also offers a means of placing on the sociological chessboard the respective positions of social and political actors. In addition, in the longer term the method aims to identify the prevailing trends of innovation and evolution.

HOW THE SOCIO-STYLES SYSTEM CAN HELP AN ORGANIZATION

Socio-cultural studies in general are an instrument for analyzing prevailing trends and the variety of needs and feelings within public opinion. It thus enables us to adapt an offering more quickly to the evolutionary rhythm and more precisely to differences between segments.

A tool for an institution's external marketing activities, it is also an internal marketing instrument for organizations, institutions and firms to improve their knowledge of their staff, workforce and partners so as to use them to better advantage.

So the socio-styles method is also a working tool for managers in organizations of all kinds and sizes, and more especially for personnel and human relations directors, training and recruitment managers, since it can analyze staff behaviour, attitudes and motivations. A wide range of information about work, the firm, the role of the employer and the work setting, remuneration and stimulation, motivation and loyalty is available in the socio-bank in the same way as facts about private life, consumer habits, etc. Work-styles is a databank managed by Mike Burke which offers developers of human potential a similar service to that available to marketing managers in the manufacturing and service sectors.

A lifestyles typology for work

First, we analyze and measure a workforce typology in the form of socio-targets specific to attitudes, motivations and behaviour towards work and the organization. This segmentation is carried out on the whole of the active working population including all types, all levels, all skills, in all trades or professions. Each of these active population segments is specific in its concept of work, its view of an ideal organization and employer, its sensitivity to a certain type of information and form of human relations in the organization, its mobility or tendency to stay put, its ambition or need for security.

For the managers of organizations it is a way of getting to know the diversity of their internal public opinions — segmented just as their public opinions or external clients are.

This workforce typology is also used in updating studies within a firm to measure precisely the weighting of each of the workforce profiles and draw a table of the homogeneity or heterogeneity of the organization's workforce.

A meteorology of ambitions among the workforce

Secondly, the socio-styles system is a general socio-cultural environmental barometer. In the areas of active life, work and leisure, remuneration and economic arbitration we can discover evolving trends in behaviour and motivations towards the organization.

Increasingly firms are able to adapt to new attitudes in the workforce to motivate them more towards certain objectives, gain their loyalty or reduce frustration and conflict. General developments in society, attitudes and lifestyles are not factors that are external to the organizations; they influence it from inside when the workforce enters the factory or office with their habits, motivations and trends.

As with commercial or social marketing we can follow socio-cultural evolutions and translate them to assist the management of human potential in organization in two ways:

❑ regular monitoring of work-style socio-targets observing which groups appear or disappear, get younger or older, become passive or rebel, become more materialistic or enthusiastic;

❑ specific questions in the form of scenarios about the firm at present and the ideal firm, today's employers, current and ideal social relations. These scenarios enable us to measure the differences between actual and ideal working life for each of the socio-styles. It is an index of aspirations for change and evolutionary trends within these populations.

Briefly, the socio-styles system offers company executives a decision making tool for recruitment and training, for social policy and motivating personnel around a collective project. Figures 7.8 illustrates this use of the typology.

HOW THE SOCIO-STYLES SYSTEM CAN ASSIST COMMUNICATION

Communication is the point of convergence of all forms of marketing and therefore of all forms of socio-styles applications. It can be communication about a product or service for commercial marketing; communication about a project, an idea, a programme or leader for social and political marketing; communication of information about culture or leisure for media marketing; communication of an enterprise or institutional image inside and outside an organization for the management of a company's culture.

This communication may take the form of newspaper information, public relations spectaculars, media publicity or direct advertising. It can also include the design of products, brands names and logos, store architecture and product labelling, packaging and staff uniforms.

All these forms of communication have a common purpose: to give information to a population about an offering. All messages therefore have to take account not only of the transmitting organization's strategic desire for information or persuasion, but also of the lifestyles and psychology of the targeted population, if they want to be noticed, understood and accepted.

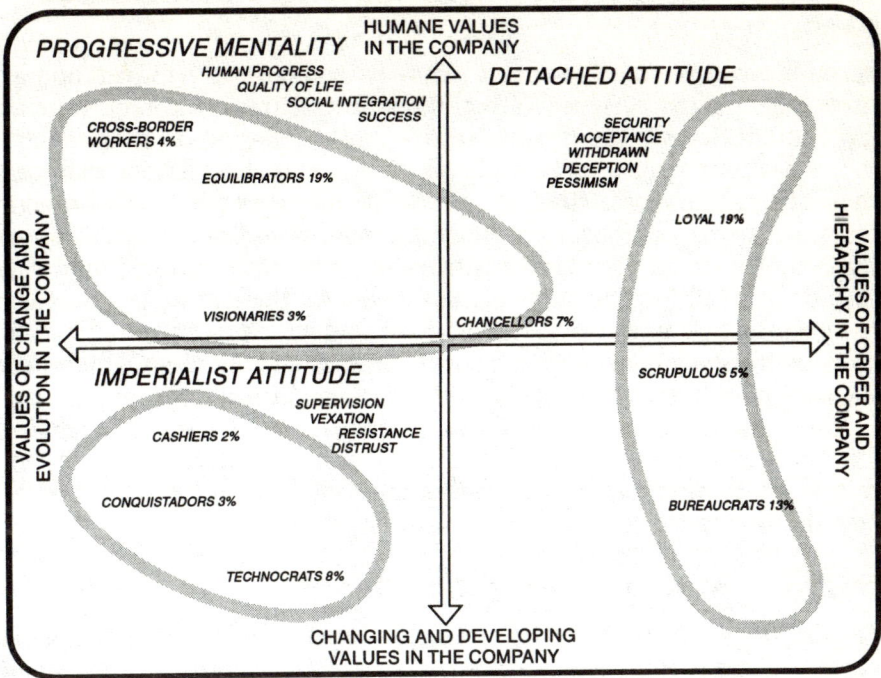

Figure 7.8   Lifestyles typology at work among management

The socio-styles system gives communication professionals several working tools which meet their needs: the socio-bank as an action tool and the Co'System as a research tool. Advertising agencies and the media were the first to support and use this method to improve the impact and targeting of their messages.

A unique criterion for media product studies

First of all, socio-styles typology gives communication professionals target audiences defined in the same terms and according to the same qualitative criteria as the target consumers of marketing companies. In effect we know each type's behaviour and purchasing motivations towards different products, responsiveness to different styles of communication and language, and behaviour towards all the media.

Media-styles studies describe the readership of journals and magazines and audiences for radio and television programmes with socio-styles portraits. This is a practical tool for use in media planning to select the best advertising support to reach a precise consumer target with the greatest impact and at the least expense.

A library of pictures, words and styles adapted to each target

Secondly, the socio-bank analyzes socio-styles language: the words and pictures, layouts and designs, packaging and promotions that motivate each target more than others. It is therefore a way of choosing the range of communication methods most suited to reaching a target population defined as socio-styles. With these studies the style of communication avoids reliance on either artistic intuition or a single mechanical test of impact. Obviously we cannot claim to provide in mathematical terms the advertising or message best suited to reach a population. However, lifestyle studies enable us to choose a style of artistic creation, information or promotion taking into account the culture of the target population and sensitivities which make them more or less responsive to a particular tone or language.

This method provides advertisers, journalists, communicators and creative people with a compass so that they can locate themselves in the mosaic of sensitivities, tastes, preferences and feelings of different populations and find the right tone to reach the right target.

Segmentation into target audiences

Thirdly, the socio-styles system provides an orientation for preparing global communication strategies in the medium and long term, both inside and outside an organization, using all the potential of the media and all forms of information. It proposes a segmentation of audiences in the form of information socio-targets (see above). Each represents a population which is unique in the themes which motivate it and the added value in information which attracts it, the tone and style of the messages which reach it and the range of multi-media with which we can reach it in an informative, questioning or entertaining manner. In this way communication planners can structure a global strategy for information and influence according to the lifestyles portrait of the population they are targeting.

Trends and methods in communication

Finally, the socio-styles system provides a social meteorology of dominant trends in information and language.

There is no one ideal way of expressing an idea, but several. The intuition of an artist and the wishes of a decision maker are not sufficient to ensure the success of a message. The impact and effectiveness of communication are largely influenced by cultural reality. Perfect aesthetics, the right sentence, an indisputable table of figures or a new joke have no value in themselves: they are received by the public more or less favourably according to the mood of the time.

When sociological fashions change the sensitivity to themes and styles of communication changes too. When lifestyles come into being they often move towards new styles of communication and new topics of information. When the socio-cultural compass is overtuned, the instrinsic quality of messages is open to question.

A dominant fashion, in the best sense of the word, is evident in information and advertising, the fashion of the dominant socio-cultural trends. As far as communication is concerned, the socio-compass measures the prevailing trends in three ways:

❏ observation and continuing analysis of the media and their audiences. This enables us to see whether the information media are becoming more or less popular than the entertainment media, to analyze the dynamics between the written word and pictures and the relative attraction of photographs or illustrations. Repeated analysis of this market of cultures and messages over the years enables us to identify languages that are retreating or making progress;

❏ detection and analysis of emerging lifestyles. The socio-bank enables creators to imagine new languages and layouts for the new audiences with known motivations and sensitivities, as well as the motivating themes for each of the subjects studied;

❏ regularly repeated testing of a large number of languages of communication in the studies: magazine covers, publicity announcements, packaging forms and illustrations, product design, press layouts, audio-visual messages. For example, the socio-scanner questionnaire of the Euro-socio-styles foundation study contained 30 pages devoted to a test of language acceptability in the graphic form of coloured photographs and drawings.

This is a 'hit parade' of regularly updated basic elements from which creators can select to try out their genius (eg black and white or colour; structured or unstructured; funny or serious).

Since the socio-styles system began, it has been intended as a practical tool for analysis and decision making in all sectors — social, cultural and economic. The socio-bank can be used for commercial, cultural and socio-political marketing, for company culture and personnel management within organizations, by communication specialists in these different sector-based activities. In over 15 years the method has shown evidence of its interest to all these sectors, both as a statistical analytical study made more interesting because it is more interpretative and also as a source of ideas and a more global vision in time and space that better synthesizes the way things are.

Figures 7.9 and 7.10 illustrate how the socio-styles can be used in media studies.

SOCIO-EXPERTISE: ARTIFICIAL INTELLIGENCE AS AN AID TO MARKETING

The growing complexity of databanks and great variety of possible processes open up greater possibilities to researchers but also run the risk of producing an information explosion. This is why the socio-bank takes two forms for different users:

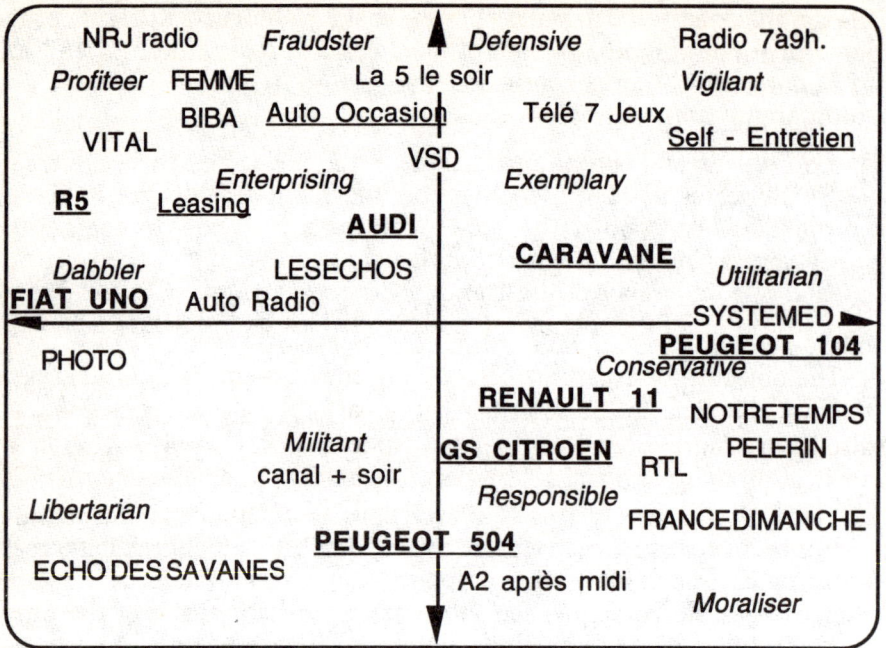

Source: Socio Styles France   © CCA 1984

Figure 7.9   Media product analysis on the socio-map

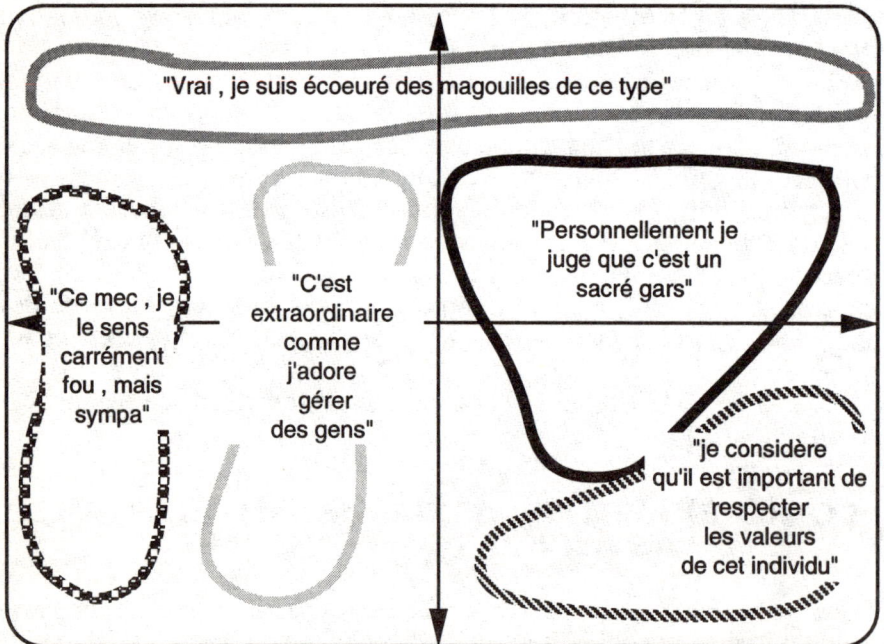

Source: LEXICO - STYLES "FRANCE"   © CCA & Infométrie1982

Figure 7.10   Language styles peculiar to different mentalities

❏   on the one hand databanks of raw statistics intended for various mathematical processes;
❏   on the other, synthetic knowledge banks intended for operational users, offering directly an interpreted view of the data and even advice, scenarios and strategic orientations. These knowledge banks are run by expert artificial intelligence systems which give faster access in an interactive dialogue with the user.

Since 1988 it has been possible for professionals to consult and use the socio-bank in the form of various expert systems in an interactive way on micro-computers.

The objective of expert artificial intelligence systems is to synthesize all the available data in the socio-bank in a particular geo-cultural zone, and also to use more extensively the knowledge and skill in interpretation and application of experts and researchers specializing in different sectors. This can be done without entering into the detail of millions of data items.

In practice the expert system interrogates the computer interactively, posing a problem and asking for advice, just as one would interrogate a human being to find out their opinion or recommendation. The expert system fulfils the same role of providing intelligence and synthesis as a well-informed expert.

The principle of a knowledge bank is to commit to memory all human or factual knowledge on a group of subjects. In the case of socio-styles the material is made up of the entire contents of the socio-bank and related studies and also the human expertise of the whole socio-styles system team.

The creation of an expert system involves organizing a very complex network of logical connections, a mixture of objective coded data taken from surveys and polls, synthetic coded data from complex statistical processes in the socio-bank, and subjective interpretative data representing experience, reflection or even intuition coming from the thoughts and experience of the researchers.

The artificial intelligence model is presented as the sum of all the knowledge from all sources concerning socio-styles in a particular geo-political zone in the form of basic raw survey data, data from specialist applications, the experience of researchers and decision makers, mathematical synthesis and human interpretation.

Finding useful information more quickly

The first application makes navigation around the databank easier, in the sense of 'knowledge navigation' suggested by J Sculley, chairman of Apple. This means organizing the research and interrogation on the computer screen using the data most useful to the user in the most automated and rapid way in relation to a set of explicit demands and implicit interests. It also involves selecting the level of synthesis or the degree of analysis required. The expert system has to make transparent tens of thousands of documents, tables, figures and maps in order to give users what is useful to them in a form which meets their requirements.

It is therefore an expert navigation system intended to assist research which then proceeds to data interpretation.

Going beyond research to work out a scenario for action

A second application is to transform the study data for a particular market in the socio-bank into a complete marketing strategy scenario describing the product, its presentation, its characteristics, its commercial distribution and its advertising — by reference to a socio-style portrait of a target population — drawn from an interactive interview with users about their objectives, potential, constraints and competitors. The socio-bank is present and active, but totally transparent; the expert system takes the necessary data and transforms it into advice. In order to do this the system has to be designed to combine raw survey data with interpretation by human experts. The expert system is as valuable as the marketing expert who has programmed it. We can clearly see that the objective is to clone the interpretative skills of an expert in order to make them freely available on a self-service basis to marketing operations.

We therefore have a strategic expert system intended for commercial managers and advertising professionals (eg Neuron Works' Market Compass).

Training in customer recognition

A third application is intended to train colleagues and make them aware of the data in the socio-bank, either in a general way concerning environmental trends and socio-styles portraits or more precisely about the socio-targets in their own market. Artificial intelligence therefore helps to transform the abstract, technical, remote study results into a living, concrete, everyday didactic tool. (Various methods can be used to take market studies out of their specialist ghetto and let them infiltrate the human networks of the organization (eg tests of knowledge, role play, strategic simulations). These expert systems have to adopt a simple form that is easy to use, even game-like, in order to become a training or self-evaluation exercise. The basic mechanism stays the same:

❑ how to recognize which socio-style or socio-target a customer belongs to;
❑ how to adapt a commercial offering and sales style to this profile.

It is an educational expert system intended for company training divisions and in particular their sales people (eg Target Test and Training, two models created by Neuron Works).

Guiding or automating sales

A fourth application uses the same procedure as above but for sales. The way the system is set up is more complex, because it has to take into account the lifestyle profiles of customers, their objective needs in relation to a product's characteristics, any possible legal restraints and the strategies of competitors. Here too human expertise within the firm combines with the knowledge in the socio-bank. The session of interactive dialogue between the computer salesperson and the potential customer begins with an interview about the customer's everyday needs, desires, current behaviour and lifestyle. It concludes with a practical proposal featuring the selection of a product and a particular line of reasoning.

This expert sales-aid system can serve as a guide to a salesperson working in isolation (eg in telephone sales) or in the presence of a customer in a shop or at home. It can also be managed on a self-service basis by customers themselves (eg an automated sales terminal in a shop).

There is also an expert promotional system designed to direct customers in a large store or reading a catalogue to innovations or products adapted to their socio-style (eg Promo-Test).

Piloting communication ideas

Another application of artificial intelligence makes media styles available at the touch of a button to advertising agencies and public relations organizations in order to generate ideas for the media plan (eg what mix of television, radio and press). This socio-media model is at the prototype stage.

X-raying innovations

To assist organizations that want to watch out for the appearance of new products in their market and evaluate their impact and competitive capacity, an expert system can carry out a detailed check on a recent product, based on the known tastes and habits of different socio-styles, in order to anticipate its potential customer base (eg product scan).

This new artificial intelligence technology opens up new applications for the databank. The socio-styles system is well prepared for this by its visual presentation and its typological and structural principle.

For users this new socio-expert tool will be a revolution in the use of research:

❑ by overcoming the explosion in the amount of data available;
❑ by spreading information within a firm in concrete, everyday, professional language;
❑ by taking strategic hypotheses from the socio-bank;
❑ by placing on every executive's desk a practical information tool;
❑ above all, by combining survey results and human experience in a knowledge bank.

CHAPTER 8
HOW TO USE THE SOCIO-BANK

AN OPEN DATABANK

Going beyond standardized reports that provide general structured and synthesized information, the socio-styles system offers decision makers the opportunity to find precise answers to their problems by interrogating the whole of the socio-styles research, relating in mathematical terms all the data from every survey. This is the most diversified of the available databanks and offers encoded information on both behaviour and psychology.

All multi-sectorial surveys are in fact carried out on the same representative sample panel of the whole population and all its sub-groups. This enables us to combine and mix the results of all the surveys in a computerized databank. In this way each variable from any survey can be cross-referenced statistically with other data from another survey.

For example, are the people who have replied to a question about the regular adoption of a new frozen food product (from a sector-based study on food) the same as those who read the magazine *Elle* (from a press readership survey)? Do these people like scientific-style publicity (from an advertising styles survey)? This type of question is put regularly to firms, journalists, teachers, marketing consultants, etc. Similar questions are also put to social and political managers in the public sector.

Combined as they are in the same unique socio-bank all the elements of every survey can be analyzed on demand according to demographic, professional and economic criteria. For example, are the people who do all the things in the previous example women rather than men, city dwellers or country dwellers, rich or poor, graduates or not?

This type of analysis enables social decision makers to identify a precise population defined both by its psychology and its behaviour on precise themes taken from the socio-bank and to describe its social, economic and cultural profile.

The same databank enables us to analyze all the sector-based data with reference to the foundation study which defined the socio-map and the socio-styles typology. Any data from any survey can be analyzed according to socio-styles. For example, are the people in the previous example 'dandies' or 'puritans'? Are they more oriented towards the conservative pole or the modernist pole on the socio-map? And are they sensitive to ecological or technological trends?

The socio-bank constitutes a source of *ad hoc, á la carte*, custom-made analyses for users of the socio-styles system, such as marketing or communication directors, social administrators, advertising and media executives, as well as sociologists. The system also offers a third service: a data source open to special statistical processing and analysis which responds precisely to specific questions.

The richness of the socio-bank lies in the combination of the complementary sector-based data which it contains and the regular updating of this data. It is a living reservoir of information on different ways of living in all areas of life and activity.

Figure 8.1 outlines the network of databanks available and figure 8.2 gives an example of cross-referencing.

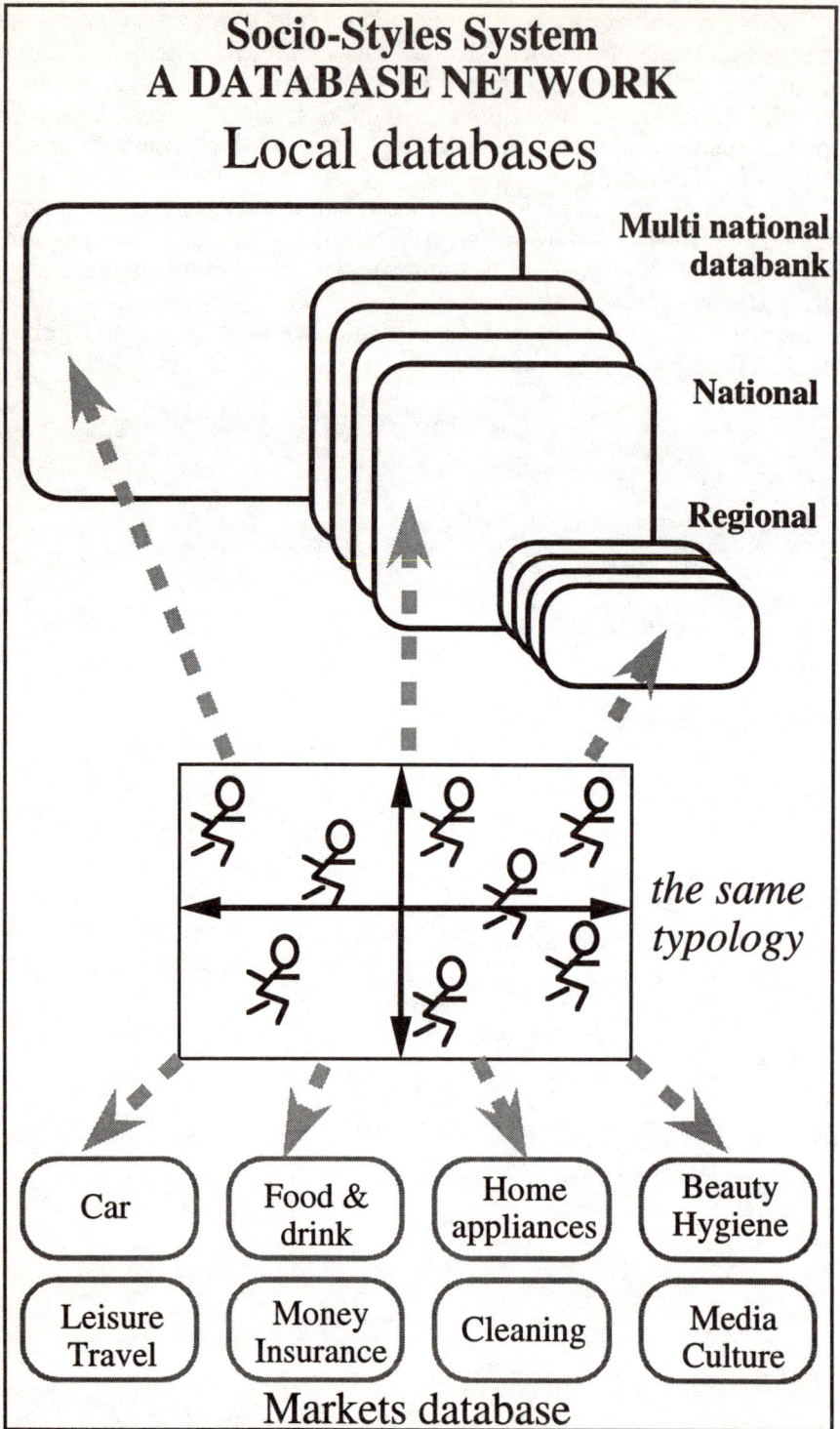

Figure 8.1   Network of databanks

EXAMPLES OF GRAPHICAL REPRESENTATION
OF CROSS-SORTS:
Reading of a newspaper (in France) crossed by the
typology of the Socio-Styles.

MAP SHOWING PENETRATION IN THE AUDIENCE

* Among 100 people in this country 1% = Regular audience and 19% = Occasional audience
* Among 100 people of each Sociostyle which are Regular or Occasional audience

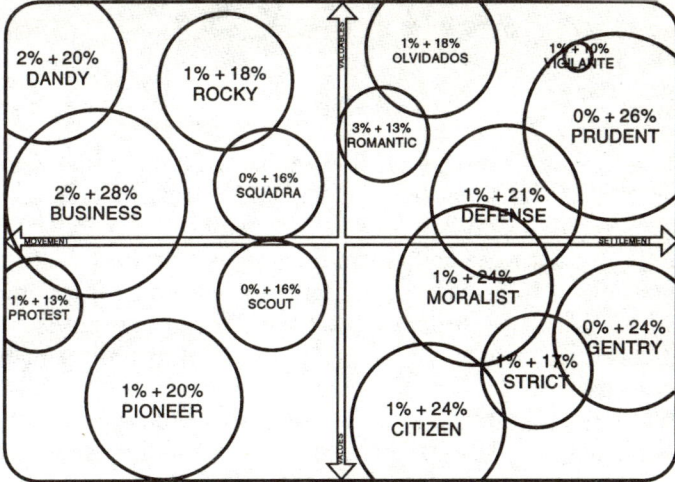

2% + 20%
DANDY

1% + 18%
ROCKY

1% + 18%
OLVIDADOS

1% + 20%
VIGILANTE

3% + 13%
ROMANTIC

0% + 26%
PRUDENT

2% + 28%
BUSINESS

0% + 16%
SQUADRA

1% + 21%
DEFENSE

1% + 13%
PROTEST

0% + 16%
SCOUT

1% + 24%
MORALIST

0% + 24%
GENTRY

1% + 20%
PIONEER

1% + 24%
CITIZEN

1% + 17%
STRICT

MAP SHOWING DISTRIBUTION OF THE AUDIENCE

* Among 100 people of the Regular audience how many belong to each Sociostyle
* Among 100 people of the Occasional audience how many belong to each Sociostyle

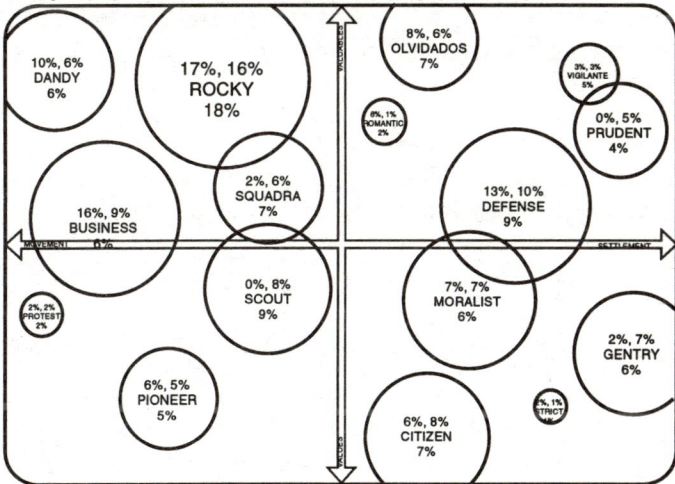

10%, 6%
DANDY
6%

17%, 16%
ROCKY
18%

8%, 6%
OLVIDADOS
7%

3%, 3%
VIGILANTE
5%

8%, 1%
ROMANTIC
2%

0%, 5%
PRUDENT
4%

16%, 9%
BUSINESS
0%

2%, 6%
SQUADRA
7%

13%, 10%
DEFENSE
9%

2%, 2%
PROTEST
2%

0%, 8%
SCOUT
9%

7%, 7%
MORALIST
6%

2%, 7%
GENTRY
6%

6%, 5%
PIONEER
5%

6%, 8%
CITIZEN
7%

2%, 1%
STRICT

Source: Euro-Socio-Styles   Copyright CCA/EUROPANEL – 1989

Figure 8.2   Graphic representation of cross-referencing (newspaper reading
crossed with socio-styles typology)

Map A shows the newspaper's penetration of each socio-style emphasizing the types which
read it more than average. Map B shows how the total readership of this newspaper is distributed among the 16 socio-style types

CHAPTER 9

APPLICATIONS FOR CONSUMER PANEL ANALYSIS

The most systematic criticism of lifestyle studies, including socio-styles, is always directed at the supposed ineffectiveness of socio-cultural criteria for analyzing the most up-to-date forms of consumer behaviour and therefore their inability to compete with socio-demographic criteria. Although socio-styles do not claim to be competitive with socio-demographic and economic analyses but rather to supplement them, this typology is particularly intended to contribute to the analysis of opinion polls and purchasing behaviour in panels.

The following examples demonstrate that socio-styles typology is very effective in explaining the purchase of different product brands or types in markets reputed to be the most influenced by behaviour, such as washing powders and food.

Whenever consumers are offered a choice, whether it involves the technical specification of a product or a brand image, socio-styles are able to discriminate between purchasing decisions that are influenced by more than simple economic or demographic criteria. While classical criteria (eg age, sex, profession) are often good at describing the consumption of a utilitarian generic product (eg detergent, pasta, shampoo), socio-styles perform the same function for purchases with specific value added to the product (eg liquid detergent, detergent with conditioner), packaging or brand.

EXAMPLE: DETERGENTS IN FRANCE*

Ways of reading the results (Figures 9.1 to 9.6)

The values of product and brand penetration in the whole sample are expressed on a base of 100, where 100 represents the penetration value of a product brand in the population. Numbers above 100 indicate which socio-styles use this product brand more and numbers below 100 which socio-styles use it less. The results are given, as always with the socio-styles system, in the form of a map which enables us to observe clusters of super-consumer.

This example deals with the market for two types of detergent products

---

* Source: Purchase of detergents in France from July 1987 to June 1988 observed on a panel of SECODIP housewives according to CCA's French socio-styles typology (1987).

(washing powders and liquid detergents) and is spread across several brands, not named here for reasons of confidentiality.

The analysis shows that:

❑ super-consumers of liquid detergent A are not the same as super-consumers of powders of the same brand; the launch of a liquid detergent by this brand has not led to competition with its powder brand, but has increased its market coverage (figures 9.1 and 9.2);
❑ liquid detergent B has a broader coverage of the market with super-consumers from a larger number of socio-styles than brand A (figures 9.2 and 9.4);
❑ liquid detergent B competes directly with the washing powder of the same brand (figures 9.3 and 9.4);

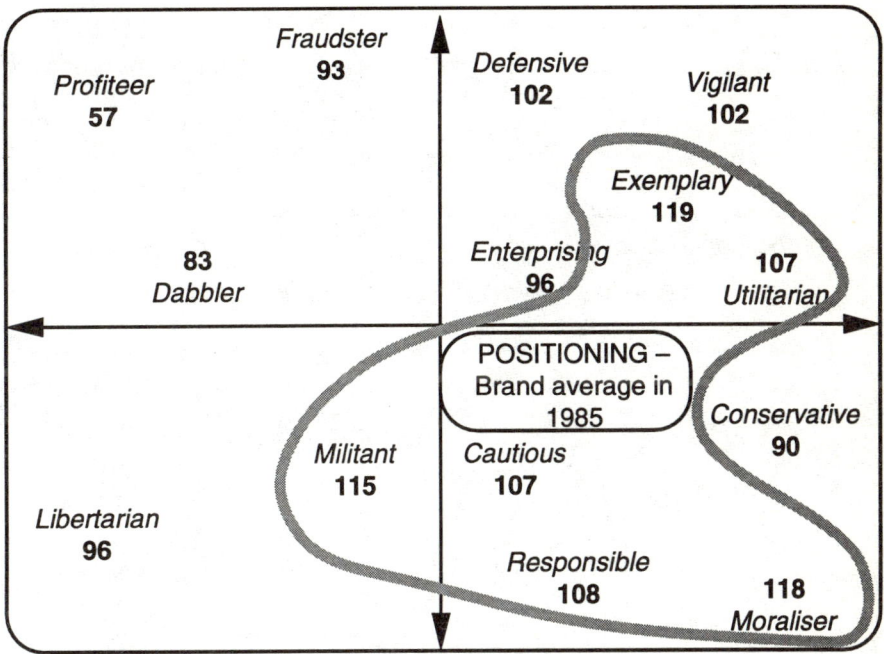

Figure 9.1   Buyers of brand A washing powder

Another example enables us to observe that two new products launched by two different brands with a similar added value (the addition of conditioners to a washing powder) did not achieve the same penetration with consumers. We can see that:

❑ the product enabled brand C to increase its penetration of the market to reach new socio-styles (at the top of the map and bottom left) (figure 9.5);
❑ the launch of product D, in contrast, enabled this brand to gain new customers on the extreme right of the map away from its starting point (figure 9.6).

The socio-bank (lifestyles in France, 1988) enables us to analyze the value of

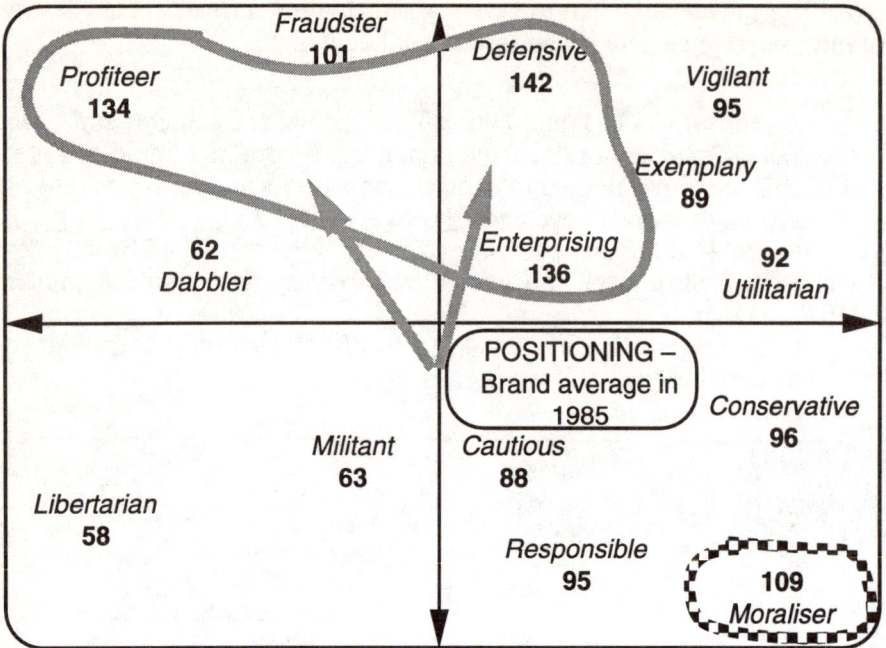

Source: panel Secodip France   © cca 1989

Figure 9.2   Buyers of brand A liquid detergent

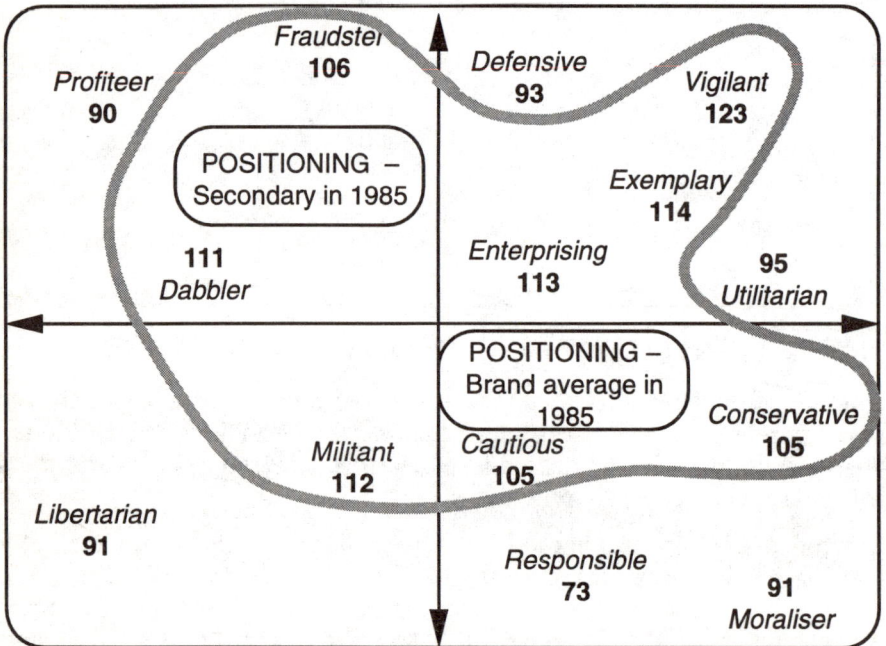

Figure 9.3   Buyers of brand B washing powder

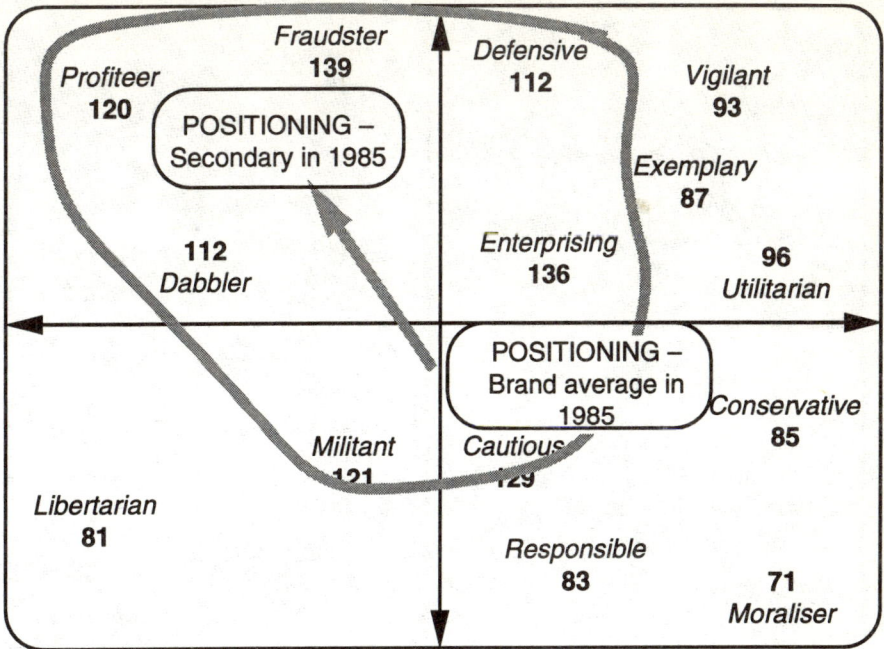

Source: panel Secodip France   © cca 1989

Figure 9.4   Buyers of brand B liquid detergent

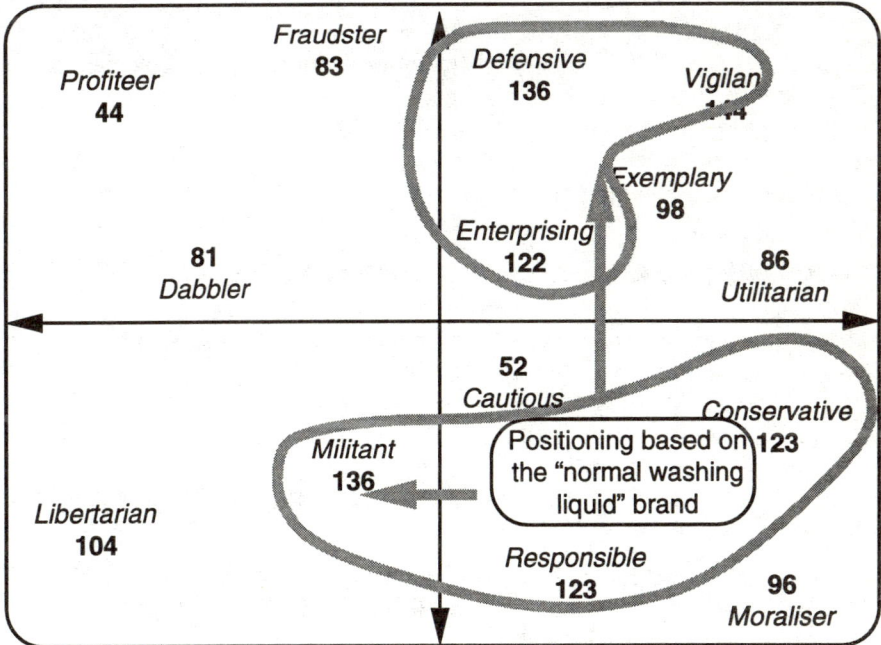

Figure 9.5   Buyers of brand C detergent with conditioner

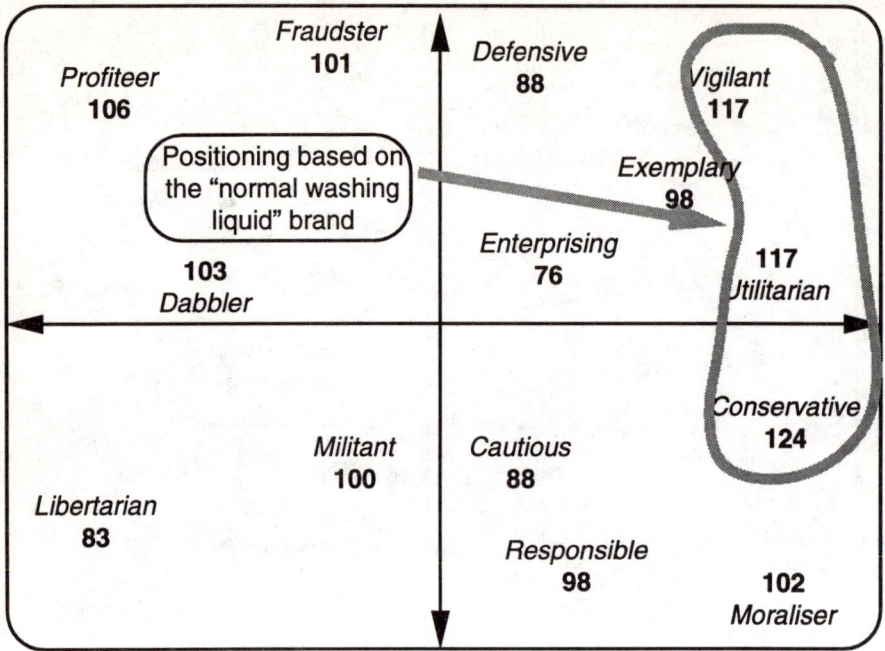

Source: panel Secodip France   © cca 1989

Figure 9.6   Buyers of brand D detergent with conditioner

the different customer groups that have been gained. The new customers gained by D, for example, are older, more rural, poorer but more loyal; while those gained by C are slightly more modern in outlook, less utilitarian, more hedonistic and more responsive to attractive packaging.

These examples and those in the following section show that socio-styles typology is effective even in analyzing markets regarded as very utilitarian and determined by objective criteria.

EXAMPLE: CONSUMER ANALYSES IN EUROPE*

This canonical typology enables us to identify clearly different consumer profiles according to their choice of product or brand. The purchase of washing materials or food products is determined not only by the requirements of socio-objective living conditions, but also by the general lifestyle equilibrium (see figures 9.7–9.10).

In the food sector we can see that the consumer profiles for dairy products are different:

❏ the main penetration of fat-free yoghurts is in the east and north of the map, among those anxious about their physical appearance;

* Source: Results from SECODIP consumer panels in France analyzed by the CCA Europanel typology of 16 European socio-styles.

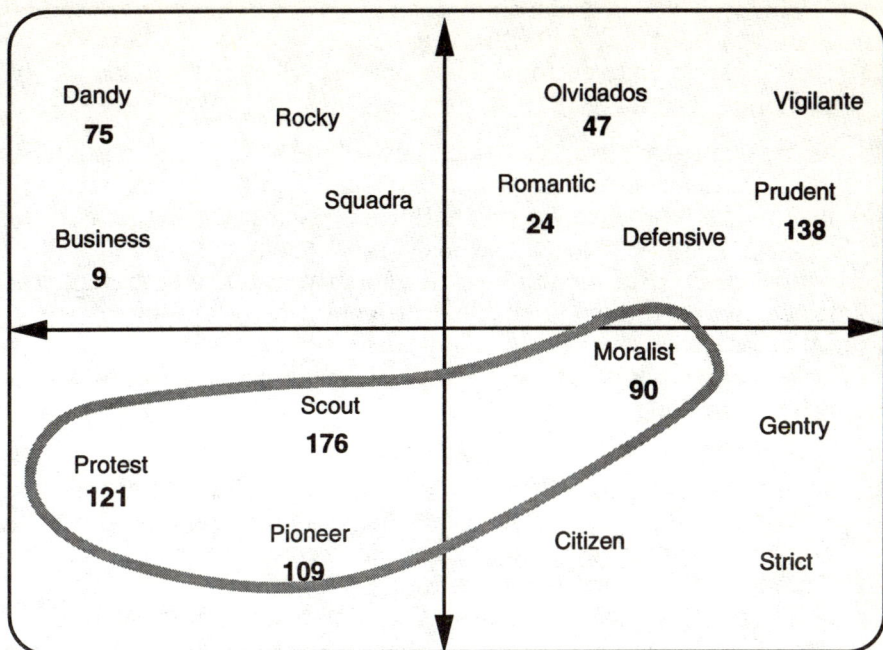

Figure 9.7   Cereal consumption

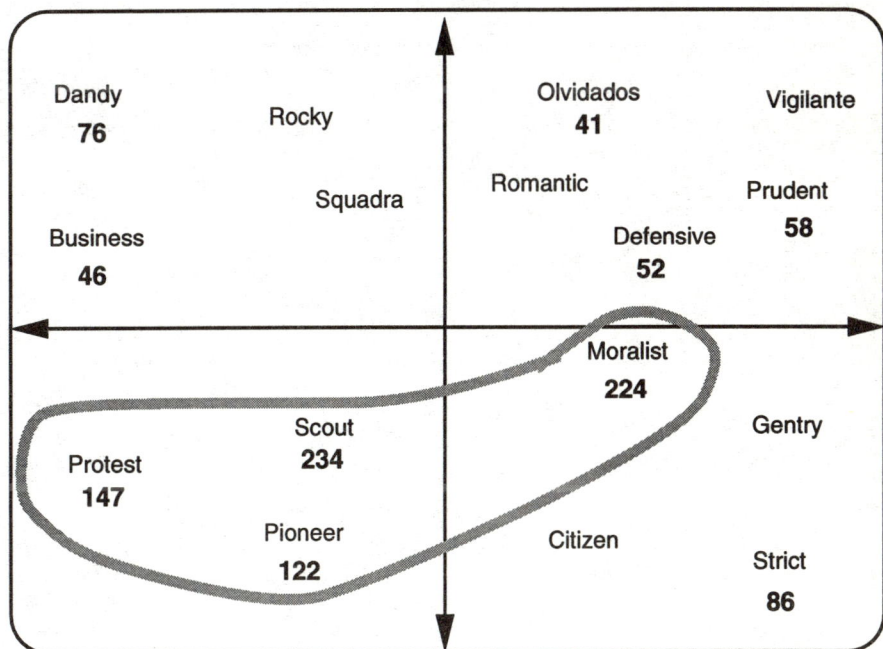

Figure 9.8   Muesli consumption

❑ bifidus-type yoghurts launched recently penetrate those in the south of the map who are more health conscious;
❑ there is a common customer base represented by types 9 and 12, who are innovators motivated by fitness.

In the breakfast market, in contrast, the analysis shows that consumers of 'ordinary' cereals and muesli do not have significantly different socio-style profiles, and both products are concentrated on consumers in the south-east of the socio-map who are spontaneously motivated by the search for fitness by natural means. But innovative consumers (types 8 and 9) are not really interested, nor are the young, middle-class gourmets (types 5 and 6).

In this case panel, analysis by socio-styles enables us to detect weaknesses in market penetration and to identify targets where an effort has to be made (figures 9.7 and 9.8).

In the detergent market the maps show:

❑ that consumers are differentiated by socio-styles according to the nature of the product — concentrated washing liquid penetrates the conservative lifestyles in the eastern section of the map; ordinary liquid detergents the modernists in the west (figure 9.9);
❑ that brands also mark out different territories for themselves — C3, C4 and C5 are famous brands; C6 is a distributor's brand (figure 9.10).

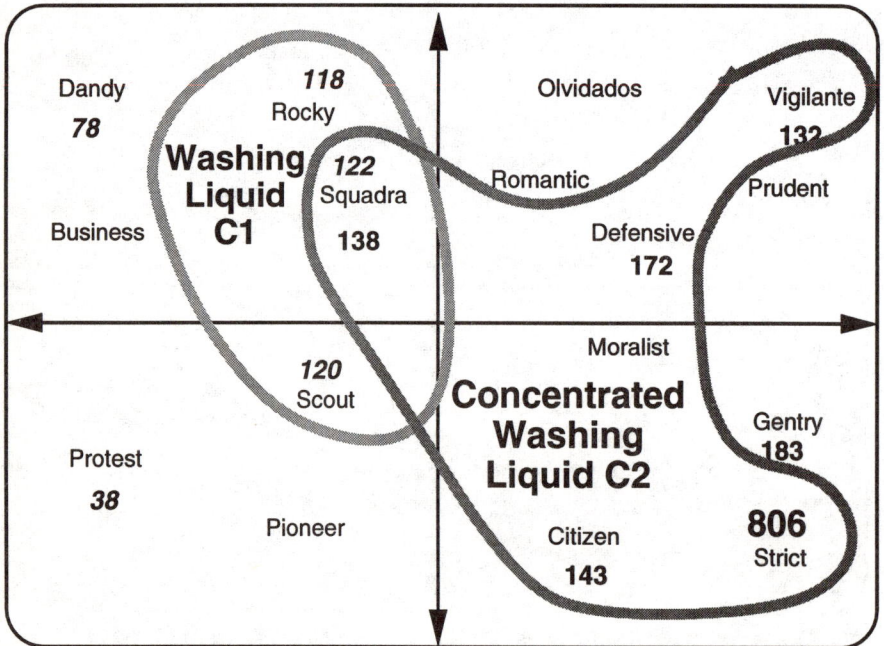

Figure 9.9   Consumers of brands of washing liquid

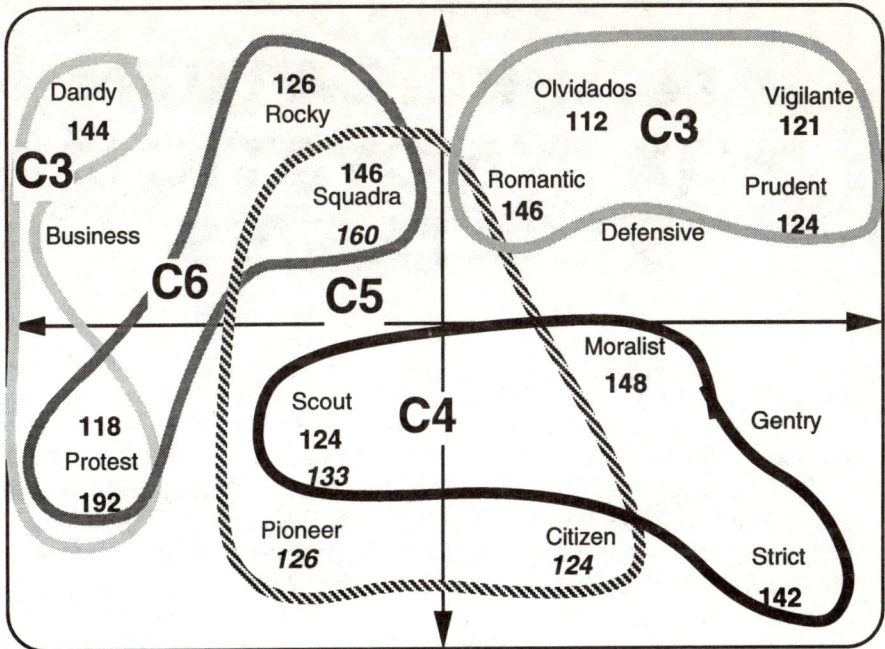

Source: Secodip France

© cca 1989

Figure 9.10   Consumers of brands of washing liquid

CHAPTER 10

AN APPLICATION FOR INNOVATION STRATEGIES

Innovation is one of the major prerequisites for business success in all sectors, but it is neither easy nor obvious. To innovate at the wrong moment — too early or too late — can lead to failure. In order to choose the right time we need to understand the cycles of fashion, trends which re-emerge periodically, attitudes and behaviour within a society which have a greater or lesser impact over a longer or shorter period.

To innovate in isolation is to run the risk of not innovating at all. To innovate effectively we need to be able to X-ray the chessboard of competitors, identify their strengths and weaknesses, and define very precisely the niche in which innovation could find a place without becoming a 'me too' product.

To innovate in a generic way is to run the risk of being ignored. In order to innovate properly we need to know how to identify a precise target of potential customers whose dissatisfaction with existing products we can cater for or whose evolving needs and lifestyles we can match.

To innovate in a laboratory is not to innovate at all. To move from an innovatory technique to a new product we have to know how to transform the innovation of the producer into an innovation perceptible to the consumer. It is necessary to keep the appearance of a product and its packaging, the introduction of a new service, advertising, sales promotion and distribution in step with the innovation and tailor them precisely to the potential client being targeted. Socio-styles studies can meet all these objectives:

❑ by identifying and measuring general socio-cultural trends in society and the dynamic evolutionary trends in consumption in a market — the social winds;

❑ by analyzing the respective competitive positions of products or services and their brands according to the most suitable consumer profiles; the socio-styles map pictures the forces that are lined up and their territories;

❑ by segmenting the general population into a typology of socio-styles in varied lifestyle portraits and segmenting each market into socio-targets of consumers with different tastes and forms of behaviour — a gallery of target portraits;

❑ by identifying the most suitable types of marketing plans for sales and communications in order to be able to achieve a position in each niche and reach each consumer profile.

All this information is available from the databank of socio-styles studies and is easily accessed using visual maps. These data enable us to build an innovation strategy step by step by successive choices of the best concept for the best market niche.

Users of the socio-styles system find in its unique databank all the information necessary for strategic and tactical reviews presented in 10 stages in the same graphic and intellectual format — the same unique ordnance survey map of society and the market *vis-à-vis* its portrait gallery of potential customers. They can:

❑ firstly, identify and study the correlations of motivations for change in this sector and the surrounding socio-cultural trends which encourage them, in order to define potential innovation niches;

❑ secondly, analyze the value of these niches, their product concepts and consumer profiles in terms of social dynamics, quantity and quality of the potential customer base, in order to choose one of the niches as a strategic terrain for innovation;

❑ finally, select the constituent elements of a marketing strategy to launch a new product: packaging, sales and promotion, image and publicity.

STAGE 1: INVENTORY AND ANALYSIS OF THE MOTIVATIONS FOR CHANGE IN THE MARKET

An initial broad study of opportunities for innovation in the market involves drawing up a checklist of different aspirations for change among consumers:

❑ negatively these aspirations can be produced by dissatisfaction with current products or services, in either technical or image terms;

❑ positively they may also be made up of motivations, utilitarian needs, or more or less realistic psychological desires which the current offering does not meet.

Classical quantitative marketing studies are too static and behavioural to meet this objective. Motivation studies carried out on small samples do not always manage to draw up a complete range of these opportunities in all their variety. Socio-styles polls devised specifically for analyzing both current behaviour and dynamic trends enable us to identify these aspirations for innovation in all markets.

We might be trying to identify for a particular sector the need for change and which people it occurs among. In each sector of the socio-styles databank devoted to a specific market or sector the user finds a map which synthesizes aspirations either in the form of psychological motivations or in the more concrete form of ideal or new products:

❑ On the map the user can immediately draw up a list of a variety of motivating innovations. Since the socio-styles study interrogates all consumer profiles it offers a broader range of concepts.

❑ On the map each of the motivating concepts is mathematically placed at the centre of gravity of a cluster of the potential customers it attracts. The socio-styles databank does not only draw up a list of a number of motivating concepts but immediately describes the consumer that will be most responsive to them. We only have to read the socio-cultural and commercial portrait in order to understand the essential characteristics of the potential consumer target.

❑ In addition, we only have to observe the position on the map of each of these concepts in order to quickly understand whether it is very specific to one, possibly marginal, population, or whether it is a mass concept on which people are in agreement.

❑ The same map reading of the respective positions of motivating concepts enables us to identify related motivations which are active in the same customer groups and which could be combined into a single product (eg motivations D, E and F in figure 10.1). On the other hand we can also see which motivating concepts placed at the opposite ends of the map are antagonistic and cannot in any way be combined or which target a single customer group (eg concepts F and B in figure 10.1).

This first stage of innovation research can be considered as opening the mind to a variety of motivations for change specific to this market whose variety, correlations and oppositions we can observe and whose potential consumer profiles we can already identify.

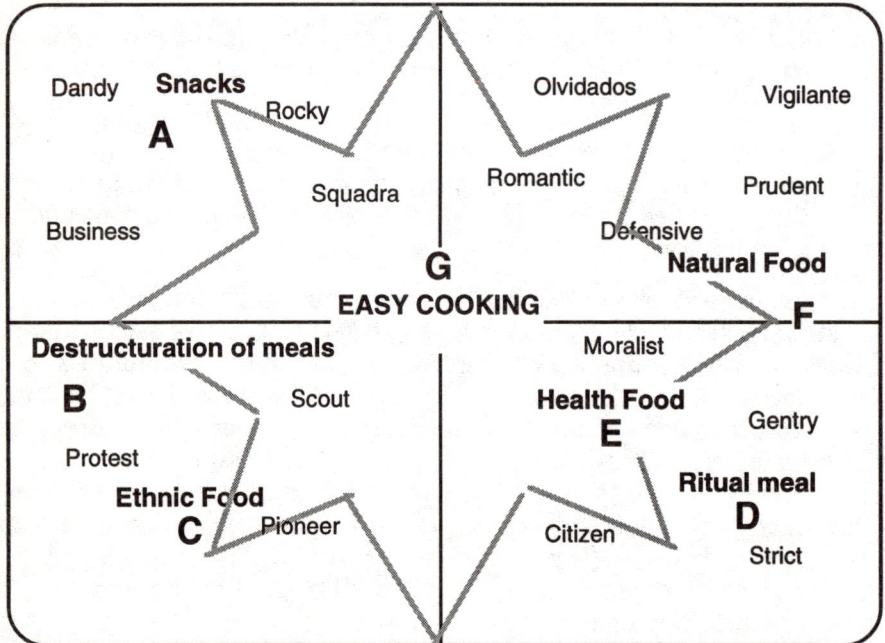

Source: Euro-Socio-Styles   © CCA 1989

Figure 10.1   Compass map of motivating trends

Reading this map therefore enables us to:

❑ measure the coefficient of attraction of a particular innovation concept for the whole sample;
❑ determine in which socio-styles family the motivation coefficient is more or less above or below average.

Certain concepts can be eliminated at this stage:

❑ either because they penetrate the whole population and the potentially interested socio-styles with too low a percentage (eg in relation to mass-market objectives;
❑ or because they reach socio-styles whose profiles are too diverse and contradictory, or types which are too specific and marginal for the organization's particular objectives.

STAGE 2: VALUE ANALYSIS OF MOTIVATING CONCEPTS IN TERMS OF SOCIO-CULTURAL DYNAMISM

It is not sufficient to identify aspirations for innovation in a given market. No market enjoys complete sovereignty and all sectors are increasingly interrelated and influence one another. In particular, all markets are influenced by socio-waves, the social winds that travel through society and influence in a general way the evolution of attitudes and customs. A market may be ahead of or behind the general evolution of society. Innovation will be more or less difficult according to whether it is encouraged by the social climate or constrained by it.

Classical market studies do not meet this objective because they focus on the behaviour and attitudes of the market studied and neglect to analyze the prevailing trends from other sectors and from the general sociological environment. Because the socio-styles system is both a socio-cultural and a market study, we can evaluate the relative interest in innovation concepts in various sectors in the light of general trends in the evolution of attitudes.

An innovation may be launched confident of a motivation for change in its particular sector, but then be held back in its development or appearance or become obsolete too early because the general socio-cultural trends which define the social climate are unfavourable or even opposed to it.

It is in the interest of all innovators to verify whether the opportunities for dynamic innovation in their own market are the same in society as a whole:

❑ If the answer is 'yes', the chances of success will be improved by a social climate universally favourable to the innovation. If the socio-cultural trend is already sufficiently established and widespread, the chances of introducing the innovation to a mass custom base will be increased; and if the prevailing environmental trend is still growing the chances of remaining fashionable will also increase.
❑ If the answer is 'no' and the motivation peculiar to this market

contradicts the main evolutionary trends in the lifestyles environment, this does not mean failure for the innovation. However, its launch will be made more difficult, since it is at odds with the general climate of ideas its mass distribution will be limited and it will run the risk of appearing old-fashioned or too advanced in comparison with current lifestyles and consumption. It is therefore up to the communication strategist to adjust the image of this innovation to make it acceptable within the environment.

The socio-styles databank offers each user information about prevailing and receding socio-waves in attitudes. It is concerned with socio-dynamic flows — social winds that sweep over society influencing the whole body of society more or less in all sectors. This does not mean that all individuals rally to it, but that it is a sort of socio-cultural common denominator to which a majority of the population tends to rally and which appears as the norm for a time.

The socio-cultural compass depicts the range of these trends; the symbol of this compass chart shows which trends are blowing in the same direction and which are in opposition. For example, in Europe today, as in the USA, the main trends can be defined as follows:

❑ a trend towards conservatism, a search for security and comfort, for guarantees and assistance, for tradition, wisdom and experience, and for nature;
❑ a trend towards rigour, which encourages the search for quality and reliability, for seriousness and professionalism, for cultural values and not only technological or economic ones, and for the establishment of secure values.

At this second stage of research it is possible for the user to eliminate some innovation concepts which appear excessively penalized by their lack of correlation with the dominant socio-cultural developments. However, the most prudent step is to note and weigh up the relative interest in different potential innovation concepts according to how much socio-cultural trends help them.

STAGE 3: DEFINITION OF INNOVATION NICHES BY A TREND MIX

The trends to be considered in defining a new product in a given market cannot be summed up in a single motivation or a single need. More often there is a set of converging needs active in the same customer profile that will assure lasting and solid success for a new product by defining several complementary and adjacent functions for it. The range of motivations and analysis of their correlations offered by the socio-styles databank enable us to consider syntheses of motivations for combination in a single product.

Innovation in a sector should not be based exclusively on the trends and needs of this market; it will be more sound if it is also based on trends in adjacent markets or sectors.

Due to the multi-sectorial character of socio-styles studies, the databank offers the opportunity to research other markets to see if trends are appearing that are likely to slow down or accentuate the needs observed in the original market. Innovation in marketing can no longer be isolated from socio-waves — socio-cultural trends which affect all ways of life and attitudes, whether social, cultural or political. A specific feature of socio-style studies and the databank is that it can analyze sociology and marketing, culture and commerce at the same time. In this way users can detect a number of general socio-cultural trends and observe how they combine with the trends specific to their own market and adjacent markets that influence it.

By comparative observation of these different innovatory market trends, the adjacent markets which exert an influence, the general socio-cultural background which defines the environmental climate, we can extract mixes of trends and motivations which constitute innovation niches that are stronger, more abundant and durable, since they are supported by a set of needs and trends.

The task of seeking convergence between motivations and trends in different sectors is made possible by the richness of socio-styles surveys and databanks. It is an intellectual task of synthesis which can be done by:

❑ the user by searching through different sectors of the databank;
❑ CCA marketing consultants and their partners;
❑ expert artificial intelligence systems which undertake systematic research into converging trends starting from an innovation hypothesis.

When this is done, the user can call on the socio-styles databank to carry out a value analysis of potential innovation niches with the aim of choosing one of them.

STAGE 4: VALUE ANALYSIS OF POTENTIAL TARGET CUSTOMER GROUPS

Quantitative analysis

This attempts to answer the question of how many will be interested. Depending on company strategy and the general opportunities offered by the economic circumstances, it may be more or less attractive:

❑ to target a small customer niche with a higher spending capacity for a new product with considerable added value in terms of use or image;
❑ to aim to become established in a much broader mass market with a compromise product and image.

For the second aim it is particularly important to appreciate the potential size of the population to be targeted.

Without resembling a sales forecast, the socio-style studies and databanks allow us to make an initial qualitative approach to a population segment that is clearly driven by motivations and trends that the new product ought to embody. For this it is sufficient to consult the sociological weighting (expressed in percentages of the general population) of each socio-style correlated with an innovation niche. This percentage appears at the top of each socio-style portrait in the basic socio-cultural background report.

This initial assessment of volume can be carried out on a market by variable geometry according to the company's area of activity:

❑ on the European market as a whole or the American market;
❑ on a national market (from the 15 available);
❑ on a region (from among 58 regions of Europe or the West Indies);
❑ on a composite market of several regions or countries;
❑ in each of these geographic groups, on the whole population or on a particular sub-group.

As a result of this stage a new evaluation of potential innovation niches can be carried out. We can add to the earlier socio-cultural score a potential market volume score.

Qualitative analysis

This attempts to answer the question of who will be attracted to this. Whether the company strategy is systematically oriented towards small niches of elitist or very specialized consumers or towards broad mass markets, it is essential to evaluate the profile of the target that the concept interests. On one hand, this consumer profile indicates the quality of the first consumers who will pioneer this innovation because of their buying power, openness to innovation or loyalty. It is a way of evaluating in advance whether the innovation is going to start off on firm, fertile ground, on shifting sands or in an economically arid desert.

On the other hand, the profile of the initial potential customer base will be valuable as an example to other customers and as an image for the product and brand. Classical market and motivation studies rarely provide this type of information. It is often necessary to wait for the first market tests to evaluate the profile of the initial customer group and analyze the value of its image.

The socio-styles studies and databanks enable this to be appreciated in advance because of the richness of the lifestyle and mentality portraits they contain. It is sufficient to read the socio-cultural and socio-commercial portrait (in the basic report) of each of the socio-styles affected by an innovation niche to have a precise and detailed idea of the personality of these potential customers. Another simpler and quicker way is to refer to the portraits of customer segments (socio-targets) defined in the specialized reports for each market. However, these reports are more specifically commercial and need to be supplemented by the socio-styles portrait in the areas of psychology and ways of life.

These portraits (which can be thoroughly investigated with the basic socio-cultural report) enable the socio-styles user to score and rank potential innovation niches according to the quality of potential customer groups — a quality that can only be judged relative to criteria specific to an organization and not in absolute terms.

STAGE 5: CHOICE OF A POTENTIAL INNOVATION NICHE SYNTHESIZED WITH VALUE ANALYSES

This value analysis may be extended to other variables, all of which are available to users in the basic reports of the socio-styles databank. When these multiple value analyses are completed, the user can choose one of the potential innovation niches.

Basically this choice is the responsibility of users/decision makers who have to integrate the objectives and constraints peculiar to their organization and its practices. However, they can be assisted by socio-styles consultants and can also use an expert artificial intelligence system which computerizes the choice.

The socio-styles system does not impose a solution. This is the result of a choice arrived at by the company decision maker from market and environmental data provided by the socio-styles databank on the one hand, and from the objectives and internal constraints peculiar to the organization on the other.

When this strategic choice has been made, the socio-styles user has:

❑ an innovation niche whose position on the map will enable the competition to be analyzed;
❑ an innovation concept, the synthesis of a whole range of sector-based and environmental motivations and trends;
❑ a portrait of the consumer target whose statistical weighting is known (in 15 countries and 80 regions of Europe) and whose demographic and economic portrait is known, as a complete socio-cultural, psychological and behavioural portrait in the food category and all other lifestyle areas.

When the strategic research phase is finished the tactical operations phase can begin. The socio-styles databank provides further practical information in order to transform this innovation concept into a new product which is as acceptable as possible to customers.

STAGE 6: MOVING FROM THE CONCEPT TO THE PRODUCT

In the socio-styles system market surveys study the attraction of different consumer profiles to product or service concepts, their physical form, realization, design and appearance.

Realization is very important in an innovation strategy, since it influences how the new product is subjectively perceived:

❏ if its appearance is too innovatory, it may shock by its excess; if it is too classical, the innovation may be imperceptible;
❏ if the form of the innovation is expressed in ways that are alien or even intolerable to the target consumer, a motivating innovation concept may sometimes become a repellent new product;
❏ if, in contrast, the perceptible way a product is realized or the introduction of a service suit the customer's world, they may make a new product both familiar and more acceptable, even though the concept was initially alien.

A product's realization has to be regarded as a way of acclimatizing a concept to the society in which it is to take root, to the micro-culture of the consumer target. The presentation of a product plays an integral part in the act of innovation.

STAGE 7: MOVING FROM THE PRODUCT TO THE PACKAGING

The packaging, wrapping, labelling, brand and all the physical attributes of product presentation (and similarly the production, décor, location and personal service style) are the logical extension of the product's physical appearance. They have to express the innovation and also be the interface acclimatizing a new product to the civilization and micro-culture of a consumer target.

For certain markets (eg food, drink, beauty products) the socio-styles databanks study the specific forms of packaging consumers prefer. More generally a whole range of information is available about the aesthetic feelings, tastes in design, labelling and image of all the socio-styles. The user can therefore draw an identikit portrait of the packaging concept that is most suitable for expressing both the innovation of a product and acclimatization to the lifestyle of a population. It is then the task of the creative professionals to move from this presentation concept to a real model which is both artistic and promotional.

STAGE 8: MOVING FROM THE FACTORY TO THE MARKET-PLACE

Obviously the choice of distribution networks only partly comes into the analysis of consumers and socio-cultural trends. It is often defined by what already exists within the firm, as well as by constraints and contractual obligations. However, it is important to discover the most effective distribution networks possible in order to reach the target consumers in the innovation niche.

There are three reasons for this:

- ❏ to reach these consumers in the shops they patronize most often;
- ❏ to reach them in a commercial venue with which they are familiar and which brings added value to the new product by relieving pressures and anxieties;
- ❏ to enable the image of the new brand to benefit from the image of a distribution outlet liked by consumers.

A particularly important stage in socio-styles surveys and an entire databank are devoted to the types of distribution preferred by consumer profiles, to the purchasing behaviour of each socio-style and its decision making style; to the most successful types of promotions and commercial campaigns with regard to the typology.

STAGE 9: MOVING FROM THE SALES NETWORK TO THE MEDIA

In the operational implementation of an innovation at the time of the product launch or its settling-in period, the choice of media, public relations or simple communication is crucial:

- ❏ to target precisely and without loss the pioneer target consumers that have been chosen;
- ❏ to make use of the value-added image that the media can confer on the new brand both in terms of prestige and credibility for the target population.

Traditional market studies — new product tests — do not usually provide this kind of information. And when a particular psycho-sociological profile has been defined as a consumer target, traditional media-planning studies that can only describe audiences in socio-demographic and economic terms do not offer sufficient information.

The socio-styles databanks enable us to make a strategic choice of media and communication support in a more coherent manner. The audiences and also the motivating images and functions of the media are analyzed according to socio-styles typology, and by country and region in the case of continental studies.

The socio-styles system user can call on a specialist databank on the media which offers information at several levels of detail. The choice of a general communication strategy using the media, then the selection of radio and television channels, then the choice of schedules and locations, develops progressively as we go into greater detail.

STAGE 10: MOVING FROM THE PRODUCT CONCEPT TO THE IMAGE MESSAGE

The success of an innovation strategy can be linked to technical originality, to the quality in use of a product or service, and also very broadly to the perception by the target public of an image stimulating in its novelty and reassuring in its closeness to their lifestyle. The whole strategy of communication, from the physical representation of the product to its packaging, from commercial promotion to visual advertising, must facilitate the take-up of a new product by its target public.

Often communication, advertising, public relations, sponsorship and the launch operation are left entirely to the creative people, to the whim of fashion or artistic temperaments whose understanding of the tastes of the target public is often haphazard. At other times we trust the brutal verdict of impact and memory tests. Rarely do market studies take time to analyze the words and images that make up the mental culture of consumer segments.

Socio-styles studies devote a large number of questions to the graphic and aesthetic sensitivities of consumers in order to understand:

❑ which of the socio-styles like and dislike publicity and therefore with which ones it is possible to communicate in an overtly commercial way;
❑ which general communication procedure is most easily accepted (eg advertising or public relations, sponsorship, packaging and design);
❑ which general tone of message is most acceptable (eg humour or seriousness, warmth or coolness, poetry or technology) and more precisely which forms of expression are regarded as most natural by each of the socio-styles and therefore by each of the market niches (eg colour, space, movement, layout);
❑ which general themes are in step with motivations (eg adventure, everyday usefulness, charm).

The socio-styles system user in each country can thus seek on the synthetic maps and more detailed mini-maps 'the communication culture of a population'. This analysis obviously does not automatically ensure the right advertising and in no way limits professional creativity. It merely offers a more precise context and objective.

Numerous maps are devoted to various forms of communication. For those responsible for the image and communication of new products, for their designers and advertising people, they constitute a reference library.

Thus in ten stages the socio-styles system has enabled us to move from a simple innovation intention to a complete marketing launch plan.

EXAMPLE: PLANNING A NEW FOOD PRODUCT FOR EUROPE

Theoretical case

Let us imagine a large company in the food sector which intends to innovate in the ready-cooked food sub-sector.

The objective is the European market. The differences in taste are such that the aim of the research is to define the architecture of the new product (concept, presentation, packaging, communication and target) on which recipes for local and national dishes will then be modelled.

The reference databank is therefore Euro-socio-styles (see figure 10.2).*

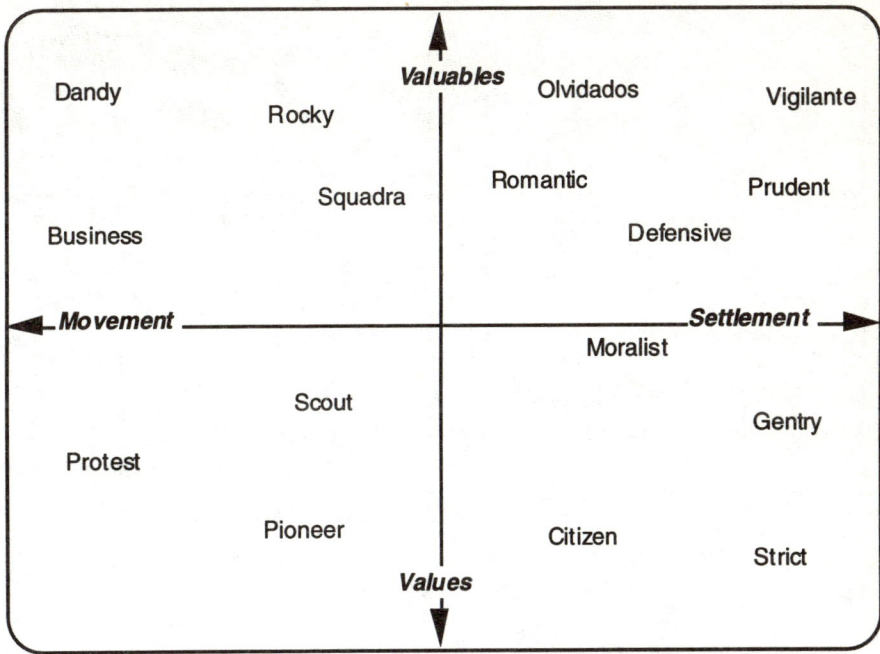

Figure 10.2   Basic socio-styles map for the European market

Inventory of motivations for innovation

In the sector on food in the Euro-socio-bank the synthetic map of motivations reveals seven trend cores for innovation still insufficiently satisfied. Several mini-maps enable us to observe the profile of the population attracted to each concept. For example, in figure 10.3 traditional cooking has a greater attraction for socio-styles in the south-east of the map.

The synthetic compass/map of motivative trend (figure 10.1) shows the spread of these concepts over the socio-styles chessboard. Here we see that:

❏   concept G (at the centre of the map and therefore the centre of gravity) is the most uniting for all populations;
❏   concept E in the south-east quadrant only partly unites a group of conservative and rigorous consumers;
❏   concept C in the extreme south-east corner, like concept A in the extreme north-west corner, is very radical and therefore relatively marginal, attracting only a few extreme socio-styles.

* NB The information on these maps is incomplete and not suitable for professional use.

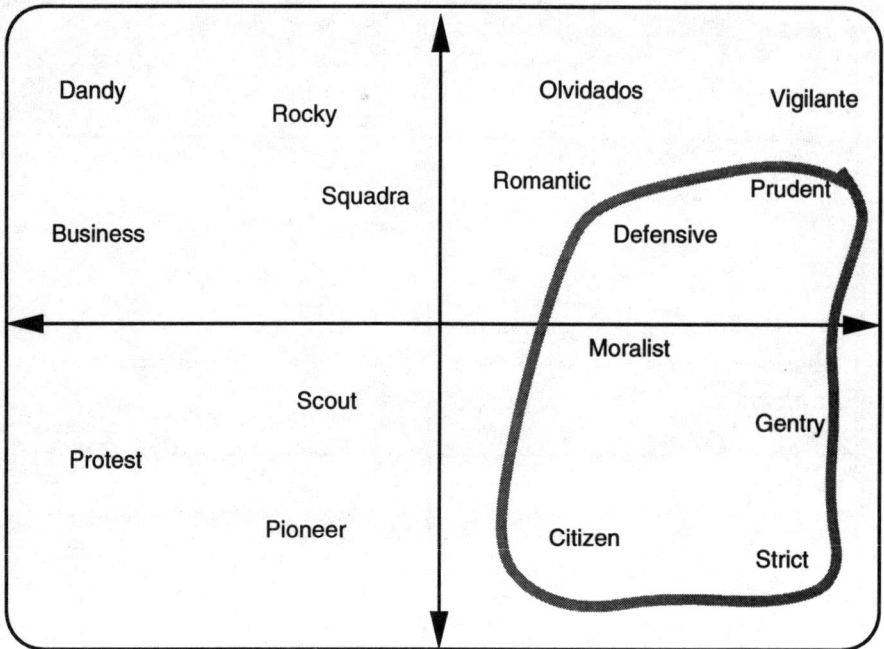

Figure 10.3   Target attracted by traditional cooking

Value analysis

By placing the socio-compass over the motivation map the sector-based trends can be compared with the general socio-cultural trends in the environment.

In figure 10.4 we see that:

❑ the motivating concepts in the food sector (A and B), if they effectively exist, are currently in opposition to the major trends that incorporate evolutions in attitudes. This does not mean that these cores of innovation should be neglected. However, to innovate using these concepts will become more difficult than before, since the general social climate of attitudes will be less spontaneously favourable to them. Even if these trends correspond to material needs linked to a new behavioural influence, their use will be less psychologically comfortable for consumers;

❑ the motivating concept C, in contrast, is encouraged by the socio-cultural trend 'rigour' which reaches the same consumer profiles;

❑ the same holds true for the innovation concept F encouraged by the socio-cultural trend 'conservatism';

❑ concepts D and E are the ones that are helped most by the general majority evolution in attitudes, because they benefit both from the trend to 'conservatism' and the trend to 'rigour'.

❑ concept G is neutral according to these trends.

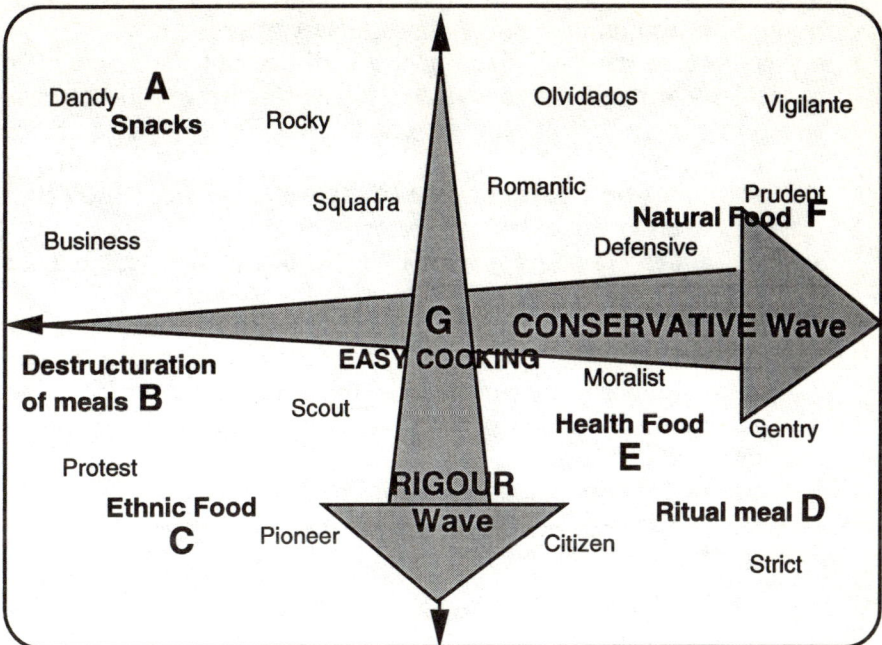

Source: Euro-Socio-Styles   © CCA & Europanel 1989

Figure 10.4   Integration map of socio-cultural trends

At this stage motivations A and B, long considered as portents of the future, are currently less included in developing attitudes.

Defining innovation niches

The synthesis of sector-based trends and general socio-cultural trends, and their correlation on the socio-map, draws together groups. Figure 10.5 indicates three innovation niches defined as sets of trends observed in several sectors among the most important group of niches revealed by the European socio-styles study:

❑   A first niche in the north-west of the map attracts principally socio-styles 7, 8, 9 and 10 (and to a lesser extent 6 and 7) to a general concept of prepared fast food dishes which can be nibbled or eaten without cutlery, without a table, by oneself at any time and while doing something else. This niche results from the convergence of sector-based trend A towards nibbling and sector-based trend B towards unstructured meals. It also reflects a trend towards less household and culinary equipment in the kitchen (taken from the household goods sector), towards working non-stop through the day (taken from the work sector), towards celibacy, towards the destruction of the family unit, towards autonomy in the lifestyle and rhythm of marriage partners and children (observed in the sector on private and family life) and socio-cultural trends towards imitation of the American way of life.

❑ A second niche can be defined in the south-west of the map which is particularly attractive to socio-style 11 (and to a lesser extent types 10 and 12) based on the concept of exotic fast food. This niche can be seen as a convergence of:

— a trend to try out exotic food and a trend towards unstructured meals (both observed in the food sector);

— a general socio-cultural trend towards open-mindedness, tolerance and curiosity regarding the outside world and its cultures;

— a trend towards less household and culinary equipment (household goods sector);

— an anti-conformist trend towards surprising others;

— a general trend towards innovation (in the general lifestyle description);

— and a pronounced and dynamic trend towards rigour which is expressed particularly among these socio-styles by a concern to find the inner truth of other civilizations.

All these trends influence the socio-styles of this niche.

❑ A third potential innovation niche can be defined in the south-east of the map including socio-styles 14, 15 and 16 (as well as 2, 12 and 13 to a lesser extent). They are attracted by the concept of traditional dishes with simplified preparation. This niche results from the convergence of several trends with various origins:

— trend D towards eating in a ritual manner at set hours as a family with select guests and not while engaged on any other activity;

— trend E towards healthy, nutritious food;

— trend F towards natural food;

— trend G towards simplifying preparation and cooking;

— a trend towards overequipping the household — in particular the kitchen (analyzed in the household goods sector);

— a trend towards reinforcing the family structure and its moments of togetherness (sector on private life);

— above all, the most pronounced and dynamic of all current socio-cultural trends towards conservatism, traditionalism, respect for past experience and another socio-cultural trend towards rigour which favours simplicity.

All these trends are active in this group of socio-styles and converge in the south-east region of the map.

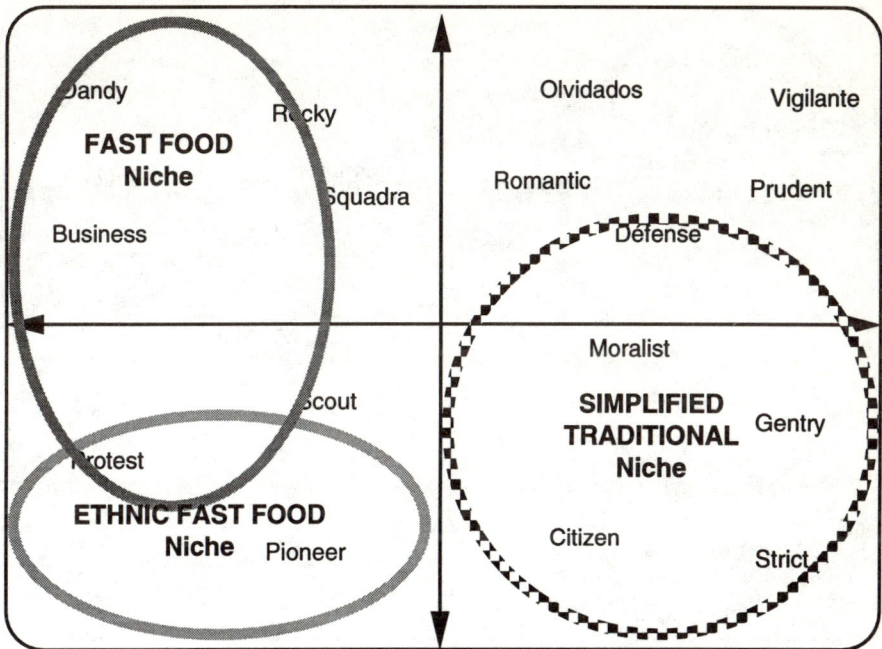

Figure 10.5   Identification map of potential innovation niches

Value analysis of target consumers

Quantitative analysis

In this example the map in figure 10.6 enables us to appreciate rapidly the following points:

❏   In order to innovate with a mass strategy for the whole European market, the fast food niche (oriented towards socio-styles in the north-west of the map) and the simplified traditional cuisine niche (oriented towards socio-styles in the south-west), while diametrically opposite, offer practically the same quantitative opportunities of potential customer volume. Yet there remain potential minority markets; indeed, the same study shows the overwhelming European attachment to traditional cuisine. In contrast, the exotic fast food innovation niche seems to represent only a distinct minority of the mass market.

❏   If the company's strategy is to concentrate more on the national dimension, the examples presented here would suggest that the fast food niche would be more profitable in Great Britain, for example.

❏   If the company's strategy is international in nature but at the same time highly segmental, this analysis reveals clearly that the fast food niche can be potentially more successful in capitals and large cities. For the prepared food market the same is true, though to a lesser extent, of the exotic fast food niche.

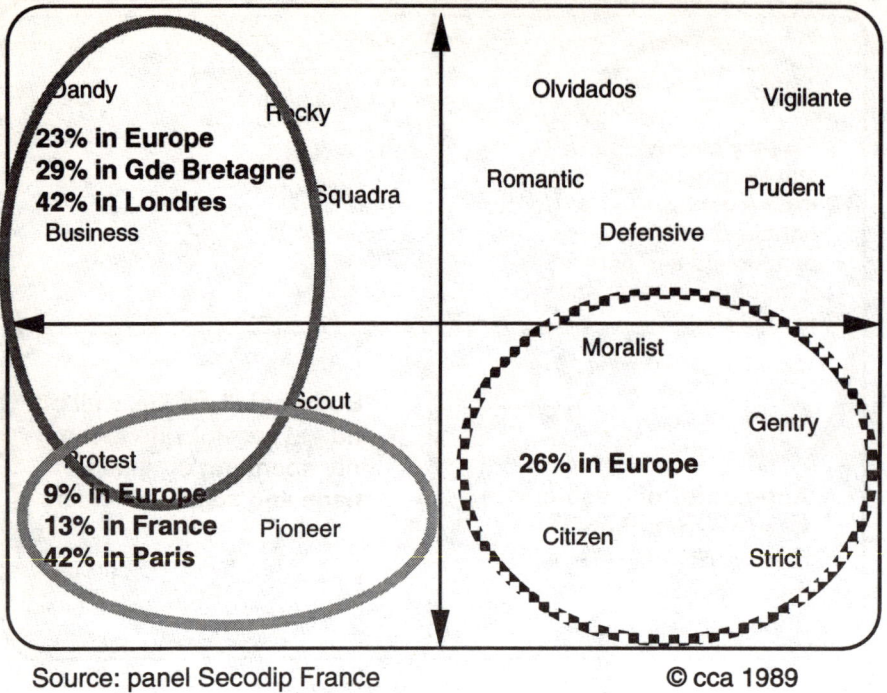

Dandy
Rocky
23% in Europe
29% in Gde Bretagne
42% in Londres
Squadra
Business

Olvidados
Vigilante
Romantic
Prudent
Defensive

Moralist

Scout

Protest
9% in Europe
13% in France
42% in Paris
Pioneer

Gentry

26% in Europe

Citizen
Strict

Source: panel Secodip France   © cca 1989

Figure 10.6   Evaluation map of consumer volumes in niches

Qualitative analysis

A profile analysis is even more important (see figure 10.7):

❑ We can see that the niche in the north-west of the map attracts in particular 'yuppie' socio-styles who are well off and educated, dynamic and
modern executives, and therefore opinion leaders, prestigious and valuable for a product or brand in its launch phase. These people are big
spenders and therefore likely to pay highly for products with high added
value; but their expenditure today is directed towards holidays and
travel, culture and leisure, beauty and clothing, dinner parties and
lunch parties at restaurants or at home rather than towards everyday
utilitarian food. They are thus consumers of exceptional rather than
normal products.

❑ In contrast, we can see that the niche in the south-east attracts more
especially a profile of middle-class socio-styles who are also well off and
educated, leaders of opinion and prestigious, but in a classical, traditional, establishment manner. They are not spenders but prudent
investors, capable of spending a lot but only on condition that the
investment is secure. This makes them extremely demanding
consumers with regard to technical and commercial services as well as
quality image.

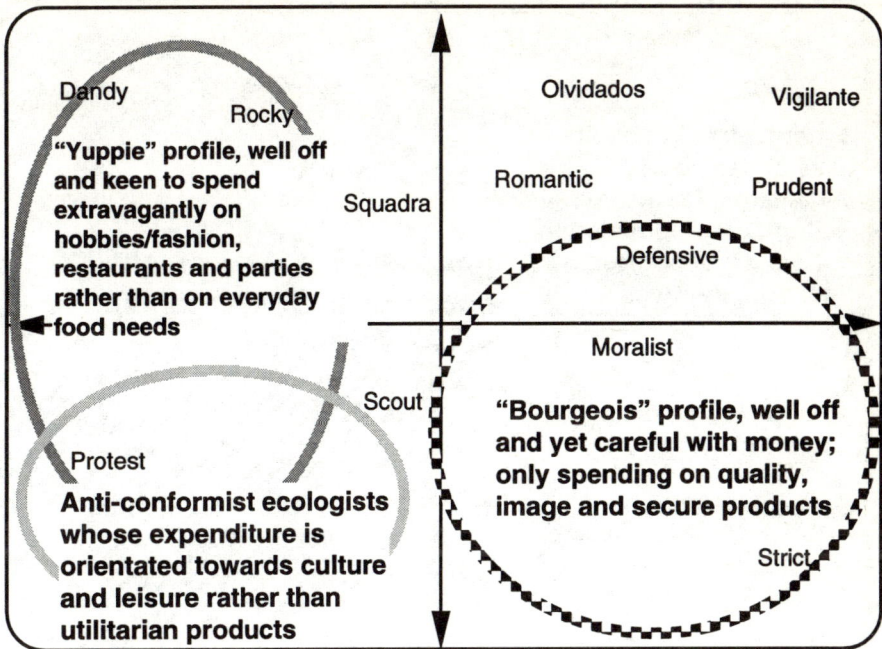

Figure 10.7   Analytical map of socio-cultural profiles of consumers

❑   We can see that the niche in the south-west offers a greater opportunity
    to develop an innovation directed towards anti-conformist consumers
    who are original, modernist and convinced ecologists and more difficult
    to seduce with industrial products. Their expenditure today is oriented
    more towards culture and leisure; any food product with a strictly utili-
    tarian connotation would be penalized.

Choice of a niche or target

In the example given here, let us imagine that the company has decided to
concentrate on the mass market (rather than on a specific minority customer group that is marginal) and also well-off, educated consumers. This is
a minimum risk strategy which eliminates opportunities for innovation
which would not be supported by a prevailing socio-cultural trend shared by
a majority of people. We can imagine that the choice will fall on the potential
innovation niche in the south-east, which is centred on a new product concept of easily prepared traditional cuisine and aimed primarily at socio-styles
14, 15 and 16 and also, to a lesser extent, 12, 13 and 2 (see figure 10.8).

    However, from the same databank and value analysis another company
might have decided to innovate for the niche in the north-west with a fast
food product. This would involve taking the risk of getting less support
from the general socio-currents but wanting to give priority to 'yuppie' customers in large cities with strong buying power and a modernist image.

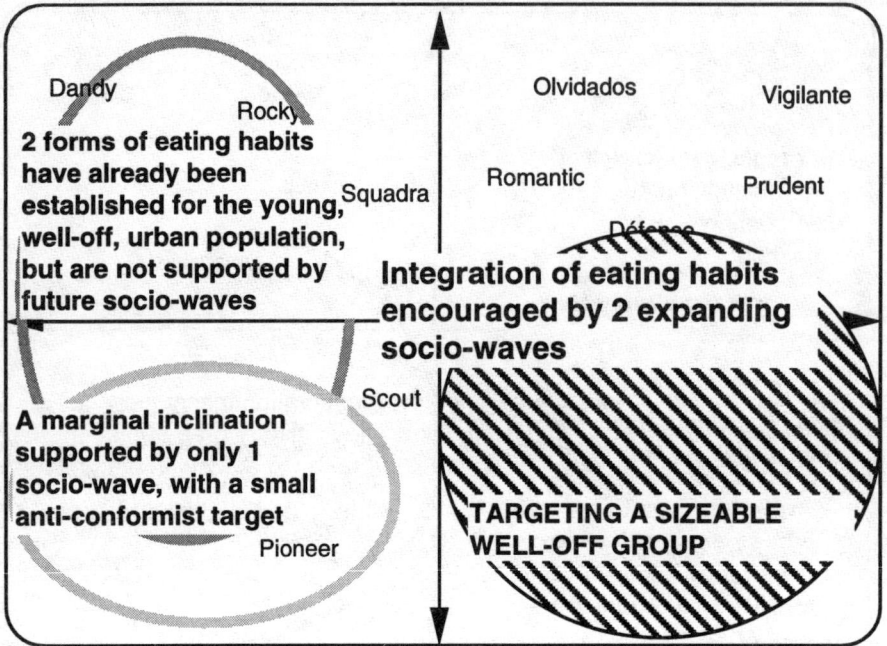

Source: panel Secodip France   © cca 1989

Figure 10.8   Map for evaluation and choice of innovation niches

In the same way, another company might have chosen the niche in the south-west and innovated in the area of exotic fast food despite a small potential volume, deciding that it can make a profit in a small niche with a high added-value product by virtue of its rarity and originality.

From the innovation niche to the product concept

Figure 10.9 summarizes the advice for realizing a new, easy to prepare, traditional cuisine product for the target consumers in the south-eastern niche. In short, it is a mixture of new preservation techniques, extremely simple preparation and natural ingredients prepared according to traditional regional recipes.

This type of information is also available in the databank for all the other socio-styles on the map. The ideal product for the south-eastern niche is prepared and partly pre-cooked, but offers variations and opportunities to add one's own ingredients; for the opposite, north-west niche wholly pre-cooked dishes requiring no preparation or personalization effort would be preferred; and for the other non-innovation niche in the north-west of the map dishes personally prepared at home using raw ingredients are always preferred.

From the product concept to its presentation

Figure 10.10 visualizes for the chosen south-eastern niche the packaging characteristics that are likely to have an impact. In short, it involves mixing

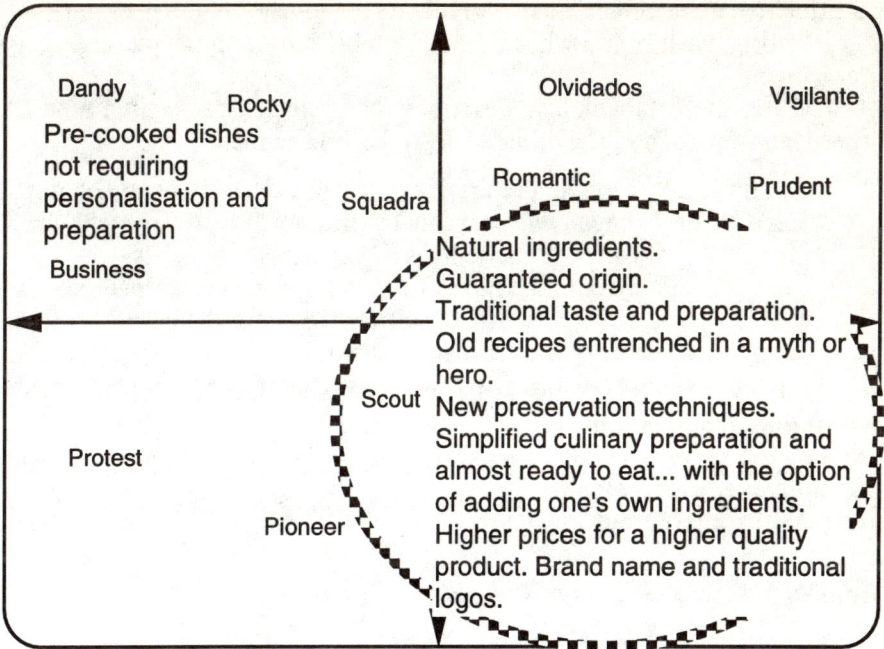

Figure 10.9   Choosing a product type suited to the target

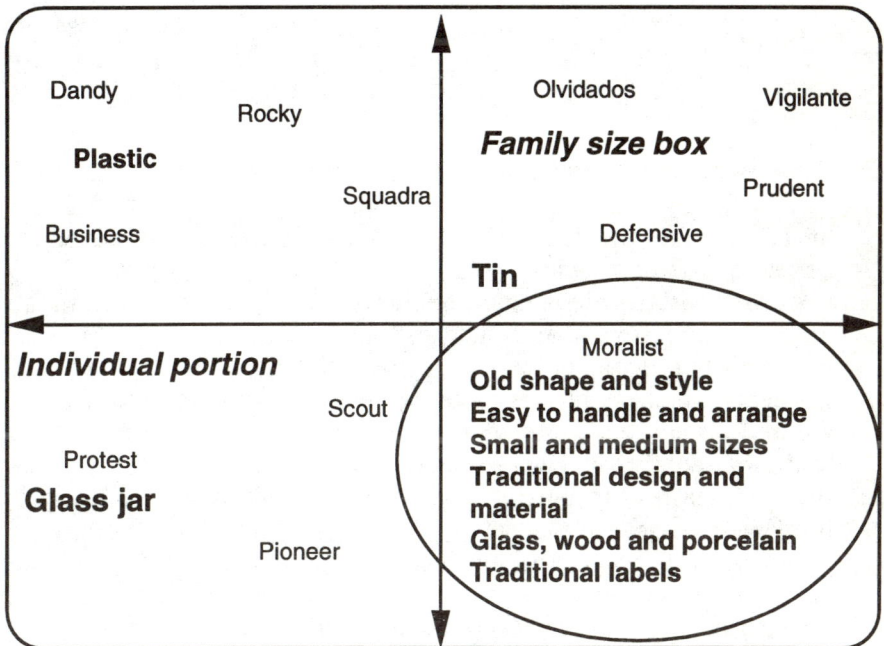

Source: panel Secodip France

Figure 10.10   Choice of packaging preferred by the target

traditional natural, high-class ingredients, a 'folksy' regional brand name and labelling, with high-tech methods, notably of functional packaging and preservation.

However, the databank also describes the preferred packaging, food and other tastes for each of the other socio-styles on the map:

❏ the south-eastern niche prefers glass or pottery containers; the north-eastern niche is happy with cardboard; the north-western niche would prefer plastic; the central niche likes metal cans;

❏ while the socio-styles from the south-eastern niche prefer medium-sized and small packaging, potential customers in the fast food niche in the west are increasingly attracted to individual portions; the more traditional socio-styles in the north-east prefer large family sizes for storage.

Of course, each of these elements can be analyzed in more detail by looking for the mini-map in the databank which describes still more precisely which socio-styles are more likely to prefer food products in glass jars.

From the factory to the market-place

The marketing toolbox provides all the necessary information on the way of reaching each socio-style.

Figure 10.11 shows the major distribution and promotion methods which appear in the socio-styles databank as being the most effective for reaching the south-western consumer niche, and market the concept of easy to prepare, traditional cuisine. We see these strategic choices contrasted with other methods of distribution and promotion which would have been more appropriate for targeting other customer bases and marketing other innovation concepts:

❏ the potential customers in the south-eastern niche can be reached by mail order, by specialist shops or wholesalers in addition to the usual food outlets, for the marketing of cooked and partly prepared food conceived as 'traditional and easy to prepare';

❏ the north-eastern niche opposite shows a tendency to buy from anywhere on impulse and according to the needs of the moment, with no loyalty to a particular outlet;

❏ the central niche, which is motivated mainly by the need for a simple life and discounts, is attracted to supermarkets and hypermarkets as well as warehouses and wholesalers;

❏ the north-eastern niche stays loyal to grocery shops and stores in the immediate neighbourhood;

❏ the targeted group in the south-east of the map appears particularly sensitive to the cleanliness of a shop and its clear layout; to personal service and especially advice; to the general quality of the products and much less to promotions;

❏ the central niche on the map is attracted particularly to special prices and promotions;

❏ the western niche in general is susceptible to the setting, atmosphere and decor, even the luxury of the shop.

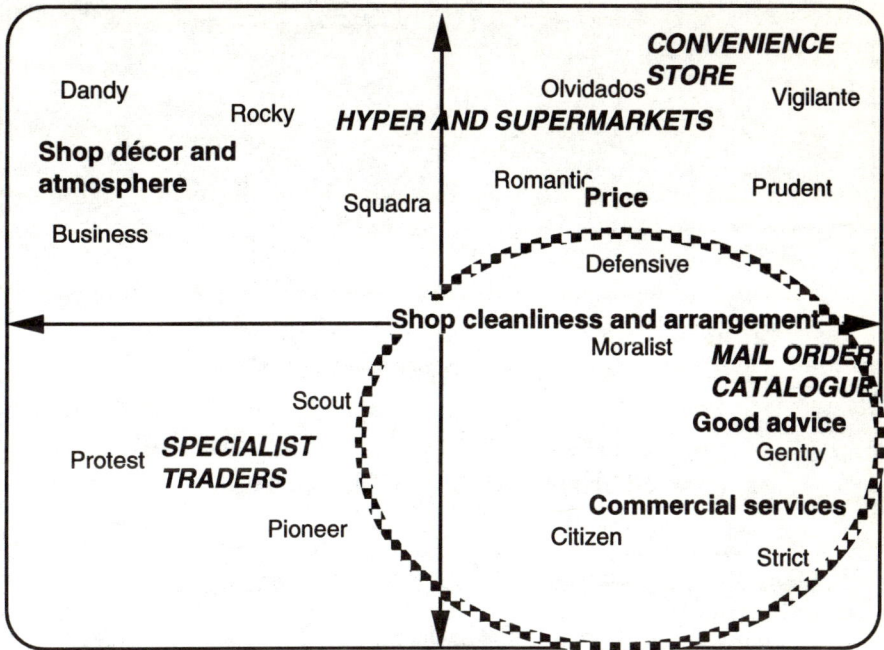

Figure 10.11 Marketing tools orientation map

Media plans

A multi-media, multi-national, multi-regional synthetic map describes in a general way which major press, radio and television types best reach which socio-style profiles and which consumer niches.

Figure 10.12 shows that to reach the target in the south-eastern niche radio seems a good medium, especially stations specializing in information, culture and news programmes. The press is also effective, particularly serious magazines dealing with culture, science, information and ideas. In contrast, television seems rather less effective, except for serious magazine programmes dealing with society, culture or news.

The same analysis shows that if the north-western consumer niche were the strategic objective we would choose television with a schedule of variety programmes, sport and serials as well as magazines devoted to fashion and beauty, sport and leisure. Radio is clearly less effective for reaching this niche, apart from stations specializing in modern music.

Other synthetic maps show the same profile of results, entering into greater detail about all aspects of a particular medium. Others offer the same multi-media choice within a particular country or region. In addition each medium is subjected to particular analysis in a mini-map which

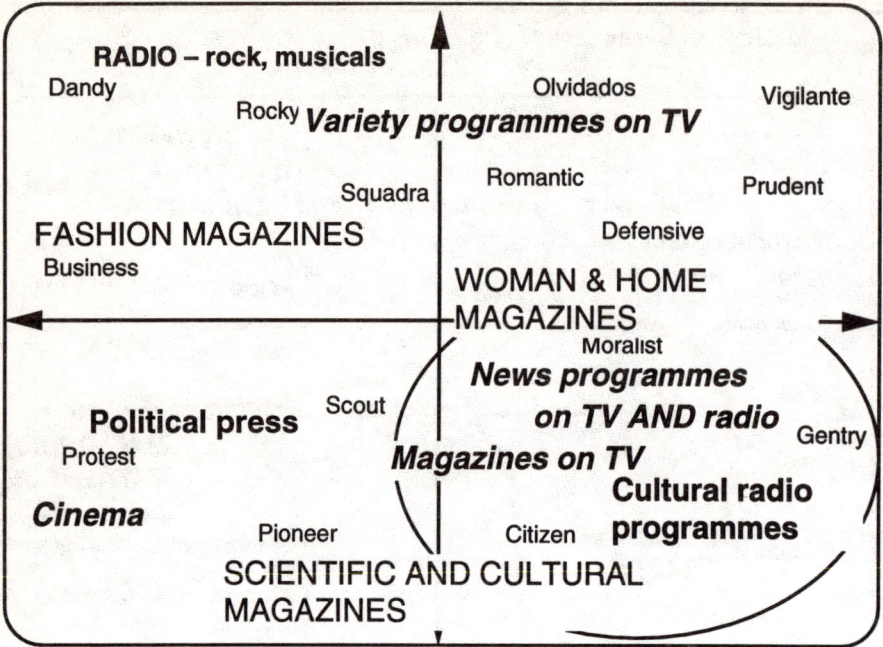

Source: Euro-Socio-Styles   © cca & europanel 1989

Figure 10.12   Choosing the media most likely to reach the target

describes in more detail which socio-styles are above average readers or listeners (figure 10.13).

From the media to the message

Figure 10.14 shows that the socio-styles in the south-eastern niche, chosen as the target in this example, are more attracted by fairly monochrome pictures and sepia tints in subdued light. In contrast audiences from the south-western niche, who also have a taste for monochrome, prefer large-scale artistic works in black and white that are very graphic in construction. The consumers in the north-eastern niche are attracted by gentle pastel colours, while socio-styles from the north-west and centre like technicolor and fluorescent colours.

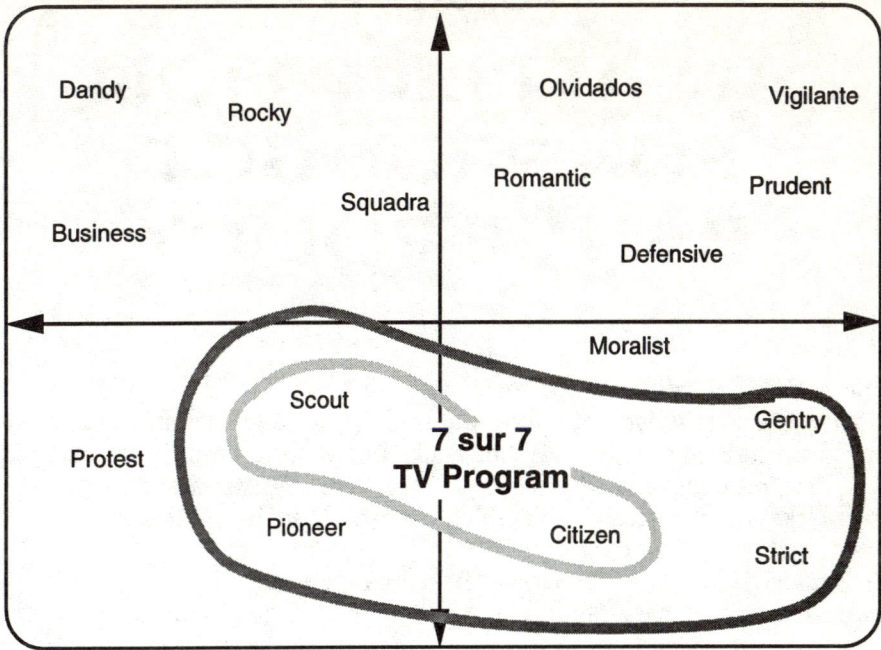

Figure 10.13   Detailed analysis of a media audience

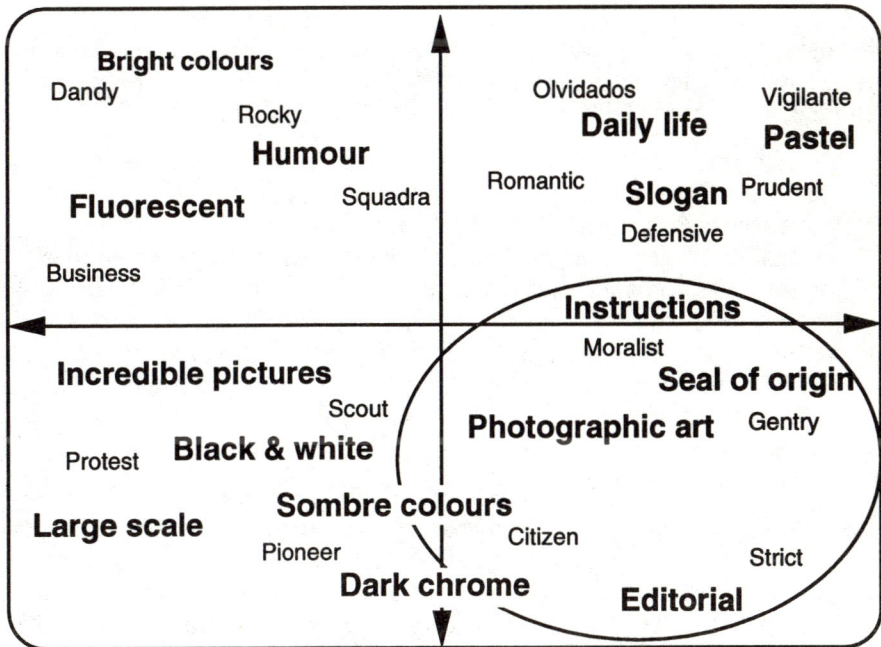

Source: Euro-Socio-Styles   © cca & europanel1989

Figure 10.14   Communication style orientation map

CHAPTER 11

AN APPLICATION FOR PRODUCT RANGE POLICY

One of the applications of the socio-styles system is for firms which are not looking specifically for a new innovation niche, or to reposition an old product in a more competitive way. Instead, they wish to co-ordinate all their activities, products and services in the most effective way in order to cover the market as extensively as possible, to maintain their profits and to secure their position against the opposition.

Similarly, whatever the market, the primary objective is to set up a range of products and services, brands and images, distribution and sales networks with consumer segmentation and market structuring into competitive niches.

STAGE 1: MARKET CHECK-UP

The user can find in each sector-based area of the socio-styles databank numerous maps which summarize different analytical topics. If, for instance, we were studying financial markets we would find:

- ❏ a check-up map of motivations with regard to money which shows the correlation between socio-styles and the psychological and social functions accorded to money that justify profit seeking;
- ❏ a check-up of views held by different socio-styles consumers about banks, insurance and finance companies, in which we can see which consumer profiles have a good or poor image of these professional institutions;
- ❏ a check-up of consumer aspirations and expectations about new services in the financial market, in which we can see which niches are most keen on innovation and of what type;
- ❏ a check-up of existing financial products where we can see contrasted consumers for gold, shares, savings products, etc.

As always, if we go beyond these maps of competitive comparison, each particular product or brand image as well as each motivation or form of behaviour can be studied more specifically by reference to the mini-map on which the consumer profile appears which owns it, does it or desires it more than average and more than all the other socio-styles.

For instance, we can discover in more precise detail which socio-styles are more likely to hold life insurance policies as financial investments. The map reveals clearly that two market niches exist, that they are relatively close as identified by the somewhat conservative and traditionalist profile in the east. Yet they are different: there is one niche of consumers who are more middle class, better off, better educated and more rational in the south-east of the map made up of the 'conservative' socio-style among others; another niche, comprising the 'peaceful' socio-style and others is more modest, less well-educated, but above all attracted by the transformation of money into consumer goods for immediate consumption and enjoyment.

However, this information is merely an analytical and detailed view of the reality of the market. From their general synthesis a global and strategic view can emerge of the niches in the sector, of consumer segments to which we must adapt the range of products, services, marketing and promotion methods.

STAGE 2: MARKET SYNTHESIS

The map of socio-targets is the most complete synthetic document put forward by the socio-styles databank and illustrates all the available information. It offers access to a detailed portrait of motivations and needs, views and preferences, current behaviour and expectations of innovation for each consumer family in its market.

We can clearly see how each socio-target is made up of a group of socio-styles which in this market represent a profile of similar consumption. It is therefore a simplification of the general socio-cultural typology. We have progressed from sixteen socio-styles to five or six segments (figure 11.1).

An evaluation of quantitative consumer potential can be carried out for each segment by adding together the socio-style percentages. (In cases where a socio-style belongs to two socio-targets its percentage can either be counted twice or divided.) This measurement of the size of the potential customer base can be carried out on a global sample, multi-regional samples, or demographic or economic sub-samples (eg young people, housewives, managers).

A more thorough analysis of the value of these socio-targets can be done with reference to the portraits of each of the socio-styles that comprise it: the socio-demographic and economic portraits as well as the socio-cultural ones. These socio-targets are customer segments and also market niches which are described in terms of the products, services and brands that are currently most well-established with these consumers, and also in terms of the product concepts, services or images which are most attractive to them.

A reading of this map and the socio-target portraits attached to it, and later a complementary reading of several socio-styles portraits, enable us to make an inventory of the main positioning opportunities in this market.

This synthetic view can be supplemented at any time by reference to the analytical maps, by simply placing the socio-targets map on any of the other competitive check-up maps or item analysis maps for this market.

It is this opportunity to move between the synthetic information and analytical documents with varying degrees of detail that makes the socio-

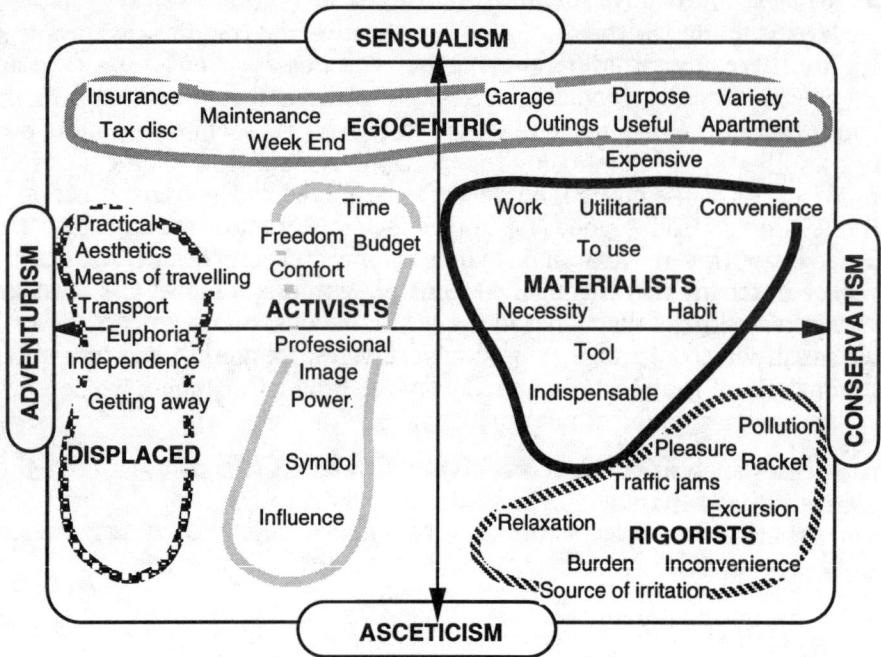

Figure 11.1   Five socio-styles clusters

styles databank so rich and extensive and provides a very flexible tool for the user. Indeed the latter always has a choice: to tackle the market analysis with a synthetic view such as the socio-targets, or with detailed analytical information about the consumer profile for a particular product.

STAGE 3: COMPETITIVE REVIEW

The first use of the socio-target map and its structure in market niches is to compare the company's current marketing and communications strategy with the table of market opportunities. It answers the following questions:

❑   Is the company represented in different niches or just one? What is the value of the consumer profile in these niches in terms of buying power, youth, leadership, loyalty, openness to innovation?

❑   Do the company's different products, services and brands cover a variety of consumer segments in a complementary way, or are they concentrated in the same niches competing with one another with the same consumers?

❑   Do the brand images of each of the company's ranges respond to the variety of motivations and sensitivities of the different socio-targets? And is each brand image quite coherent with the motivations and sensitivities of its consumer segment?

❏ What is the relative market coverage on this ordnance survey map of territories for conquest?

❏ Are there any attractive and dynamic consumer segments on the map where today the company has no presence? Has it anything to offer this niche?

The same review has to be conducted on competitors using the same questions, and will enable us to do two things:

❏ analyze the strengths and weaknesses of each competitor in relation to the company's strengths and weaknesses in market coverage revealed above;

❏ see in which niches there is a concentration of competitors, in which ones there is almost a monopoly by one product or brand, which ones are underexploited or not exploited at all.

In all cases analysis of the socio-target portraits enables us to evaluate the relative value of these niches and thus the relative advantage of being positioned there.

This review can be conducted in several ways:

❏ from statistical information available in the socio-styles databank;
❏ from databanks linked to the socio-styles system and therefore offering an analysis of comparable consumer profiles (eg the consumer study panels of the Europanel network in Europe);
❏ from *ad hoc* complementary qualitative or quantitative studies;
❏ through an exercise of expertise using the socio-checkboard grids directly derived from socio-styles studies. Analysis of the contents of these grids enables us to position marketing strategies in relation to the map of this market.

FROM DIAGNOSIS TO STRATEGY DEFINITION

The socio-styles system offers the opportunity to conduct a dynamic review not only of the present market situation but also of its opportunities for the user. This is thanks to the information available on general socio-cultural currents, trends peculiar to this market, new profiles of emerging lifestyles, consumer segments undergoing expansion, rejuvenation or increased affluence.

The socio-target map (figure 11.2) can be used to elaborate a general strategy for market coverage:

❏ by adopting a diversification scenario for products, services or brands in order to improve coverage of the various segments;
❏ by deciding to withdraw from a niche because it seems too unprofitable in terms of consumer profile or volume, or because it is too saturated with competitors;
❏ by deciding to attack a niche whose consumer profiles seem interesting and where the competition is not yet firmly entrenched.

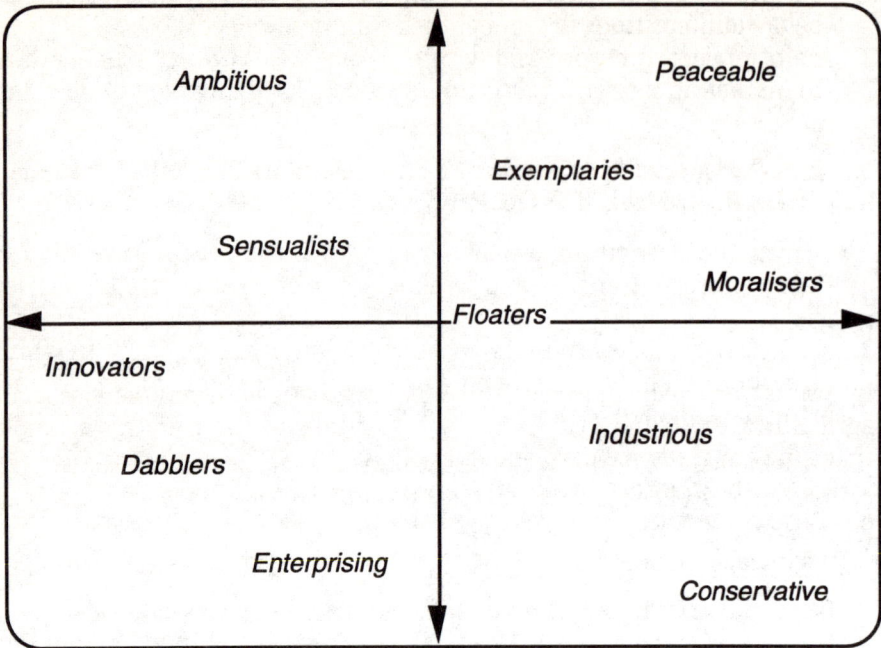

Figure 11.2   Basic socio-styles map (France in the 1970s)

These decisions are dependent on company strategy. The socio-styles data-bank, particularly in the form of the socio-target map, provides a classification of choices in the form of a consumer and niche typology, and can assist the decision process by weighing up these opportunities according to potential consumer volume, level of wealth, socio-cultural dynamism and general consumption profile.

At the end of this appraisal and strategic orientation using the sector-based socio-target map as the main tool, the user is in a position to define a priority niche for development (eg defensive stabilization or offensive conquest) for each range, product, service or brand, and then successive secondary niches.

As demonstrated in the innovation example above and using the same process, the socio-styles databank can be used downstream to develop a tactical plan of action:

❏   A precise consumer portrait corresponds to each niche — a socio-target portrait completed by portraits of its socio-styles. It is the point of departure for extracting all the available information on this target population from the databank in order to respond better to its needs, speak its language and become better acquainted.

❏   Each niche can be located precisely on the socio-map as a region of the ordnance survey map. The user can reinterpret all the other maps in the databank by placing them over it, and quickly identify what needs to be known about the niche (eg current consumer motivations and behaviour, positions of competitors, innovation needs). Above all it is a point of departure for seeking out ways of action in the stages devoted to marketing tools.

EXAMPLE: REORIENTING A STRATEGY FOR FINANCIAL PRODUCTS AND SERVICES IN FRANCE

This type of strategic application depends strictly on the nature and strategy of each organization. We will take as an example the strategic thinking that might have taken place during the 1970s in the banking and financial sector in France for Crédit Agricole. This is a large bank with mutual status and agricultural and rural origins, based historically in the countryside and at that time engaged on a development policy.

The socio-styles databank for France (1974 to 1976) revealed a typology of 11 socio-styles (figure 11.2).

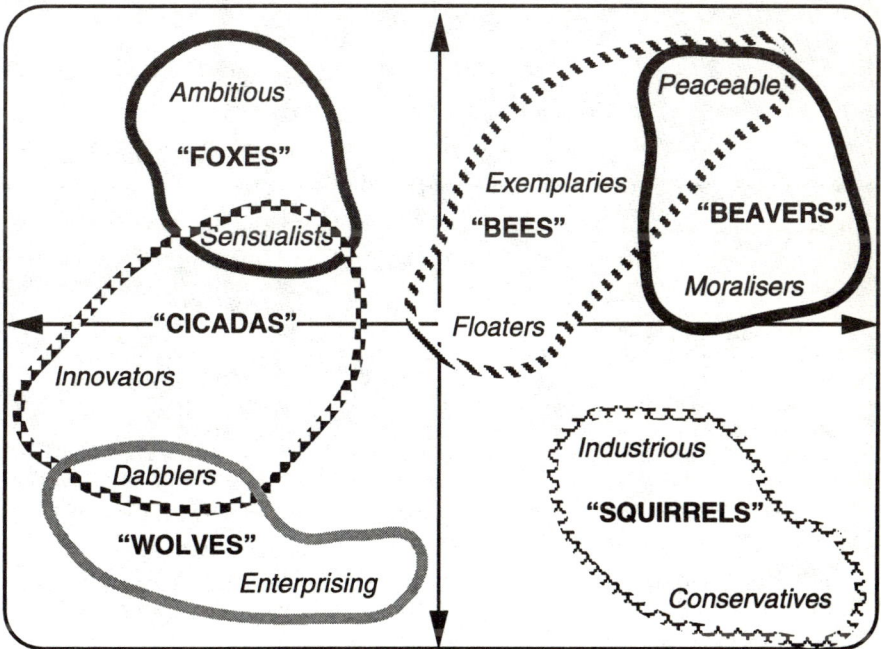

Source: Socio Styles France   © CCA 1976

Figure 11.3   Socio-target map of the banking sector

Market background

On this basic social map the databank devoted to the financial sector revealed a synthesis of six socio-targets and described their portraits (figure 11.2).

Review of the company's market coverage

Figures 11.3 and 11.4 show that at that time Crédit Agricole penetrated the 'ecureuil' (squirrel) and 'castor' (beaver) customer segments in particular. We can see that the market coverage is very partial and mainly concentrated on consumer profiles that are very isolated, badly off and in the countryside — socio-styles that are ageing, becoming impoverished and losing any leadership to the urban areas.

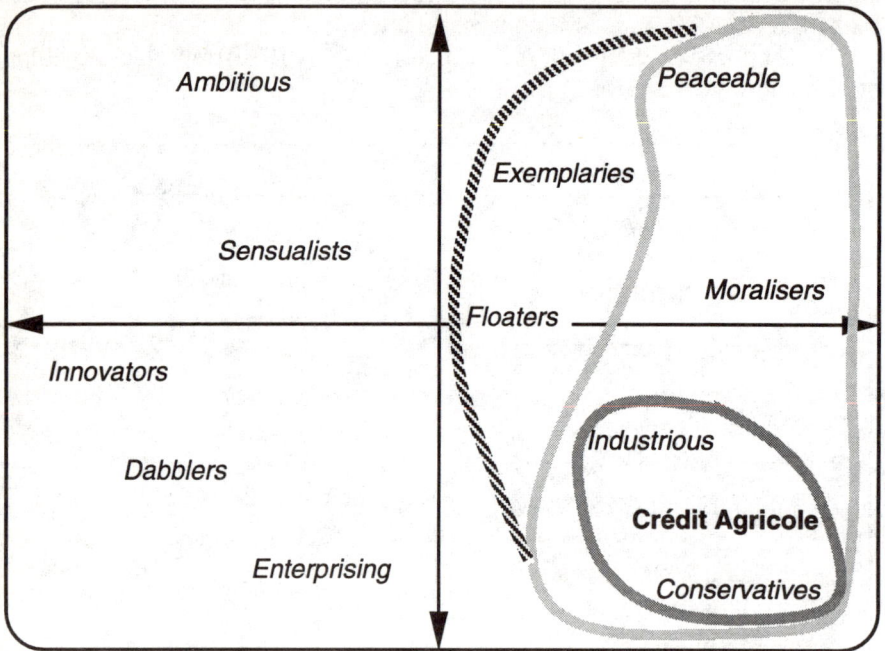

Figure 11.4   Mini-map showing penetration of the market by Crédit Agricole

Review of competitors' market coverage

Figure 11.5 shows that Crédit Agricole is in competition in its own territory with other organizations that are state-owned or belong to the social economy sector. In contrast, nationalized banks, which benefit from being regarded as private banks, have a better penetration of other customer segments such as 'renards' (foxes) which are more urban, better off, younger, better qualified, expanding and getting richer (see figure 11.5).

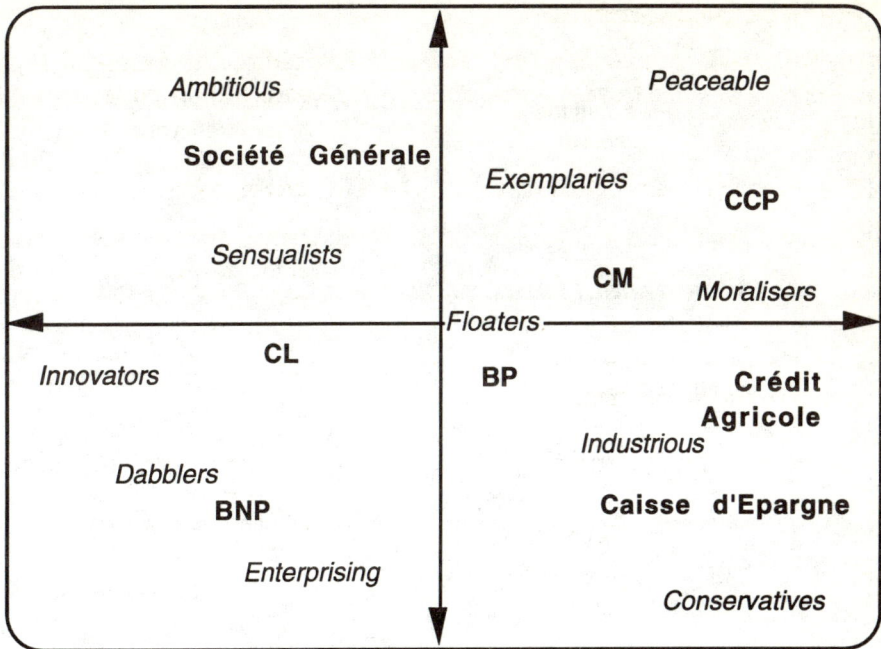

Source: Socio Styles France   © CCA 1976

Figure 11.5   Map of competitive positionings

Appraisal of the strategic synthesis

This rapid analysis shows the problems that the socio-styles databank can address for a company. In the current example the following picture emerges:

❑ the bank only partially occupies the social terrain, concentrated on the business capital of humble and isolated consumers facing recession, old age and impoverishment;
❑ it is in competition with other financial organizations with the same status and image;
❑ more dynamic and solvent consumer profiles shun it, being courted strongly by another group of finance and banking organizations (figure 11.5).

The problem at the time for Crédit Agricole and other organizations in a similar position was as follows (see figures 11.6 and 11.7):

❑ either to stay in the position inherited from the past, to strengthen it as much as possible by staying with financial products in everyday use, managing small accounts and offering loans for professional equipment and consumer goods, and giving priority to an extensive distribution network;
❑ or to embark on a policy of financial product diversification, establishing distribution outlets in urban and suburban areas, a considerable

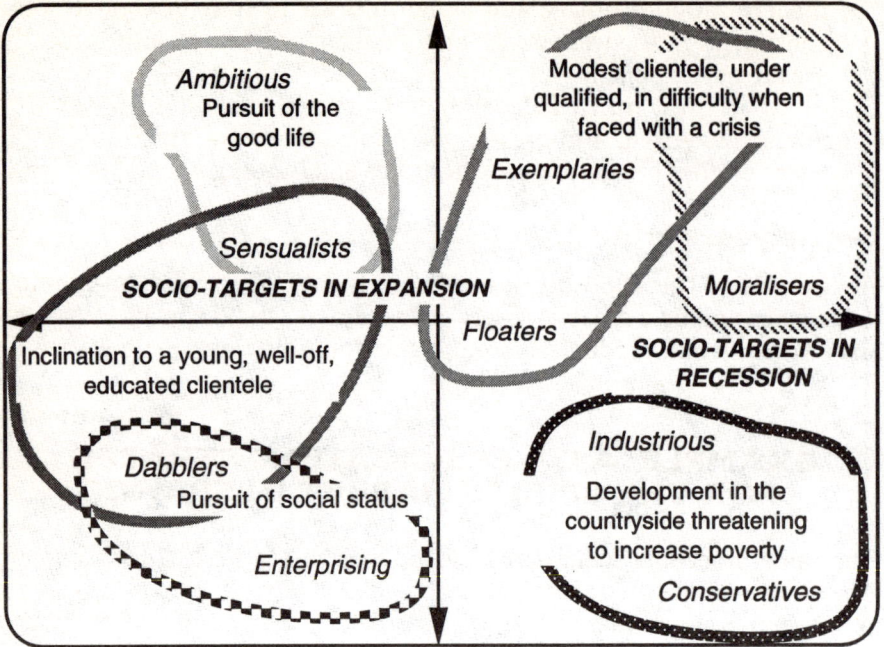

Figure 11.6   Analytical map of the trend value of niches

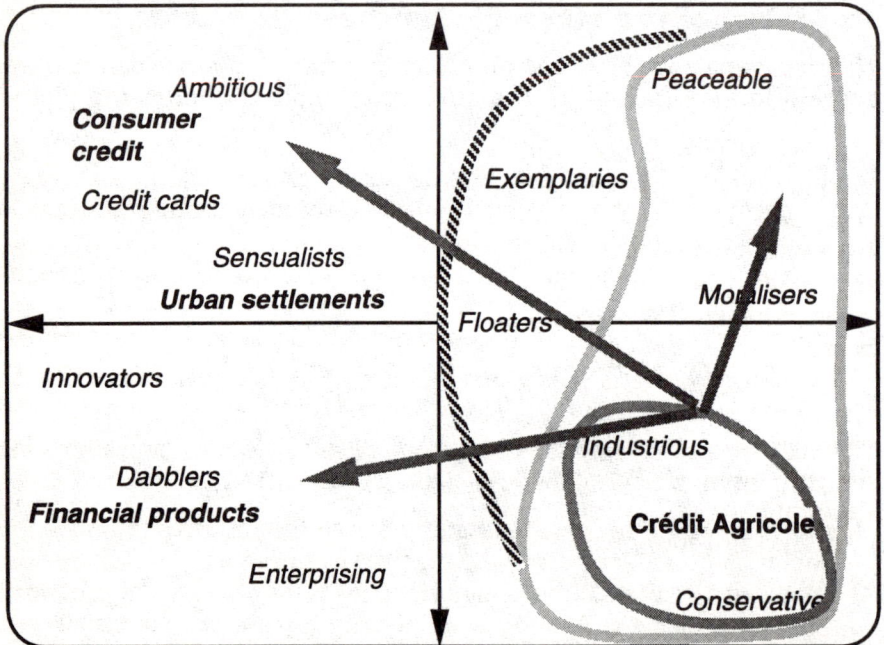

Source: Socio Styles France   © CCA 1976

Figure 11.7   Strategic reorientation scenarios

modernization of image and brand in order to start to conquer other consumers in the west of the lifestyle map, competing with banks that are already established there;

❏ or to attempt limited development without abandoning territory already acquired, aiming to shift progressively towards more socio-styles profiles by opening new branches and introducing new services.

Some years later ...

At the end of the 1980s, 15 years after this survey, Crédit Agricole is established among a greater variety of consumers over the whole socio-style map with different products and more diversified distribution networks.

EXAMPLE: A DIVERSIFICATION STRATEGY FOR THE SPIRITS MARKET IN FRANCE

The same procedure which enabled the firm in the preceding example to carry out a competitive appraisal of a market, identify its niches and distribute several product lines and brands, can also be applied to a diversification strategy. This application can be of use to firms or professional organizations currently represented in the market by a single product based on generic know-how. The socio-styles system can help them identify all opportunities for making use of this know-how in the form of diversified products or services which meet the needs of different consumer categories not reached by the basic product.

The procedure

The first stage is a check-up of all the market niches to pick out which product groups seem to respond successfully to the motivations of various socio-targets. Each of these niches can be analyzed as a model of responses to motivations and lifestyles. Analysis of socio-contrasts enables us to gain a better understanding of the nature of motivations and needs and the added value of the different types of products which share this commercial chessboard.

The second stage is to position the basic product on the commercial chessboard by analyzing the relevant mini-map. We can therefore evaluate which 'market surface' it is capable of covering today, which consumer profile and volume it attracts today and which segments it has not managed to penetrate.

At the third stage there are some questions to be asked:

❏ Why has the basic product not managed to satisfy other socio-targets? What does it lack? Analysis of the motivation maps of different socio-styles will provide the answer.

❏ Can we take from this basic product any sub-products which would

satisfy adjacent socio-targets by a simple change of presentation, packaging, brand or advertising? Analysis of the contrasts between market niches will provide the answer.
❏ Does the firm have the know-how to respond to the needs of these other consumers? Are there products already in existence which might suit them?
❏ Do we have to innovate more radically?

It often happens that professional know-how is underestimated or limited to a small number of products inherited from the past, whereas there are potential new products at the prototype stage or being produced secretly in small quantities. Both might offer opportunities for development through diversification at less cost than innovation. A check-up of market expectations combined with systematic internal research into all the company's know-how may provide some clues.

Application

Let us take as an example West Indian rum and its marketing in the French metropolitan market.* Figure 11.8 gives the general map of socio-styles in France.

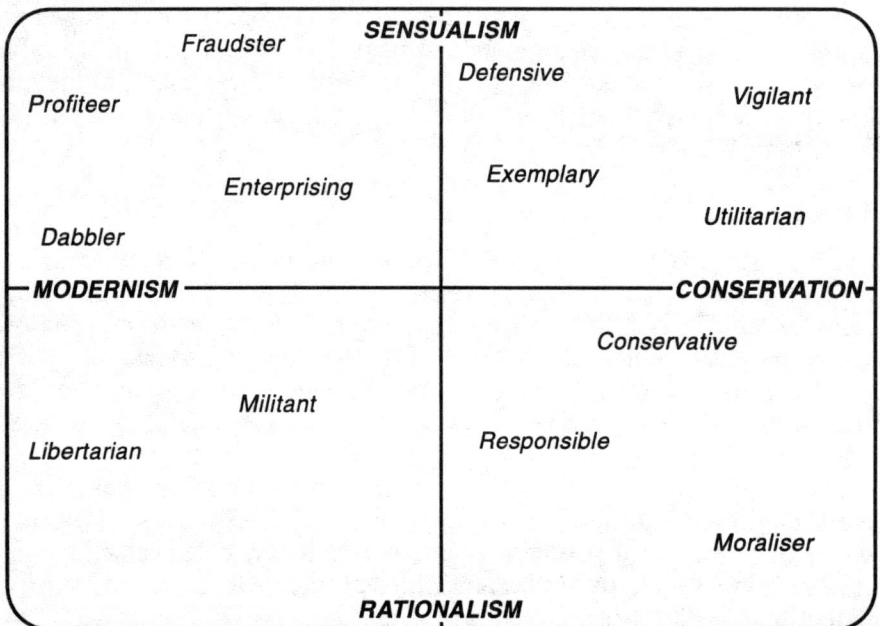

Source: Socio Styles FRANCE 1984   Copyright: CCA

Figure 11.8   General map of socio-styles in France

* Source: Socio-bank of lifestyles in France in the 1980s, particularly the sections concerned with alcoholic drinks.

Analysis of the principal competitive niches in the alcoholic drinks market (figure 11.9) shows that rum as a single product is confined to just one market niche, while the tendency for other alcoholic drinks is to penetrate several socio-targets in the form of different levels in the range and increasingly in the form of specialist drinks. We note in particular the wide diversification of whisky-type products. We also see rapid development among white alcohols, such as vodka, aquavit and tequila, which have grown from their 'folksy' consumption linked to everyday meals to become liqueurs for some consumers, aperitifs for others. We see a market for cocktails developing in an interesting way.

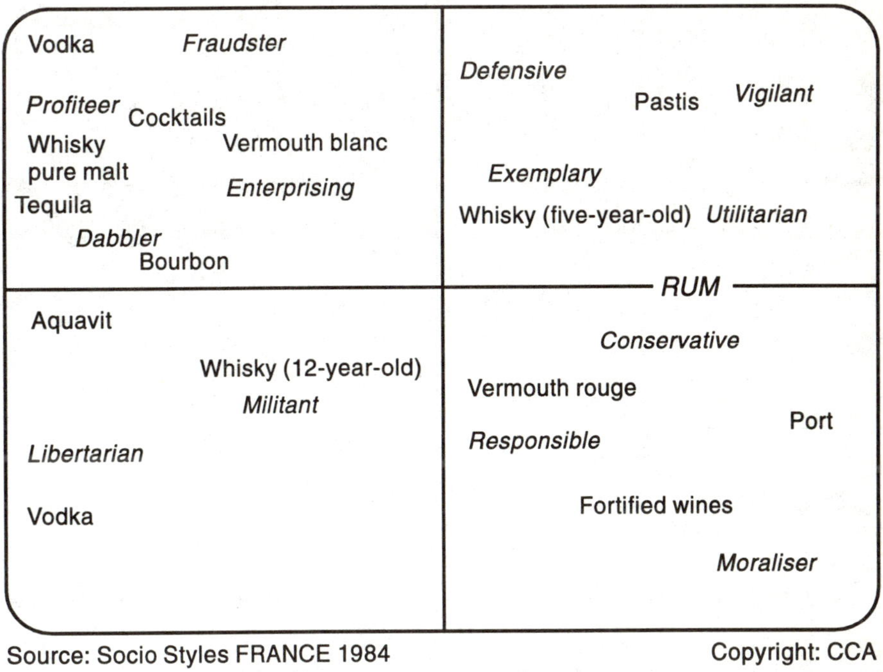

Vodka   Fraudster
 	
Profiteer Cocktails
Whisky   Vermouth blanc
pure malt
          Enterprising
Tequila
     Dabbler
          Bourbon
	Defensive
	
	                    Pastis *Vigilant*
	
	Exemplary
	
	Whisky (five-year-old) *Utilitarian*

Aquavit
 	
          Whisky (12-year-old)
               Militant
 	
Libertarian
 	
Vodka
	——— RUM ———
	          Conservative
	
	Vermouth rouge
	                         Port
	Responsible
	
	          Fortified wines
	
	               Moraliser

Source: Socio Styles FRANCE 1984   Copyright: CCA

Figure 11.9   Competitive niches in the alcoholic drinks market

We can therefore move on to an identification on the map (figure 11.10) and a territorial analysis of the current customer base for West Indian rum in France. This is actually industrial brown rum, a bottom-of-the-range product whose flavour has not changed and which is relatively cheap. The mini-map devoted to Negrita, the flagship brand, shows that it is well established among 'materialist' socio-styles — a popular, modest type, who go out relatively little, are not leaders of opinion, and are above all a socio-portrait in decline, ageing and tending towards poverty. In contrast, we find that this rum only slightly penetrates the better-off segments and is therefore seldom present among the super-consuming socio-targets (eg 'rigorist') or the innovative ones (eg 'marginal').

The position is therefore as illustrated in figure 11.11. There is a prevailing market which is keen on top-of-the-range products that are elaborate and sophisticated in taste, natural and expensive:

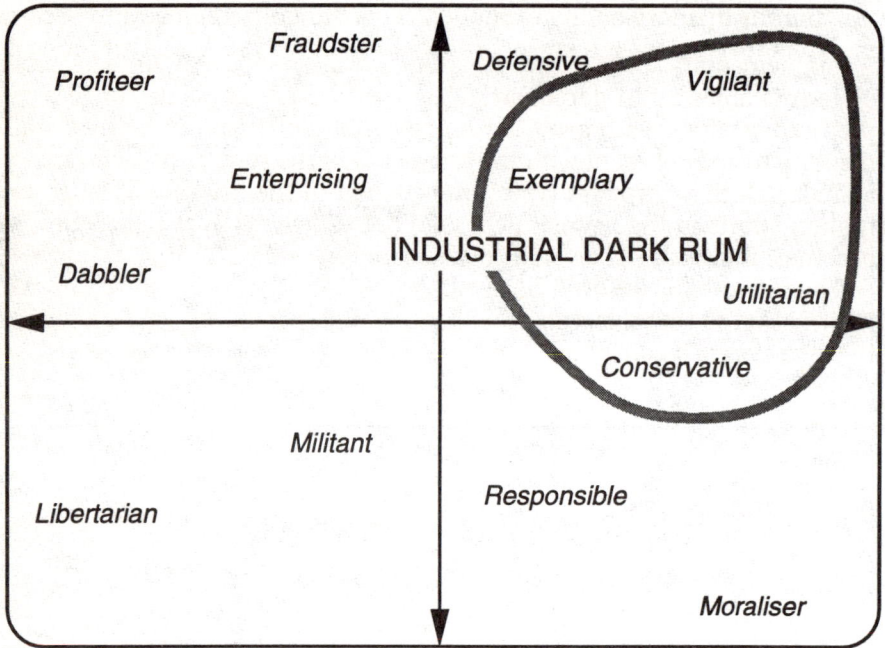

Figure 11.10   Mini-map showing the penetration of Negrita (industrial dark) rum

❑ in niche A this would be a gastronomic alcohol to be sipped like a liqueur catering for socio-styles of the 'rigorist' mentality;
❑ in niche B it would be used as a celebratory drink for creating atmosphere as an aperitif or at parties for the socio-target of the 'fringe' mentality in the west of the map;
❑ for niche C in the extreme north a less expensive product is required, simple but frivolous, serving as a base for long drinks and cocktails.

An audit of professional know-how was able to show that there were plenty of rum products which until then had mainly been limited to local consumption. These responded to the needs of different socio-targets which had not been reached and which were likely to be integrated into different competing niches:

❑ white agricultural rum already introduced on a modest scale into the metropolitan market, likely to enter the niches of cocktail bases;

❑ straw rum, almost unknown in the market, especially old rums which offer qualities of taste and naturalness capable of gaining them entry to socio-styles interested in liquors;

❑ rarer specialities, such as '*le coeur de chauffe*', a product resulting from the first distillation of the sugar cane, which has a very high alcohol content (more than 60 per cent) and is potentially attractive to 'let's get high' niches, a market small in volume but important in terms of image and the financial ability to pay highly for élitism based on rarity.

A complementary study of the research innovation model by the socio-styles system enables us to demonstrate in addition the opportunity to create prepared cocktails with a white rum base and exotic fruit in a way complementary to and coherent with the know-how of the rum manufacturers.

Today all these product types can be found in the market, although promotion efforts in the newest niches are not sufficient. West Indian rum has become a multi-target, diversified basic product.

The socio-bank offers the producers of these brands quite concrete information so that they can adapt their products and even sales methods to the tastes of each consumer.

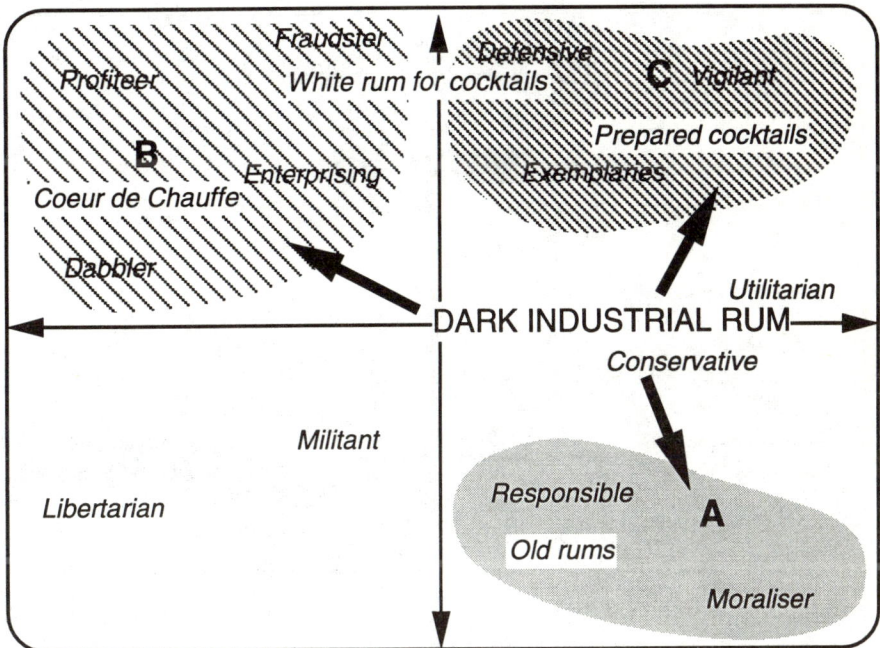

Source: Socio Styles France   © CCA 1984

Figure 11.11   Analytical map showing the value of consumer niches

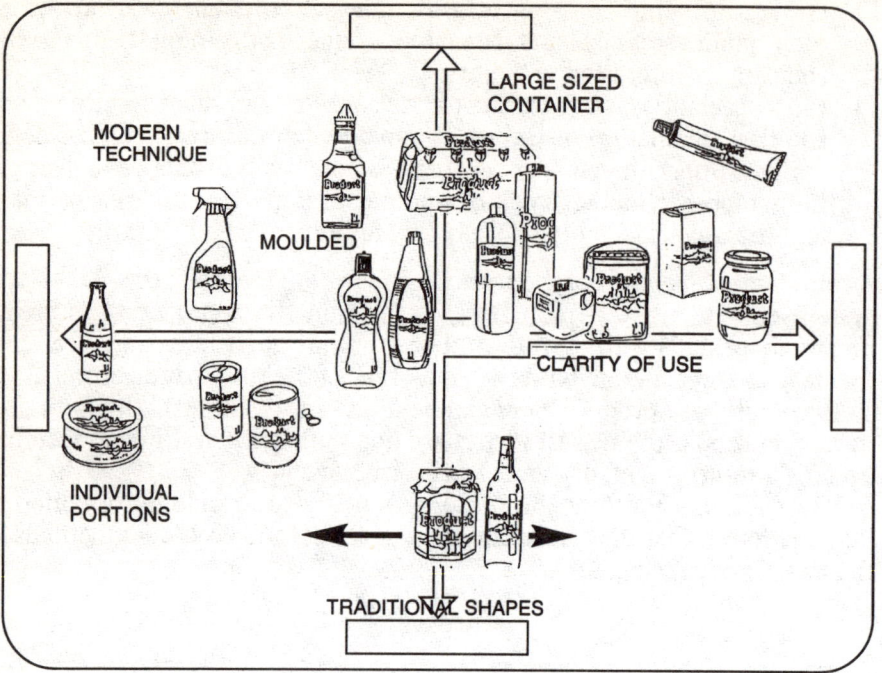

Figure 11.12   Packaging

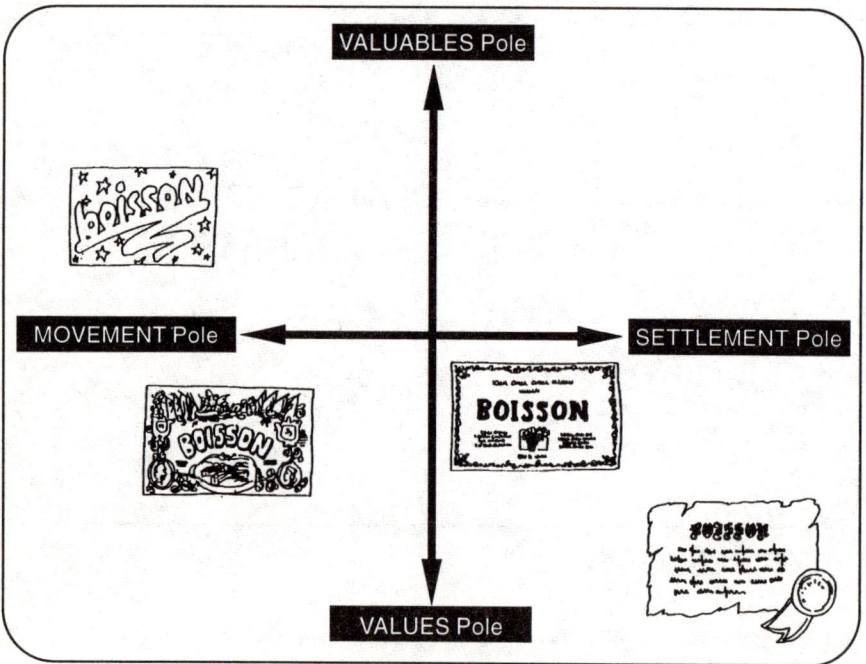

Figure 11.13   Drink labelling styles

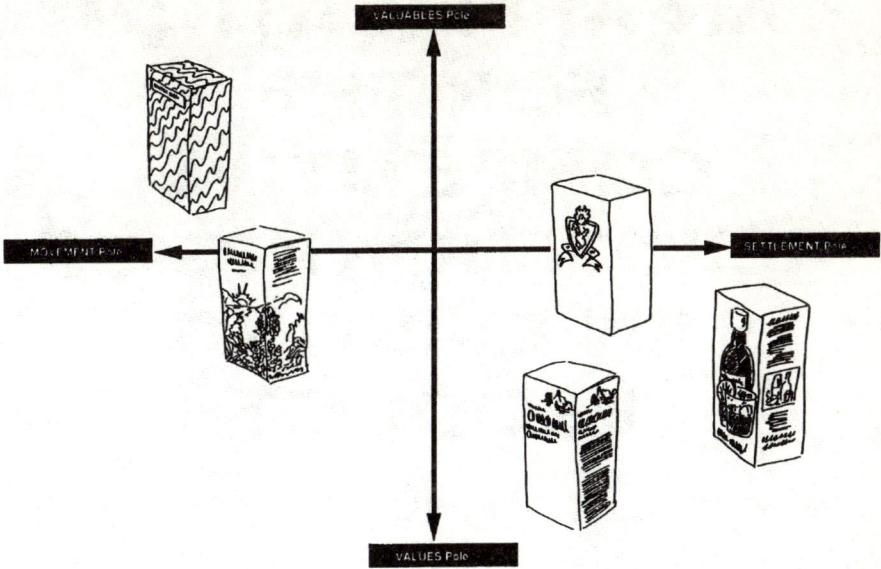

Schéma 162 — STYLES D'EMBALLAGE POUR UNE BOISSON

Figure 11.14   External packaging for drinks

CHAPTER 12

AN APPLICATION FOR THE COMPETITIVE REPOSITIONING OF AN EXISTING PRODUCT

Socio-styles studies aim to be both static and dynamic. The diagnosis and measurement of socio-cultural trends in the evolution of mentalities, the identification and measurement of future scenarios or innovation concepts are intended for the preparation of new products or new socio-political initiatives. However, the main part of the socio-bank and particularly of the associated databanks (consumer panels, for instance) is devoted to a picture of the current state of society and the markets.

One of the most frequent applications of this tool in marketing is in managing existing products and brands in a competitive situation in order to optimize their positioning. This procedure can be described in several main steps and calls on all the resources of the socio-bank.

STAGE 1: PRODUCT CHECK-UP

The profile of the current customer base for a product or service is identified and positioned in its territory on the typological socio-styles map. If the brand and product in question are included in the socio-styles databank, in an associated databank or in an *ad hoc* study using the same typology, the check-up will be direct and therefore very precise. However, if this information is not available it is possible make an approximation by looking for the positioning and consumer profile of the product and brand nearest to it, an analogical check-up.

This study relies on the mini-map, the most analytical type of document in the socio-styles databank, which visualizes the penetration rate of an item in the different socio-style families by emphasizing above-average penetration of the general sample (ie the socio-styles who own more equipment, who consume more of a product, who read a newspaper more, who liked a brand more, etc).

After this stage we can obtain the answers to a number of questions:

❏ Is the population for this product homogeneous (made up of adjacent socio-styles on the map which designate a single and unique territory) or heterogeneous (made up of two or three socio-styles at distant or even opposite points on the map)?
❏ Is the consumer profile or audience profile concentrated on a small number of socio-styles that are well above average, or spread over a larger number of types who differ only slightly from the average?
❏ Is the territory of the product or brand in a central position on the map, off-centre or somewhat marginal but very specific?

The more central the territory of the product, brand image or medium and the more widespread it is over a large number of socio-styles, the more chance it has of constituting a mass market, though weak in personality and specificity. By contrast, the smaller, more homogeneous, concentrated and marginal the cluster is on the map, the greater the importance of its unique added value potential. The more homogeneous the consumer profile, the stronger and more specific the promotion and image policy can be, since it is addressed to a very precise population. If, on the other hand, the target seems heterogeneous — made up of antagonistic socio-styles — it will be more difficult to develop a strong image. A compromise is often unsatisfying for one or other of the targets and the dual language is disturbing. One solution may be to diversify from the basic product into two brands, two images, two distinct commercial offerings each addressed to a more homogeneous target.

A preliminary diagnosis of market coverage can be carried out on the mini-map of each item.

STAGE 2: VALUE ANALYSIS OF THE CUSTOMER BASE

When the socio-styles profile of the customer base for a product is known, the user can refer to the socio-cultural databank to evaluate the relative interest of this core group. The socio-styles portraits provide several elements for consideration:

❏ the size of the population concerned;
❏ its socio-demographic profile;
❏ its psychological profile;
❏ its social profile;
❏ its micro-economic and commercial profile (eg financial behaviour, buying methods);
❏ its shopping portrait (eg brand loyalty, patronage of retail outlets);
❏ its media portrait.

From these variables available in the socio-cultural report, a marketing manager has criteria for evaluating the relative strategic interest of this population. This judgement relies on both socio-economic and psychological variables which are qualitative and quantitative. The value of the customer base can be analyzed both in terms of financial profitability and prestige, as well as the ease of commercial action and long-term loyalty. Beyond this general data we must also take into account attitudes, trends and behaviour specific to this customer group in this market. For this the sector-based databank provides maps which indicate the dominant characters in the target map by simple superimposition. We can then make a further evaluation:

❑ What is the current level of expenditure of customers in this sector and what are their future spending intentions?
❑ Are they already overequipped or saturated?
❑ How far apart are product performance and their ideal motivations?
❑ Does the firm have the means to respond to their innovation needs?

STAGE 3: COMPETITIVE ANALYSIS

After evaluating the nature and value of the existing population, socio-styles system users can then turn to the databank to evaluate their specific positioning against their competitors. The competitive positioning niche map is one of the key databank elements in each sector. We can see how different products are spread out or grouped together according to their existing customer profile. Competitive niches are then drawn up composed of several products and brands which currently reach the same population profile, and complementary niches are drawn for products that are bought by different populations.

We can therefore carry out another comparative value analysis of the product's positioning:

❑ Is the product in question the only one in its niche, in its customer territory, or does it share it with a considerable number of competitors?
❑ Are the other products and brands in the same niche direct competitors in terms of function or usage, and what is the competitive capacity of the product in comparison with the others?
❑ Are the adjacent products simply competing economically in the same market offering an alternative consumer product to the same population? If so, is this alternative more innovatory, more prestigious or more fashionable?
❑ Do some of the adjacent products belong to the same company or group as the product in question, thus competing against themselves?
❑ Does the price range of the competing products and the product in question conform to the economic capacity of the consumers and their consumption tendencies?

This procedure enables decision makers to evaluate the relative degree of interest in competing in this niche, depending on whether they benefit from an almost exclusive monopoly or are up against strong competition from very competitive products.

STAGE 4: STRATEGIC SCENARIOS

Following this appraisal the marketing manager can proceed to a general scan of market opportunities. This is provided by the map of competitive positioning niches for all the products and brands.

In order to clarify the strategic choices raised by this map, the databank offers a group of maps which describe the contrasts between the niches which impose choices about the nature of the product or image.

To translate this chessboard of competitive niches into a landscape of potential target consumers, the socio-bank also provides a sector-based map of socio-targets. The latter describes the consumer segments specific to this market, paints their portraits and measures their importance.

This inventory enables users to envisage theoretically but with full knowledge of the situation what profit there would be in operating in each of these niches and market segments. They carry out a value analysis of each of the niches:

❑ by consulting the portrait of each consumer socio-targets which is later supplemented by a portrait of the component socio-styles;
❑ by analyzing the nature of the demand in each niche which is explained by the behavioural map and the map of consumer motivations;
❑ by observing the number and kind of competitors in each niche.

This strategic check-up on all the market opportunities can be supplemented by a simulation exercise. We have to imagine what needs to be done to transfer the product in question from its current positioning to each of the other market niches:

❑ Is it possible in terms of the technical nature, performance or use of a product or service, relative to the needs and motivations of this consumer segment, and what modifications would have to be made to the product?
❑ Is it possible in terms of price relative to the buying power and consumption trends of the consumer target, and relative to the pricing policy of competitors? And what modifications does this scenario imply for the price or promotion strategy?
❑ Is it possible in terms of commercial distribution?
❑ Is it possible in terms of image relative to the motivations of this socio-target, and relative to the image strategy of the competitors in the niche? What changes does this imply in advertising strategy?

A large proportion of the data necessary for the strategic simulation is available in the socio-styles databank — concerning needs, motivations and behaviour, buying power and consumer trends. It needs to be supplemented by information about competitors and also any additional qualitative studies.

STAGE 5: STABILITY OR REPOSITIONING

After this review, assisted by the sector-based and general socio-styles data-bank, strategists for a product or brand can choose one of the following courses of action:

❏ to pursue their commerical action plan in the niche in which they are already established;
❏ to attempt a gradual extension from this positioning towards an adjacent customer group;
❏ to begin a progressive change of niche to a competitive niche and a new consumer socio-target.

In these final two cases the socio-bank can still help to define precisely the tools for this extension or evolution. Every positioning movement on the socio-styles map corresponds to a change of target and therefore to a change in consumer demand. We have to adapt by modifying (actually or symbolically) the added value attached to the product and brand image. The conquest of a new territory often coincides with the discovery of new customer groups through their commercial habits and responsiveness to advertising. If the opportunity arises the commercial distribution network can be modified, the language and communication method changed, the media plan adapted.

All this information is available:

❏ if we transfer the current niche and objective niche to the motivation check-up map (figure 12.1), we can evaluate the need to transform the product, its design, symbolism, etc;
❏ if we trace this strategic evolutionary movement on the map showing distribution networks and methods of commercial promotion, we can see if it is necessary to change the distribution network and promotional strategy (figure 12.2).

The same applies to advertising style (figure 12.3) and media utilization (figure 12.4).

This method of applying the socio-styles system to the positioning of a product and brand starts from the most analytical information on this product to integrate progressively comparative data and synthetic maps. An opposite procedure beginning with the socio-target map, the most synthetic diagram of market analysis, can be applied to the positioning of a group of products and brands in a firm's policy for diversification and general market coverage (see chapter 11).

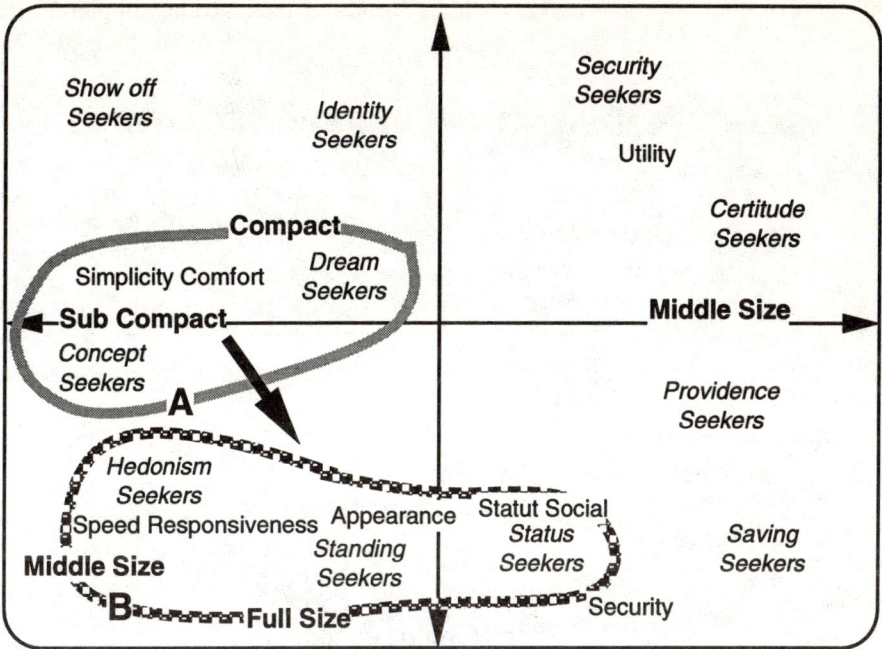

Source: US Socio-Styles   © US Mapping 1988

Figure 12.1   Consumer needs and motivations

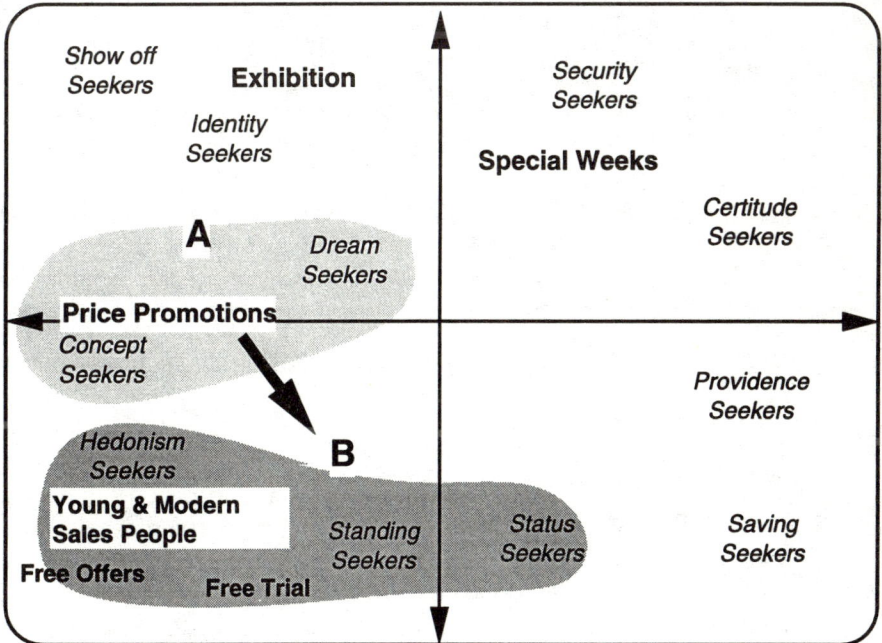

Figure 12.2   Consumer receptiveness to promotions

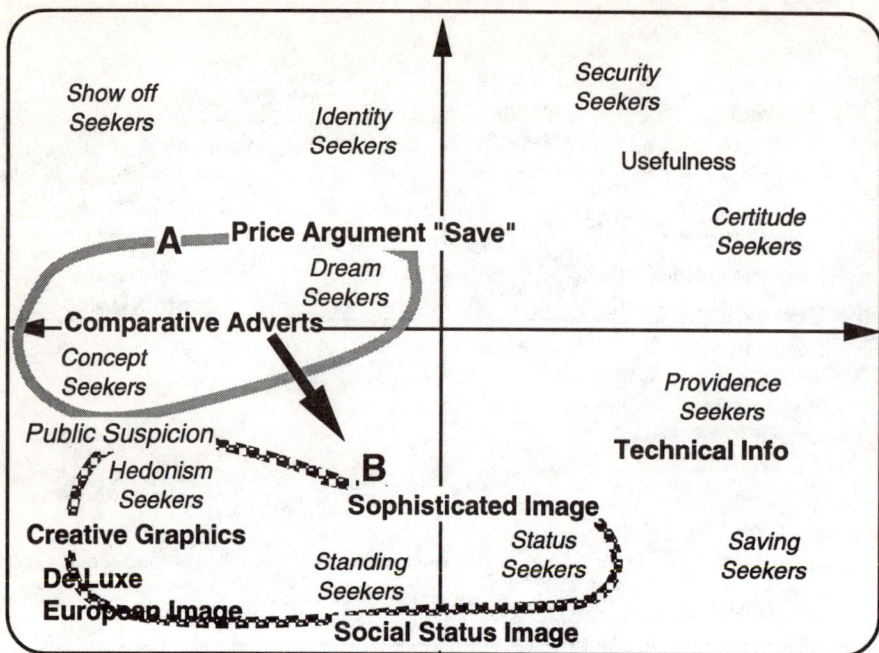

Source: U.S. Socio-Styles   © US Mapping 1988

Figure 12.3   Consumer sensitivity to advertising

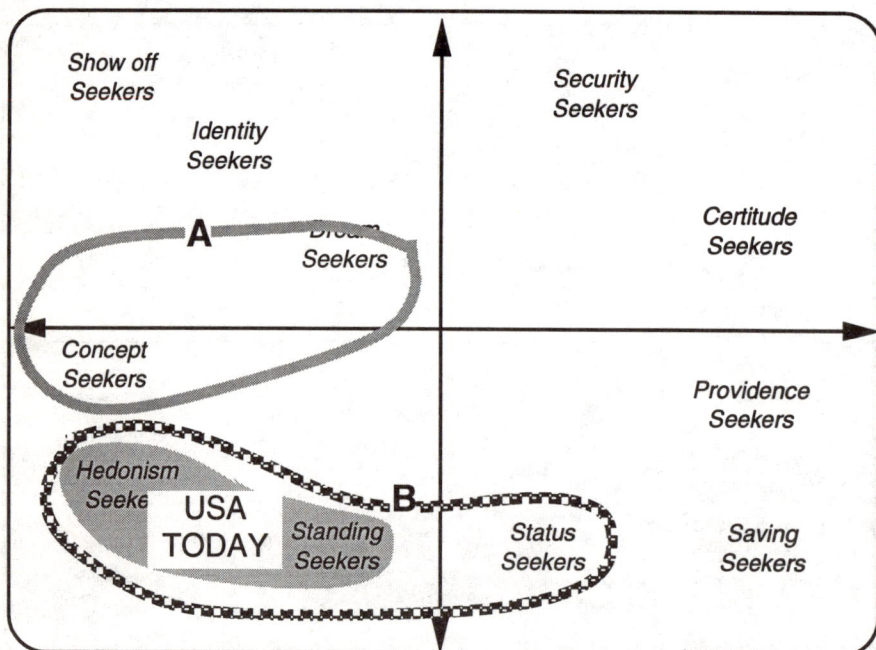

Source: US Socio-Styles   © US Mapping 1988

Figure 12.4   Mini-map of the readership of *USA Today*

EXAMPLE: REPOSITIONING OF A EUROPEAN CAR MODEL IN THE USA

This example concerns a fictitious product because of the confidential nature of this type of analysis. However, the market data referred to is accurate, although partial. It is taken from the US-socio-styles databank on the automobile market in the USA. Figure 12.5 gives the general socio-styles map.

Let us imagine a mid-range saloon car from Europe imported into the American market with a relatively weak rate of penetration for the past ten years. The first stage of the product check-up shows that its market penetration, although weak in quantitative terms, is very specific and homogeneous, very concentrated and relatively marginal, principally among socio-styles 9 and 10 (see figure 12.6).

Value analysis of the consumer target shows that they are mainly young urban dwellers of quite a high educational and socio-cultural level with average buying power. They have a rather anti-conformist, anti-establishment mentality, are very open to the whole world and foreign products, but are weak on loyalty. They are more likely to spend on cultural pursuits and sport, and show themselves to be rather anti-advertising.

For a manager of product X the advantage of this customer group is its openness to imported products, but it also has drawbacks: the difficulty of inspiring loyalty, reticence about paying a large amount for the added value

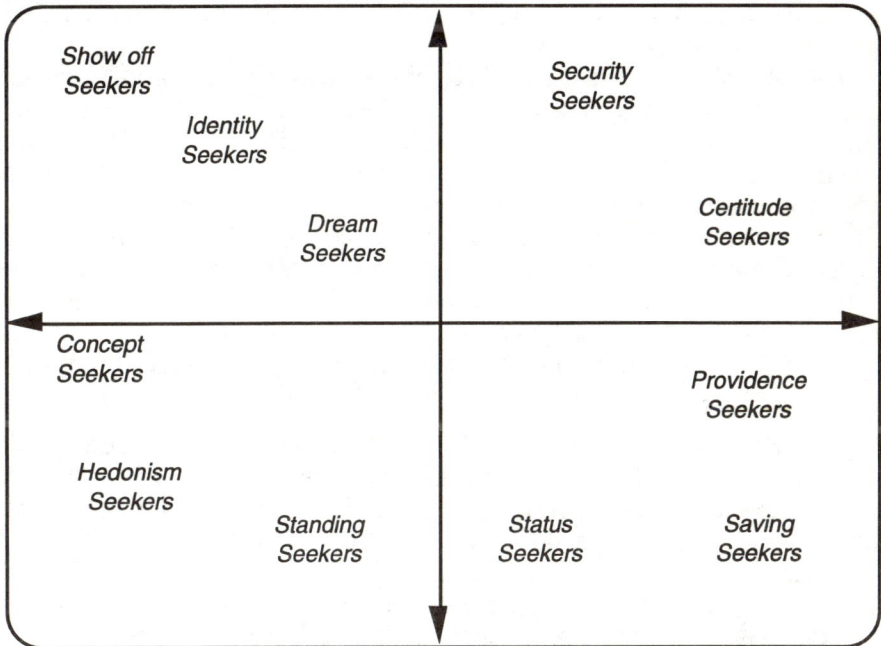

Figure 12.5   General socio-styles map of the American market

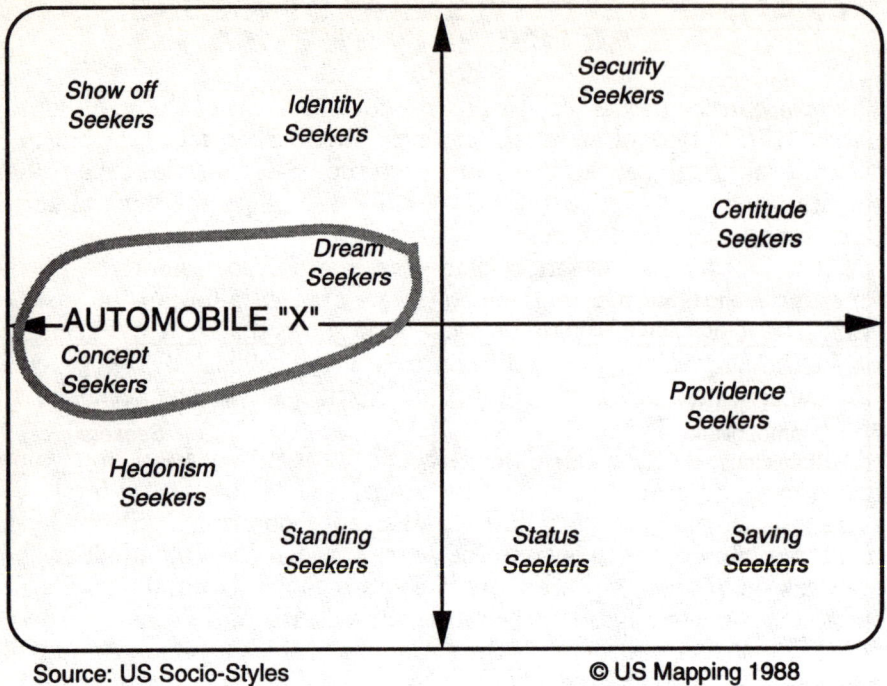

Source: US Socio-Styles   © US Mapping 1988

Figure 12.6   Map showing the penetration of socio-styles by a product

of the product, and a weak capacity for leadership and being an example to other consumer (figure 12.7).

The next stage — the competitive check-up — shows that product X is placed in an extremely competitive niche, where all the Japanese manufacturers are established with fairly similar mid-range models (figure 12.8). Documentary analysis of the market supplements these observations by showing that these brands have a policy of fairly low prices and quite sophisticated equipment, with a model design copied from American car styles. The product X marketing manager may ask what point there is in continuing to operate in this niche because of the considerable competitive density and the commercial qualities of the competition.

On the map of brand niches a systematic scan of market niches and analysis of these opportunities shows that:

❑ niches D, E and F in the east of the map seem to be wedded to the brands and models of American manufacturers, and analysis of the consumer socio-targets confirms their rejection of imported foreign models;

❑ the north-western socio-target C is too poor to be commercially viable, being mainly buyers of second-hand cars;

❑ niche B in the south-west, represented by socio-styles 1, 6 and 2 in particular, offers a more promising strategic scenario. It is a population of well-off 'yuppies', high spenders particularly on cars, opinion leaders who are examples to the middle classes, relatively open to imported

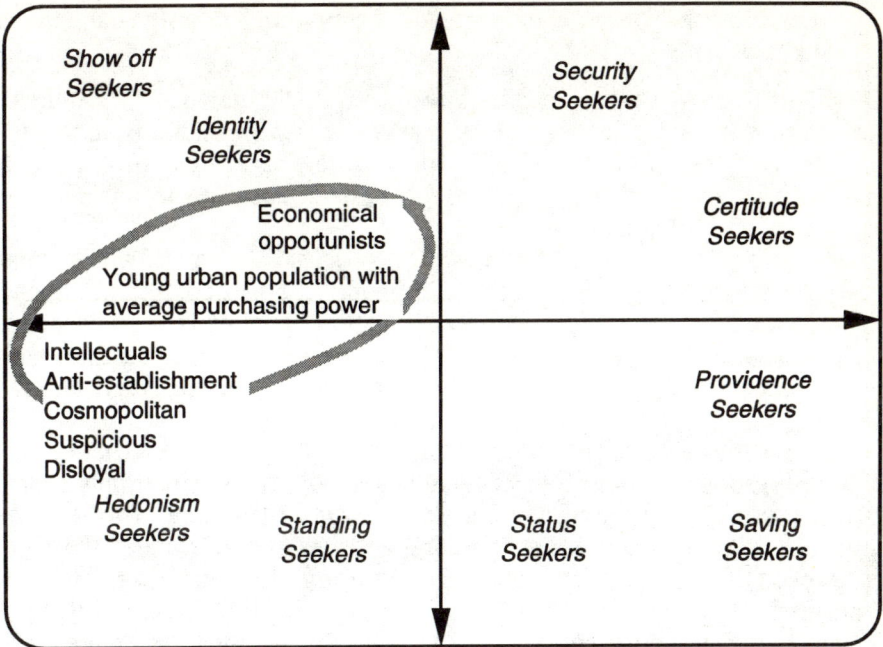

Figure 12.7 Value analysis of the current customer base

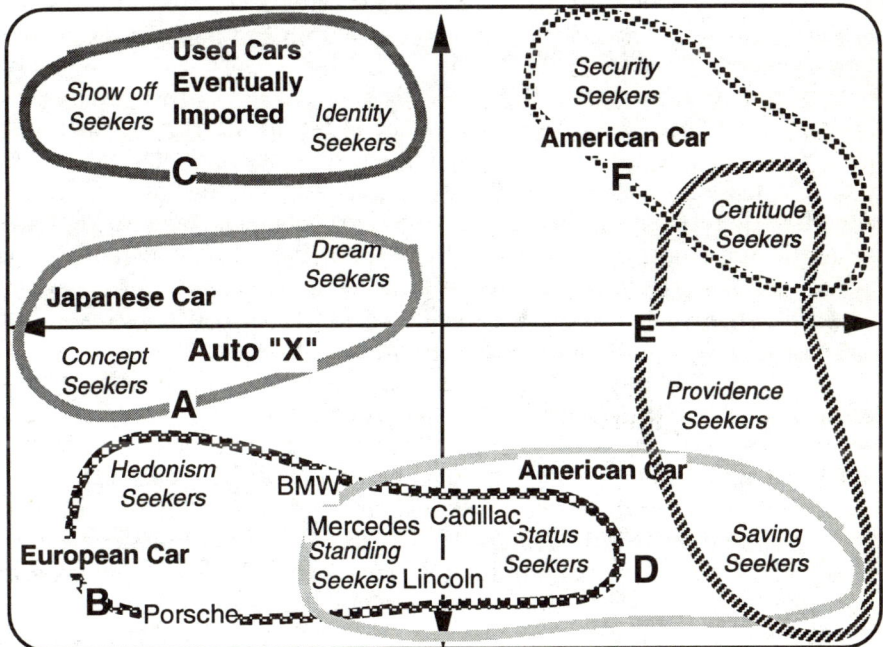

Source: U.S. Socio-Styles   © US Mapping 1988

Figure 12.8 Positioning of competing makes of car

goods. Observation of the competition shows that it is strong here, but more with European cars as well as prestigious, top-of-the-range, local models.

At the fifth stage we can imagine that the strategic manager for product X will decide to shift progressively from niche A towards niche B, to position the product higher up the range with a more prestigious customer base. This will escape a price war against Japanese competition for disloyal consumers in the current niche.

Analysis of motivations (figure 12.1) shows that the movement of socio-target A towards segment B implies a notable change in demand. There is less demand for comfort, economical use and ease of driving and more for elegance, speed and sportiness. If the model is capable of meeting these requirements, its presentation, commercial logic and adveritising will have to change.

Analysis of the tastes in style of different socio-targets shows that target A is more responsive to a compact design — small cars with a simple appearance. Potential target B, in contrast, wants larger, medium-sized cars especially with a smoother shape, long and low-slung, evoking sportiness and speed. If product X is already related through its design to the tastes of consumer B, its positioning will evolve naturally. But if this is not the case, it will be necessary to consider either a design modification or the use of decorative accessories likely to give the car a sportier look.

The superimposition of other maps from the socio-bank enable us to analyze the receptiveness to promotion and commercial behaviour of socio-target B. It shows the great importance of salespeople who are expected to be young and dynamic, quick and effective, fond of sports cars — the image of their potential customers (figure 12.2).

Analysis of their receptivity to advertising (figure 12.3) reveals that this new customer group dislikes advertising and despises very aggressive advertising campaigns, yet is very demanding artistically and fond of unusual advertising creations. What is required is European-style advertising that is aesthetic and emotional to inspire dreams; not the rational, demonstrative, almost consumerist type preferred by target A.

Various maps concerning the media (eg figure 12.4) can be taken from the databank to select the tools for a communication strategy.

We can make the hypothesis in this case study that the marketing director of product X for the American market, after judging the acceptable constraints, would decide on a change of positioning from niche A to niche B and work out a three-year strategic plan based on the above observations.

During this change *ad hoc* qualitative and quantitative studies based on socio-styles system methodology could enable us to monitor the evolution of the image and the profile of the new customers. During the preparation periods internal working tools such as socio-check-boards can be used to verify that all design, promotional and advertising activity is properly directed towards to the new niche.

CHAPTER 13

THE SOCIO-STYLES SYSTEM: A MULTI-FUNCTION, INTEGRATED TOOL

In summary, what is the socio-styles system and how does it operate?

This tool and its databank enable us to link a whole range of operations for consumer detection, analysis and selection. They are based on an X-ray of competitive positions for offerings and demand opportunities so that we can then select the most effective means of action for the target we are aiming for (figure 13.1).

The socio-styles system enables us to do the following:

❏ segment a population within a sector into a variety of populations and customer bases according to motivations, attitudes and current behaviour at the same time;
❏ identify which segments are influenced by which socio-cultural, commercial and economic trends and trends in taste;
❏ observe which market niches are saturated or untouched, and which consumer segments are satisfied or awaiting innovation:
❏ define which types of marketing these segments of populations favour;
❏ choose the forms of promotion, advertising and media that suit each socio-style.

The socio-styles system offers decision makers an instrument panel to help them pilot their strategy into the archipelago of public diversity and the meteorology of social trends. On this instrument panel we find:

❏ three basic environmental indicators: social climate, segmentation and lifestyles;
❏ a variable geometry reading: national, international and regional;
❏ regular updating
❏ an interface with each sector or market to describe its innovation trends, its target populations and its competing niches.

The system can be compared to a radar.

a Socio-map	a typology of Socio-styles	a Socio compass
as a general **positioning** *tool*	*as a general* **segmentation** *tool*	*as a general* **innovation** *tool*
the same basic chess board to compare marketing, media and ads, shops...	the same basic lifestyles classification to target any topic in any market	the same basic sociocultural trends to identify new opportunities

for sectorial applications ...

to analyse the positions of competitors in market niches	to define the consumers Socio-targets	to detect and measure behavioural and psychological trends

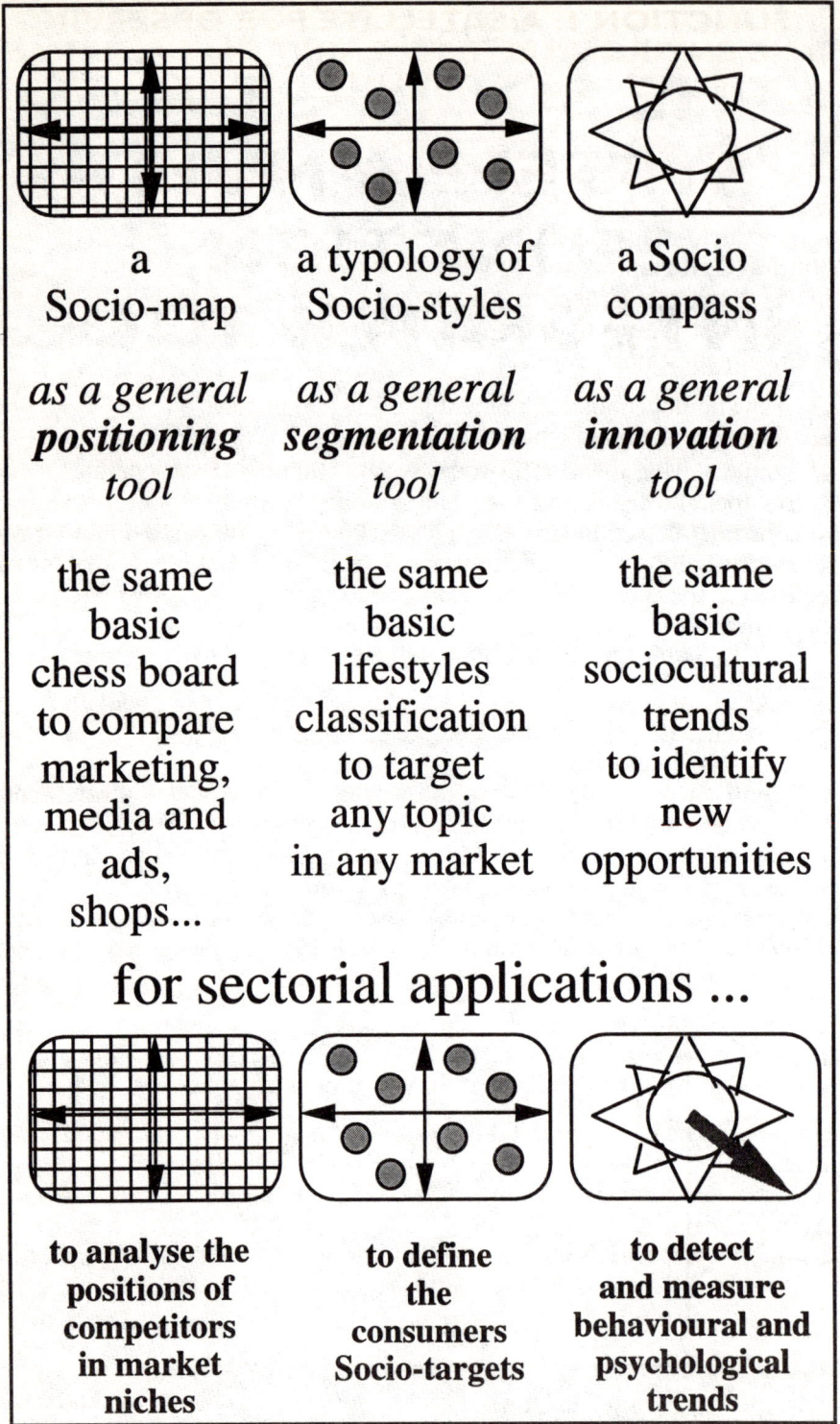

Figure 13.1   Three general multi-sectional tools

FUNCTION I: A SATELLITE FOR OBSERVING THE ENVIRONMENT TO CARRY OUT A MARKET AUDIT

The general socio-style surveys function as a kind of satellite photography which draws a landscape map identifying environmental islands, either to avoid them or to reach them without having to navigate blind (figure 13.2).

The socio-map and its socio-styles typology are the product of socio-cultural cartography which paints the landscape of the social environment in which pilots of large firms and organizations have to choose their route.

This first glance at the social background enables us to answer the following questions:

❏ How homogenous or fragmented is the population?
❏ What are the main types?
❏ What is the structure that explains this diversity (eg social class, demography, culture)?
❏ How is this diversity organized, according to which axes and on which contrasting themes (socio-structure and socio-map)?

And in a particular market:

❏ Is there a mass market or several micro-markets?
❏ What are the main consumer segments (socio-targets)?
❏ What is the portrait of each one of these?
❏ In which areas are they contrasted and similar?

Use socio-styles as a satellite to draw up an objective map of your environment and your sector.

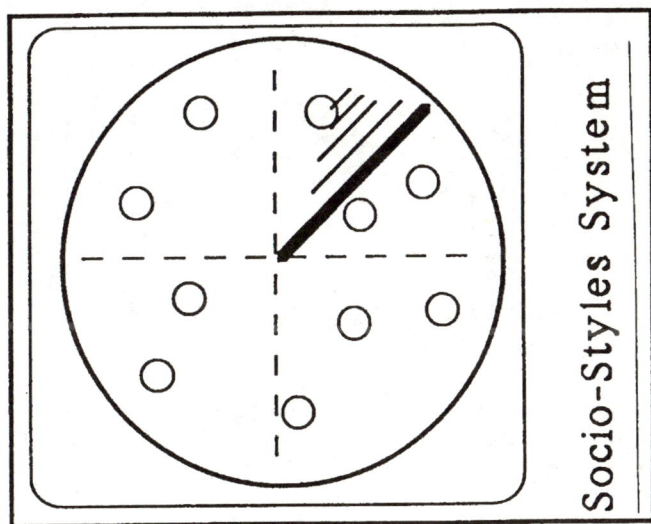

Figure 13.2 Function 1: A satellite for observing the environment to carry out a market audit

FUNCTION 2: AN X-RAY SCANNER FOR A CHECK-UP ON COMPETITIVE POSITIONS

Beyond identifying islands of individuals and consumer families, socio-styles sector-based studies also describe the variety of positionings for existing offerings (figure 13.3).

The socio-bank answers the following questions:

❑ Are the products and brands concentrated precisely on a small number of segments or spread throughout the typology?
❑ What are the main niches that gather them together into families of offerings?
❑ Where are the messages, advertisements and images located?
❑ What is the positioning of each firm on this chessboard?
❑ How coherent is the positioning of product, brand image, communication, distribution and promotion?
❑ How specific is each positioning?
❑ What is the analysis of its value according to the profile of the population concerned?

Use socio-styles for an audit of competitive positioning in your market.

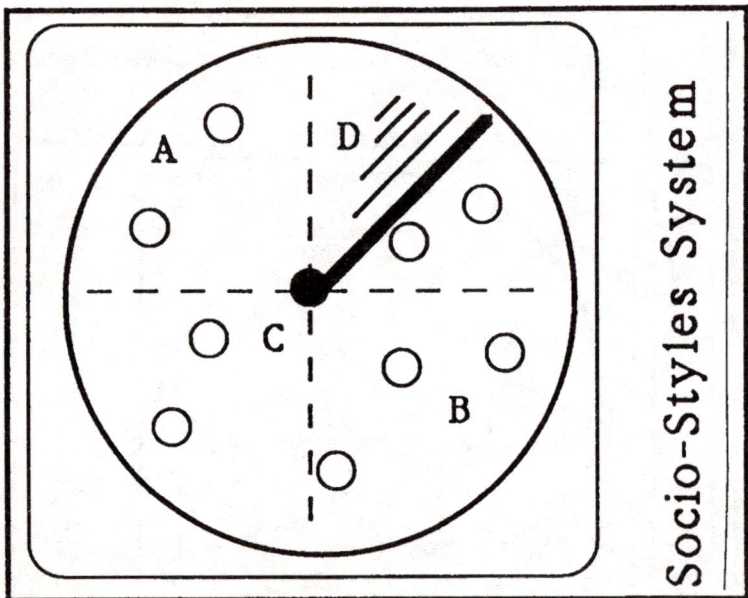

Figure 13.3   Function 2: An X-ray scanner for a check-up of competitive positions

FUNCTION 3: AN APPROACH RADAR FOR ANTICIPATING INNOVATIONS

The aim of socio-styles studies is to follow the developments of attitudes and habits and to anticipate them by detecting innovation needs in all sectors (figure 13.4).

The socio-bank answers the following questions:

- Which segments are satisfied or dissatisfied with their current products?
- According to which main criteria?
- Which products and brands are at risk because of this dissatisfaction?
- Which segments demonstrate new requirements?
- What ideal offering do they dream of in terms of product, design, performance, use?
- In what form do they want commercial and advertising presentation?
- What new innovation concepts are emerging?
- Are these mass-market products for the majority or well-targeted minority products?
- With which existing products and brands would they be in competition?

Use socio-styles to detect opportunities for innovation in your market.

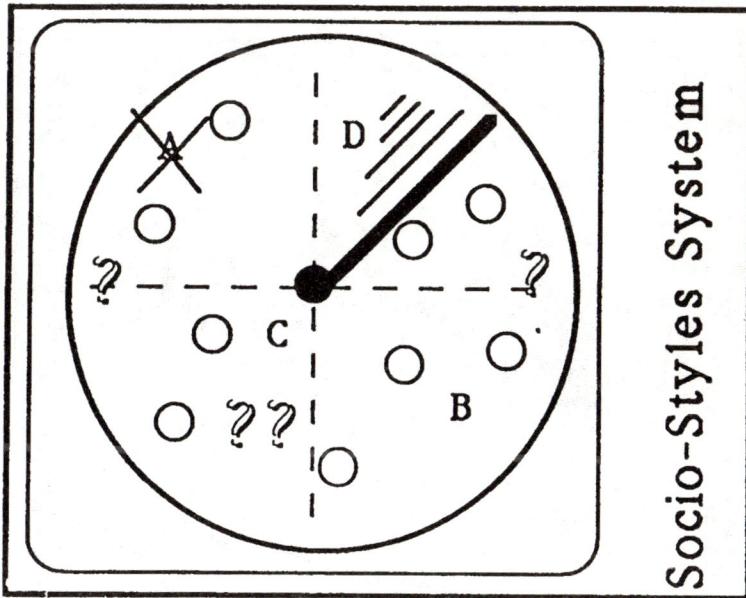

Figure 13.4   Function 3: An approach radar for anticipating innovations

FUNCTION 4: A SOCIO-DYNAMIC METEOROLOGY FOR NAVIGATING WITH THE PREVAILING WINDS

Socio-styles studies function as a barometer which follows the evolution of attitudes, value systems, interests, motivating themes in the current environment (figure 13.5).

The socio-bank answers the following questions:

❑ What makes up the 'hit parade' of most attractive, fashionable values, principles and topics?
❑ What are the dominant ideas held by the majority?
❑ What are the topics of disagreement that are divisive?

And with respect to a particular market:

❑ Which product or brand image positionings are encouraged or discouraged by socio-cultural trends?
❑ Which potential innovations would go in the direction of these trends?
❑ Which consumer profiles (socio-targets) and which plans of consumption are going to be encouraged or discouraged by these social winds?
❑ Which forms of communication can correct an out-of-date positioning in order to ride the prevailing winds?

Use socio-styles to navigate more quickly, more comfortably, at less risk and with the wind in your favour.

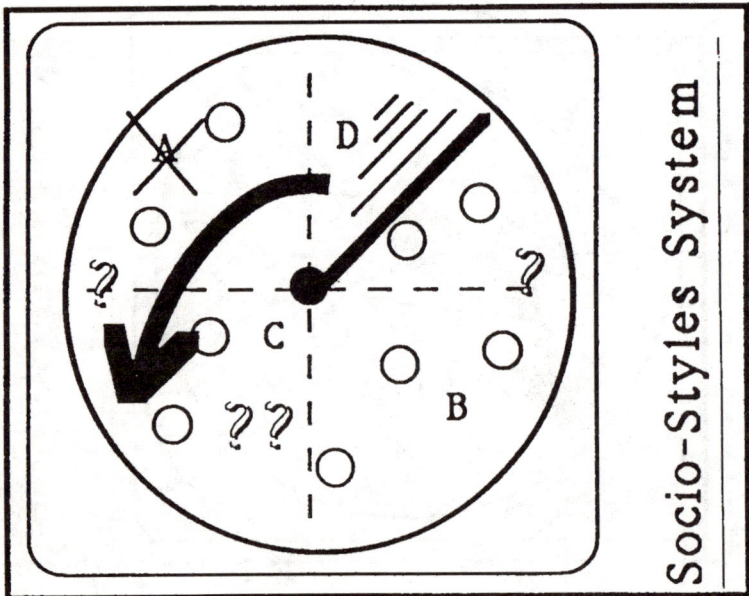

Figure 13.5   Function 4: A socio-dynamic meteorology for navigating with the prevailing winds

FUNCTION 5: A MARKETING TOOLBOX FOR MORE EFFECTIVE ACTION ON A TARGET

The foundation and extension studies of the socio-styles system, and the related databank panels, are an important reference library on the habits and tastes of different populations according to their lifestyle profile. They pay particular attention to consumers' commercial habits, taste in advertising, responsiveness to promotions and behaviour with regard to information (figure 13.6).

When a target population has been defined according to the above check-ups, the socio-bank offers a wide range of courses of action for this precise segment:

- ❏ In which outlets should the product be sold and with what additional services?
- ❏ What kind of presentation, commercial encouragement and promotion is needed?
- ❏ What packaging, design and communication should be used?
- ❏ What advertising and public relations strategy should support it?
- ❏ Which style, tone, words and images should be used in this strategy?
- ❏ Which media should be used?

Finally, use socio-styles to provide a more coherent offering to a better-defined group of customers.

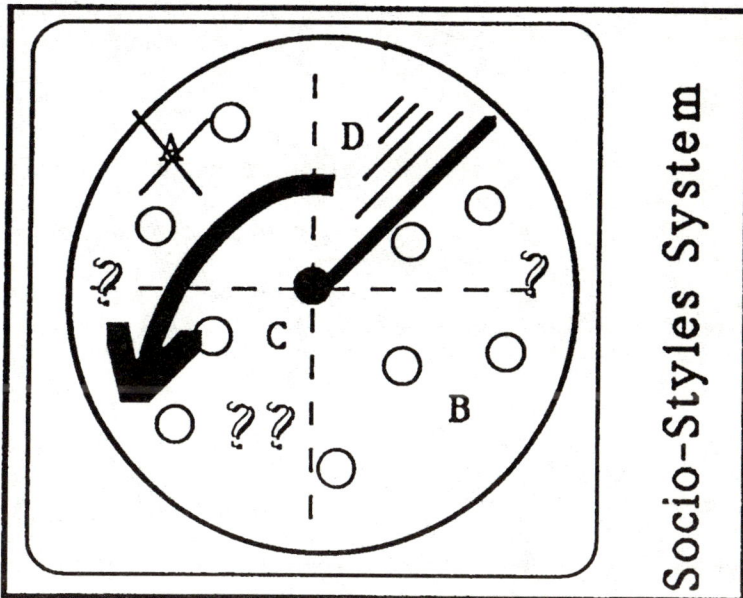

Figure 13.6   Function 5: A marketing toolbox for more effective action on a target

GLOSSARY

A. EURO-SOCIO-STYLES

Business   wealthy, spendthrift young professionals seeking leadership in a competitive leisure society

Citizen   community organizers seeking leadership in social activities

Dandy   hedonist youth with modest income seeking welfare structures

Defensive   small-town xenophobes that seek assistance and protection

Gentry   middle-class ultra-conservatives seeking law and order

Moralist   quiet, religious, middle-class people seeking to bring up their children quietly

Olvidados   retired catholic housewives threatened by the growing complexity of the world who seek protection and guidance

Pioneer   young, well-off, extremely tolerant intellectuals seeking social justice

Protest   young, intellectual libertarians seeking social justice

Prudent   resigned, retired, modest people seeking security

Rocky   working-class youths who feel excluded and seek integration through making money

Romantic   sentimental, young, working-class couples seeking progress through traditional methods and values

Scout   middle-aged, tolerant conservatives seeking orderly social progress

Squadra   tolerant, fairly young suburban couples seeking a secure life of sports and leisure

Strict   overly repressive puritans in favour of social control

Vigilante   frustrated, urban, blue-collar savers that seek to preserve their identity

B. US SOCIO-STYLES

Hedonism Seekers   youthful, dynamic adventurers, motivated by money and pleasure

Status Seekers   mature, settled, responsible and pragmatic, have the means and habit of buying the best

Providence Seekers   life revolves around micro-local religious community, reject modern culture

Show-off Seekers	Idealist, uninvolved status seekers, open to new technology
Standing Seekers	'born leaders of a marching America', attentive to 'politics, business, lifestyle'
Certitude Seekers	isolated from events and developments, motivated by family and religion
Security Seekers	religious, traditional and active on a micro-local level, pessimistic for future
Dream Seekers	seek a balanced quality of life between family and work while still making it to the top
Identity Seekers	seek a peaceful balance of technology/nature, big clients for fashion
Saving Seekers	believe in hard work, service to God and family, world turns around local life
Concept Seekers	the defence of private life is most important, peaceful and high-priority pleasure spenders

C. FRENCH SOCIO-STYLE MENTALITIES IN THE 1980s

Activists	Go-getter + militant Middle-aged city-dwellers with good professional qualifications
Ego-centries	Pretender + defensive + vigilante Young working-class people from industrial cities with few technical qualifications
Materialists	Utilitarian + exemplary + expectant Elderly people of modest means and with few professional qualifications living in the country or small towns
Rigorists	Conservative + moralist + responsible People of modest means and a low standard of education living in medium-sized towns
Syncs	Libertarian + dilettante + advantage-taker Young, educated, well-off executives or would-be executives living in cities and urban areas

D. EUROPEAN MENTALITIES

Ambitious	Dandy + rocky + business Accord priority to dynamism, investing for success
Contestors	Protester + pioneer Accord priority to ideals and permissiveness in order to lead a meaningful life in spite of their natural scepticism

Dreamers	Romantic + squadra
	Accord priority to the building of a harmonious life
Militants	Scout + citizen
	Accord priority to protecting the community from extremism
Notables	Moralist + gentry + strict
	Accord priority to family and traditional values against a modern world shaken by economic crises and decline
Withdrawn	Defensive + olvidados + prudent + vigilante
	Accord priority to family life and efforts for a better micro-social quality of life

FURTHER INFORMATION

FOUNDERS OF THE SOCIO-STYLES SYSTEM

CCA (Centre de Communication Avancé)

A subsidiary of EURO RSCG, one of the leading communication groups in Europe and worldwide. Founded in Paris in 1971 by Bernard Cathelat and Mike Burke together with Claude Matricon, it was one of the first companies to organize lifestyle studies in Europe directed by Jean de Nicolaÿ.

CCA has been developing applications of the socio-styles system for advertising, commercial marketing and socio-political research for the longest time and to the greatest extent.

One particular application of the system has been developed for studying and modelling of methods of communication under the direction of Robert Ebguy; and another application, Work Styles, has been developed under the direction of Mike Burke.

CCA International serves as a technical adviser for applications of the socio-styles system worldwide in collaboration with local research organizations.

CCA
8 rue de l'Hotel de Ville
92200 Neuilly sur Seine
France
Tel: (33) 1 47 47 14 14   Fax: (33) 1 47 47 64 79
Contacts: Jean de Nicolaÿ, Bernard Cathelat, Mike Burke, Robert Ebguy.

USERS OF THE SOCIO-STYLES SYSTEM

The leading networks of market research institutes in Europe specializing in consumer panels — GFK (Germany), SECODIP (France) and their respective subsidiaries.

GFK Group

A German company covering several European countries with a coordinating centre based in Nuremberg, under the direction of Andreas Winkler for Eurosociostyle applications.

Austria:

GFK & Co
Franz-Josefs-Kal 47
A-1010 Wien
Mr Bretschneider
Tel: (43) 1 534 96   Fax: (43) 1 534 96 175

Belgium:

GFK Belgium
1, rue Paul Lautess
1050 Brussels
Mr Pierre Dewinter/Mr Boschloos
Tel: (32) 2 649 00 55   Fax: (32) 2 647 41 21

Denmark:

Observa
Toldbodgade 10
1253 Copenhagen
Mr Erik Christiansen
Tel: (45) 33 93 17 40   Fax: (45) 33 13 07 40

Germany:

GFK AG
Lebensstilforschung Nordwestring 101
8500 Nurnberg 90
Mr Andreas Winkler
Tel: (49) 911 395 36 35   Fax: (49) 911 395 40 24

Norway:

Norsk Forbrukerpanel A/S
Kr. Augusts Gate 19
0164 Oslo 1
Mr Espen Moen
Tel: (47) 2 67 09 04   Fax: (47) 2 67 03 18

Sweden:

GFK Marknadsforkning AB
Box 401 - St Lars Vag 46

22100 Lund
Mr Roland Kruuse
Tel: (46) 46 18 16 00   Fax: (46) 46 11 67 71

SECODIP Group

A French market research company also covering Spain and Portugal, under the coordination of François Hovart.

France:

SECODIP SA
2, rue Francis Pédron
78241 Chambourcy
Mr François Hovart/Mr Manfred Hertl
Tel: (33) 1 39 65 56 56   Fax: (33) 1 39 65 12 19

Portugal:

Euroteste Marketing e Opiniao SA
Rua engr. Arantes de Oliveira 5 s/loja Porta E
1900 Lisbon
Mr José Vidal de Oliveira/Mr Joao Marques
Tel: (351) 1 847 10 80   Fax: (351) 1 80 79 95

Spain:

Dympanel SA
Avenida de Roma 6-10
08015 Barcelona
Mr Jose Ignacio Butina Jimenez/Mr Alberto de Pablo
Tel: (34) 3 22 62 478   Fax: (34) 3 22 65 723

IHA Group

A Swiss company under the direction of Dr Kurt Heller, specializing in panel and *ad hoc* research.

IHA Institut fur Marktanalysen
Obermattweg 9
6052 Hergiswil
Dr Kurt Heller/Mrs Irene Marty
Tel: (41) 41 95 94 51   Fax: (41) 41 95 91 24

EURO RSCG Group

The leading advertising group in Europe and sixth in the world, with agencies covering the different fields of advertising, promotion, public relations and direct marketing. CCA developed socio-styles research during the 1970s within this framework, especially in the field of media, achieving for Euromedia a computerized system of strategic planning.

Euromedia
11, Square Léon Blum
92806 Puteaux
Mme Brigitte Amiot
Tel: (33) 1 46 93 33   Fax: (33) 1 46 93 32 53

M CONSULTANTS

A market research and management consulting company established in the Antilles (French West Indies), working throughout the Caribbean region. It adopted the socio-styles system for the first lifestyles study in Guadelupe and Martinique in 1986 in cooperation with CCA International.

M CONSULTANTS
Habitation Desfourneaux
97212 St Joseph
Martinique
Mr Alain Rozenfeld/Mr Jean François Meyer
Tel: (596) 57 72 62   Fax: (596) 57 93 20

US MAPPING

An American company created by GMF and a team of researchers directed by Bernard Allien to develop market studies. It adopted the socio-styles system for the first application study in the USA, now managed by NFO.

NFO

An American company specializing in *ad hoc* research and owner of US sociostyles.

PO Box 315
Toledo
Ohio
Mr Richard Spitzer/Mr Bruce Johnson
Tel: 419 666 88 00

APPLICATIONS OF THE SOCIO-STYLES SYSTEM

Euro-Socio-Styles

Begun on the initiative of CCA, this is the first multi-sectorial pan-European socio-styles study — carried out in 1988–89, co-produced and distributed by CCA International and Europanel.

A first survey of 4,000 interviews enabled us to define a typology of 16 European socio-styles. A second regionalized survey of 20,000 interviews measured this typology in 15 countries (European Community, Austria, Switzerland, Norway, Sweden) and 80 regions applying it to 15 commercial sectors.

This is the first 'variable geometry' socio-bank to make the study results available in a continental, national, regional or multi-regional dimension according to choice.

This databank is enhanced by sectorial maxi-scans. Expert systems can be taken from it for an operational application. Modular reports are available from GO and CCA on subscription.

US socio-styles bank

A socio-styles system study of the population of the USA carried out on the initiative of US Mapping with technical collaboration from CCA International under the direction of Bernard Allien and Bernard Cathelat. A first qualitative and quantitative foundation study was produced in 1986–87 using the Market Facts panel and then updated in 1989–90 in collaboration with NFO.

This research, incorporating 2,500 interviews, and its updating enabled a typology of 11 socio-styles to be defined. This socio-bank was the first to be transformed into an expert system by Neuron Works. It is distributed by NFO on subscription.

Socio-styles in the Antilles (French West Indies)

In 1986 the first foundation study in Guadeloupe and Martinique was carried out on the initiative of M Consultants with the technical collaboration of CCA International under the direction of Bernard Cathelat, Alain Rozenfeld and Jean-François Meyer. 1,200 interviews (600 per island) enabled us to define an original typology of 11 West Indian socio-styles to be used as a study tool by firms, administrations and regional media. Updated in 1990, this databank is available on subscription from M Consultants.

Socio-expertise: Artificial intelligence and socio-styles

Development of artificial intelligence and multi-media information programs using socio-styles typology in interactive reception, information, sales and training terminals.

Generally an expert system is an information model which attempts to reproduce human thinking through software which collects data in interactive dialogue with the user or the environment. It then integrates them into a group of logical rules, whose automatic functioning provides a solution. The first applications were technological, but more recently expert systems have made their entrance into marketing and sociology.

To facilitate and optimize the operational uses of the socio-styles system Bernard and Monique Cathelat together with Walfroy Dauchy of ARIA have developed various expert systems using Nexpert-Object and Aivision software:

❑ The Socio-Targeting Tool: a navigation system within the socio-bank intended for study specialists to help them research and read the results according to their needs. The US socio-styles bank is available in this form.

❑ The Market Compass: an automatic definition system of marketing strategy starting from the user's needs and objectives, based on the socio-bank which remains invisible.

❑ Target Tests and Training: systems for training personnel in socio-styles typology or the segmentation of socio-targets in a market, by Test-Game.

❑ Sales Force model: an expert sales-aid system which interviews the potential customer before suggesting products accompanied by a specific rationale. It is intended for automated sales or as an aid to the salesperson.

❑ The Promo-Test: a self-service test-game for customers of a shop or mail order catalogue directing them towards promotions relating to their tastes and needs.

❑ The Socio-Media model: this generates media plans for advertisers.

❑ The Scan Product: this is to evaluate the market impact of new products.

All these expert system models are based on a socio-styles typology. They can be developed for various kinds of micro-computers.

Socio-styles studies

The general lifestyle surveys began in France in 1972 and have been updated regularly (1974, 1976, 1978, 1980, 1982, 1984, 1987, 1990, 1992) and supplemented by media audience analyses (every two years) and sector-based market studies:

❑ Lifestyles of Young People, 1978 and 1984 in France.

❑ Lifestyles of Farmers, 1982 with BVA (JP and G Ville) and 1987 in France.

❑ Lifestyles of Salespeople in France.

CCA METHODS ASSOCIATED WITH THE SOCIO-STYLES SYSTEM

Quorum

A qualitative study method of collective motivations and values devised by Bernard Cathelat and Mike Burke of CCA in 1974. It consists of an analysis of convergences and divergences in psychology between groups of different socio-styles combined and confronted simultaneously and interactively.

The Co'System

An analytical and creative model for communication messages of all kinds devised by Bernard Cathelat and Robert Ebguy of CCA.

Its principle is that all communication is a remodelling of the referent by the transmitter in order to confer an added value perceptible and acceptable to the public receiver.

The Co'System plan describes three added value registers (utilitarian, social and psychological) corresponding with three communication registers (demonstrative, conative and evocative) and three tones (rational, emotional, fantasmatic) which can be applied in three areas (valorization of the transmitter, the referent object or the target receiver). In this way 60 communication modules are described. (See *Styles de Pub, 60 manières de communiquer* by Bernard Cathelat and Robert Ebguy, Editions d'Organisation, Paris 1988.)

Media information functions

The work of Bernard Cathelat and Mike Burke of CCA has distinguished several functions corresponding to various audience motivations: the Echo function (reassuring mirror of everyday reality), Ampli (watching over the present), Focus (reflection), Antenna (destabilizing and stimulating information), Prism (training and advice). These functions are studied on a regular basis in the media studies of the socio-styles system. (See *Publicité et Société* by Bernard Cathelat, Editions Payot, Paris 1987.)

Star and Socio-check-board

Skilled techniques for the socio-cultural positioning of an object, brand, personality, institution, media or message on the lifestyles chessboard of populations by simple analysis of the contents. These tools were devised by Bernard Cathelat and Robert Ebguy at CCA.

Ethno

A method of participant observation of actual lifestyles on location, developed by the socio-styles system team since 1975, notably Jean-Pierre Grard.

Work Styles

Studies on organizational and management styles, the lifestyles of staff and workers developed by Mike Burke of CCA. These concepts are used in internal audit studies of motivation within an organization to define human relations strategies, internal communication and company plans.

See *Portraits de Famille* (1983), *A chacun son style d'entreprise* (1987), Inter-Editions, *Styles de Pouvoir* (1992) Dunod — all by Mike Burke.

BIBLIOGRAPHY

Adler, A (1929) *The Science of Living*

Alper, L and Gelty, R (1969) 'Product positioning by behavioral life-styles', *Journal of Marketing*, Vol 33, No 2

Ansbacher, H 'Life Style: A Historical and Systematic Review', *Journal of Individual Psychology*, Vol 23, pp 191–212

Berget, P and Luckmann, T (1966) *The Social Construction of Reality*, Doubleday, New York

Bouchet, D (1986) 'Kompleksitetsparadigmet', *Paradigma*, Vol 1, No 1, Aarhus

Broadbent, S and Linton (1974) *L'extension des études de Styles de Vie aux marchés européens*, /17/, Paris

Castoriadis, C (1986) *L'imaginarie: la création dans le domaine social-historique*, Seuil, Paris

Cathelat, B and Burke, M (1975) *Les Styles de Vie pour un marketing dynamique*, CCA Document, Neuilly sur Seine

Cathelat, B and Cadet, A (1976, 1987) *Publicité et Société*, Payot, Paris

Cathelat, B (1985) *Les Styles de Vie*, Vols 1 and 2, Éditions d'Organisation, Paris

Douglas, S and Acquin, A (1977) *Utilisation des notions de courants socio-culturels et de Styles de Vie dans le choix des supports*, CESA Document, Paris

Fromm, E (1955) *The same society*, New York

Grard, J P (1980) *Essai d'épistémologie des Styles de Vie*, CCA Document, Neuilly sur Seine

Herman, J (1983) *Les languages de la sociologie*, PUF, Paris

Hustad, T P *Industry's use of life-styles analysis*

Institut des Recherches Publicitaries (1974) *Report of a seminar on Life Styles*, Paris

Krech, D and Crutchfield, R (1952) *Théories et problèmes de la psychologie sociale*, PUF, Paris

Lazer, W (1963) 'Life Style Concepts and Marketing', *Towards Scientific Marketing*, Proceedings of American Marketing Association

Levy, S (1959) 'Symbols for Sale', *Harvard Business Review*, Vol 37

Mitchell, A (1983) *The Nine American Life Styles*, Macmillan, New York

Moscovici, S (1976) *Social Influence and Social Change*, Academic Press, London

Plummer, J T (1974) *Aspects of life styles research to the creation of advertising campaigns*

Rokeach, M (1970) *Beliefs, attitudes and values*, Jossey Bass Inc, San Francisco

Rokeach, M (1967) *The Rokeach Value System*, Sumyrale-California-Malgren Test

Scardigli, V (1974) *Modes de vie et évolution de la société française*, /17/, Paris

Truchot, D and Bonnell, R (1978) 'Les noveaux critères media', *Stratégie*, No 170, Paris

Urban, C H (1975) *Life-Style patterns of Women in the United States and United Kingdom*

Weber, M (1948) *Essays in Sociology*

Wells, W D *et al* (1972) *Life styles and psychographics*, University of Chicago

Yankelovich, D (1971) 'What new life-styles mean to market planners', *Marketing Communications*, Vol 299, No 6 (June), New York

INDEX